SUPERMAN

THE WRATH OF
GOG

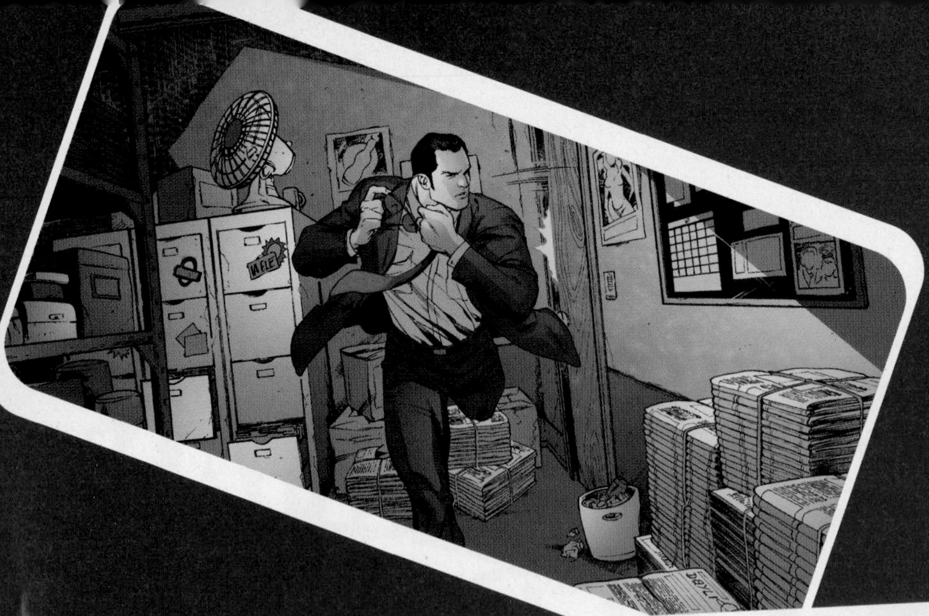

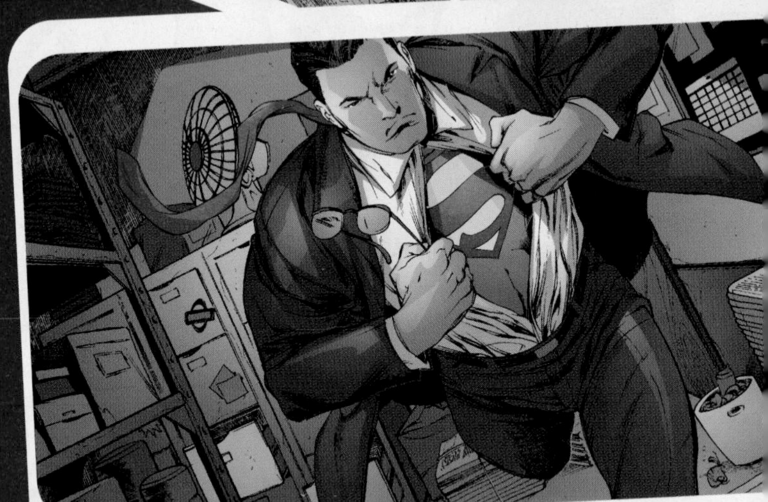

SUPERMAN: THE WRATH OF GOG

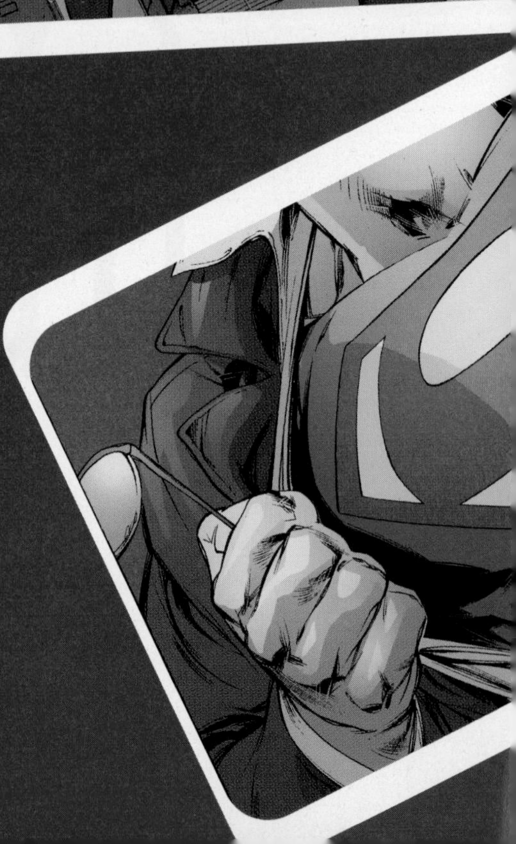

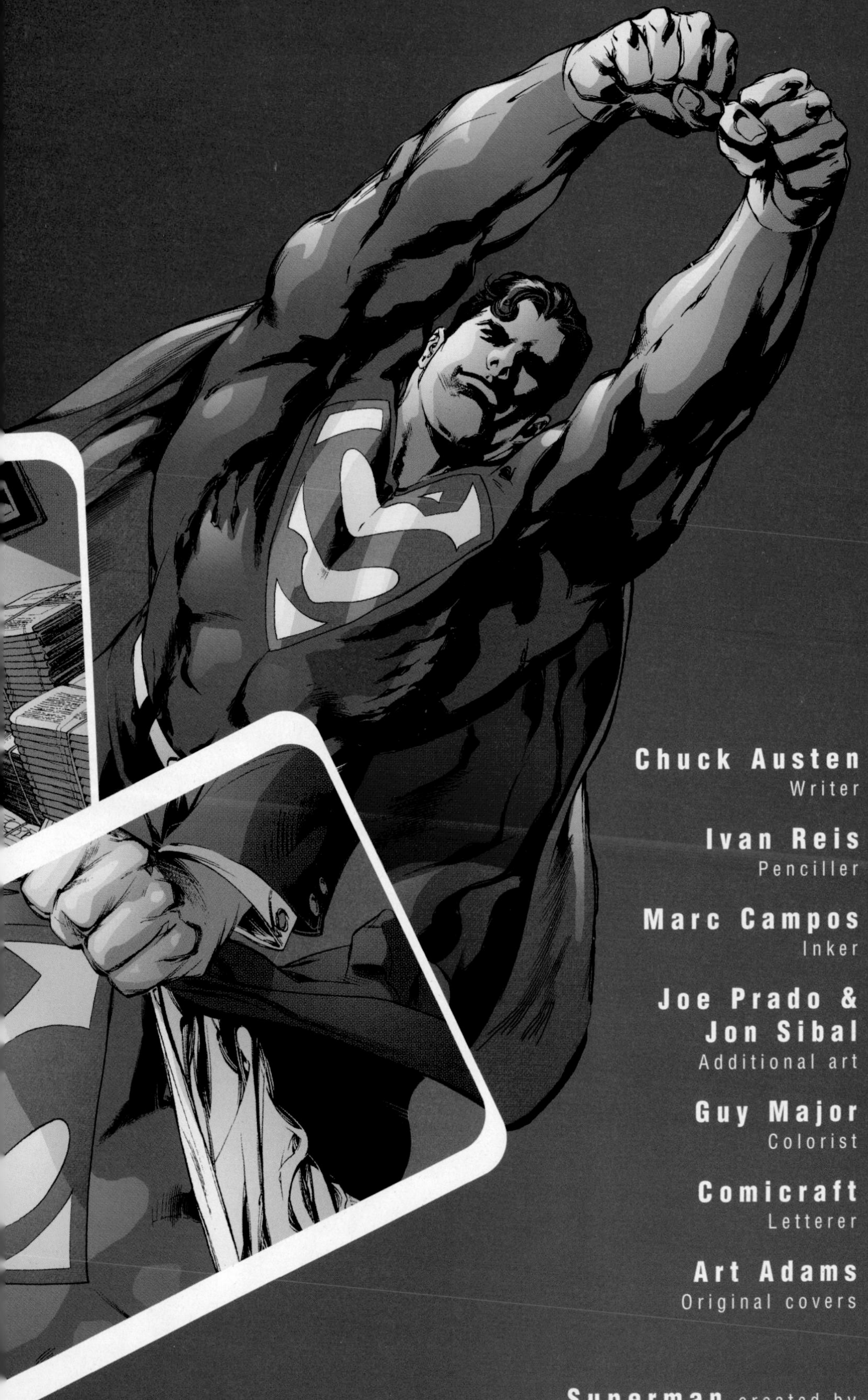

Chuck Austen
Writer

Ivan Reis
Penciller

Marc Campos
Inker

Joe Prado &
Jon Sibal
Additional art

Guy Major
Colorist

Comicraft
Letterer

Art Adams
Original covers

Superman created by
Jerry Siegel &
Joe Shuster

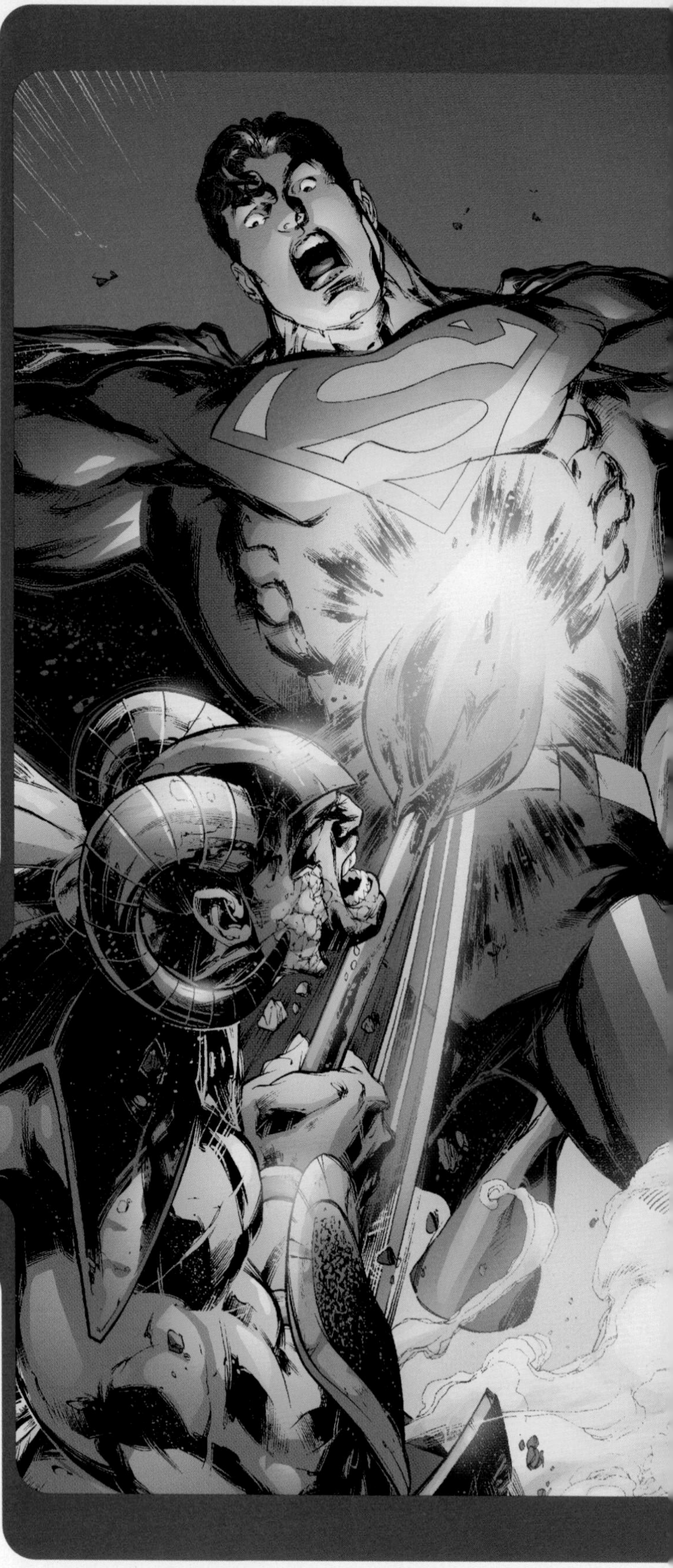

SUPERMAN: THE WRATH OF GOG

Published by DC Comics. Cover and compilation copyright © 2005 DC Comics. All Rights Reserved. Originally published in single magazine form in ACTION COMICS #812-819. Copyright © 2004 DC Comics. All Rights Reserved. All characters, their distinctive likenesses and related elements featured in this publication are trademarks of DC Comics. The stories, characters and incidents featured in this publication are entirely fictional. DC Comics does not read or accept unsolicited submissions of ideas, stories or artwork. DC Comics, 1700 Broadway, New York, NY 10019. A Warner Bros. Entertainment Company. Printed in Canada. First Printing. ISBN: 1-4012-0450-3. Cover art by Ivan Reis & Marc Campos, with colors by Dave Stewart. Publication design by John J. Hill

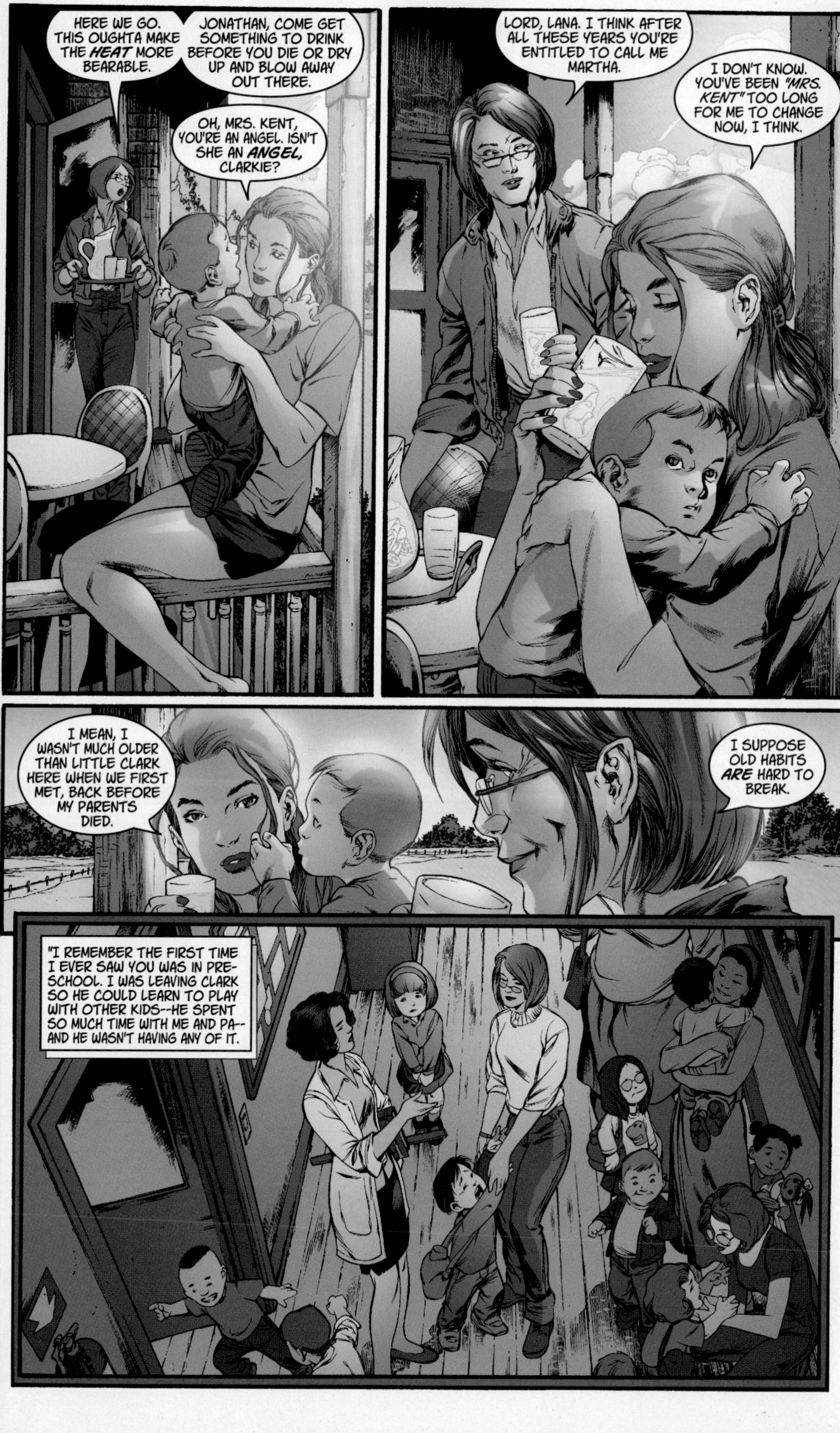
HERE WE GO. THIS OUGHTA MAKE THE HEAT MORE BEARABLE.
JONATHAN, COME GET SOMETHING TO DRINK BEFORE YOU DIE OR DRY UP AND BLOW AWAY OUT THERE.
OH, MRS. KENT, YOU'RE AN ANGEL. ISN'T SHE AN ANGEL, CLARKIE?
LORD, LANA. I THINK AFTER ALL THESE YEARS YOU'RE ENTITLED TO CALL ME MARTHA.
I DON'T KNOW. YOU'VE BEEN "MRS. KENT" TOO LONG FOR ME TO CHANGE NOW, I THINK.
I MEAN, I WASN'T MUCH OLDER THAN LITTLE CLARK HERE WHEN WE FIRST MET, BACK BEFORE MY PARENTS DIED.
I SUPPOSE OLD HABITS ARE HARD TO BREAK.
"I REMEMBER THE FIRST TIME I EVER SAW YOU WAS IN PRE-SCHOOL. I WAS LEAVING CLARK SO HE COULD LEARN TO PLAY WITH OTHER KIDS--HE SPENT SO MUCH TIME WITH ME AND PA--AND HE WASN'T HAVING ANY OF IT.

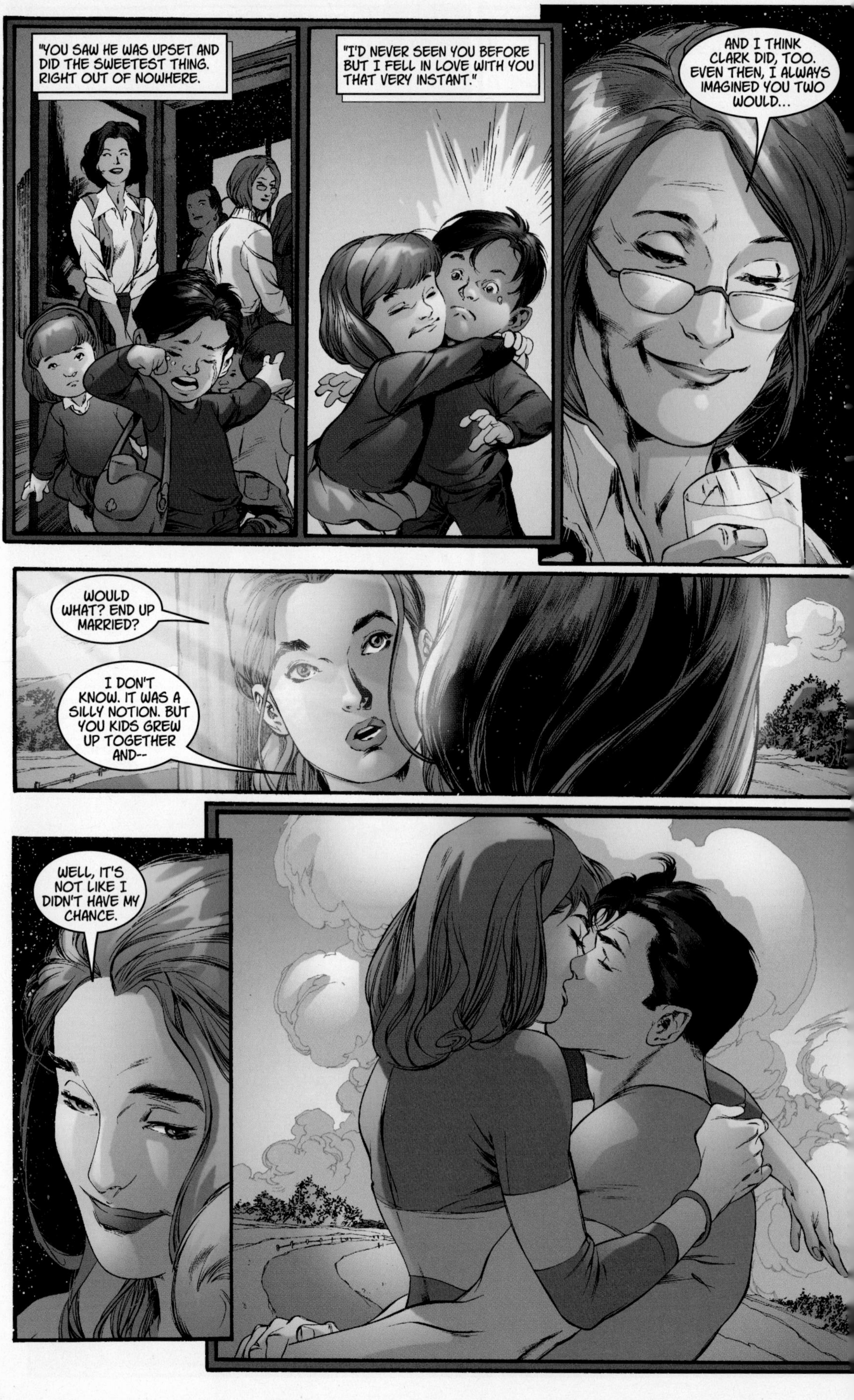
"YOU SAW HE WAS UPSET AND DID THE SWEETEST THING. RIGHT OUT OF NOWHERE.
"I'D NEVER SEEN YOU BEFORE BUT I FELL IN LOVE WITH YOU THAT VERY INSTANT."
AND I THINK CLARK DID, TOO. EVEN THEN, I ALWAYS IMAGINED YOU TWO WOULD...
WOULD WHAT? END UP MARRIED?
I DON'T KNOW. IT WAS A SILLY NOTION. BUT YOU KIDS GREW UP TOGETHER AND--
WELL, IT'S NOT LIKE I DIDN'T HAVE MY CHANCE.

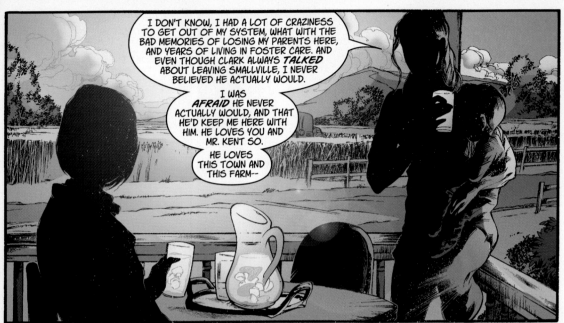

I DON'T KNOW, I HAD A LOT OF CRAZINESS TO GET OUT OF MY SYSTEM, WHAT WITH THE BAD MEMORIES OF LOSING MY PARENTS HERE, AND YEARS OF LIVING IN FOSTER CARE. AND EVEN THOUGH CLARK ALWAYS *TALKED* ABOUT LEAVING SMALLVILLE, I NEVER BELIEVED HE ACTUALLY WOULD.

I WAS *AFRAID* HE NEVER ACTUALLY WOULD, AND THAT HE'D KEEP ME HERE WITH HIM. HE LOVES YOU AND MR. KENT SO.

HE LOVES THIS TOWN AND THIS FARM--

NOW THAT I'VE BEEN AWAY, I FINALLY UNDERSTAND WHY. I WISH I COULD GO BACK AND DO THINGS DIFFERENTLY.

I'M SORRY THINGS DIDN'T WORK OUT BETTER WITH PETE. DO YOU THINK YOU'LL MOVE BACK? NOW THAT YOU TWO ARE GETTING A DIVORCE?

I CAN'T. I'D LIKE TO. IT'S SO MUCH MORE PEACEFUL HERE, AFTER ALL I'VE GONE THROUGH WITH PETE, AND NOW HIS DECISION TO--

I DON'T KNOW. THE ONLY WORK I COULD GET WAS IN METROPOLIS, ANYWAY.

SO AT LEAST YOU'LL BE NEAR CLARK AGAIN.

I'M SORRY. I DIDN'T THINK THAT WOULD BE A SORE SUBJECT.

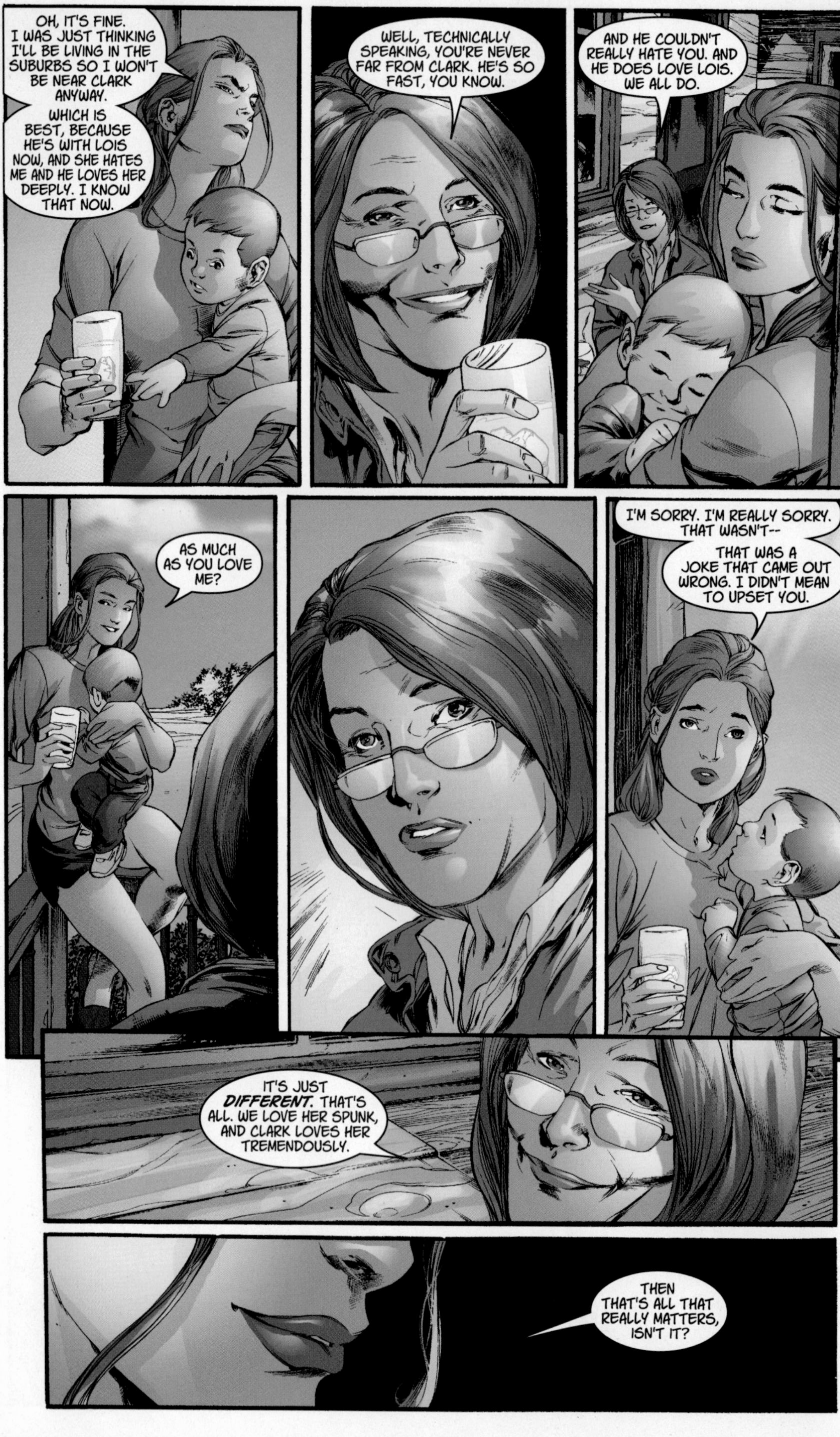
OH, IT'S FINE. I WAS JUST THINKING I'LL BE LIVING IN THE SUBURBS SO I WON'T BE NEAR CLARK ANYWAY.
WHICH IS BEST, BECAUSE HE'S WITH LOIS NOW, AND SHE HATES ME AND HE LOVES HER DEEPLY. I KNOW THAT NOW.
WELL, TECHNICALLY SPEAKING, YOU'RE NEVER FAR FROM CLARK. HE'S SO FAST, YOU KNOW.
AND HE COULDN'T REALLY HATE YOU. AND HE DOES LOVE LOIS. WE ALL DO.
AS MUCH AS YOU LOVE ME?
I'M SORRY. I'M REALLY SORRY. THAT WASN'T--
THAT WAS A JOKE THAT CAME OUT WRONG. I DIDN'T MEAN TO UPSET YOU.
IT'S JUST *DIFFERENT.* THAT'S ALL. WE LOVE HER SPUNK, AND CLARK LOVES HER TREMENDOUSLY.
THEN THAT'S ALL THAT REALLY MATTERS, ISN'T IT?

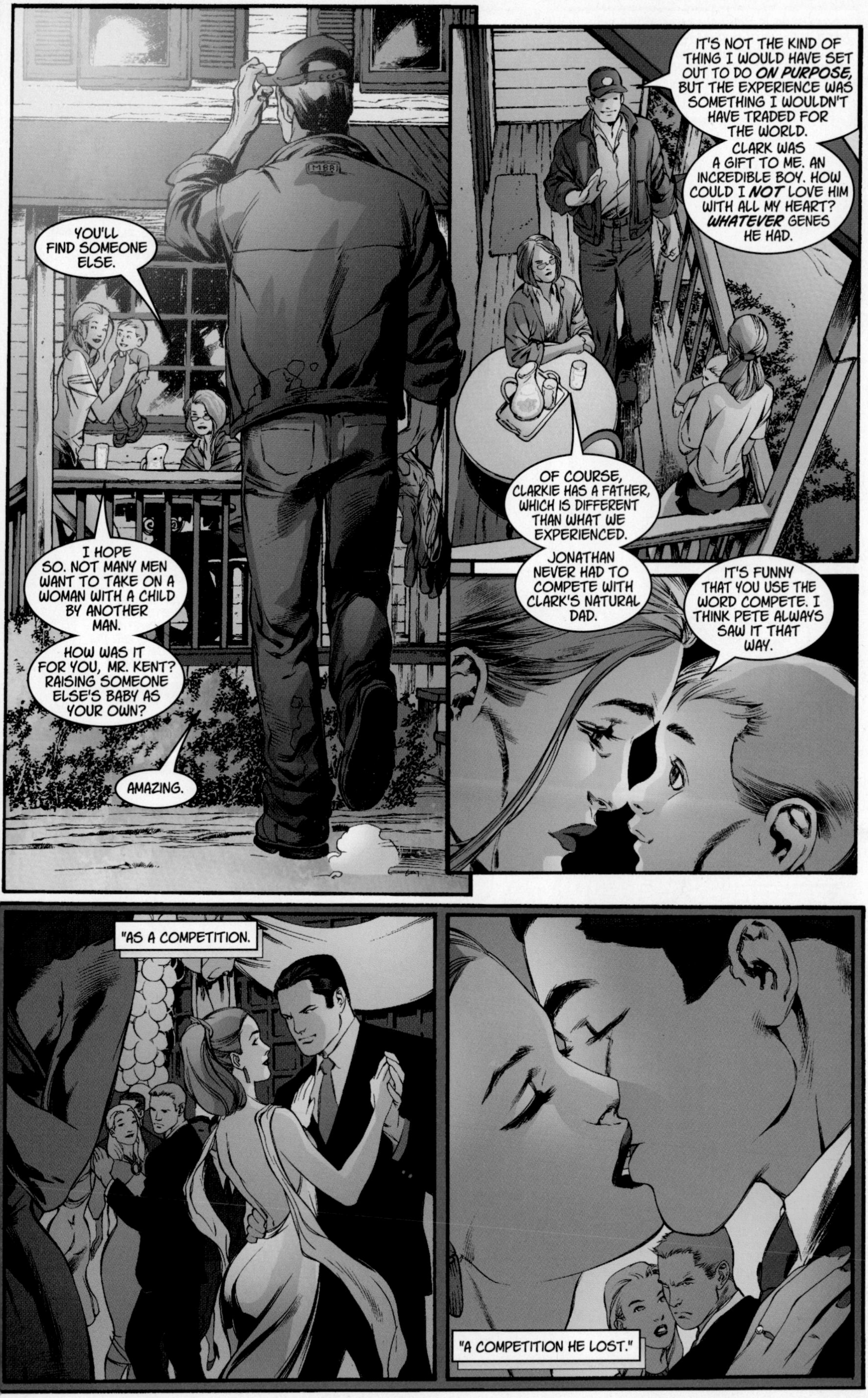
YOU'LL FIND SOMEONE ELSE.
I HOPE SO. NOT MANY MEN WANT TO TAKE ON A WOMAN WITH A CHILD BY ANOTHER MAN.
HOW WAS IT FOR YOU, MR. KENT? RAISING SOMEONE ELSE'S BABY AS YOUR OWN?
AMAZING.
IT'S NOT THE KIND OF THING I WOULD HAVE SET OUT TO DO *ON PURPOSE,* BUT THE EXPERIENCE WAS SOMETHING I WOULDN'T HAVE TRADED FOR THE WORLD.
CLARK WAS A GIFT TO ME. AN INCREDIBLE BOY. HOW COULD I *NOT* LOVE HIM WITH ALL MY HEART? *WHATEVER* GENES HE HAD.
OF COURSE, CLARKIE HAS A FATHER, WHICH IS DIFFERENT THAN WHAT WE EXPERIENCED.
JONATHAN NEVER HAD TO COMPETE WITH CLARK'S NATURAL DAD.
IT'S FUNNY THAT YOU USE THE WORD COMPETE. I THINK PETE ALWAYS SAW IT THAT WAY.
"AS A COMPETITION.
"A COMPETITION HE LOST."

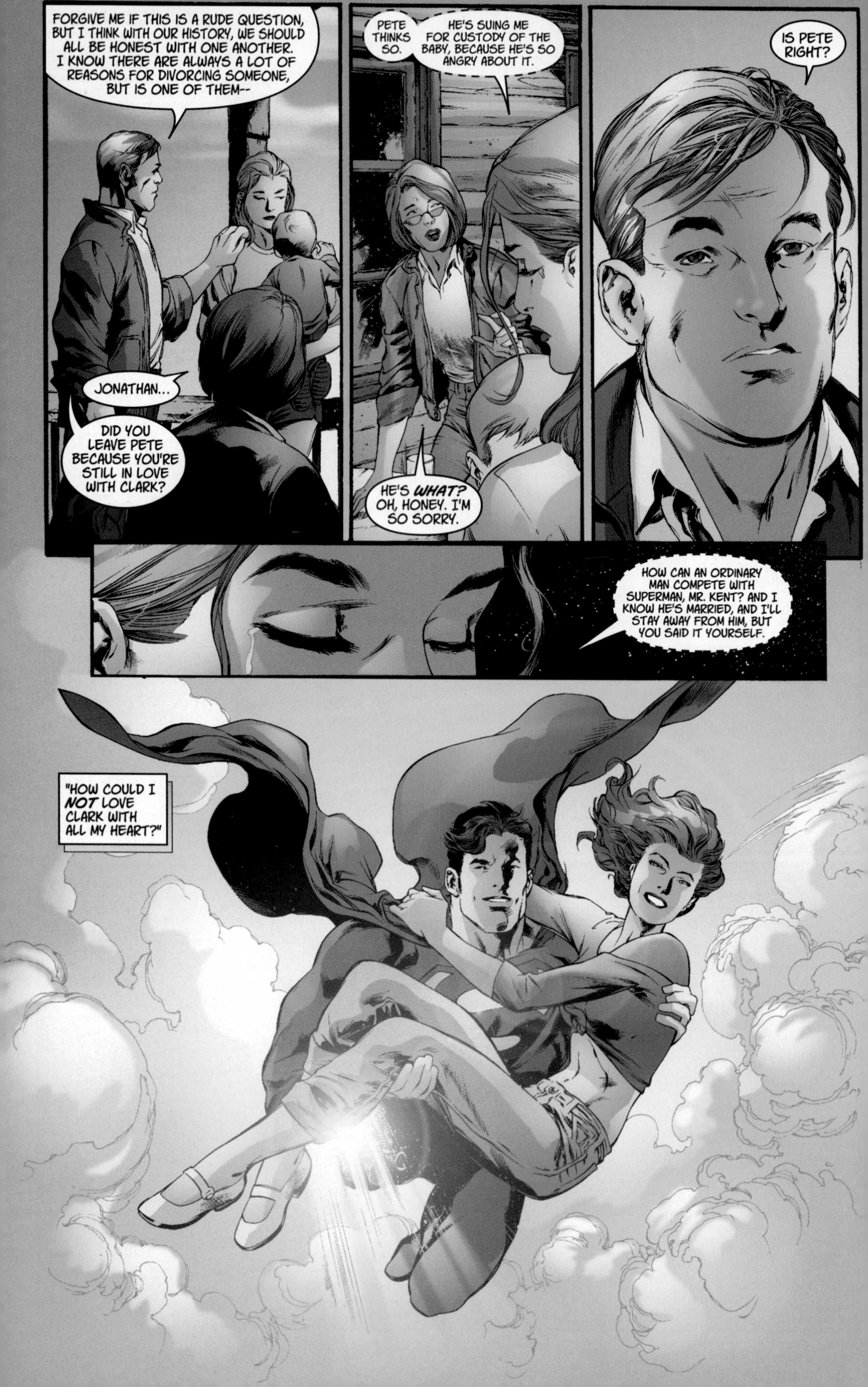
FORGIVE ME IF THIS IS A RUDE QUESTION, BUT I THINK WITH OUR HISTORY, WE SHOULD ALL BE HONEST WITH ONE ANOTHER. I KNOW THERE ARE ALWAYS A LOT OF REASONS FOR DIVORCING SOMEONE, BUT IS ONE OF THEM--
JONATHAN...
DID YOU LEAVE PETE BECAUSE YOU'RE STILL IN LOVE WITH CLARK?
PETE THINKS SO.
HE'S SUING ME FOR CUSTODY OF THE BABY, BECAUSE HE'S SO ANGRY ABOUT IT.
HE'S WHAT? OH, HONEY. I'M SO SORRY.
IS PETE RIGHT?
HOW CAN AN ORDINARY MAN COMPETE WITH SUPERMAN, MR. KENT? AND I KNOW HE'S MARRIED, AND I'LL STAY AWAY FROM HIM, BUT YOU SAID IT YOURSELF.
"HOW COULD I NOT LOVE CLARK WITH ALL MY HEART?"

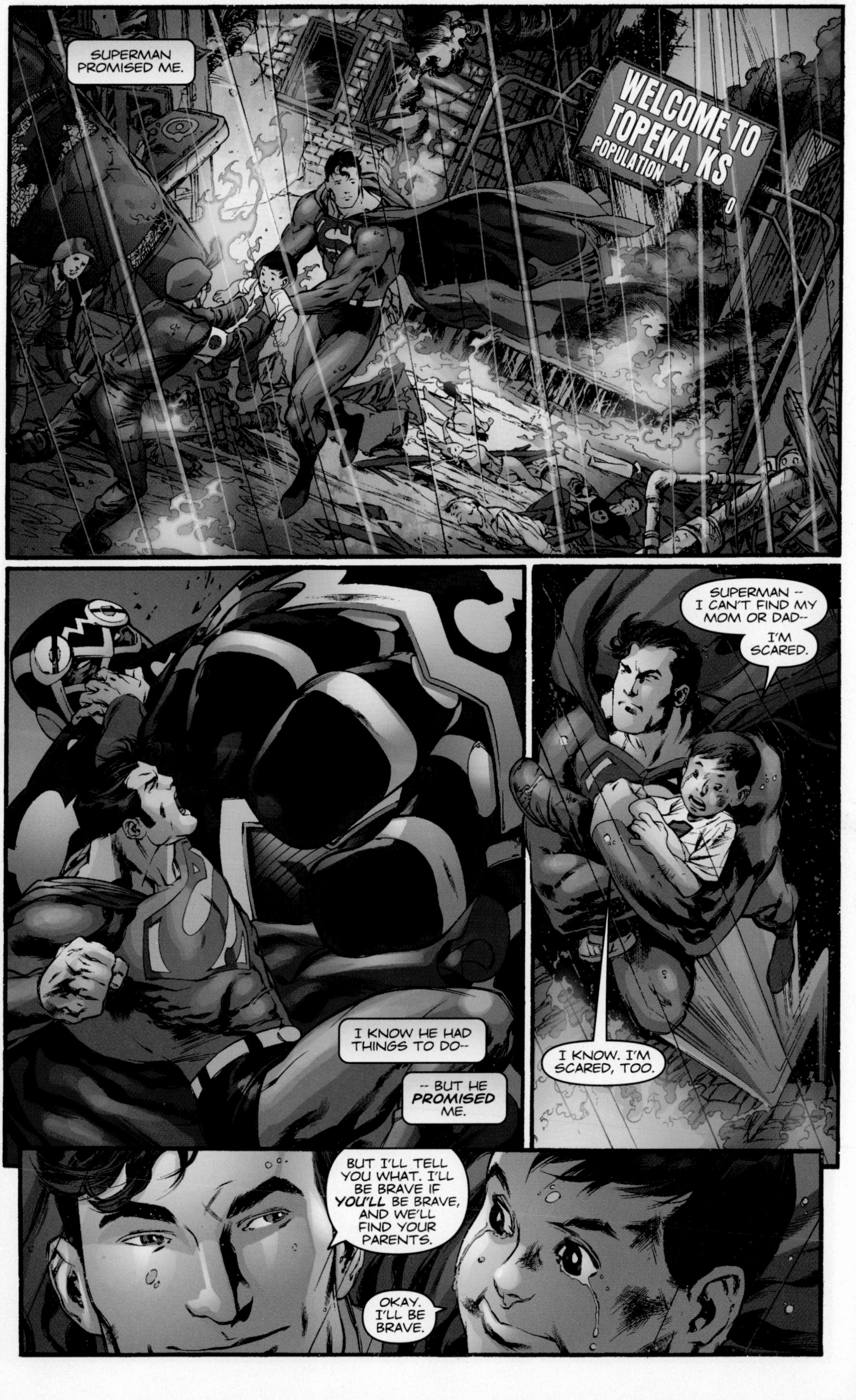

SUPERMAN PROMISED ME.
WELCOME TO TOPEKA, KS POPULATION 0
I KNOW HE HAD THINGS TO DO--
-- BUT HE PROMISED ME.
SUPERMAN -- I CAN'T FIND MY MOM OR DAD-- I'M SCARED.
I KNOW. I'M SCARED, TOO.
BUT I'LL TELL YOU WHAT. I'LL BE BRAVE IF YOU'LL BE BRAVE, AND WE'LL FIND YOUR PARENTS.
OKAY. I'LL BE BRAVE.

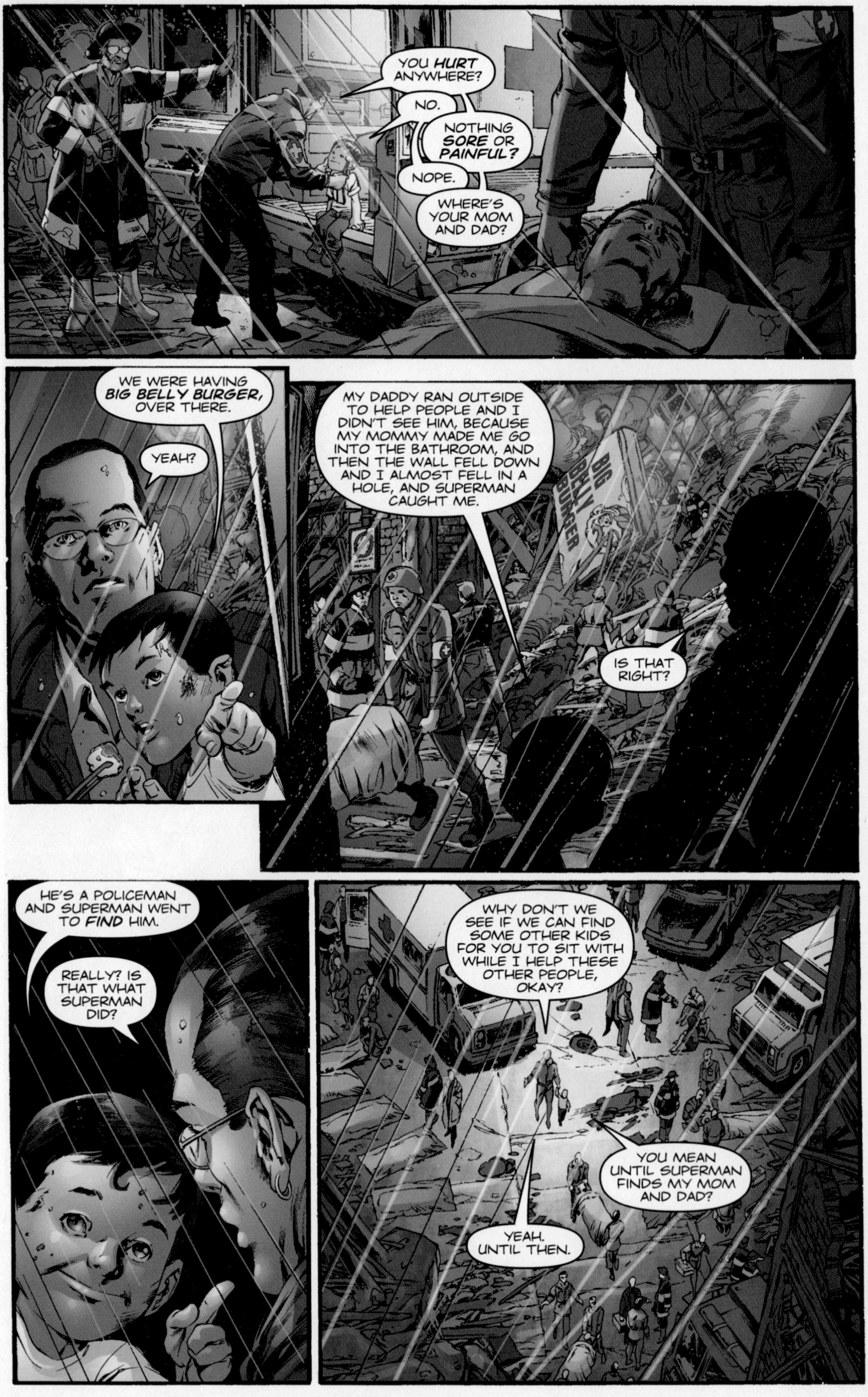

YOU HURT ANYWHERE?
NO.
NOTHING SORE OR PAINFUL?
NOPE.
WHERE'S YOUR MOM AND DAD?
WE WERE HAVING BIG BELLY BURGER, OVER THERE.
YEAH?
MY DADDY RAN OUTSIDE TO HELP PEOPLE AND I DIDN'T SEE HIM, BECAUSE MY MOMMY MADE ME GO INTO THE BATHROOM, AND THEN THE WALL FELL DOWN AND I ALMOST FELL IN A HOLE, AND SUPERMAN CAUGHT ME.
BIG BELLY BURGER
IS THAT RIGHT?
HE'S A POLICEMAN AND SUPERMAN WENT TO FIND HIM.
REALLY? IS THAT WHAT SUPERMAN DID?
WHY DON'T WE SEE IF WE CAN FIND SOME OTHER KIDS FOR YOU TO SIT WITH WHILE I HELP THESE OTHER PEOPLE, OKAY?
YOU MEAN UNTIL SUPERMAN FINDS MY MOM AND DAD?
YEAH. UNTIL THEN.

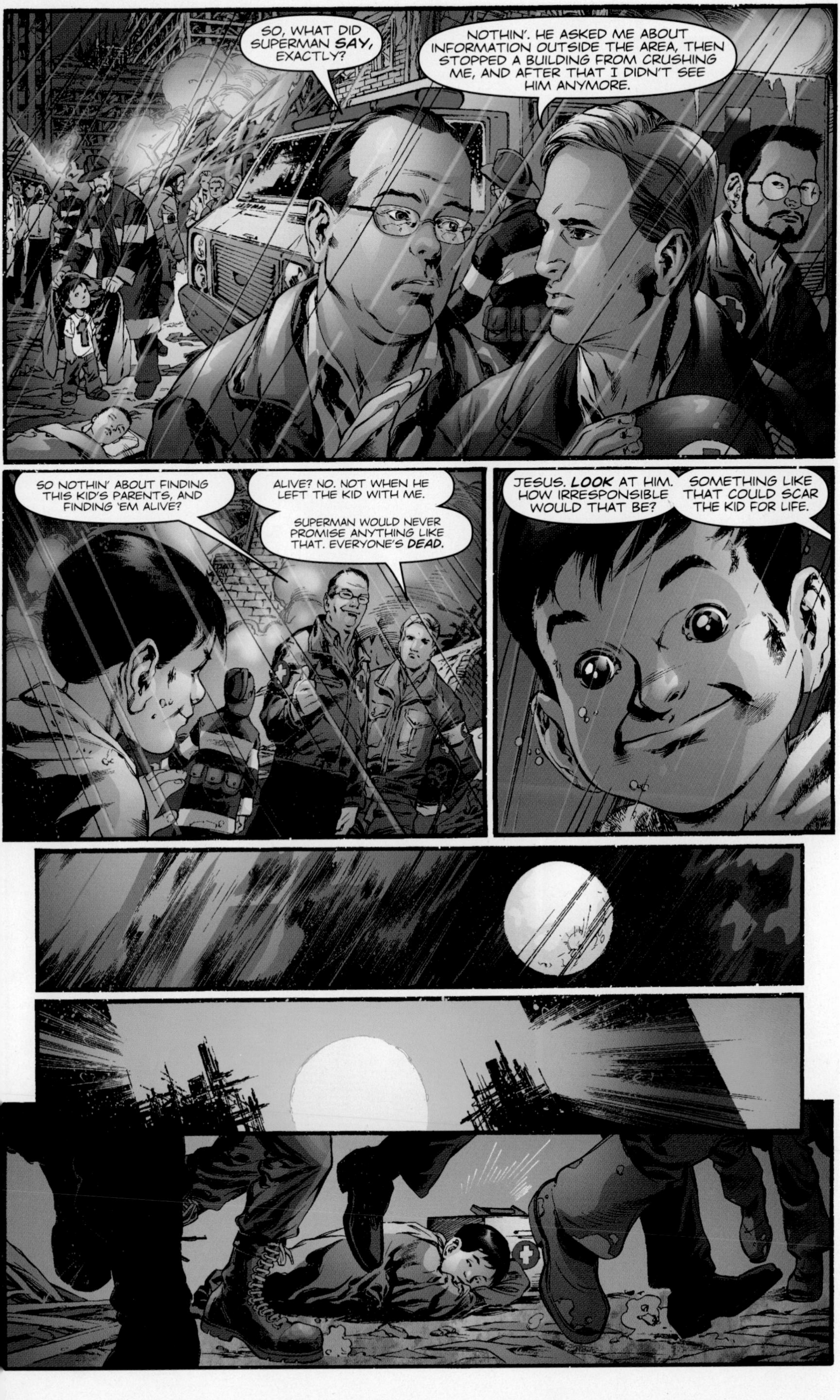
SO, WHAT DID SUPERMAN SAY, EXACTLY?
NOTHIN'. HE ASKED ME ABOUT INFORMATION OUTSIDE THE AREA, THEN STOPPED A BUILDING FROM CRUSHING ME, AND AFTER THAT I DIDN'T SEE HIM ANYMORE.
SO NOTHIN' ABOUT FINDING THIS KID'S PARENTS, AND FINDING 'EM ALIVE?
ALIVE? NO. NOT WHEN HE LEFT THE KID WITH ME.
SUPERMAN WOULD NEVER PROMISE ANYTHING LIKE THAT. EVERYONE'S DEAD.
JESUS. LOOK AT HIM. HOW IRRESPONSIBLE WOULD THAT BE?
SOMETHING LIKE THAT COULD SCAR THE KID FOR LIFE.

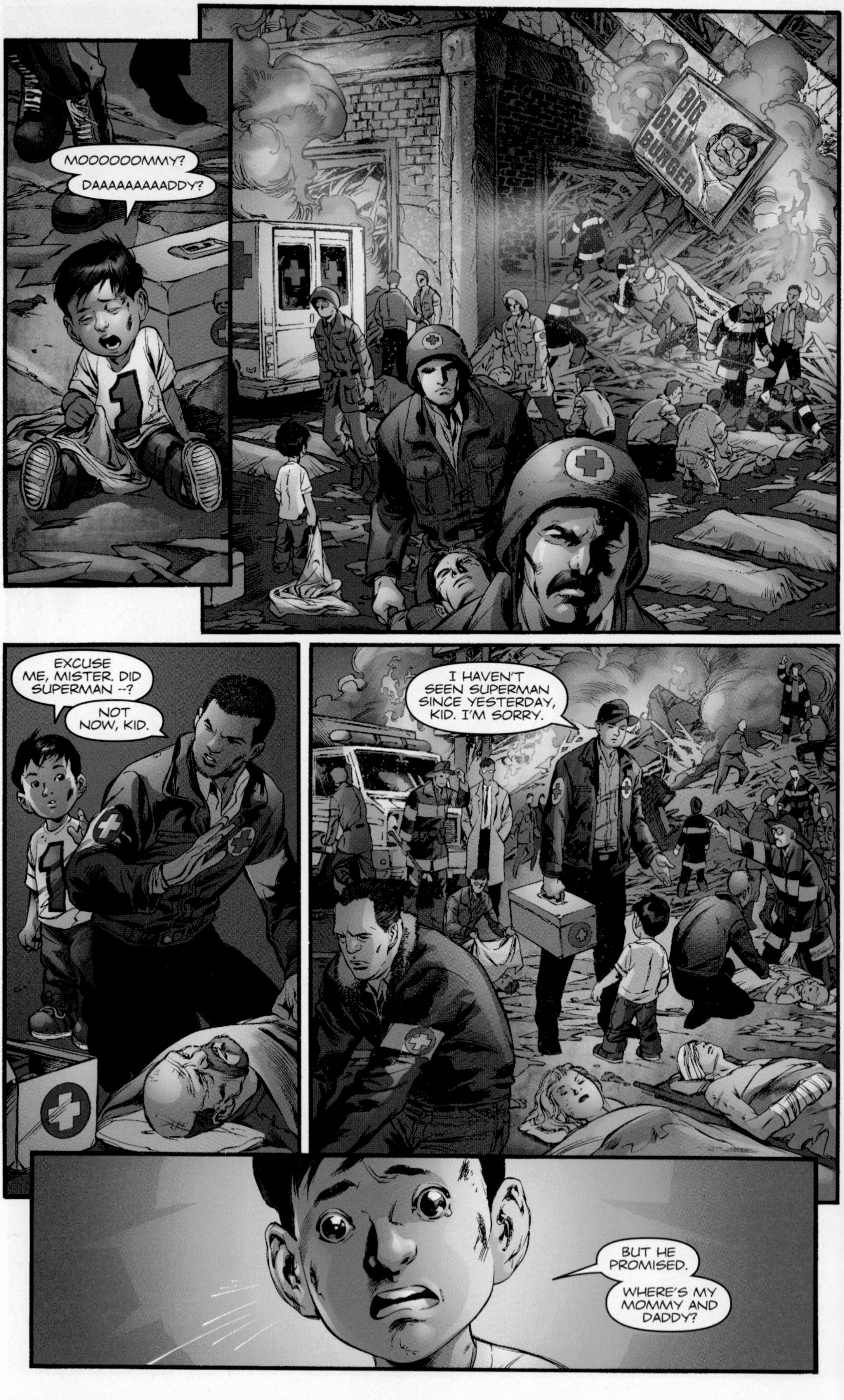
MOOOOOOMMY?
DAAAAAAAAADDY?
BIG BELLY BURGER
EXCUSE ME, MISTER. DID SUPERMAN --?
NOT NOW, KID.
I HAVEN'T SEEN SUPERMAN SINCE YESTERDAY, KID. I'M SORRY.
BUT HE PROMISED.
WHERE'S MY MOMMY AND DADDY?

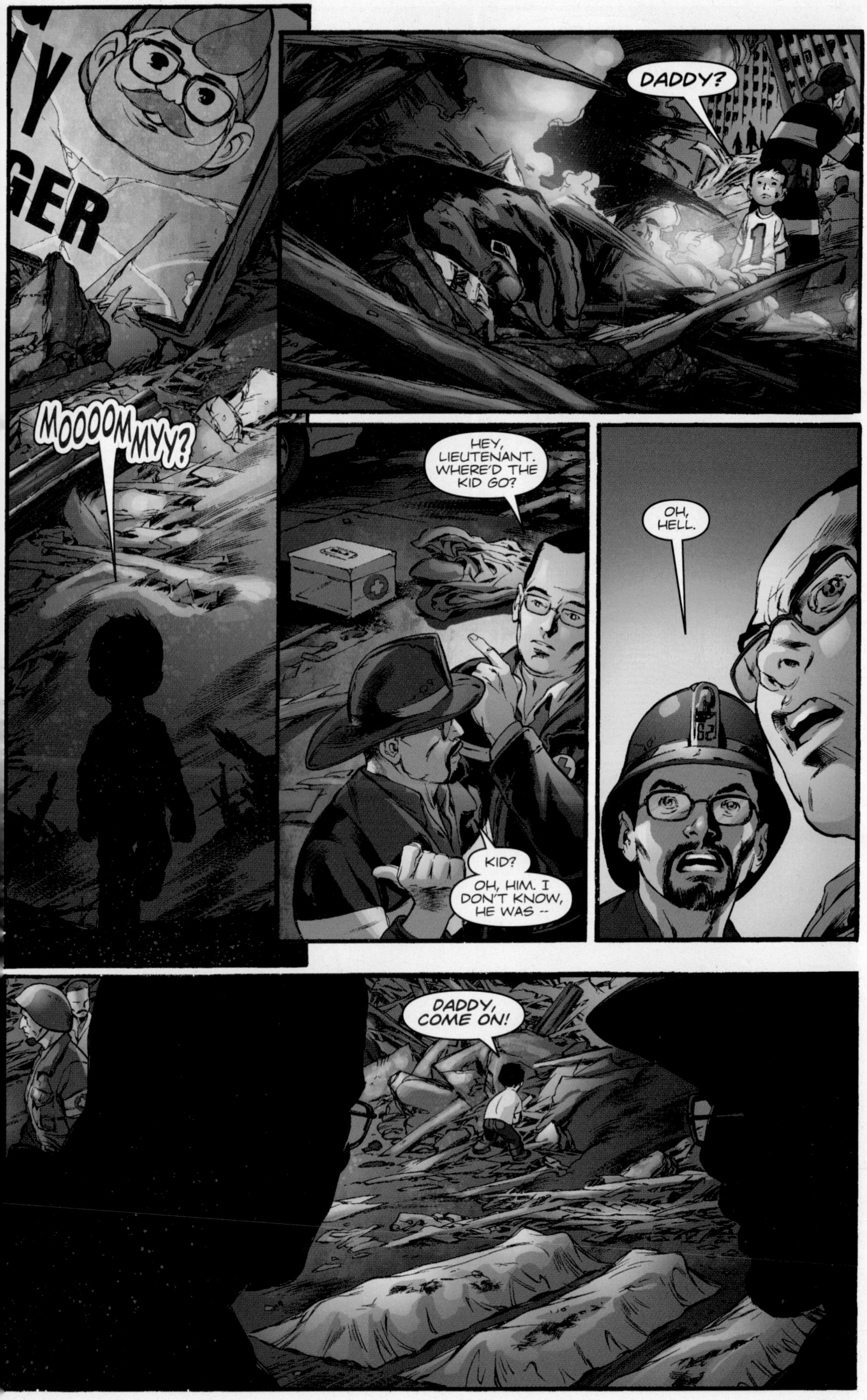
DADDY?
MOOOOMMYY?
HEY, LIEUTENANT. WHERE'D THE KID GO?
KID?
OH, HIM. I DON'T KNOW, HE WAS --
OH, HELL.
DADDY, COME ON!

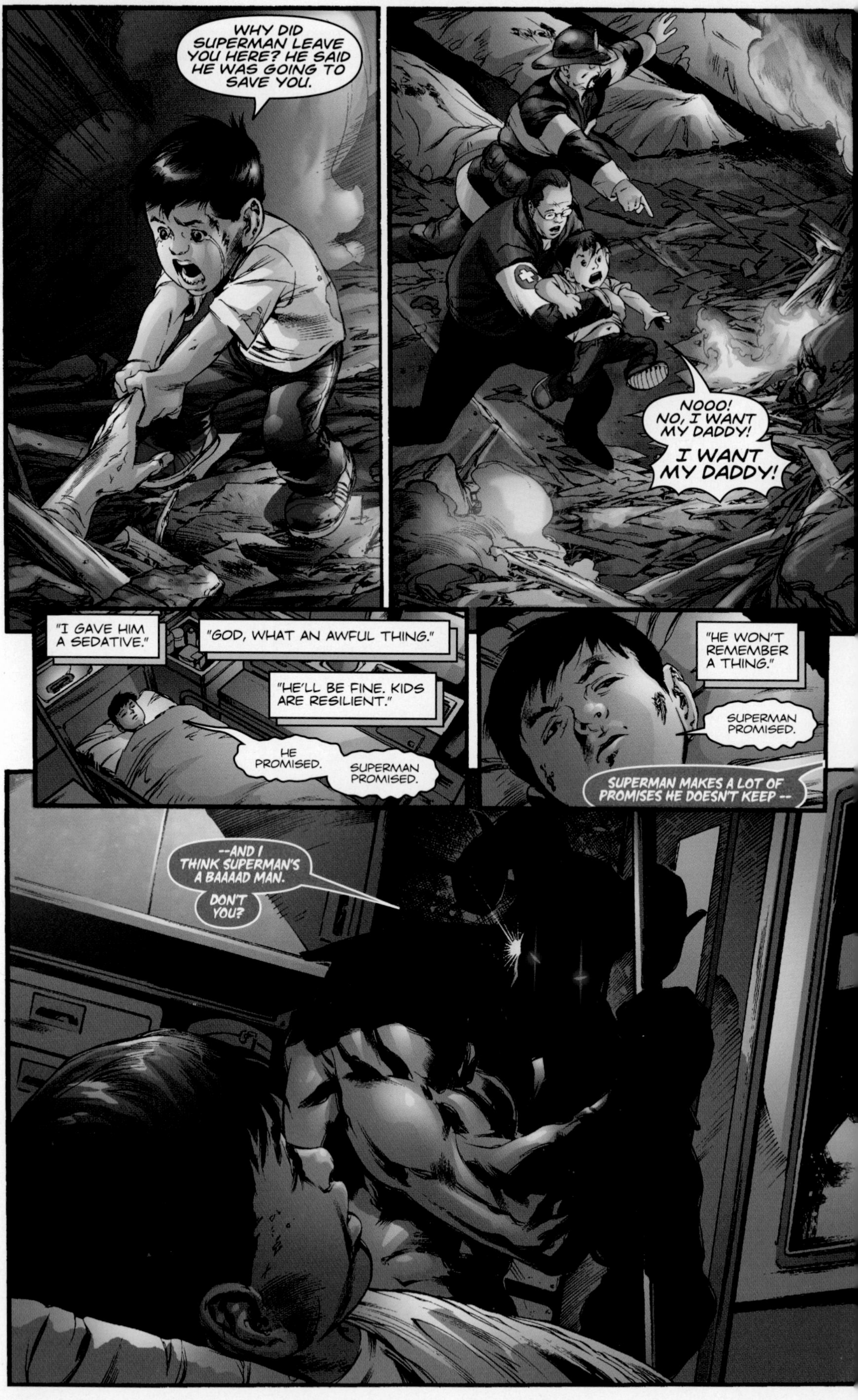
WHY DID SUPERMAN LEAVE YOU HERE? HE SAID HE WAS GOING TO SAVE YOU.
NOOO! NO, I WANT MY DADDY!
I WANT MY DADDY!
"I GAVE HIM A SEDATIVE."
"GOD, WHAT AN AWFUL THING."
"HE'LL BE FINE. KIDS ARE RESILIENT."
HE PROMISED.
SUPERMAN PROMISED.
"HE WON'T REMEMBER A THING."
SUPERMAN PROMISED.
SUPERMAN MAKES A LOT OF PROMISES HE DOESN'T KEEP --
--AND I THINK SUPERMAN'S A BAAAAD MAN.
DON'T YOU?

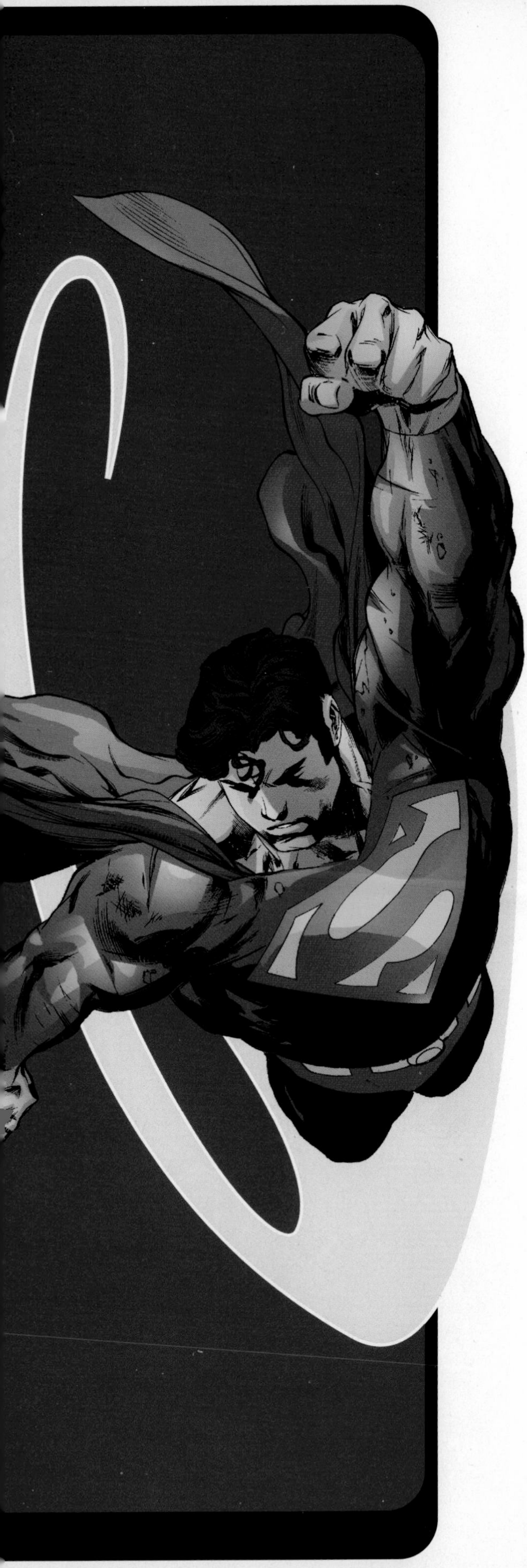

THE STORY THUS FAR...

Faster than a speeding bullet, more powerful than a locomotive, able to leap the tallest buildings with a single bound...**Superman** is known to all as the world's greatest super-hero. While he has faced many challenges that have tested his heroic abilities, the Man of Steel now finds himself in a situation that has its roots in several of his past adventures...

Although he is a protector of all mankind, Superman calls **Metropolis** home. A sprawling city teeming with skyscrapers and bustling with activity, Metropolis is known to many as the City of Tomorrow.

Superman found himself manipulated by the enigmatic **Futuresmiths**, cloaked beings who used Metropolis's futuristic technology to change the course of time. In an effort to confuse and distract the Man of Steel from their true plans, they engineered many events, including the creation of **Cir-El** — a new Supergirl who claimed to be Superman's daughter — and a robotic Superman from a far-flung future who warned of an impending technological doom thanks to the Futuresmiths.

Clark Kent and his *Daily Planet* editor Perry White faked Kent's firing, allowing him to go undercover to look for proof that President Lex Luthor was engaged in criminal activities. Shortly thereafter, Superman and Batman began an assault on Luthor to bring him down once and for all. Luthor, in turn, once more tried to turn the populace against its otherworldly protector by proclaiming a meteor approaching Earth was from Krypton and could wipe out humanity. The heroes prevailed, bringing down the president. Vice President Pete Ross was sworn in as president to complete the term.

Perry rehired Clark to return to the *Planet*, but in a lesser role. Before Clark could reestablish himself, Metropolis was thrust into a new crisis.

The **Robot Superman** took Kal-El into the time stream itself to witness how his actions in the present were all planned to bring about the Futuresmiths and unleash a deadly nanotech virus upon humankind. Finally, thousands of years in the future, Superman confronted the Futuresmiths, who were revealed to be merely servants of another consciousness: Brainiac 12. This iteration of the green-skinned despot used Cir-El to take hold in the present (disguised as the one thing Superman would not attack: his offspring) and ensure a world overrun by machines that would give rise to an even more powerful Brainiac 13. Locked in a struggle with Brainiac 12, Superman was knocked into the time stream, where he left his foe trapped inside a temporal anomaly, imprisoned in a sort of phantom zone. This act of heroism left Superman adrift through time, tumbling through a multitude of possible realities until he found his way home.

With Superman gone, Earth was troubled. A hero from another reality, Majestic, briefly helped out, seeing to it that time corrected itself and Metropolis was returned to its normal 21st-century splendor. Superman's friends and especially his wife, Lois, felt adrift. His return signaled a fresh start.

Almost immediately upon the restoration of the time stream, the asteroid crashed into the ocean and brought with it Kal-El's cousin Kara. Over a period of weeks, she acclimated herself to Earth, currently training with the Amazons on Themyscira.

Meantime, life continued as White hired Jack Ryder to fill Kent's investigative reporting slot. When Clark Kent was finally ready to return to work, he had to settle for something lower on the food chain.

Accounts of these events can be found in the following collections:

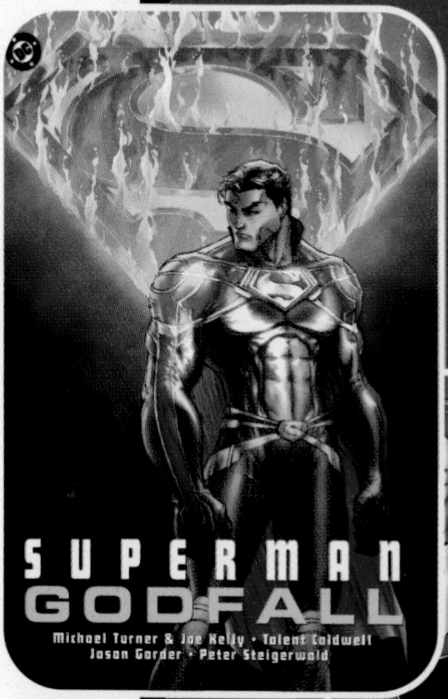
SUPERMAN
GODFALL
Michael Turner & Joe Kelly • Talent Caldwell
Jason Gorder • Peter Steigerwald

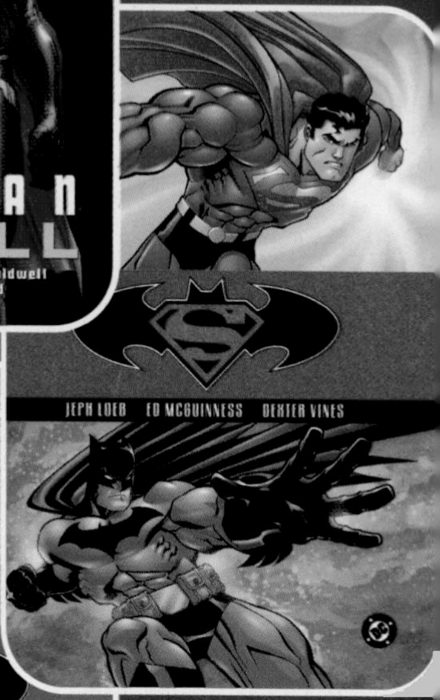
JEPH LOEB ED MCGUINNESS DEXTER VINES

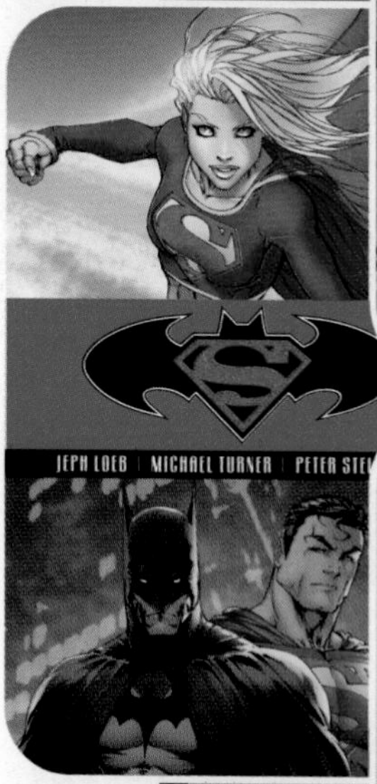
JEPH LOEB | MICHAEL TURNER

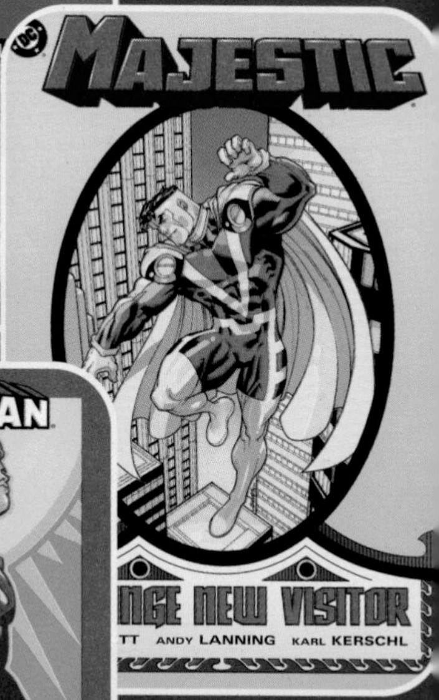
MAJESTIC
ANDY LANNING KARL KERSCHL

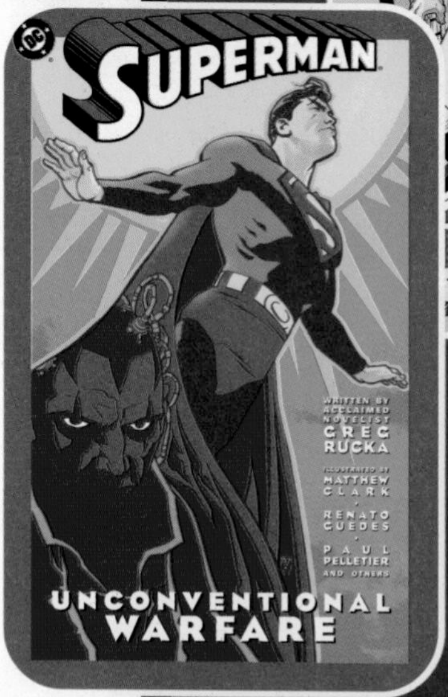
SUPERMAN
WRITTEN BY ACCLAIMED NOVELIST GREG RUCKA
ILLUSTRATED BY MATTHEW CLARK
RENATO GUEDES
PAUL PELLETIER AND OTHERS
UNCONVENTIONAL WARFARE

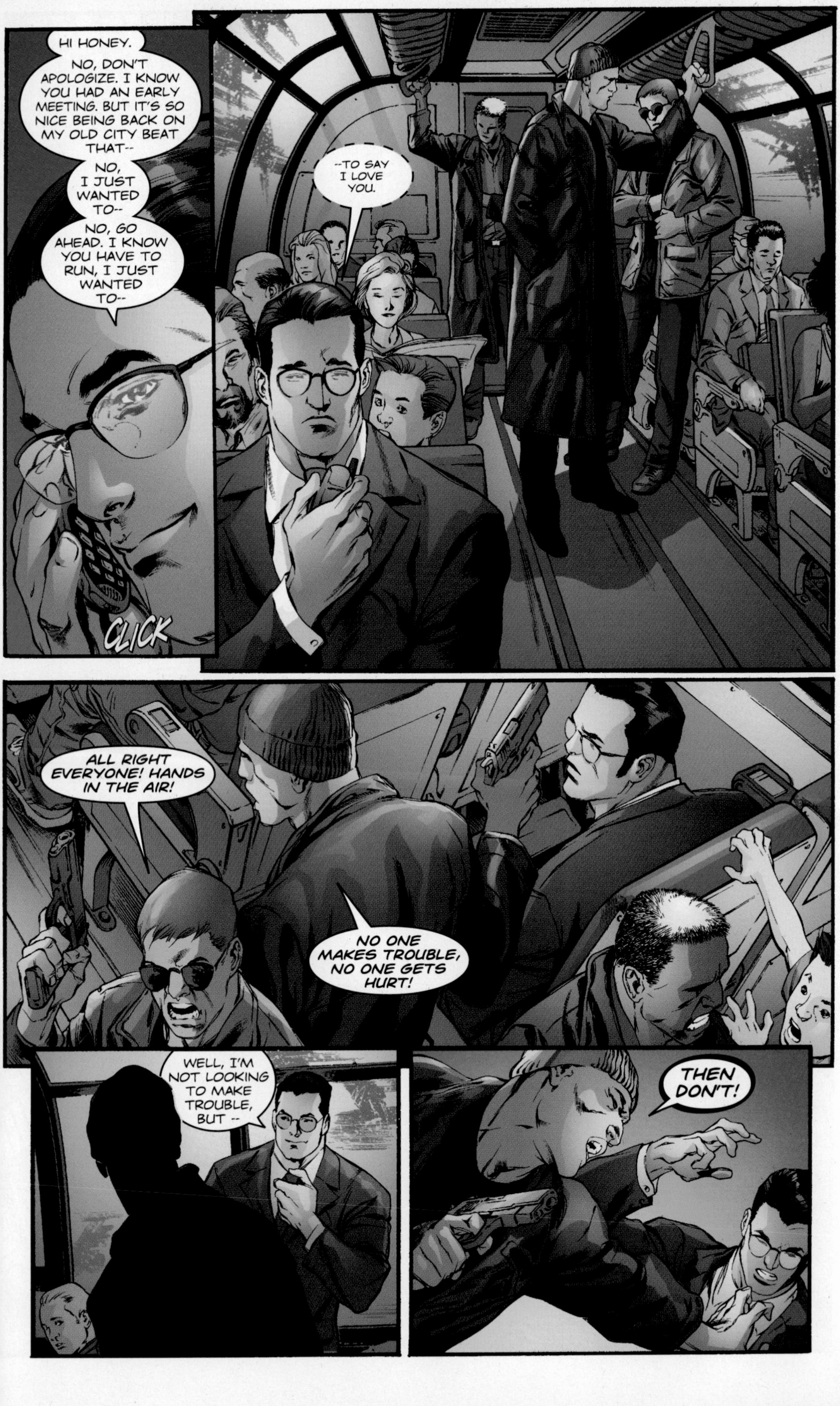
HI HONEY.
NO, DON'T APOLOGIZE. I KNOW YOU HAD AN EARLY MEETING. BUT IT'S SO NICE BEING BACK ON MY OLD CITY BEAT THAT--
NO, I JUST WANTED TO--
NO, GO AHEAD. I KNOW YOU HAVE TO RUN, I JUST WANTED TO--
CLICK
--TO SAY I LOVE YOU.
ALL RIGHT EVERYONE! HANDS IN THE AIR!
NO ONE MAKES TROUBLE, NO ONE GETS HURT!
WELL, I'M NOT LOOKING TO MAKE TROUBLE, BUT --
THEN DON'T!

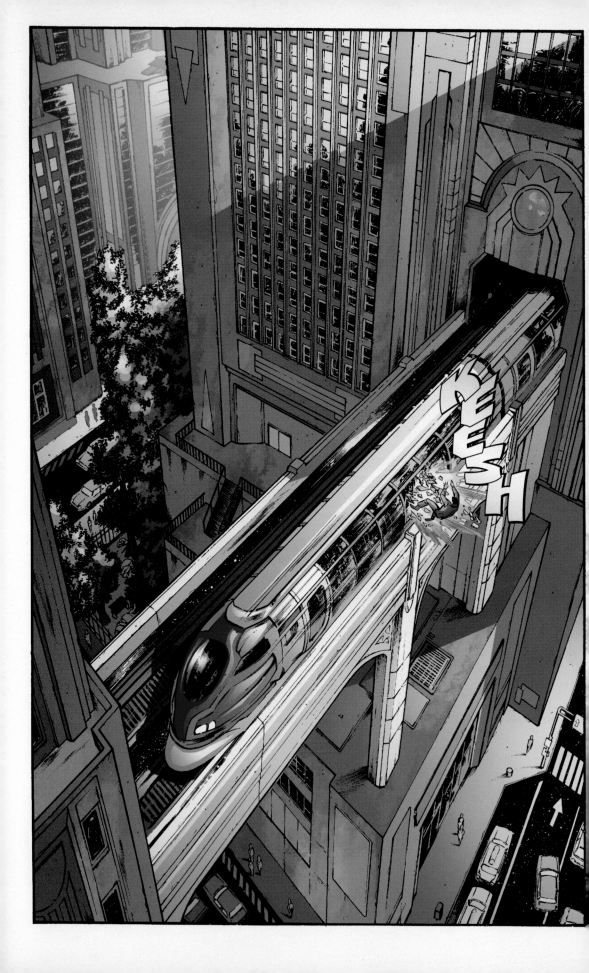

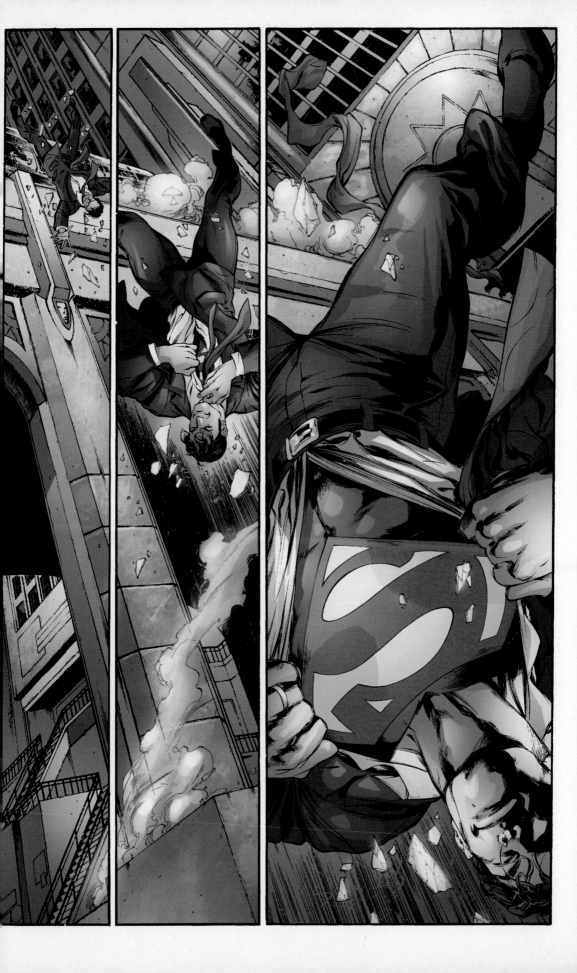

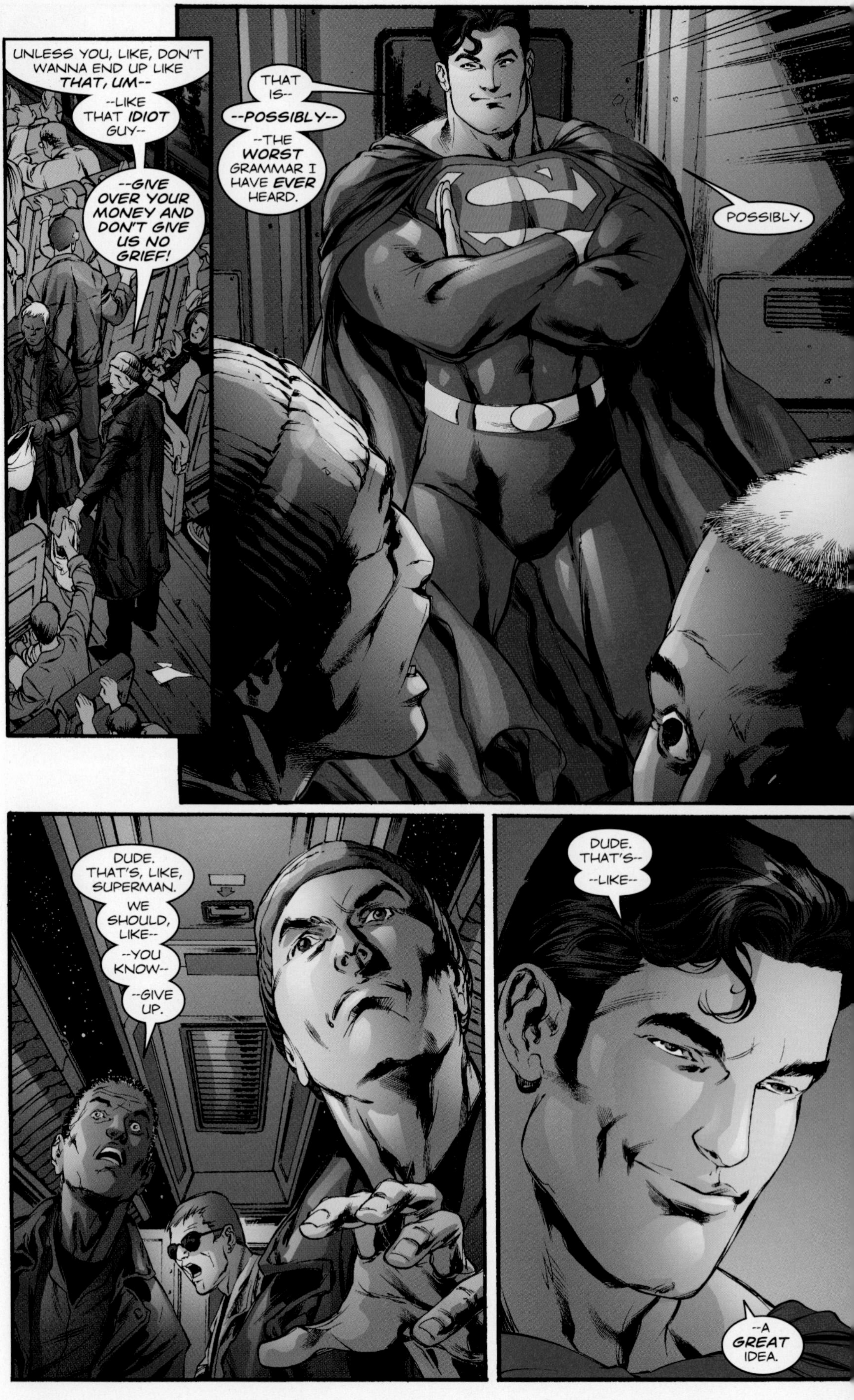

UNLESS YOU, LIKE, DON'T WANNA END UP LIKE THAT, UM--
--LIKE THAT IDIOT GUY--
--GIVE OVER YOUR MONEY AND DON'T GIVE US NO GRIEF!
THAT IS--
--POSSIBLY--
--THE WORST GRAMMAR I HAVE EVER HEARD.
POSSIBLY.
DUDE. THAT'S, LIKE, SUPERMAN.
WE SHOULD, LIKE--
--YOU KNOW--
--GIVE UP.
DUDE. THAT'S--
--LIKE--
--A GREAT IDEA.

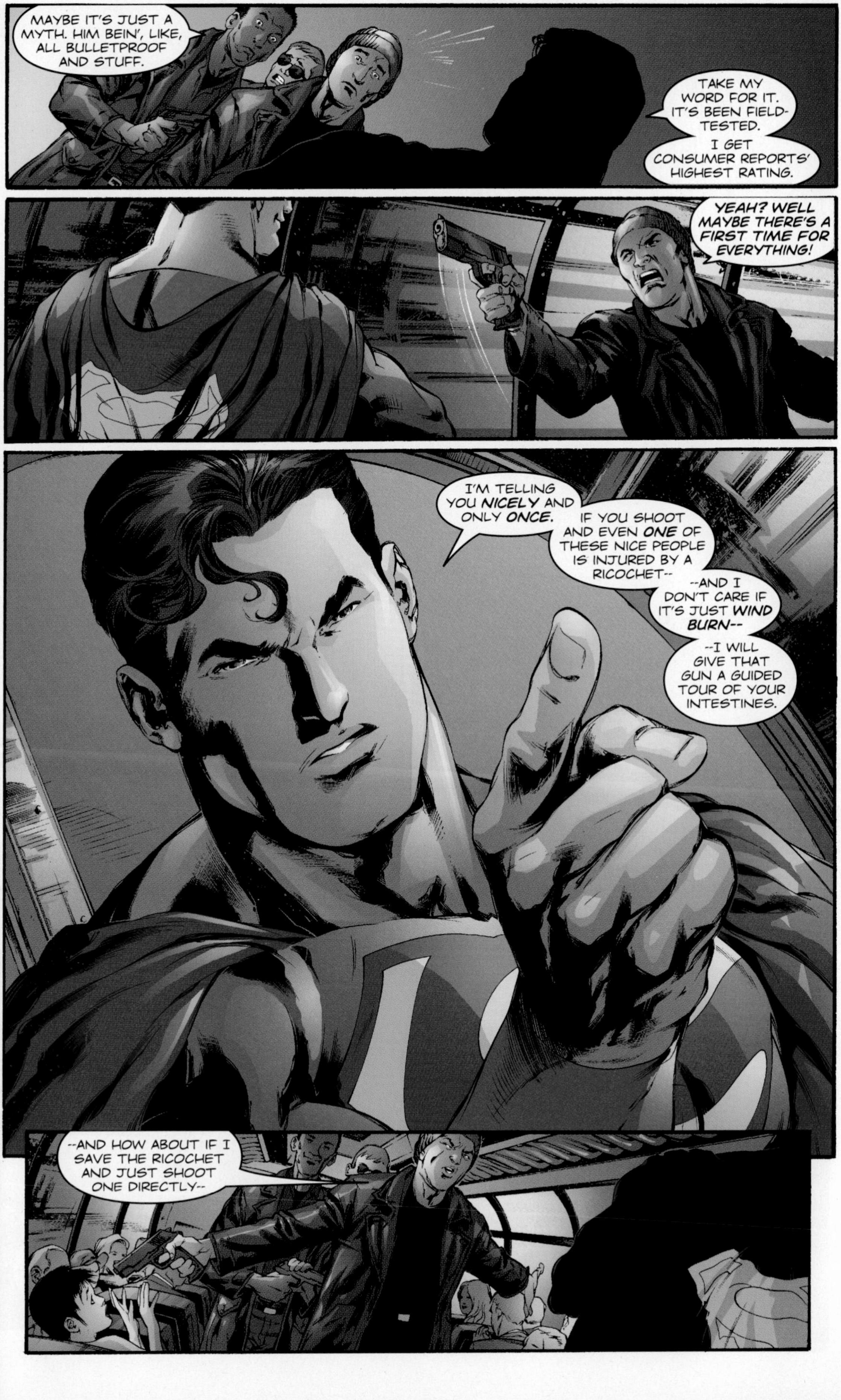
MAYBE IT'S JUST A MYTH. HIM BEIN', LIKE, ALL BULLETPROOF AND STUFF.
TAKE MY WORD FOR IT. IT'S BEEN FIELD-TESTED.
I GET CONSUMER REPORTS' HIGHEST RATING.
YEAH? WELL MAYBE THERE'S A FIRST TIME FOR EVERYTHING!
I'M TELLING YOU NICELY AND ONLY ONCE.
IF YOU SHOOT AND EVEN ONE OF THESE NICE PEOPLE IS INJURED BY A RICOCHET--
--AND I DON'T CARE IF IT'S JUST WIND BURN--
--I WILL GIVE THAT GUN A GUIDED TOUR OF YOUR INTESTINES.
--AND HOW ABOUT IF I SAVE THE RICOCHET AND JUST SHOOT ONE DIRECTLY--

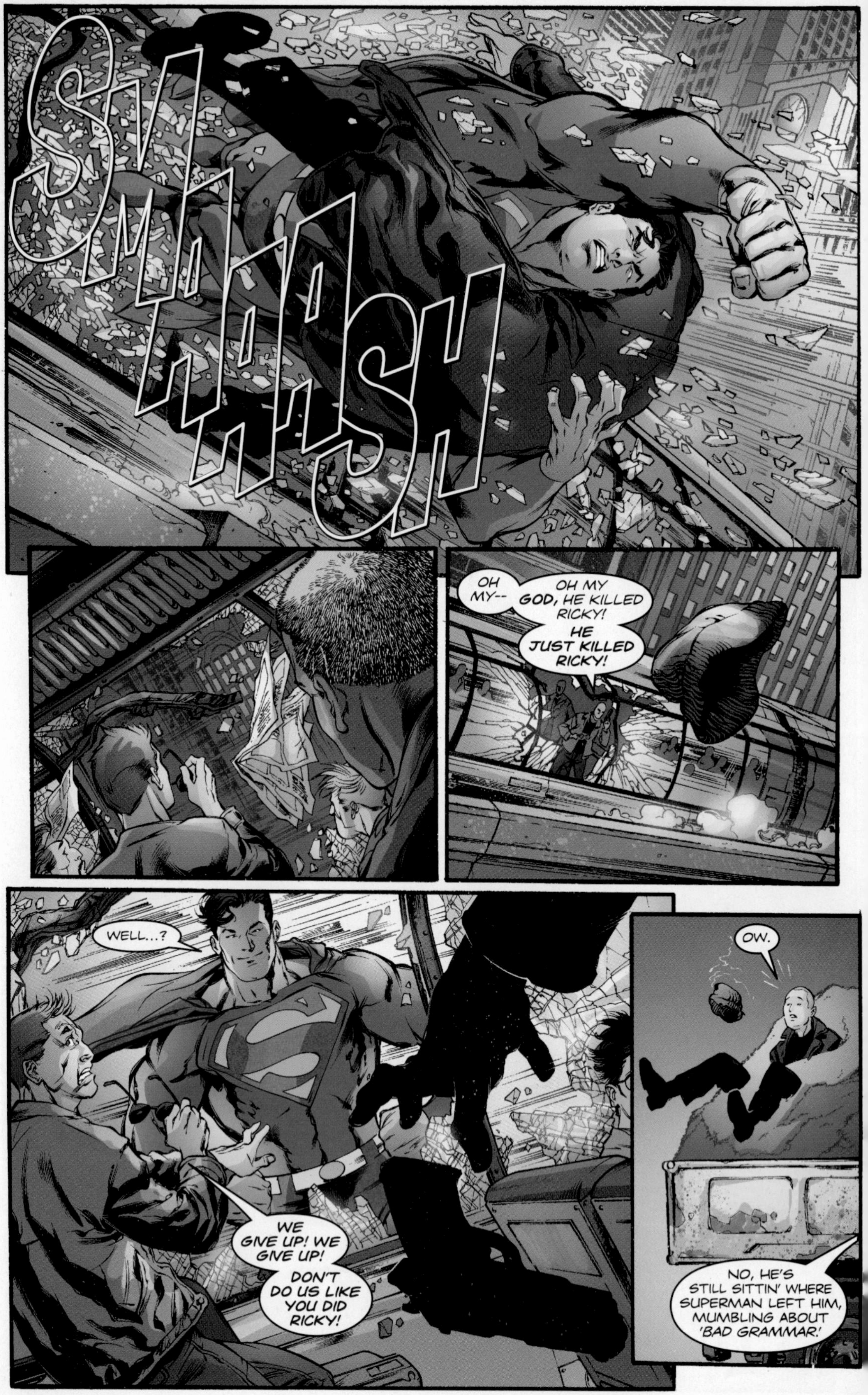
SMAASH
OH MY--
OH MY GOD, HE KILLED RICKY!
HE JUST KILLED RICKY!
WELL...?
WE GIVE UP! WE GIVE UP!
DON'T DO US LIKE YOU DID RICKY!
OW.
NO, HE'S STILL SITTIN' WHERE SUPERMAN LEFT HIM, MUMBLING ABOUT 'BAD GRAMMAR.'

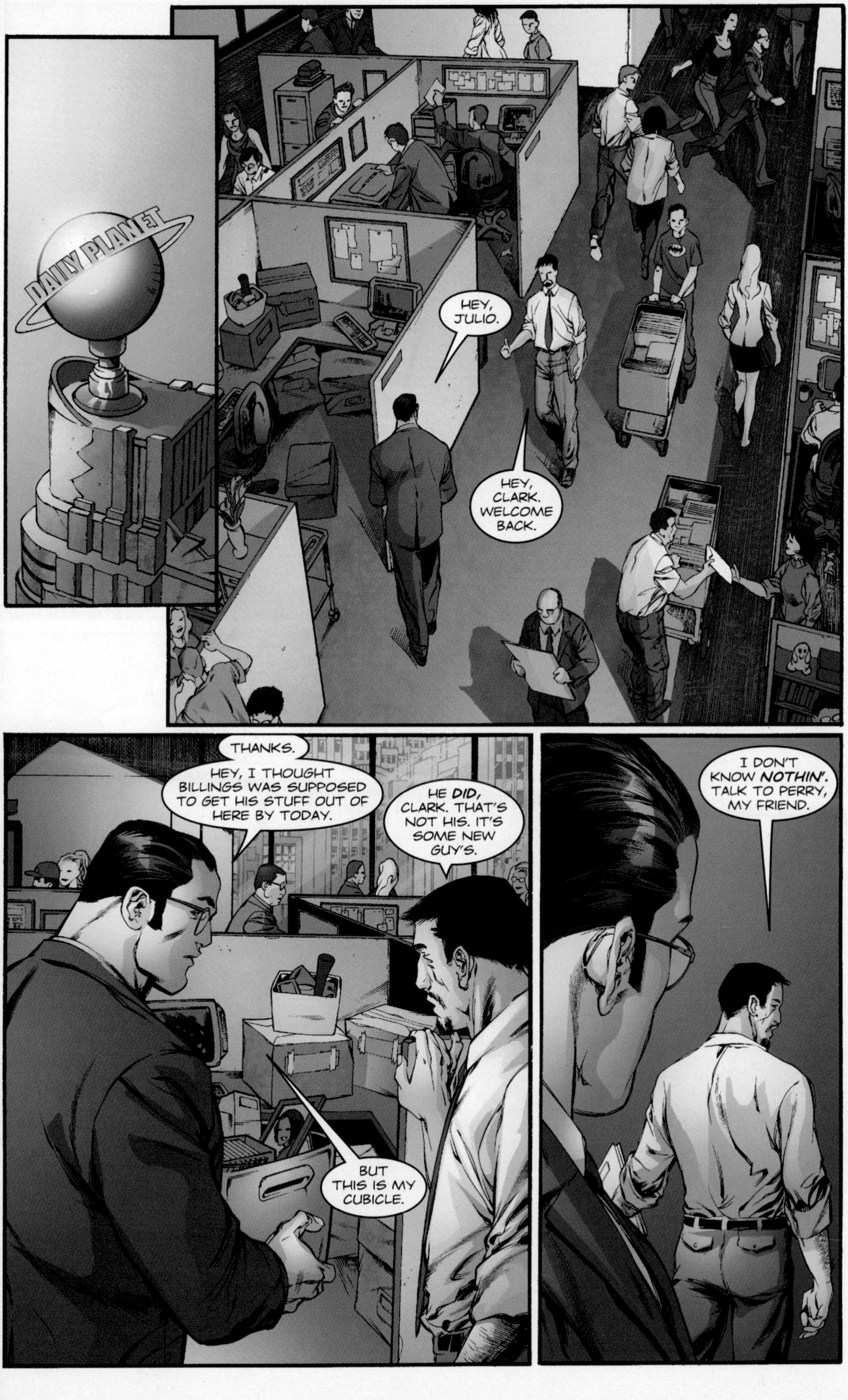
DAILY PLANET
HEY, JULIO.
HEY, CLARK. WELCOME BACK.
THANKS.
HEY, I THOUGHT BILLINGS WAS SUPPOSED TO GET HIS STUFF OUT OF HERE BY TODAY.
HE *DID*, CLARK. THAT'S NOT HIS. IT'S SOME NEW GUY'S.
BUT THIS IS MY CUBICLE.
I DON'T KNOW ***NOTHIN'***. TALK TO PERRY, MY FRIEND.

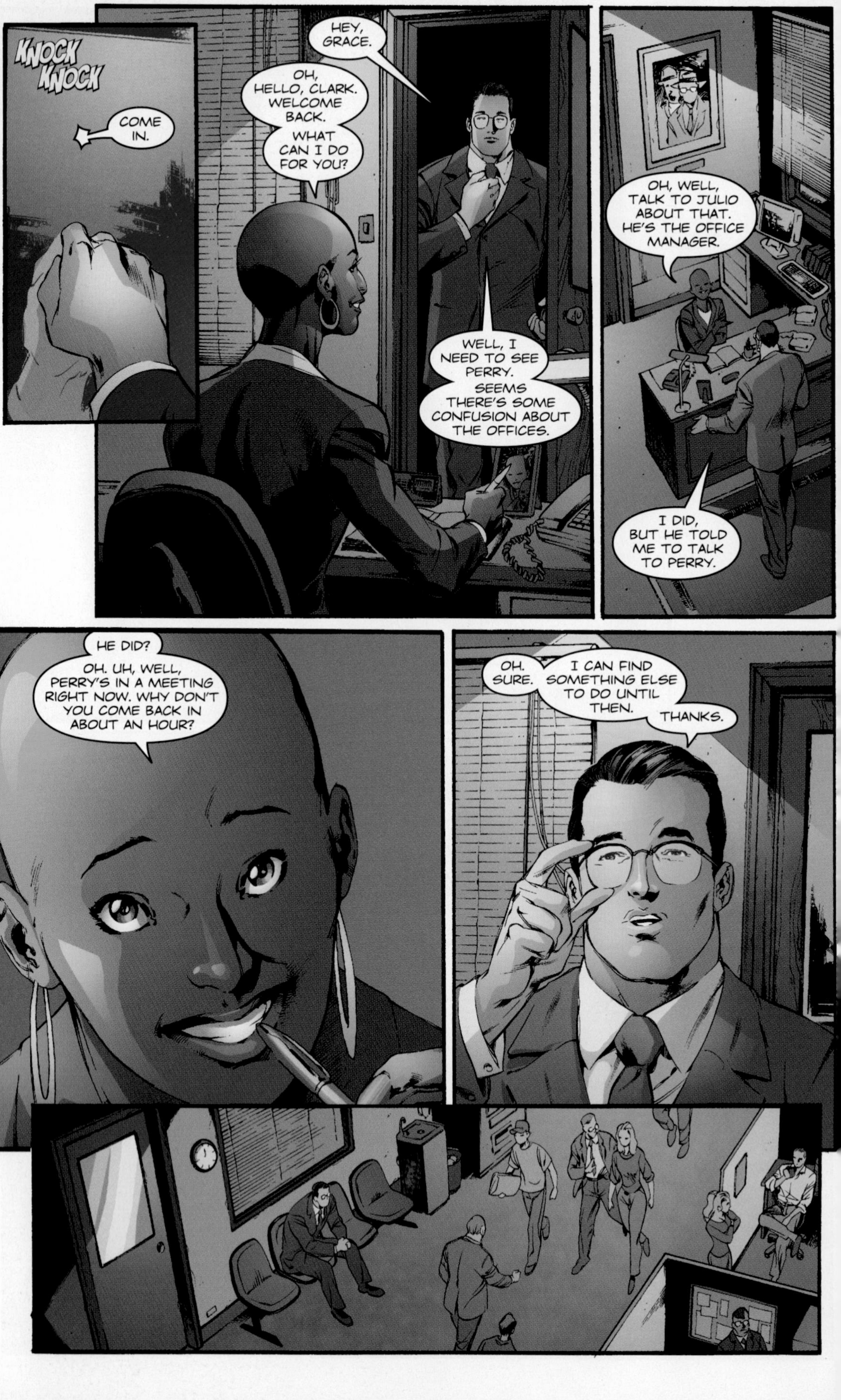
KNOCK KNOCK
COME IN.
HEY, GRACE.
OH, HELLO, CLARK. WELCOME BACK.
WHAT CAN I DO FOR YOU?
WELL, I NEED TO SEE PERRY.
SEEMS THERE'S SOME CONFUSION ABOUT THE OFFICES.
OH, WELL, TALK TO JULIO ABOUT THAT. HE'S THE OFFICE MANAGER.
I DID, BUT HE TOLD ME TO TALK TO PERRY.
HE DID?
OH. UH, WELL, PERRY'S IN A MEETING RIGHT NOW. WHY DON'T YOU COME BACK IN ABOUT AN HOUR?
OH. SURE.
I CAN FIND SOMETHING ELSE TO DO UNTIL THEN.
THANKS.

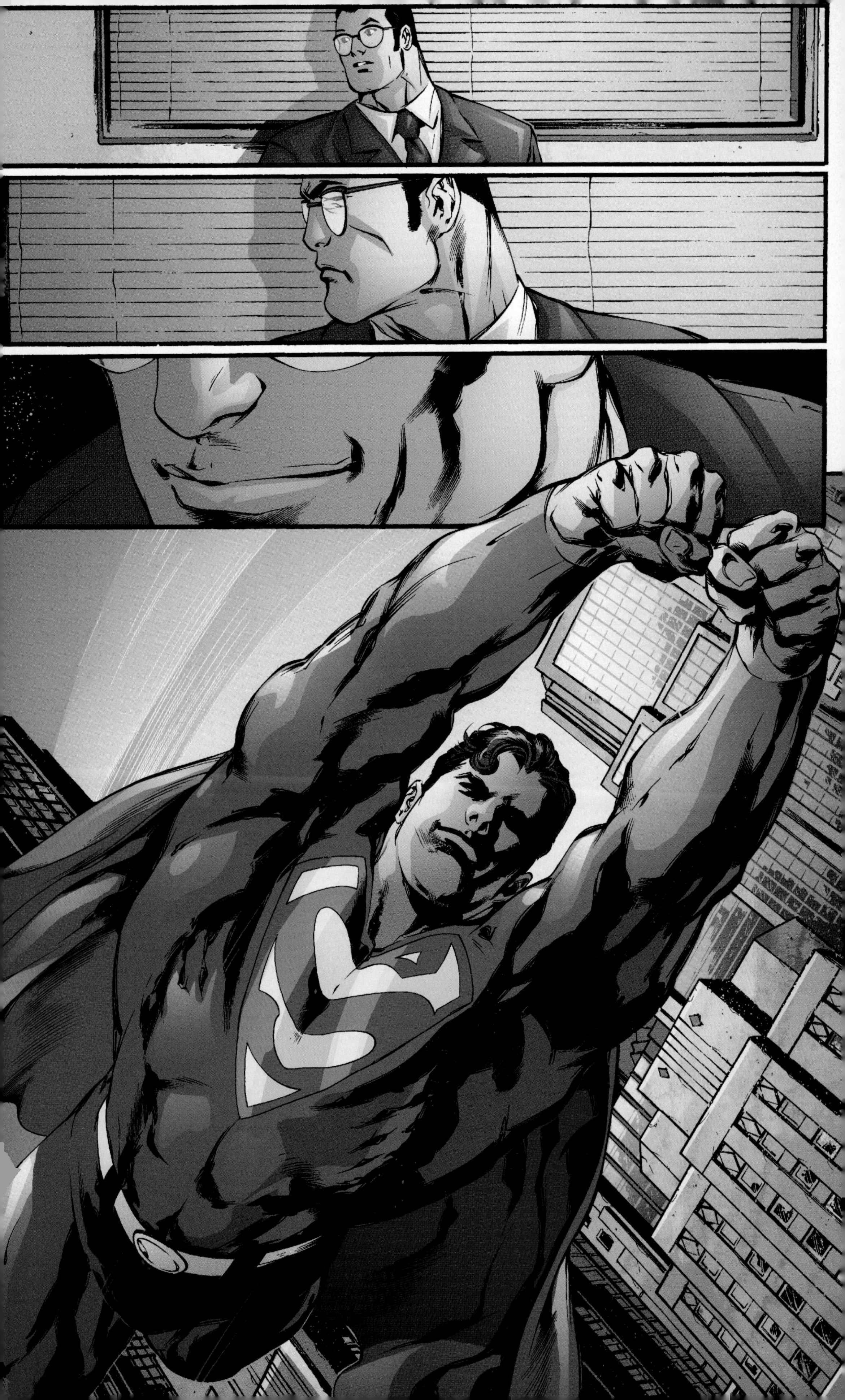

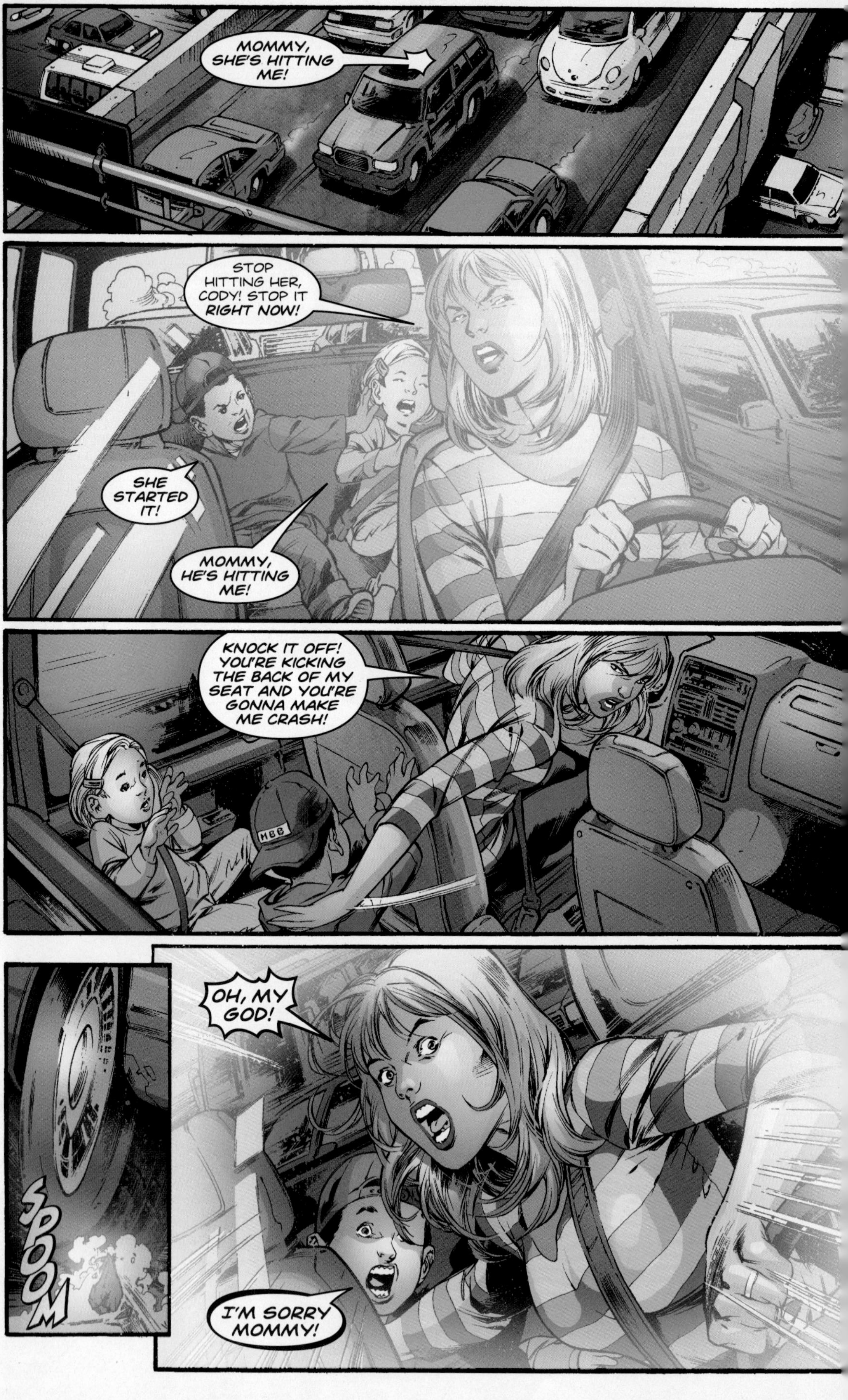
MOMMY, SHE'S HITTING ME!
STOP HITTING HER, CODY! STOP IT RIGHT NOW!
SHE STARTED IT!
MOMMY, HE'S HITTING ME!
KNOCK IT OFF! YOU'RE KICKING THE BACK OF MY SEAT AND YOU'RE GONNA MAKE ME CRASH!
MBB
SPOOM
OH, MY GOD!
I'M SORRY MOMMY!

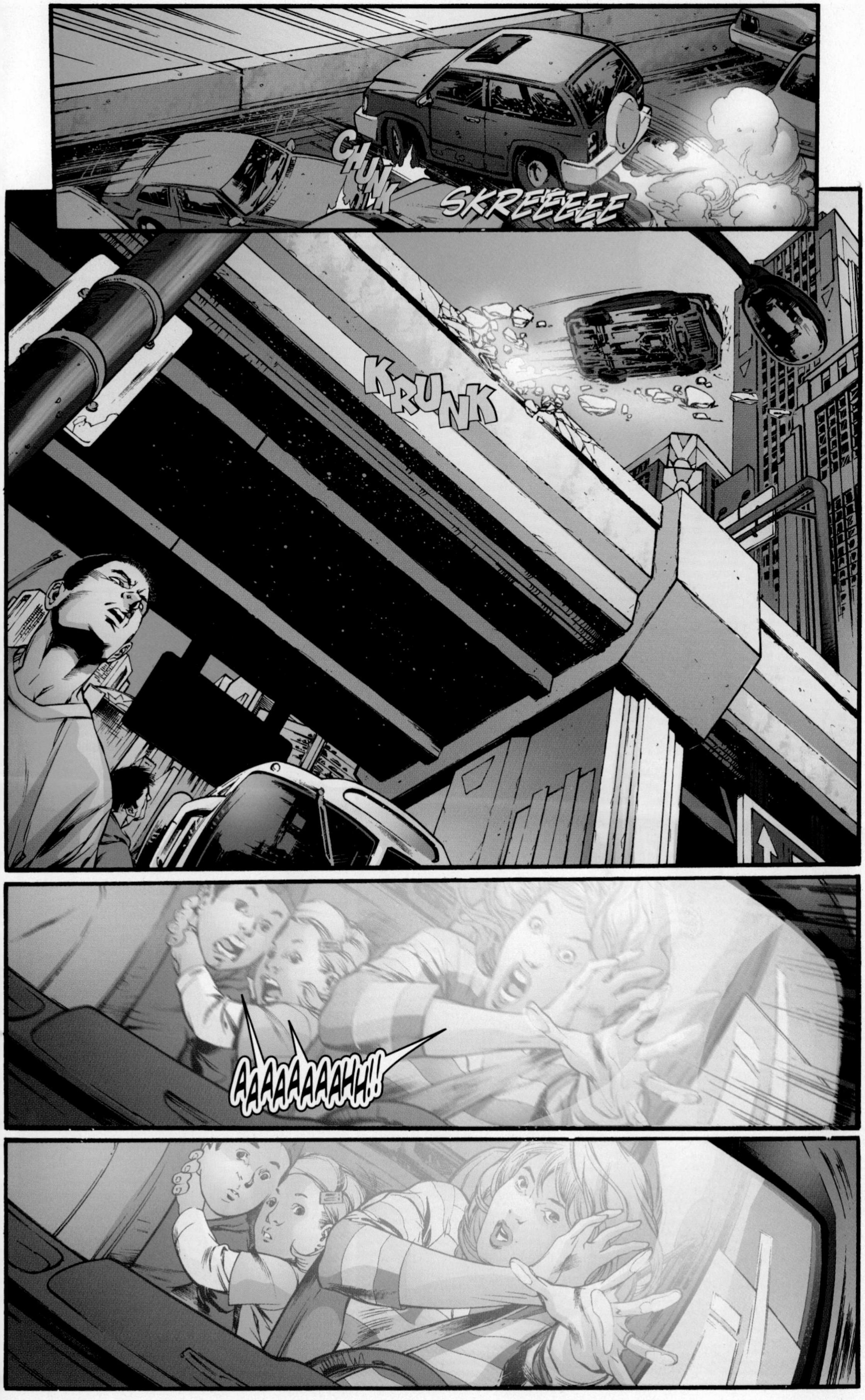
CHUNK
CHUNK
SKREEEEEE
KRUNK
AAAAAAAAH!!

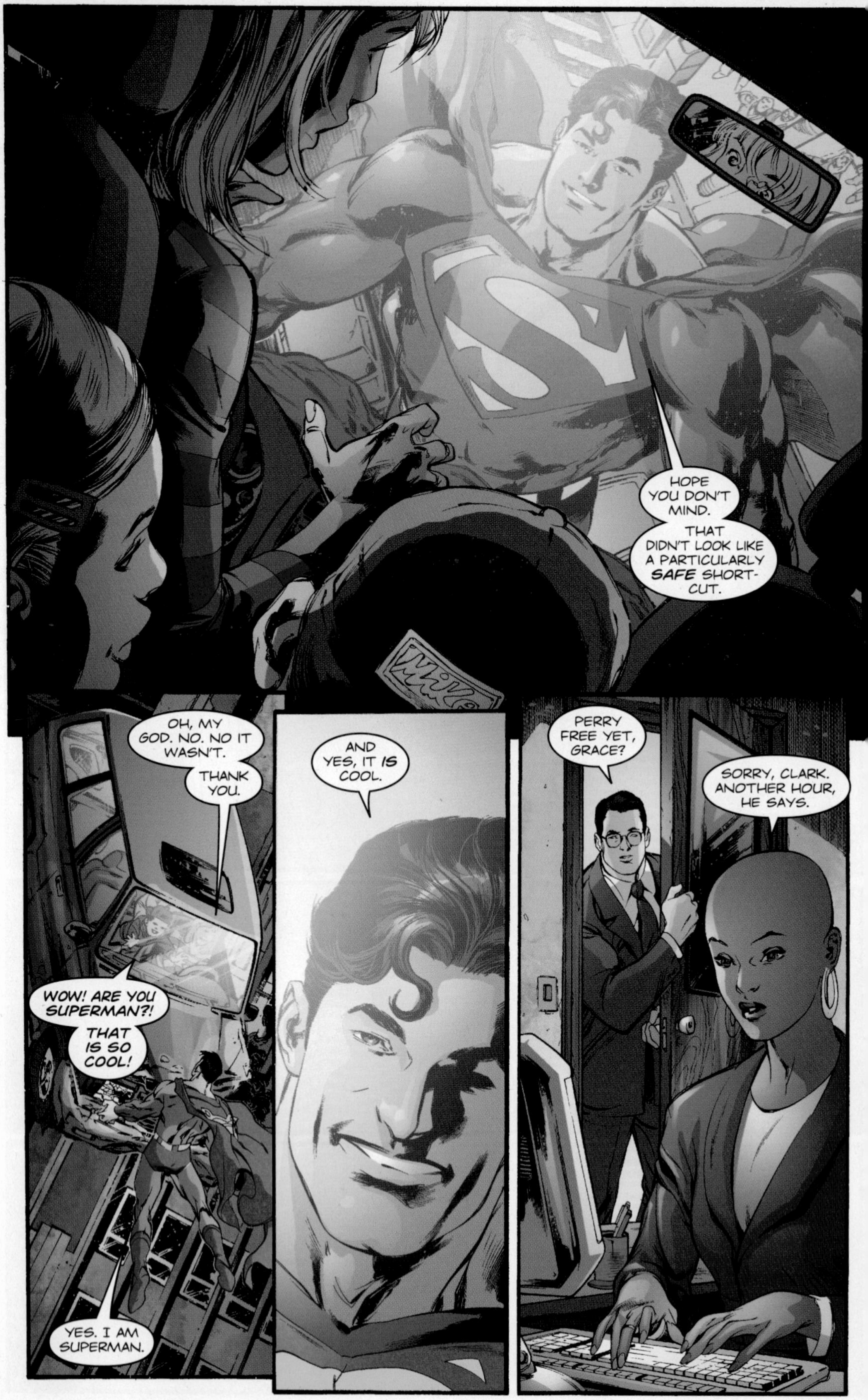
HOPE YOU DON'T MIND.
THAT DIDN'T LOOK LIKE A PARTICULARLY **SAFE** SHORT-CUT.
OH, MY GOD. NO. NO IT WASN'T.
THANK YOU.
WOW! ARE YOU SUPERMAN?!
THAT IS SO COOL!
YES. I AM SUPERMAN.
AND YES, IT **IS** COOL.
PERRY FREE YET, GRACE?
SORRY, CLARK. ANOTHER HOUR, HE SAYS.

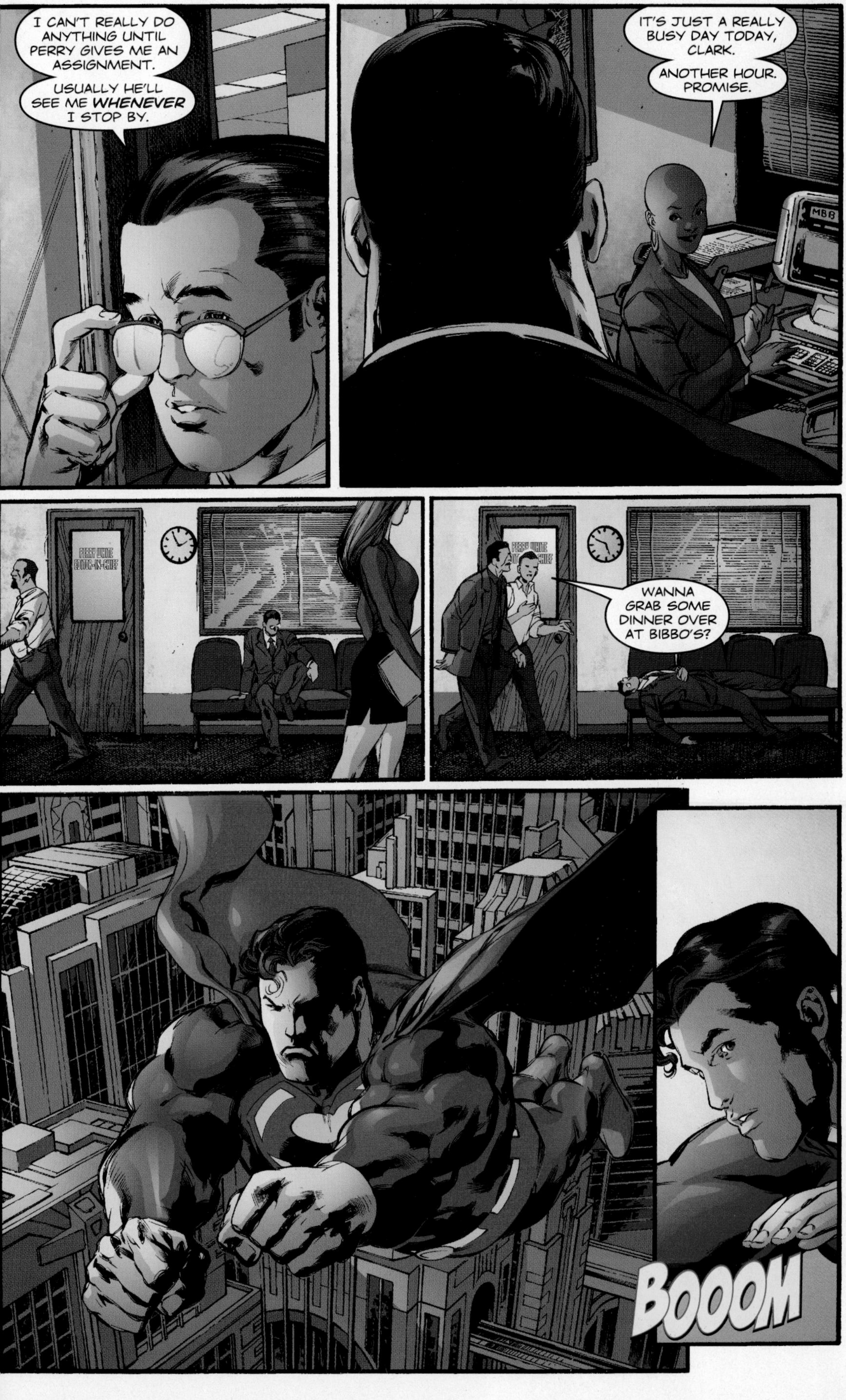
I CAN'T REALLY DO ANYTHING UNTIL PERRY GIVES ME AN ASSIGNMENT.
USUALLY HE'LL SEE ME *WHENEVER* I STOP BY.
IT'S JUST A REALLY BUSY DAY TODAY, CLARK.
ANOTHER HOUR. PROMISE.
MBB
PERRY WHITE EDITOR-IN-CHIEF
WANNA GRAB SOME DINNER OVER AT BIBBO'S?
BOOOM

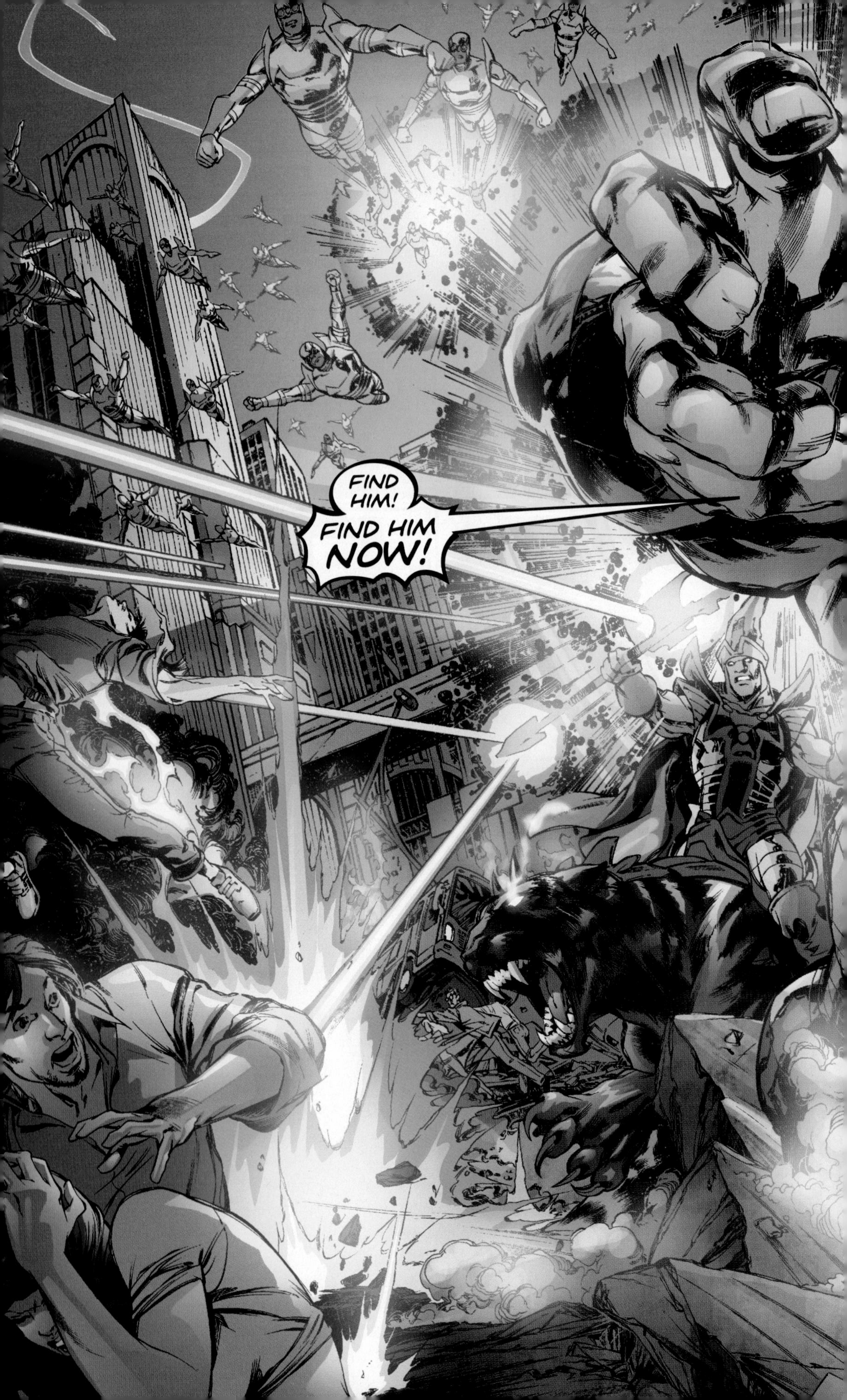
FIND HIM!
FIND HIM NOW!

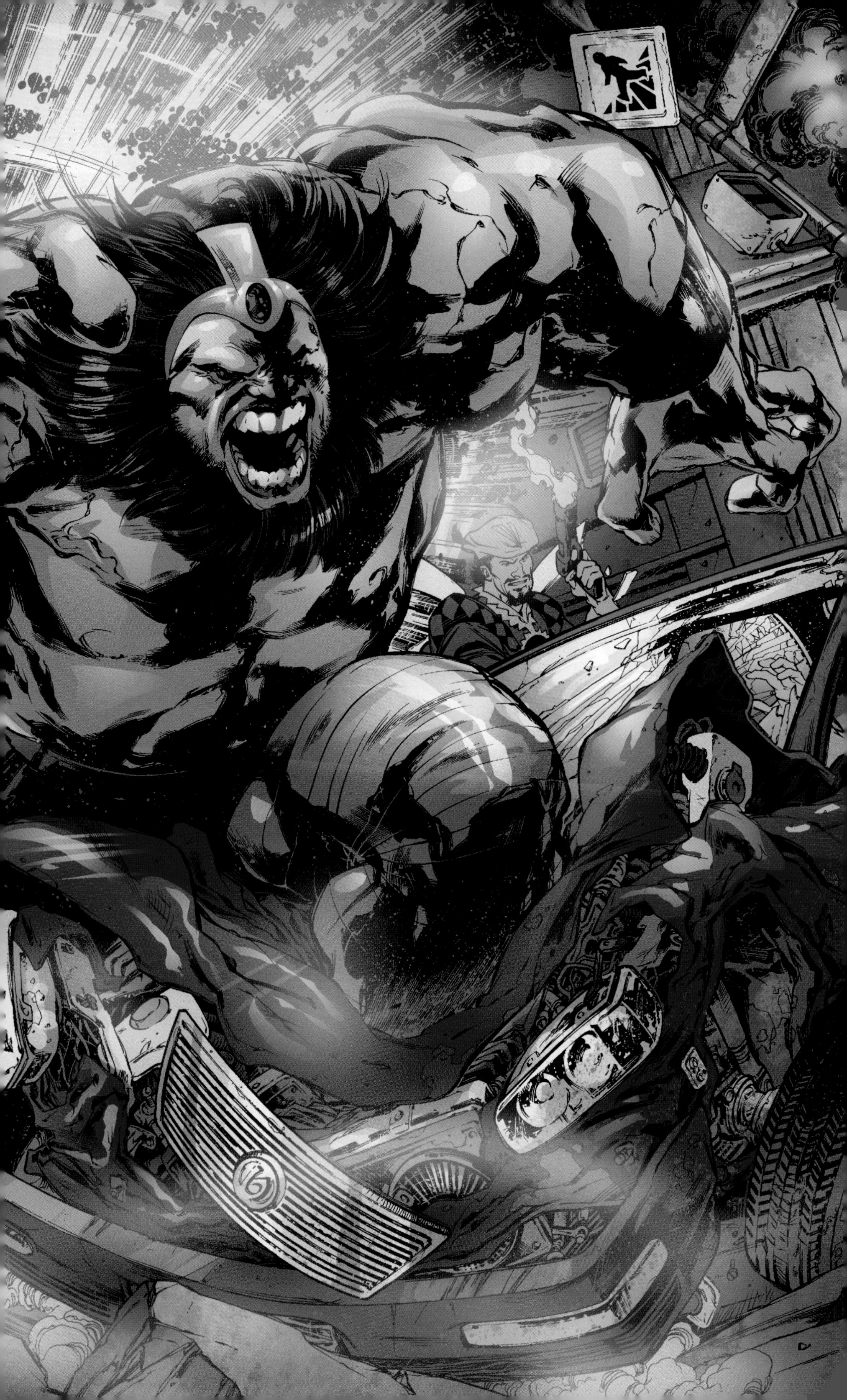

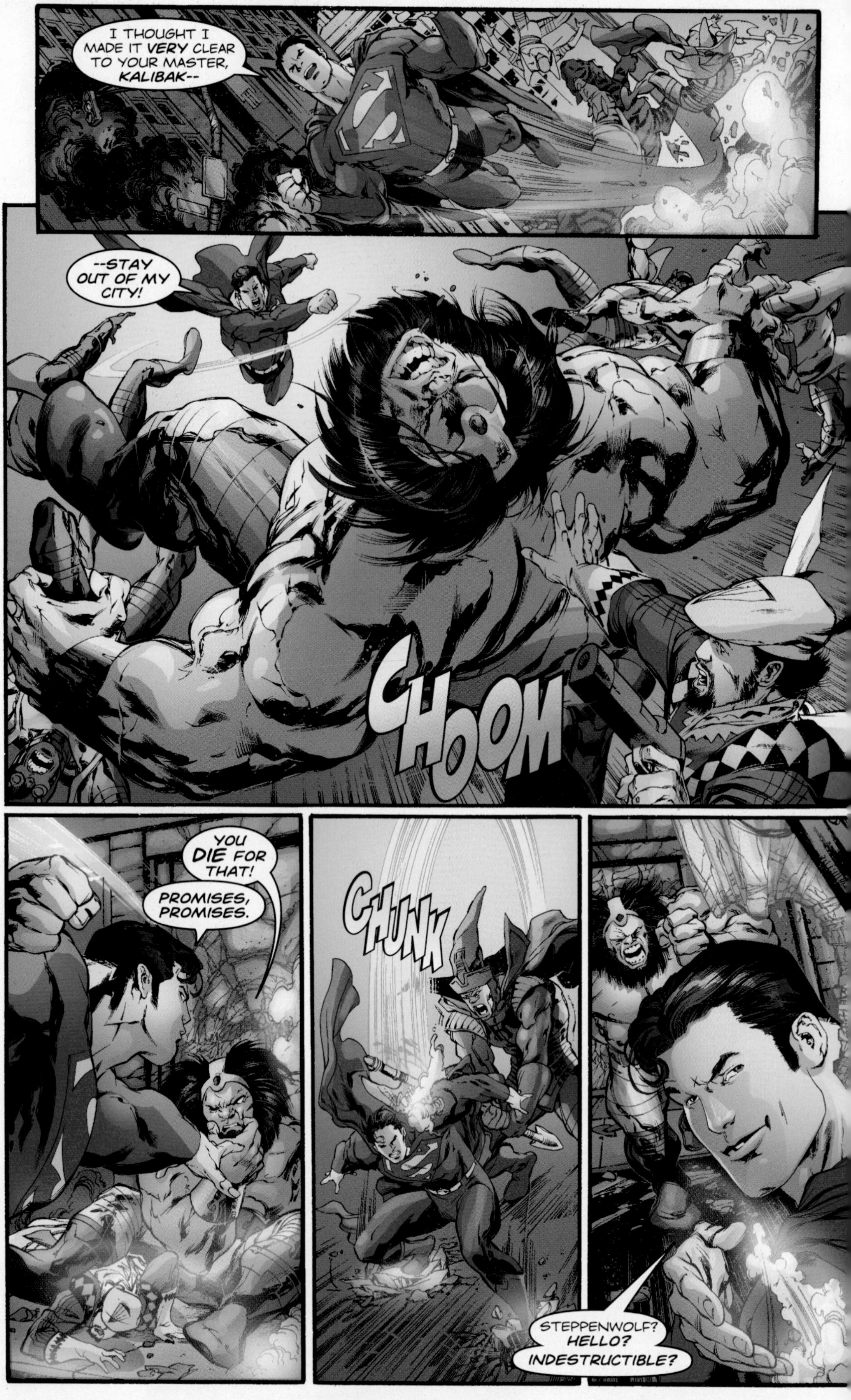
I THOUGHT I MADE IT VERY CLEAR TO YOUR MASTER, KALIBAK--
--STAY OUT OF MY CITY!
CHOOM
YOU DIE FOR THAT!
PROMISES, PROMISES.
CHUNK
STEPPENWOLF? HELLO? INDESTRUCTIBLE?

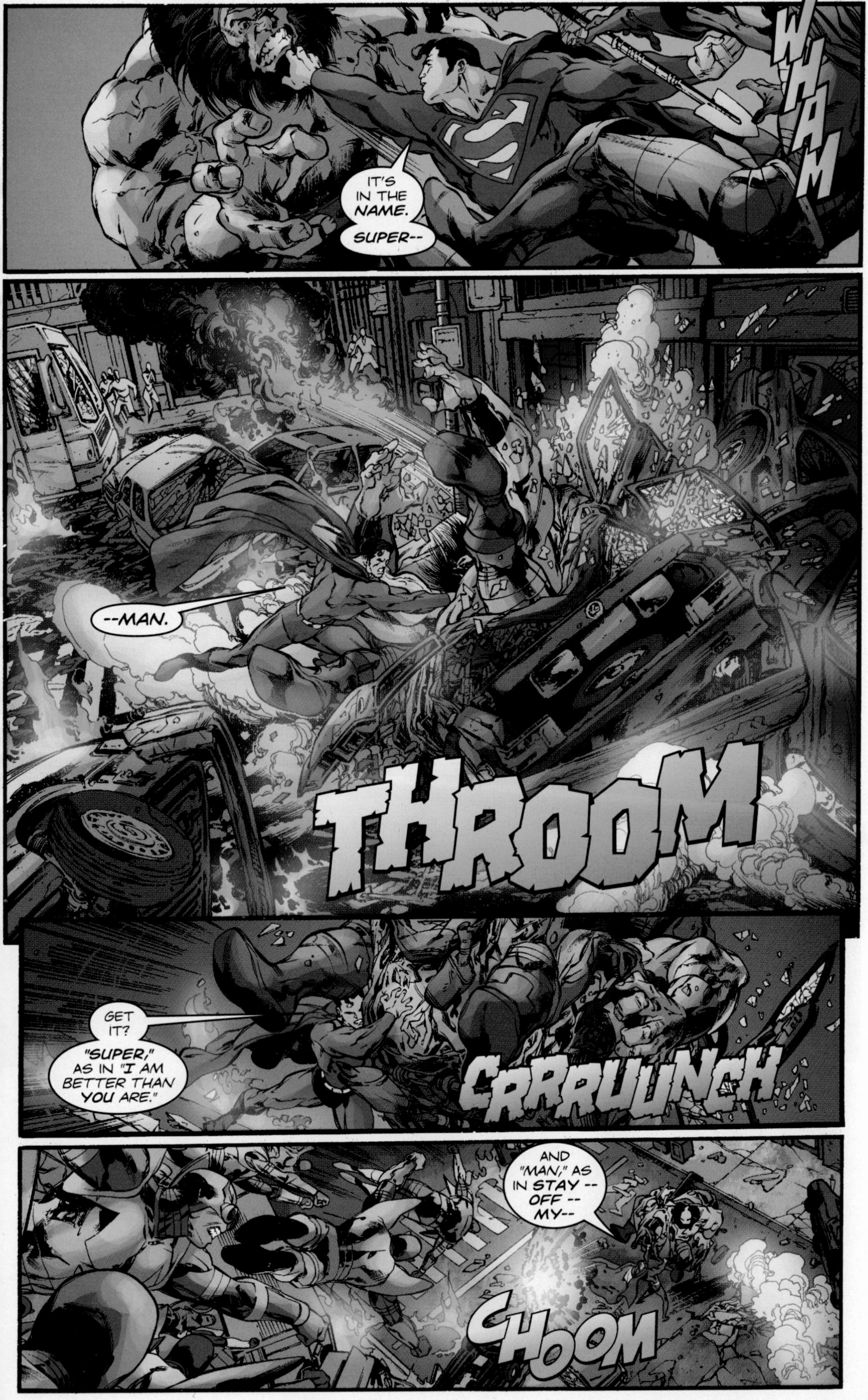
WHAM
IT'S IN THE NAME.
SUPER--
--MAN.
THROOM
GET IT?
"SUPER," AS IN "I AM BETTER THAN YOU ARE."
CRRRUUUNCH
"AND "MAN," AS IN STAY -- OFF -- MY--
CHOOM

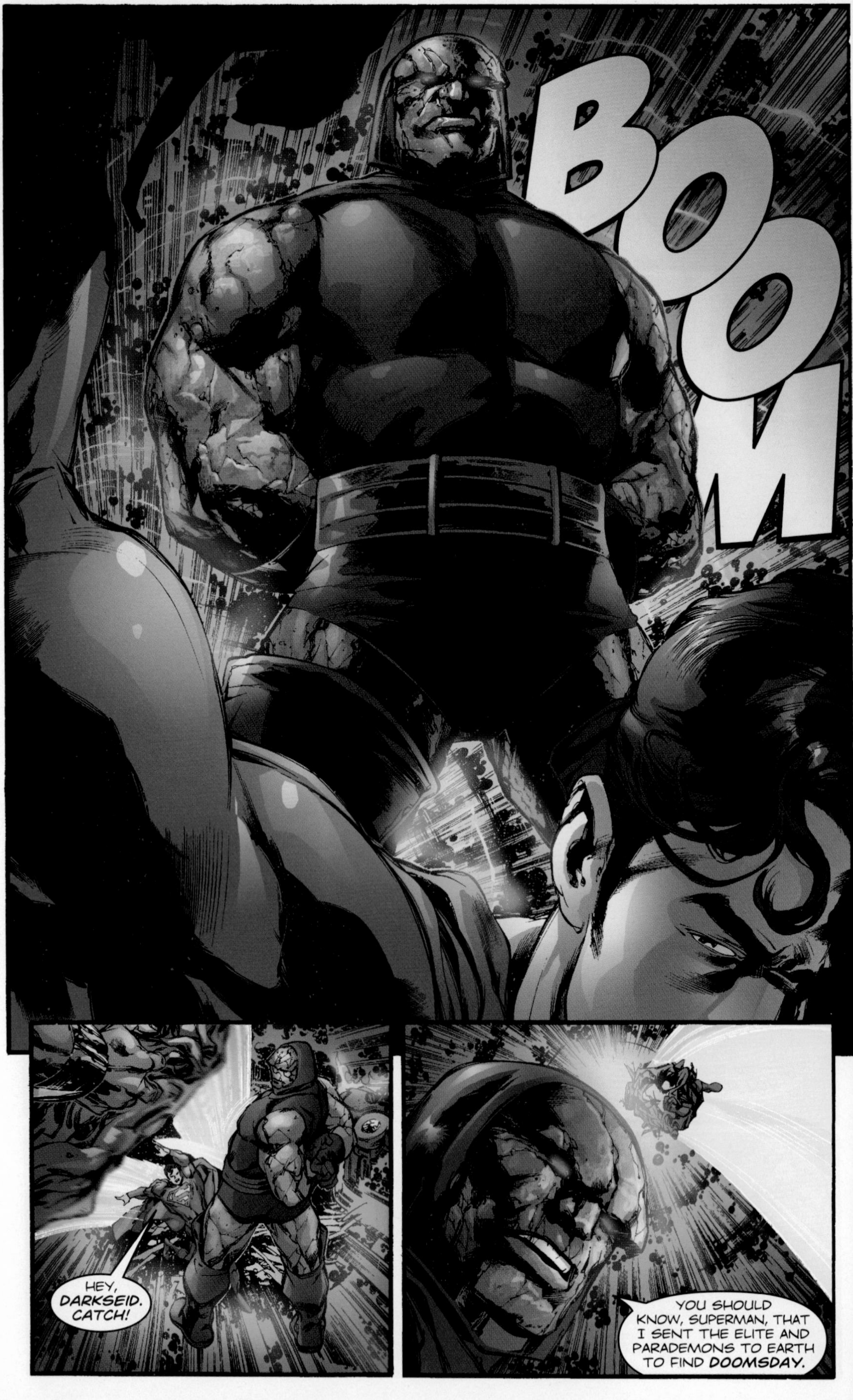
BOOM
HEY, DARKSEID. CATCH!
YOU SHOULD KNOW, SUPERMAN, THAT I SENT THE ELITE AND PARADEMONS TO EARTH TO FIND DOOMSDAY.

WHAT? DOOMSDAY?!

YOU LOST HIM?!

IT WAS NOT *I* WHO LOST HIM, SUPERMAN, BUT RATHER SOME INFERIORS WHO ARE NO LONGER WITH US.

THEY WERE TRAINING HIM TO BECOME MY ULTIMATE WEAPON, AND FOUND THE ONLY SKILL HE LACKED WAS *INTELLECT.*

ONCE DOOMSDAY GAINED THAT INTELLECT AND REALIZED IT WAS THE ONLY THING REMAINING HE MIGHT NEED TO DEFEAT YOU --

--HE FOUND THE MEANS TO RETURN TO EARTH.

I DIDN'T HEAR ANY BOOM TUBE BEFORE *YOUR* TWO.

I SAID HE HAD *GAINED* INTELLECT. HE KNOWS YOU'D HEAR THE TUBE.

HE MUST HAVE COME IN SOMEWHERE ELSE, AND WILL EVENTUALLY MAKE HIS WAY *HERE.*

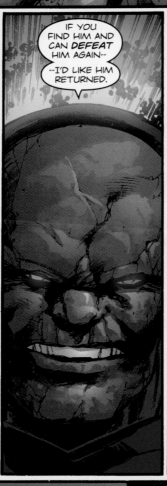

IF YOU FIND HIM AND CAN *DEFEAT* HIM AGAIN--

--I'D LIKE HIM RETURNED.

AND I'D *LIKE* YOU TO GET OFF MY PLANET AND STAY OFF, AS I'VE TOLD YOU REPEATEDLY.

DO NOT ORDER ME LIKE SOME MEANINGLESS *VASSAL,* SUPERMAN.

I AM DARKSEID. I GO WHERE I PLEASE.

GOSH. I DON'T SEEM TO BE COMMUNICATING *EFFECTIVELY* HERE.

HOW CAN I MAKE THIS *CLEARER* TO YOU?

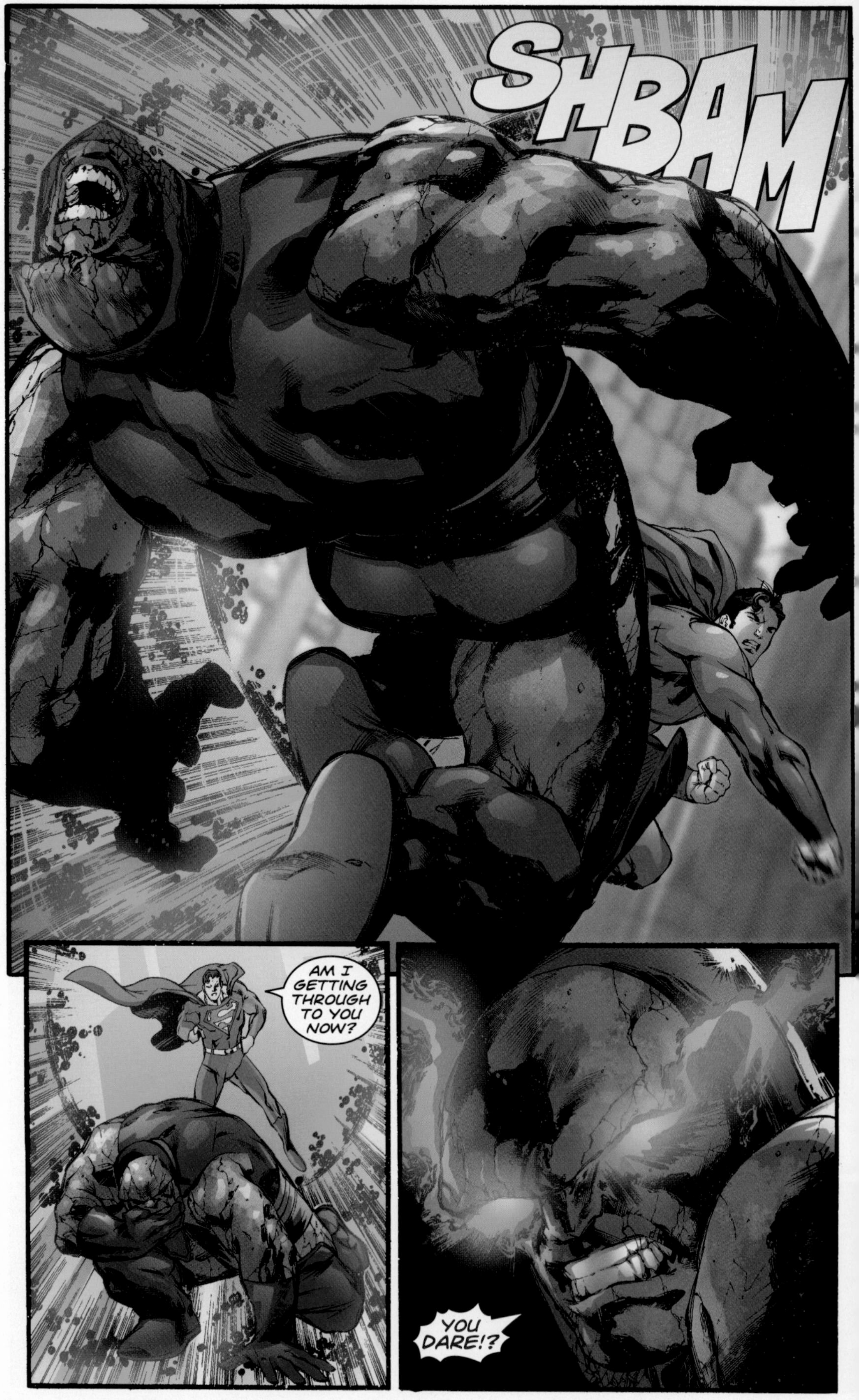
SHBAM
AM I GETTING THROUGH TO YOU NOW?
YOU DARE!?

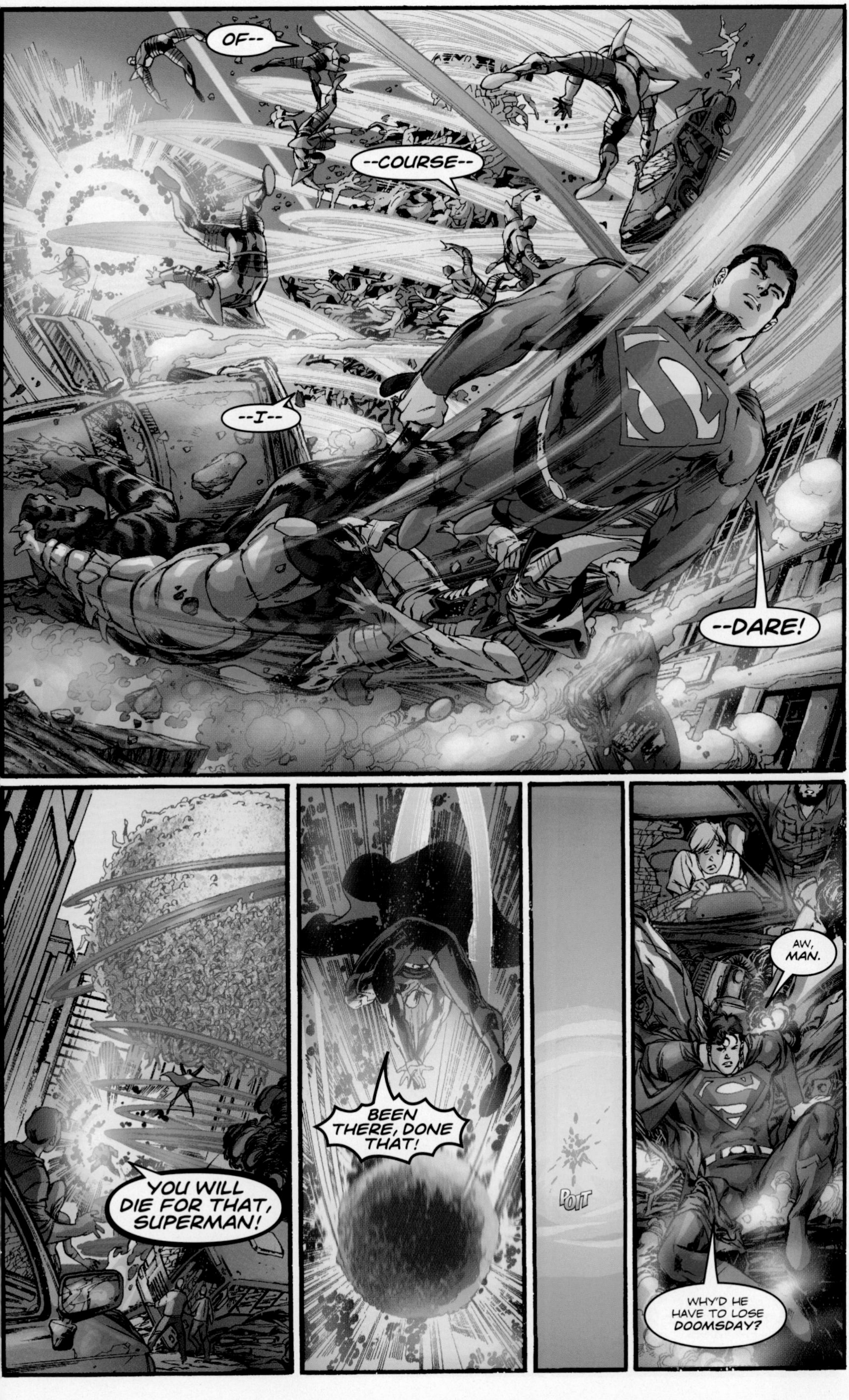
OF--
--COURSE--
--I--
--DARE!
YOU WILL DIE FOR THAT, SUPERMAN!
BEEN THERE, DONE THAT!
POIT
AW, MAN.
WHY'D HE HAVE TO LOSE DOOMSDAY?

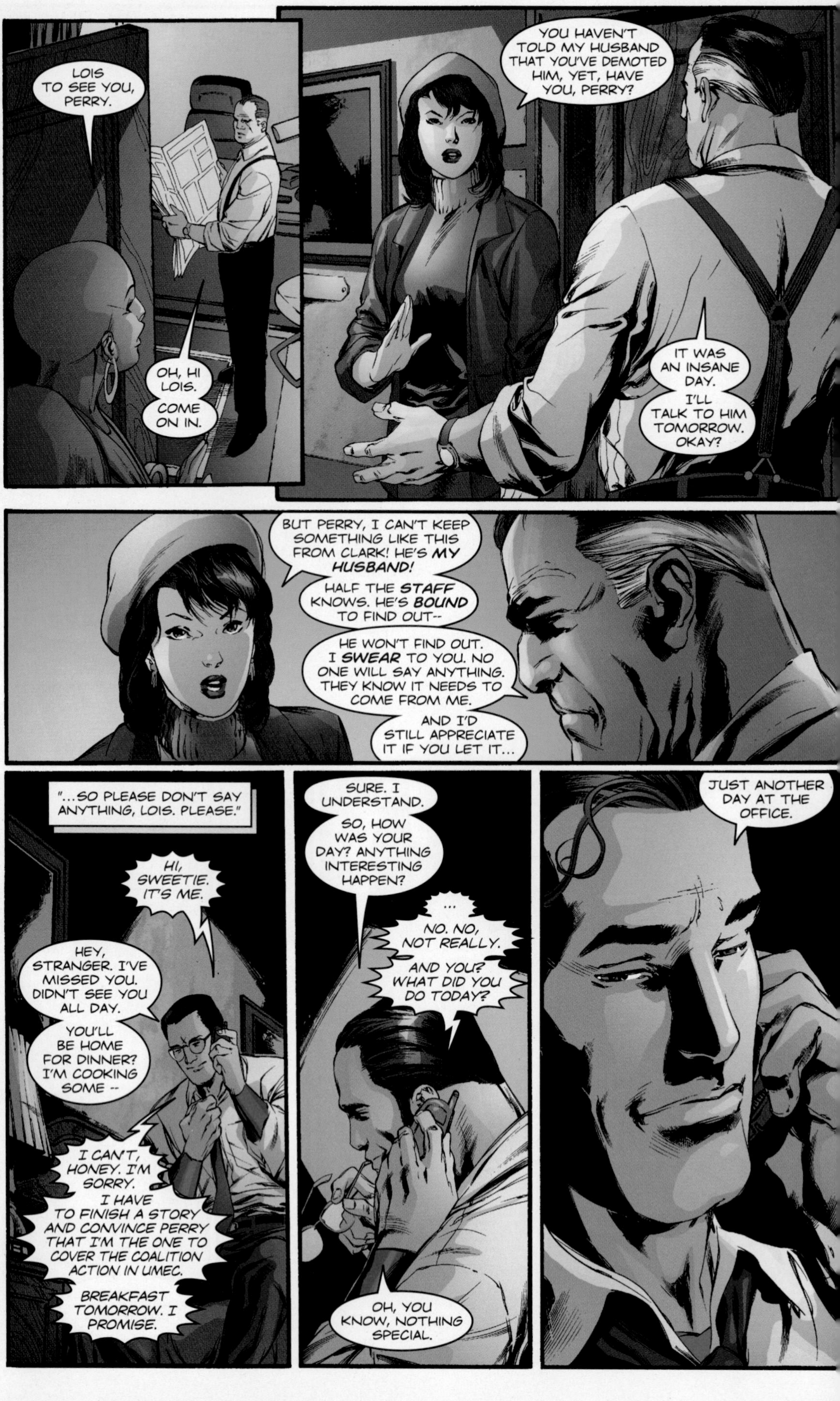

LOIS TO SEE YOU, PERRY.
OH, HI LOIS.
COME ON IN.
YOU HAVEN'T TOLD MY HUSBAND THAT YOU'VE DEMOTED HIM, YET, HAVE YOU, PERRY?
IT WAS AN INSANE DAY.
I'LL TALK TO HIM TOMORROW. OKAY?
BUT PERRY, I CAN'T KEEP SOMETHING LIKE THIS FROM CLARK! HE'S MY HUSBAND!
HALF THE STAFF KNOWS. HE'S BOUND TO FIND OUT--
HE WON'T FIND OUT. I SWEAR TO YOU. NO ONE WILL SAY ANYTHING. THEY KNOW IT NEEDS TO COME FROM ME.
AND I'D STILL APPRECIATE IT IF YOU LET IT...
"...SO PLEASE DON'T SAY ANYTHING, LOIS. PLEASE."
HI, SWEETIE. IT'S ME.
HEY, STRANGER. I'VE MISSED YOU. DIDN'T SEE YOU ALL DAY.
YOU'LL BE HOME FOR DINNER? I'M COOKING SOME --
I CAN'T, HONEY. I'M SORRY.
I HAVE TO FINISH A STORY AND CONVINCE PERRY THAT I'M THE ONE TO COVER THE COALITION ACTION IN UMEC.
BREAKFAST TOMORROW. I PROMISE.
SURE. I UNDERSTAND.
SO, HOW WAS YOUR DAY? ANYTHING INTERESTING HAPPEN?
...
NO. NO, NOT REALLY.
AND YOU? WHAT DID YOU DO TODAY?
OH, YOU KNOW, NOTHING SPECIAL.
JUST ANOTHER DAY AT THE OFFICE.

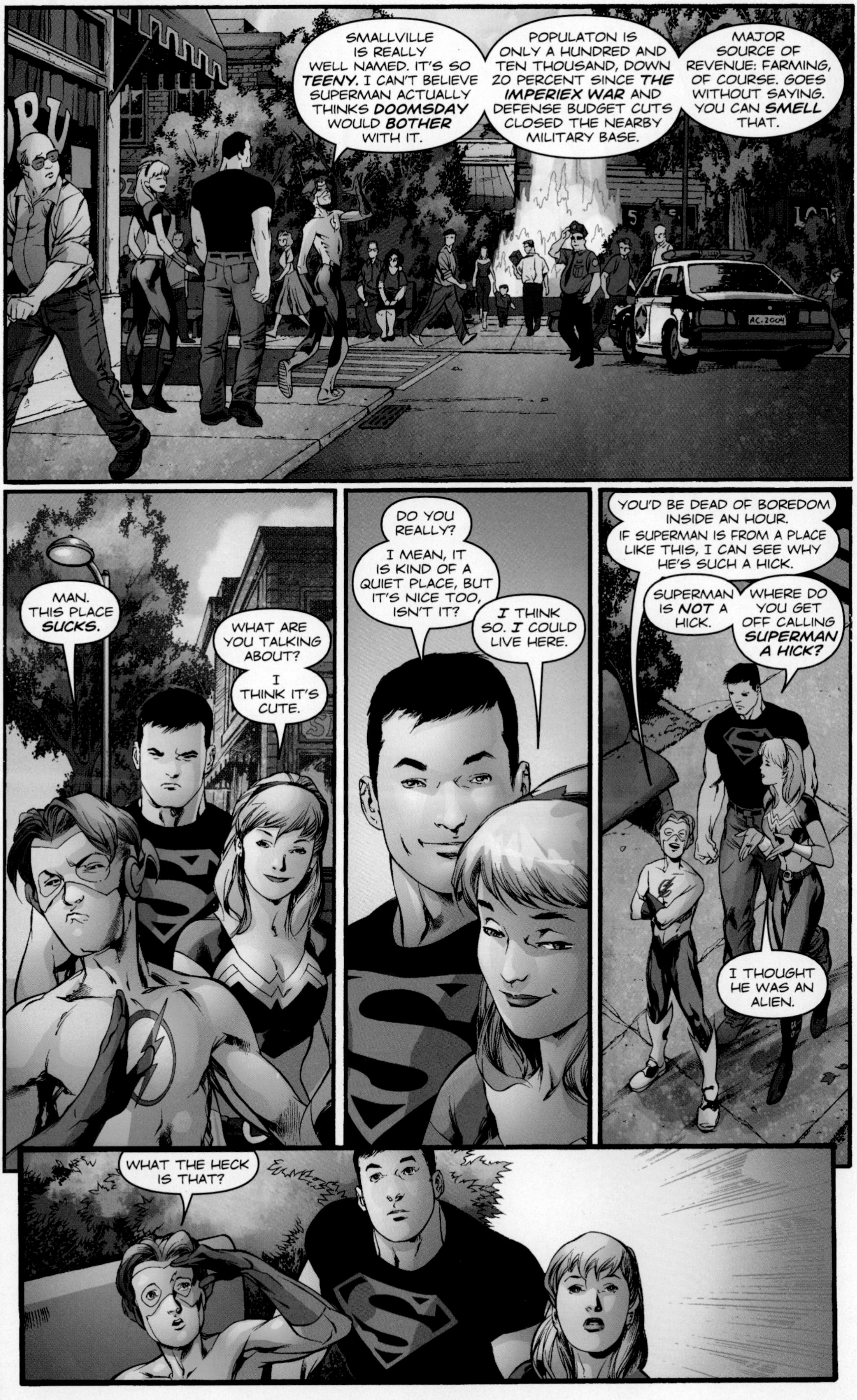
SMALLVILLE IS REALLY WELL NAMED. IT'S SO TEENY. I CAN'T BELIEVE SUPERMAN ACTUALLY THINKS DOOMSDAY WOULD BOTHER WITH IT.
POPULATON IS ONLY A HUNDRED AND TEN THOUSAND, DOWN 20 PERCENT SINCE THE IMPERIEX WAR AND DEFENSE BUDGET CUTS CLOSED THE NEARBY MILITARY BASE.
MAJOR SOURCE OF REVENUE: FARMING, OF COURSE. GOES WITHOUT SAYING. YOU CAN SMELL THAT.
AC.2004
MAN. THIS PLACE SUCKS.
WHAT ARE YOU TALKING ABOUT?
I THINK IT'S CUTE.
DO YOU REALLY?
I MEAN, IT IS KIND OF A QUIET PLACE, BUT IT'S NICE TOO, ISN'T IT?
I THINK SO. I COULD LIVE HERE.
YOU'D BE DEAD OF BOREDOM INSIDE AN HOUR.
IF SUPERMAN IS FROM A PLACE LIKE THIS, I CAN SEE WHY HE'S SUCH A HICK.
SUPERMAN IS NOT A HICK.
WHERE DO YOU GET OFF CALLING SUPERMAN A HICK?
I THOUGHT HE WAS AN ALIEN.
WHAT THE HECK IS THAT?

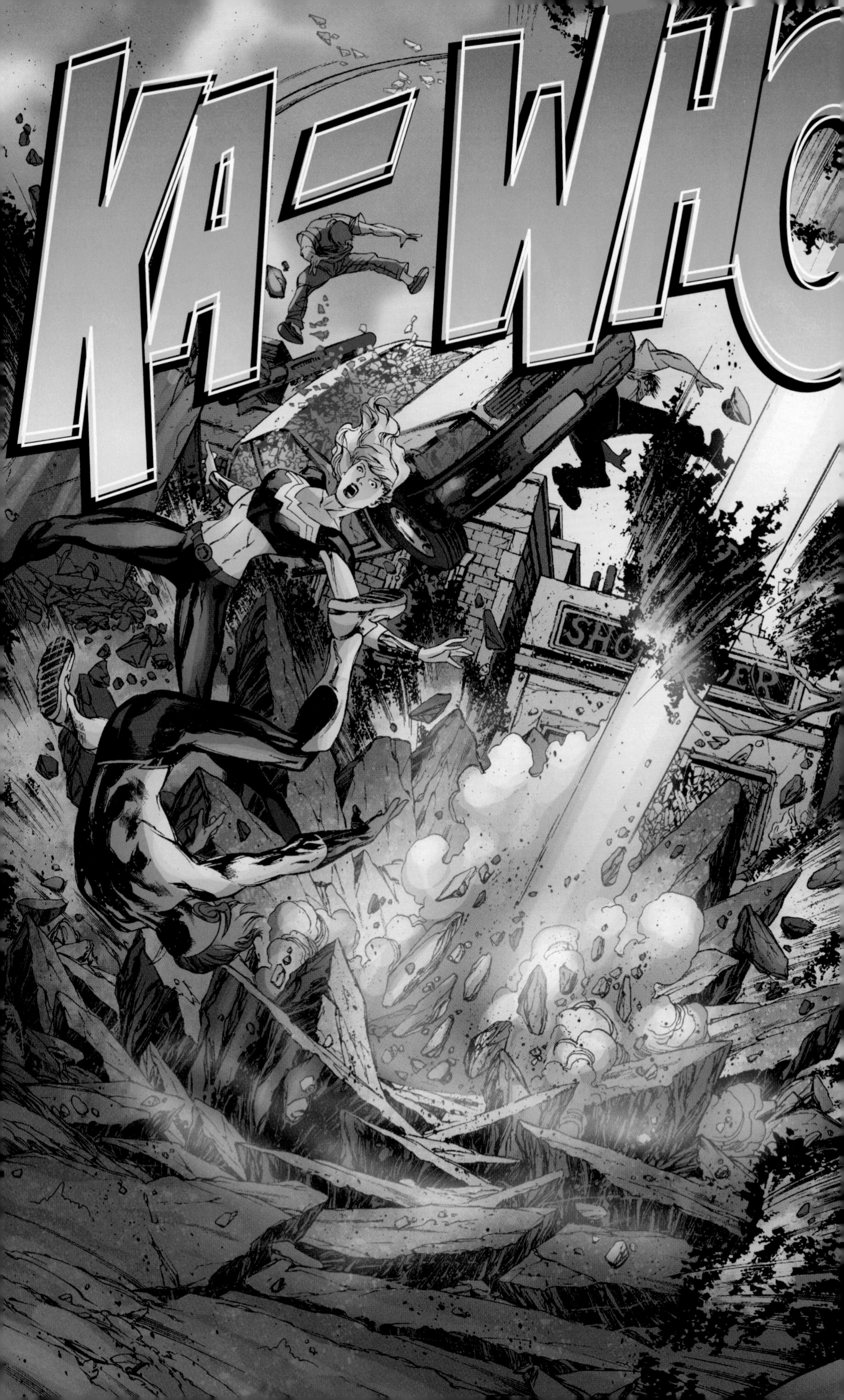
KA-WHO

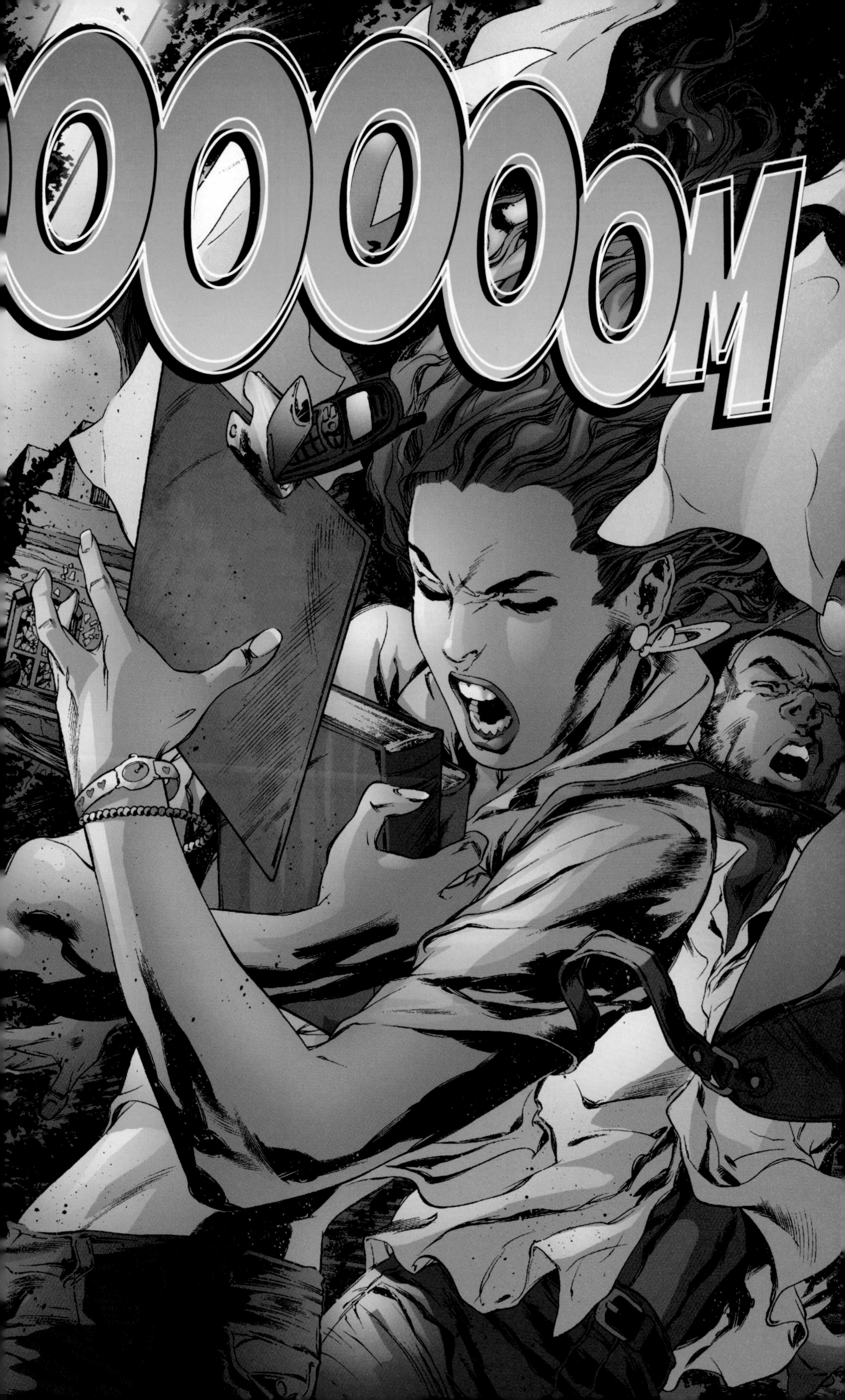
OOOOOM

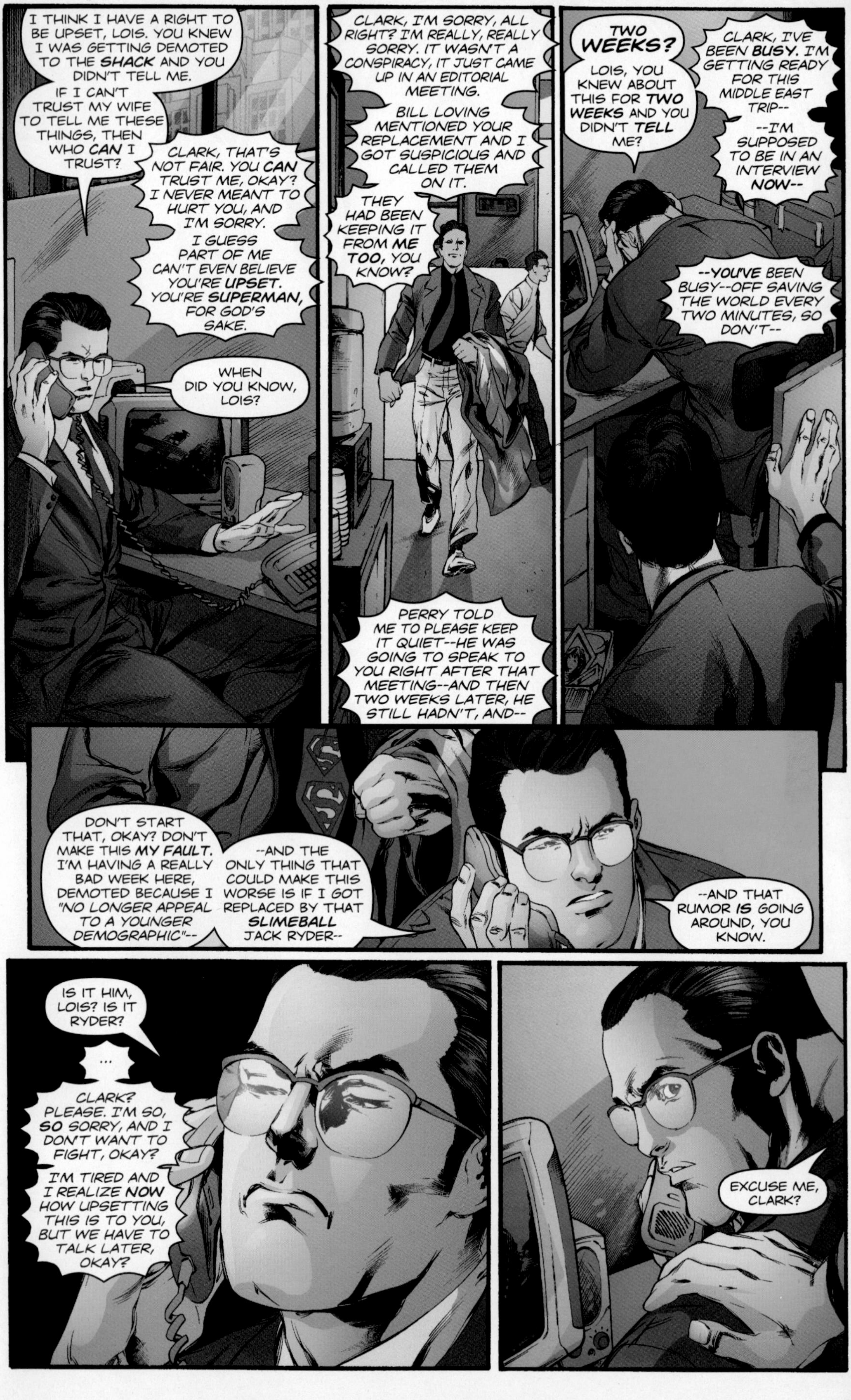
I THINK I HAVE A RIGHT TO BE UPSET, LOIS. YOU KNEW I WAS GETTING DEMOTED TO THE SHACK AND YOU DIDN'T TELL ME.
IF I CAN'T TRUST MY WIFE TO TELL ME THESE THINGS, THEN WHO CAN I TRUST?
CLARK, THAT'S NOT FAIR. YOU CAN TRUST ME, OKAY? I NEVER MEANT TO HURT YOU, AND I'M SORRY.
I GUESS PART OF ME CAN'T EVEN BELIEVE YOU'RE UPSET. YOU'RE SUPERMAN, FOR GOD'S SAKE.
WHEN DID YOU KNOW, LOIS?
CLARK, I'M SORRY, ALL RIGHT? I'M REALLY, REALLY SORRY. IT WASN'T A CONSPIRACY, IT JUST CAME UP IN AN EDITORIAL MEETING.
BILL LOVING MENTIONED YOUR REPLACEMENT AND I GOT SUSPICIOUS AND CALLED THEM ON IT.
THEY HAD BEEN KEEPING IT FROM ME TOO, YOU KNOW?
PERRY TOLD ME TO PLEASE KEEP IT QUIET--HE WAS GOING TO SPEAK TO YOU RIGHT AFTER THAT MEETING--AND THEN TWO WEEKS LATER, HE STILL HADN'T, AND--
TWO WEEKS?
LOIS, YOU KNEW ABOUT THIS FOR TWO WEEKS AND YOU DIDN'T TELL ME?
CLARK, I'VE BEEN BUSY. I'M GETTING READY FOR THIS MIDDLE EAST TRIP--
--I'M SUPPOSED TO BE IN AN INTERVIEW NOW--
--YOU'VE BEEN BUSY--OFF SAVING THE WORLD EVERY TWO MINUTES, SO DON'T--
DON'T START THAT, OKAY? DON'T MAKE THIS MY FAULT. I'M HAVING A REALLY BAD WEEK HERE, DEMOTED BECAUSE I "NO LONGER APPEAL TO A YOUNGER DEMOGRAPHIC"--
--AND THE ONLY THING THAT COULD MAKE THIS WORSE IS IF I GOT REPLACED BY THAT SLIMEBALL JACK RYDER--
--AND THAT RUMOR IS GOING AROUND, YOU KNOW.
IS IT HIM, LOIS? IS IT RYDER?
...
CLARK? PLEASE. I'M SO, SO SORRY, AND I DON'T WANT TO FIGHT, OKAY?
I'M TIRED AND I REALIZE NOW HOW UPSETTING THIS IS TO YOU, BUT WE HAVE TO TALK LATER, OKAY?
EXCUSE ME, CLARK?

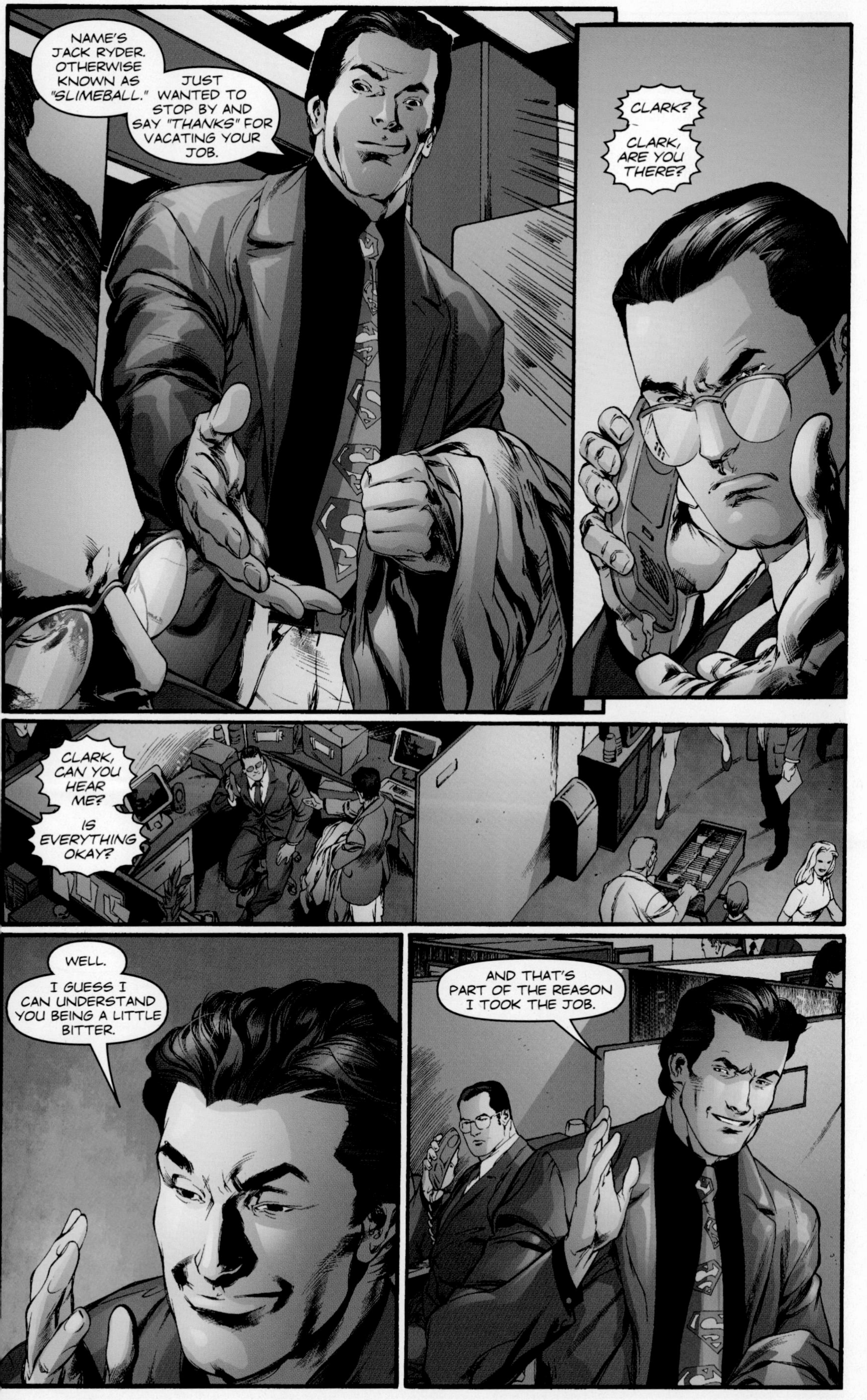
NAME'S JACK RYDER. OTHERWISE KNOWN AS "SLIMEBALL."
JUST WANTED TO STOP BY AND SAY "THANKS" FOR VACATING YOUR JOB.
CLARK?
CLARK, ARE YOU THERE?
CLARK, CAN YOU HEAR ME?
IS EVERYTHING OKAY?
WELL. I GUESS I CAN UNDERSTAND YOU BEING A LITTLE BITTER.
AND THAT'S PART OF THE REASON I TOOK THE JOB.

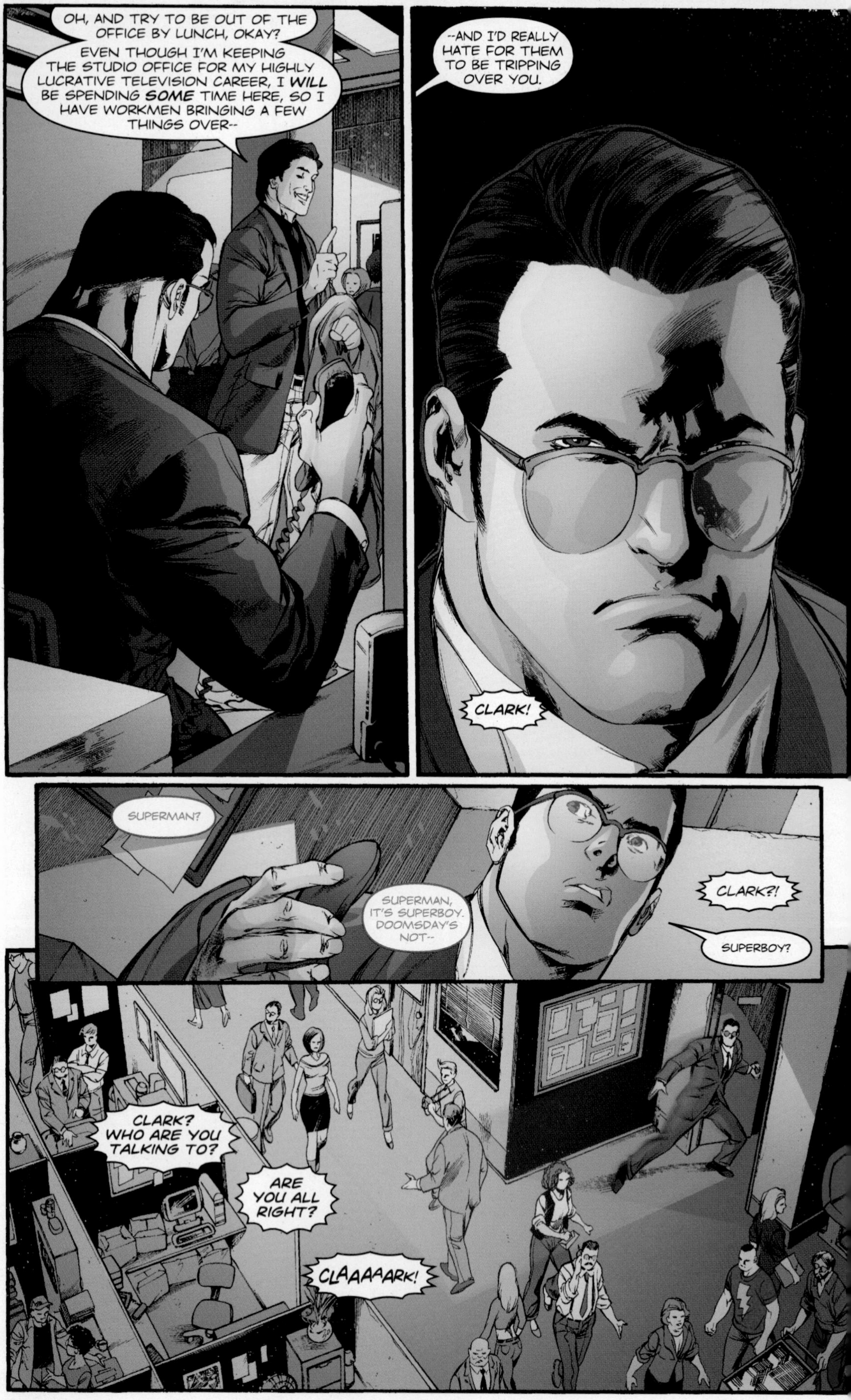
OH, AND TRY TO BE OUT OF THE OFFICE BY LUNCH, OKAY?
EVEN THOUGH I'M KEEPING THE STUDIO OFFICE FOR MY HIGHLY LUCRATIVE TELEVISION CAREER, I WILL BE SPENDING SOME TIME HERE, SO I HAVE WORKMEN BRINGING A FEW THINGS OVER--
--AND I'D REALLY HATE FOR THEM TO BE TRIPPING OVER YOU.
CLARK!
SUPERMAN?
SUPERMAN, IT'S SUPERBOY. DOOMSDAY'S NOT--
CLARK?!
SUPERBOY?
CLARK? WHO ARE YOU TALKING TO?
ARE YOU ALL RIGHT?
CLAAAAARK!

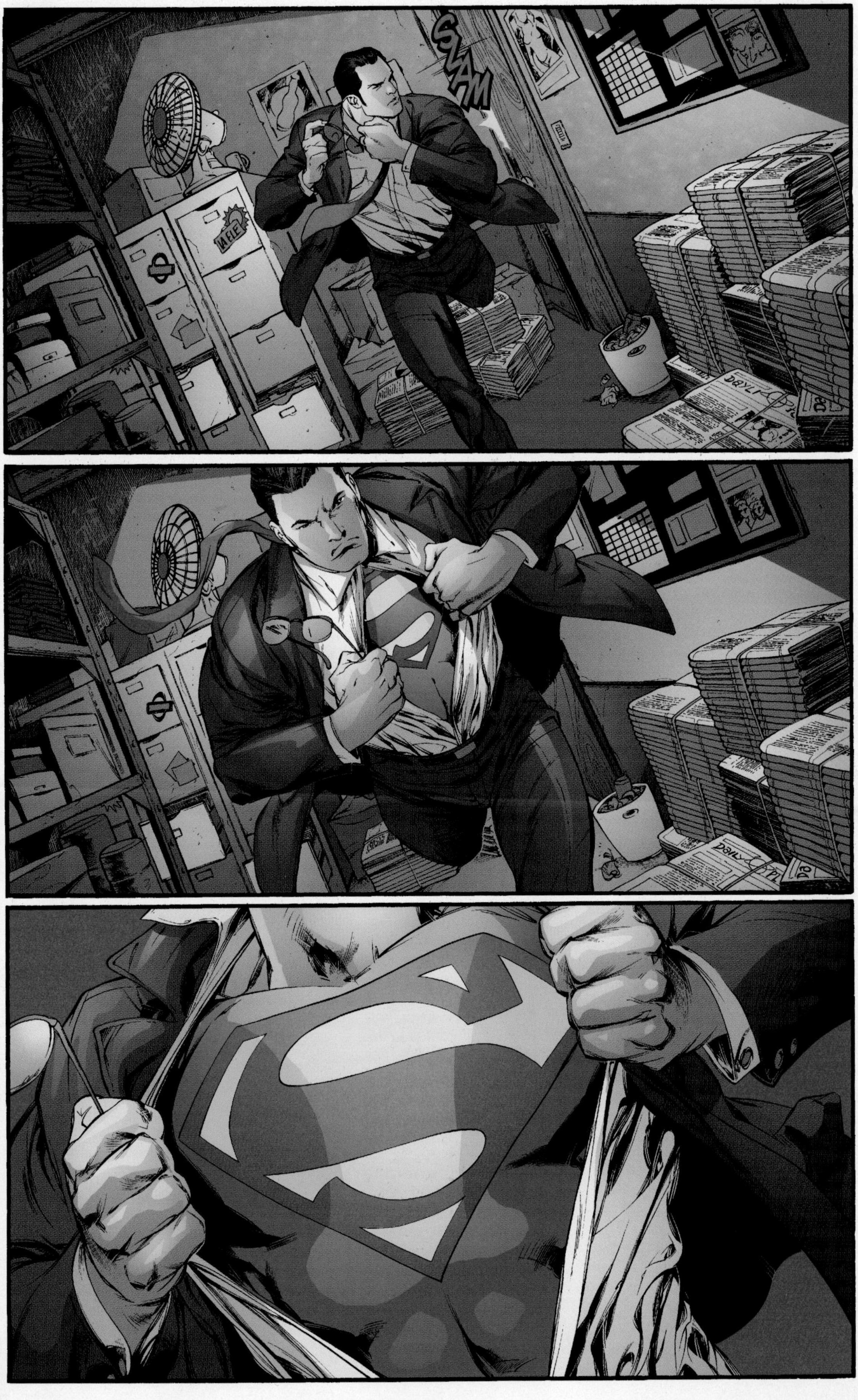
SLAM

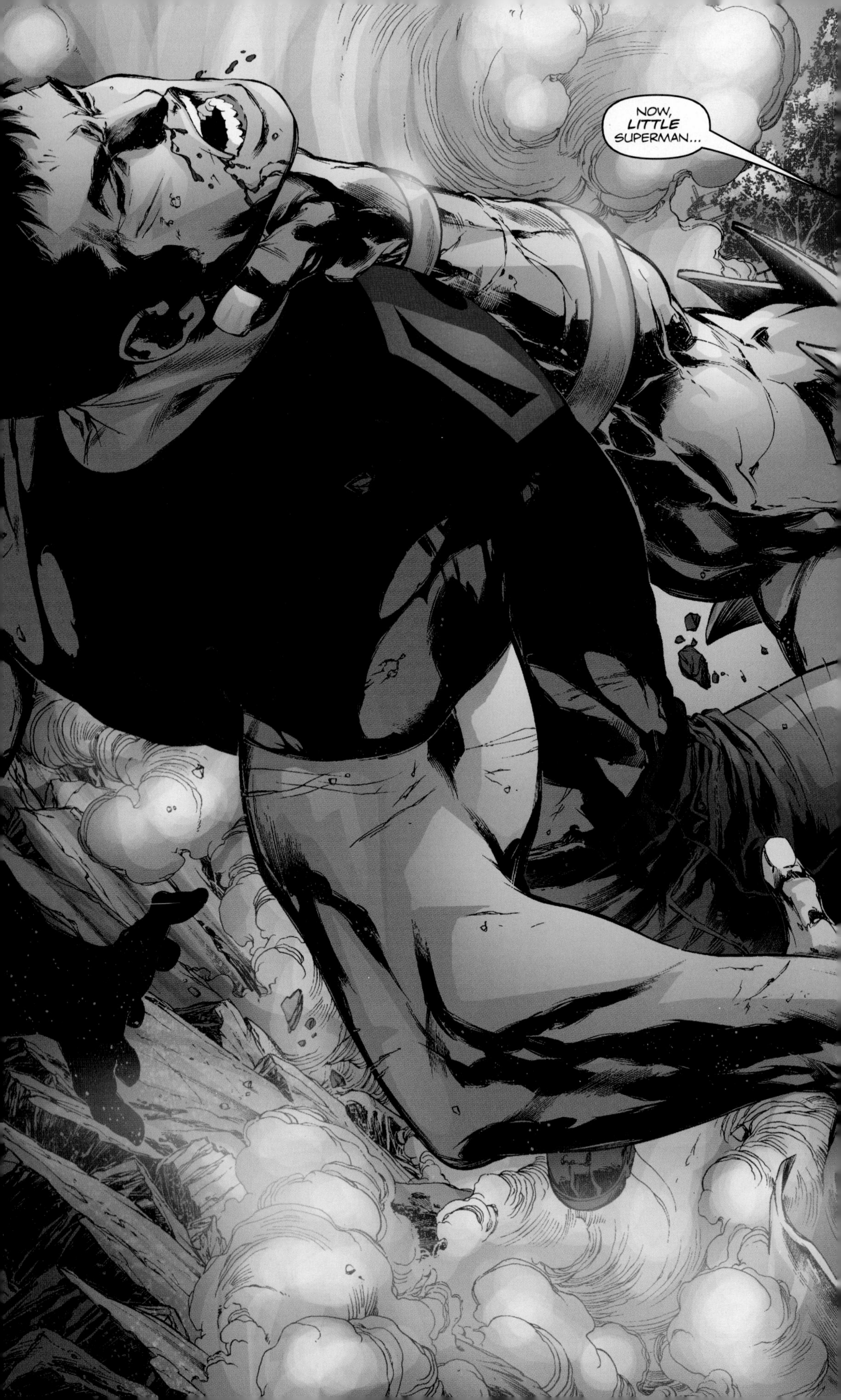
NOW, LITTLE SUPERMAN...

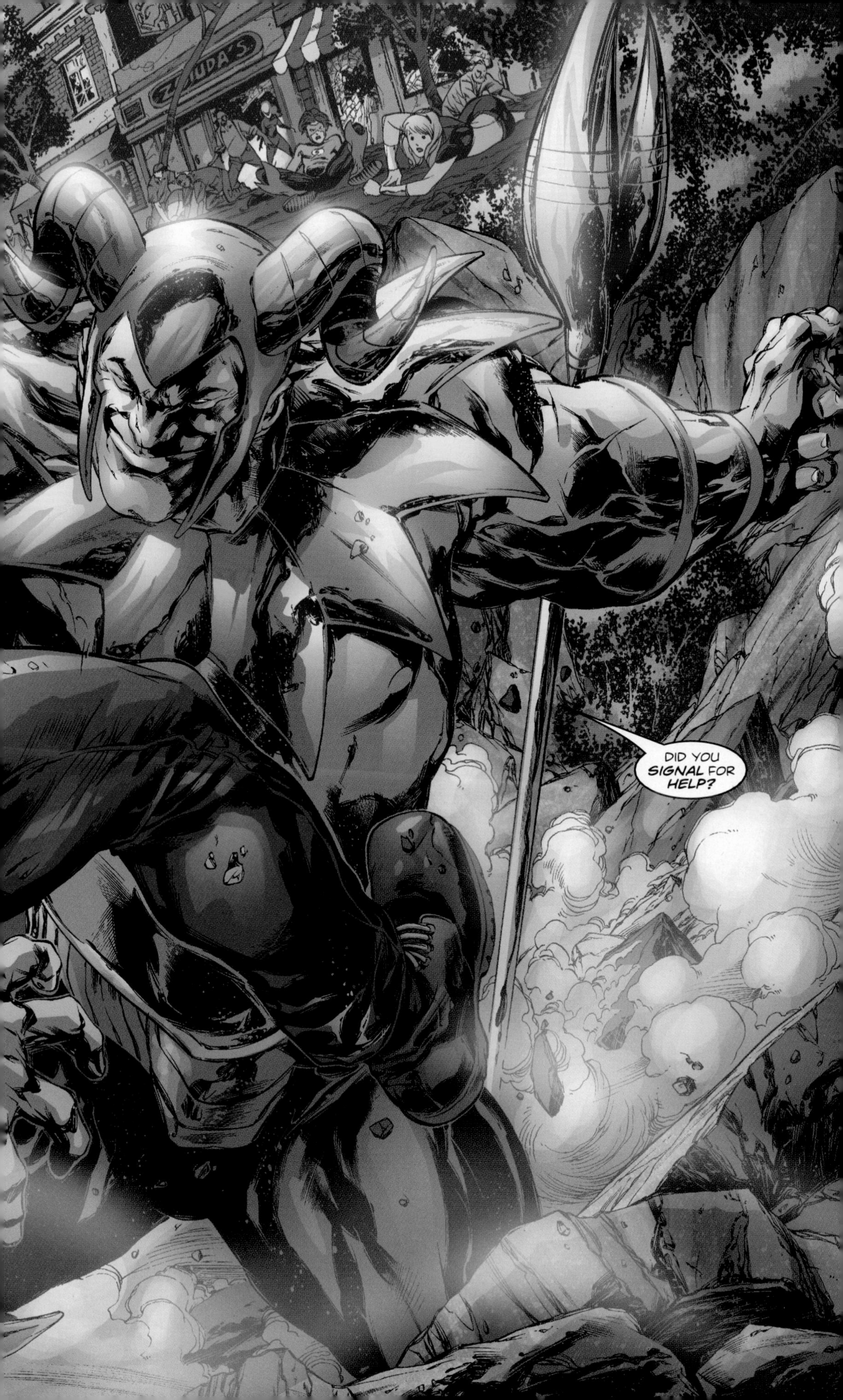
DID YOU SIGNAL FOR HELP?

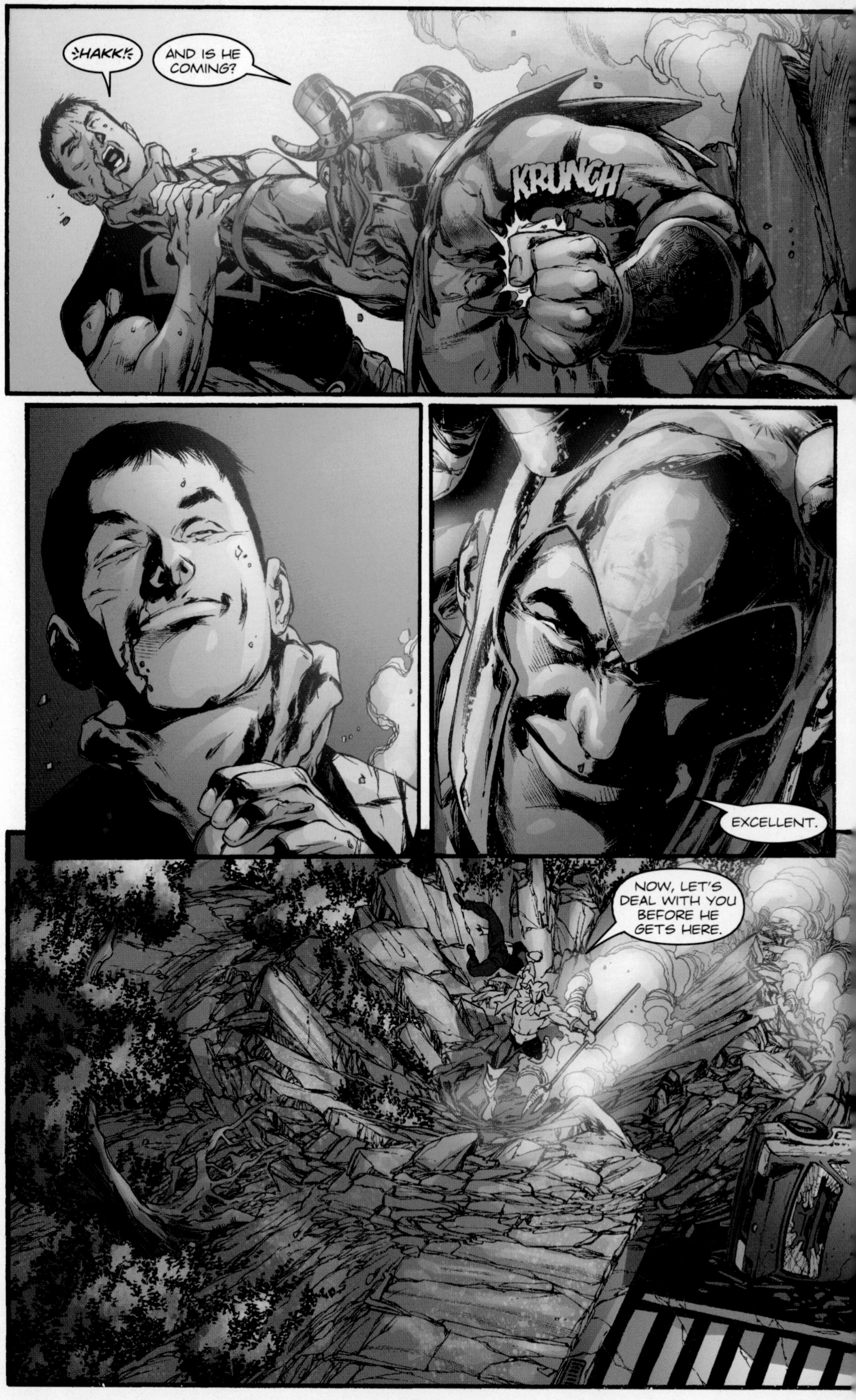
HAKK!
AND IS HE COMING?
KRUNCH
EXCELLENT.
NOW, LET'S DEAL WITH YOU BEFORE HE GETS HERE.

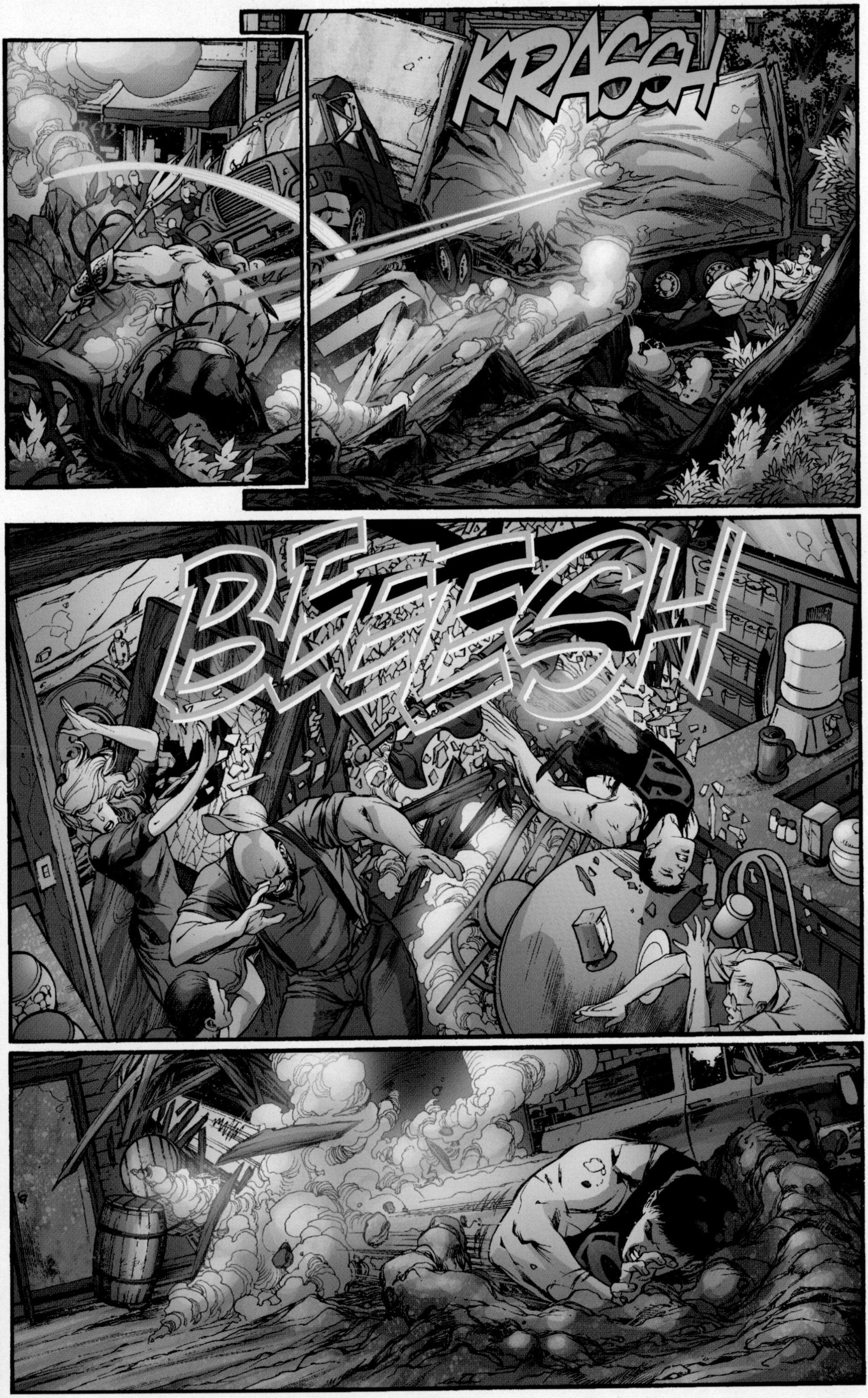

KRASSH
BEESH

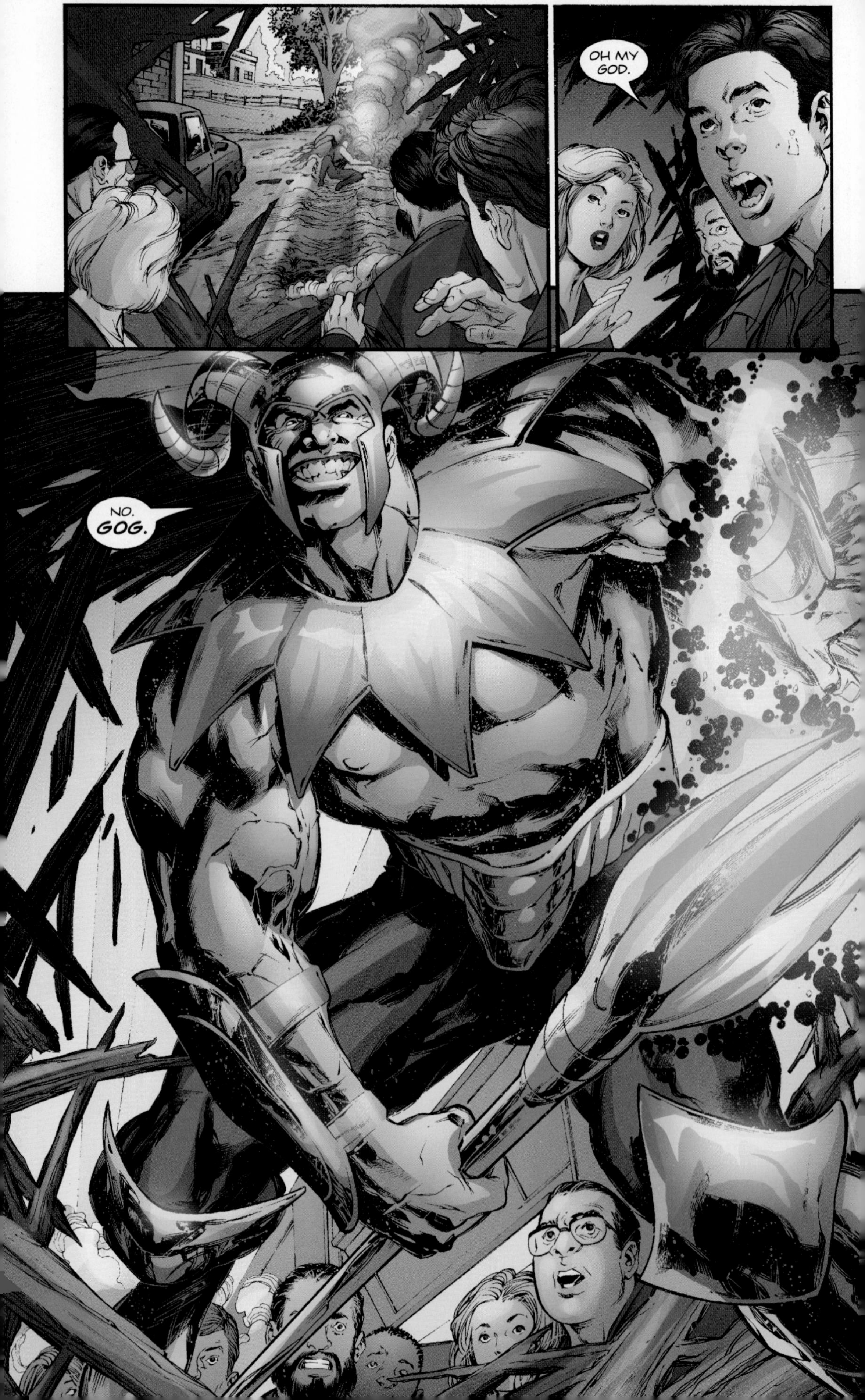
OH MY GOD.
NO. GOG.

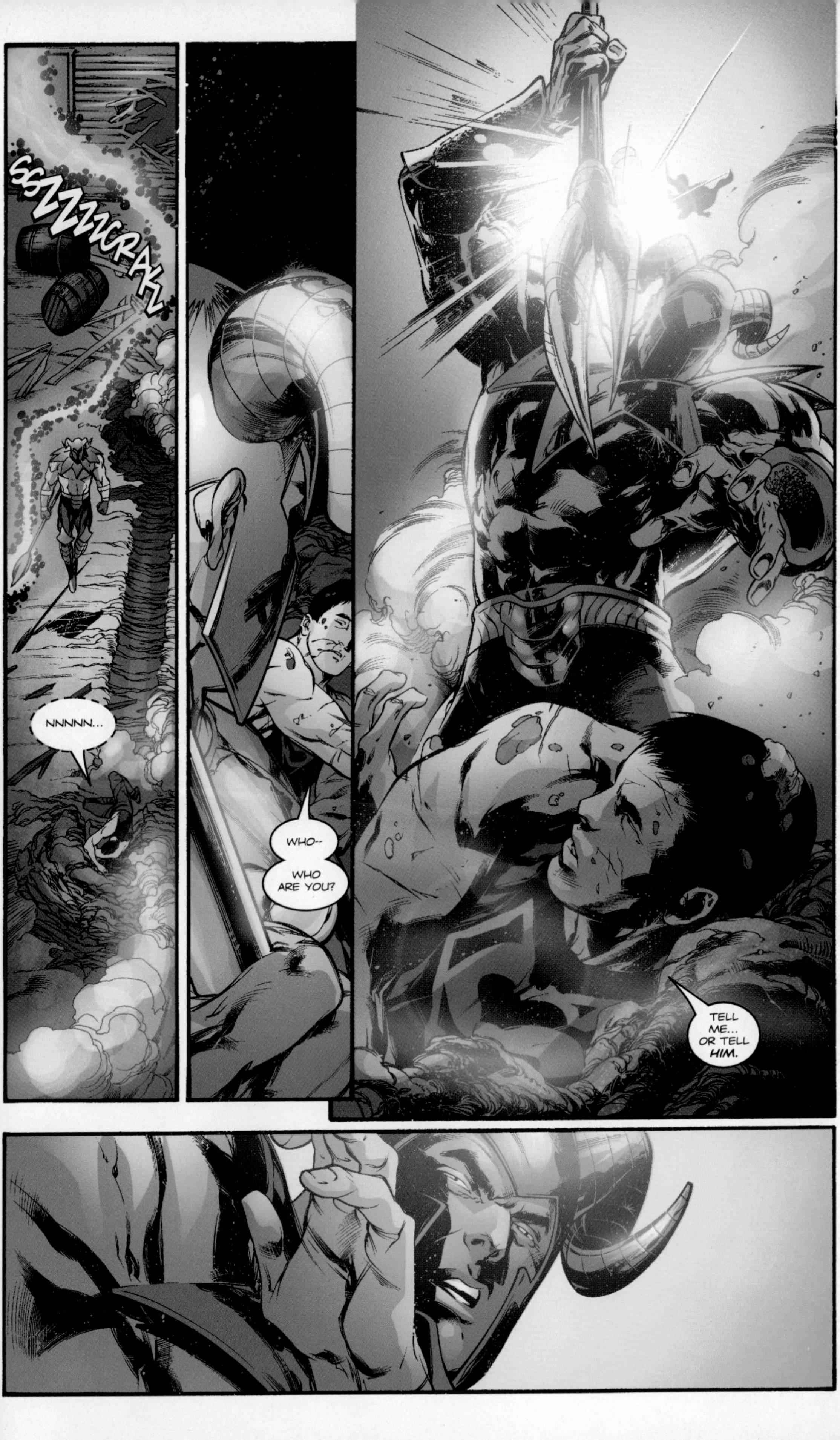
SSZZZZCRAKL
NNNNN...
WHO--
WHO ARE YOU?
TELL ME... OR TELL HIM.

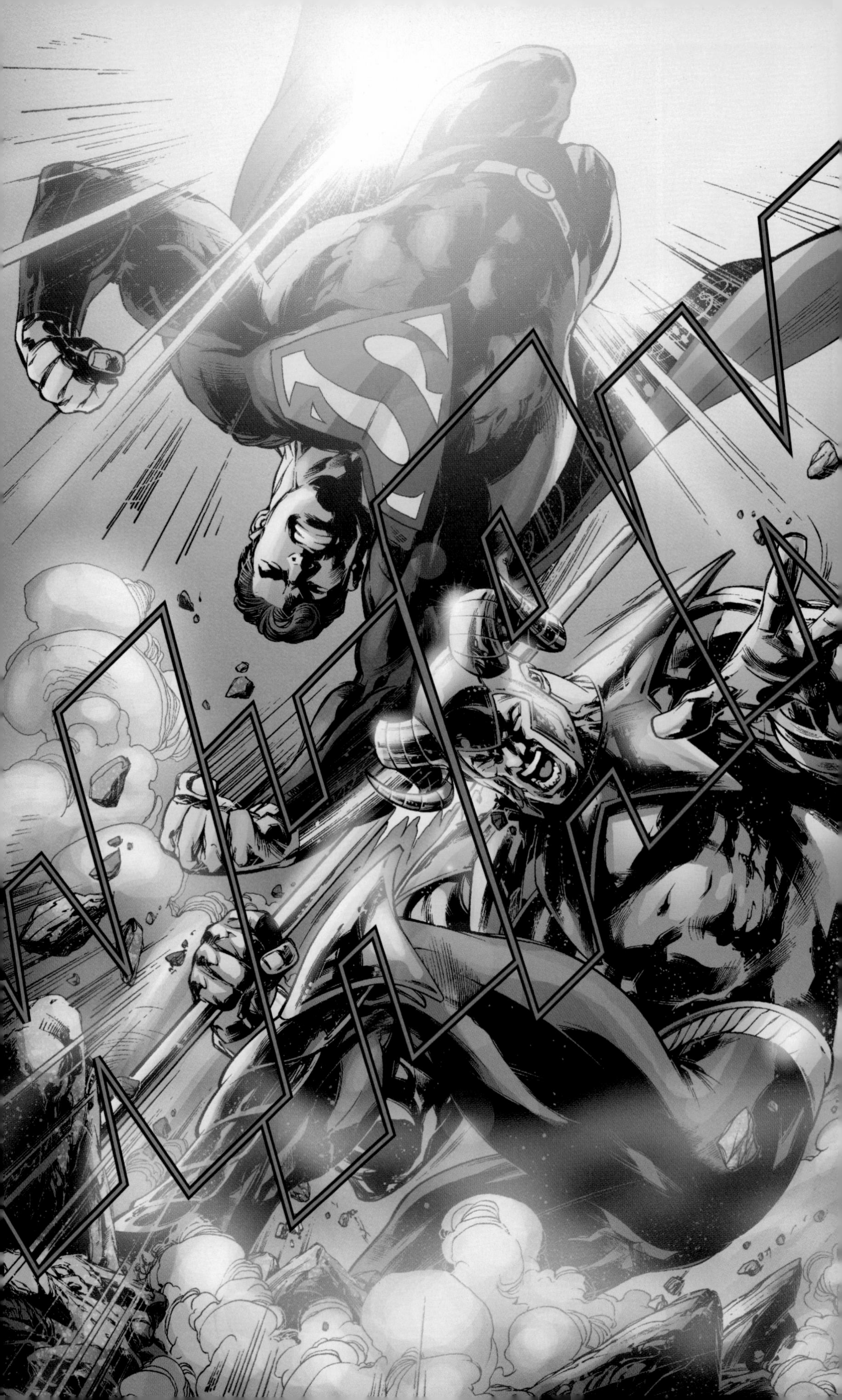

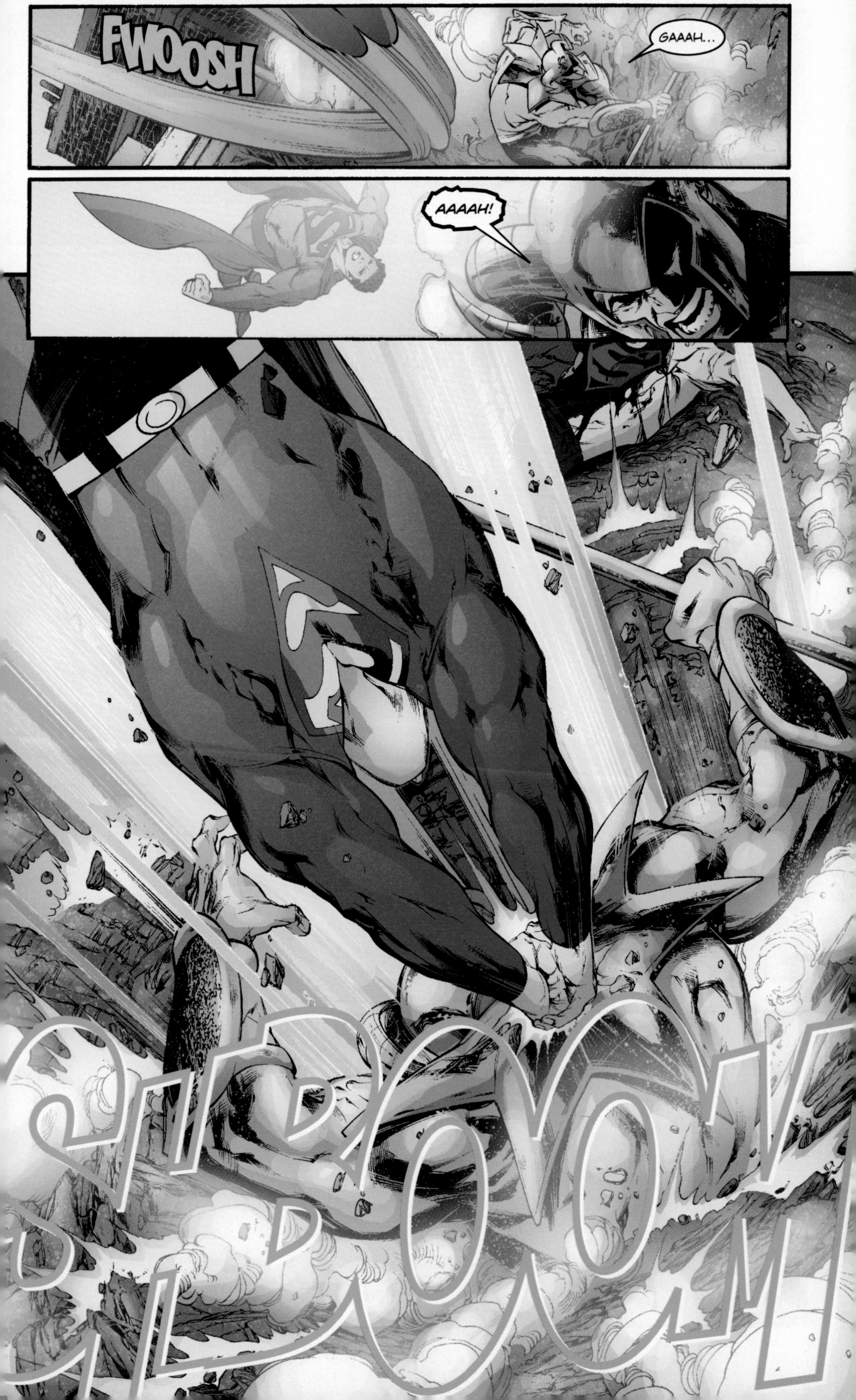

FWOOSH
GAAAH...
AAAAH!
SHBOOM

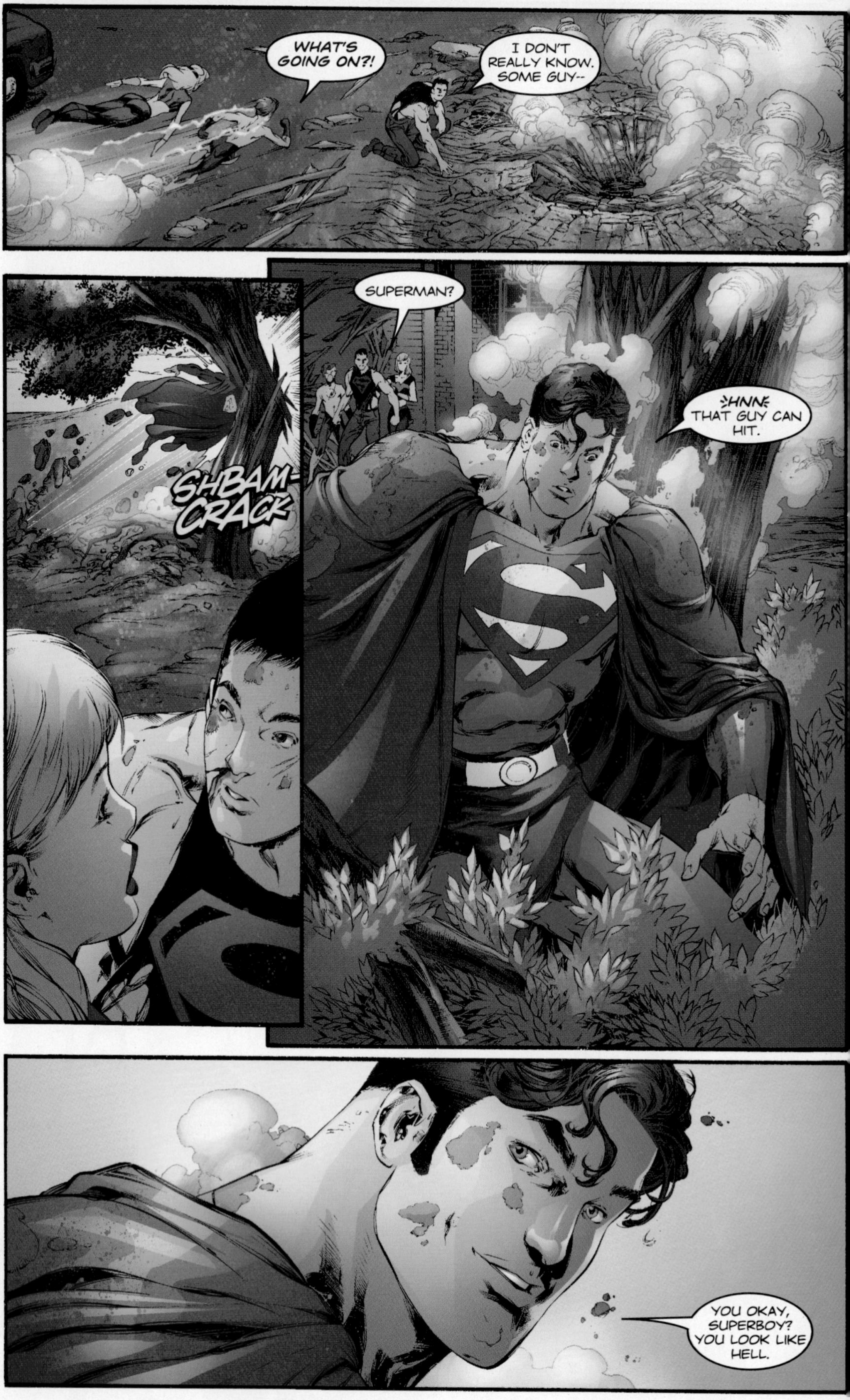

WHAT'S GOING ON?!
I DON'T REALLY KNOW. SOME GUY--
SUPERMAN?
SHBAM-CRACK
HNN. THAT GUY CAN HIT.
YOU OKAY, SUPERBOY? YOU LOOK LIKE HELL.

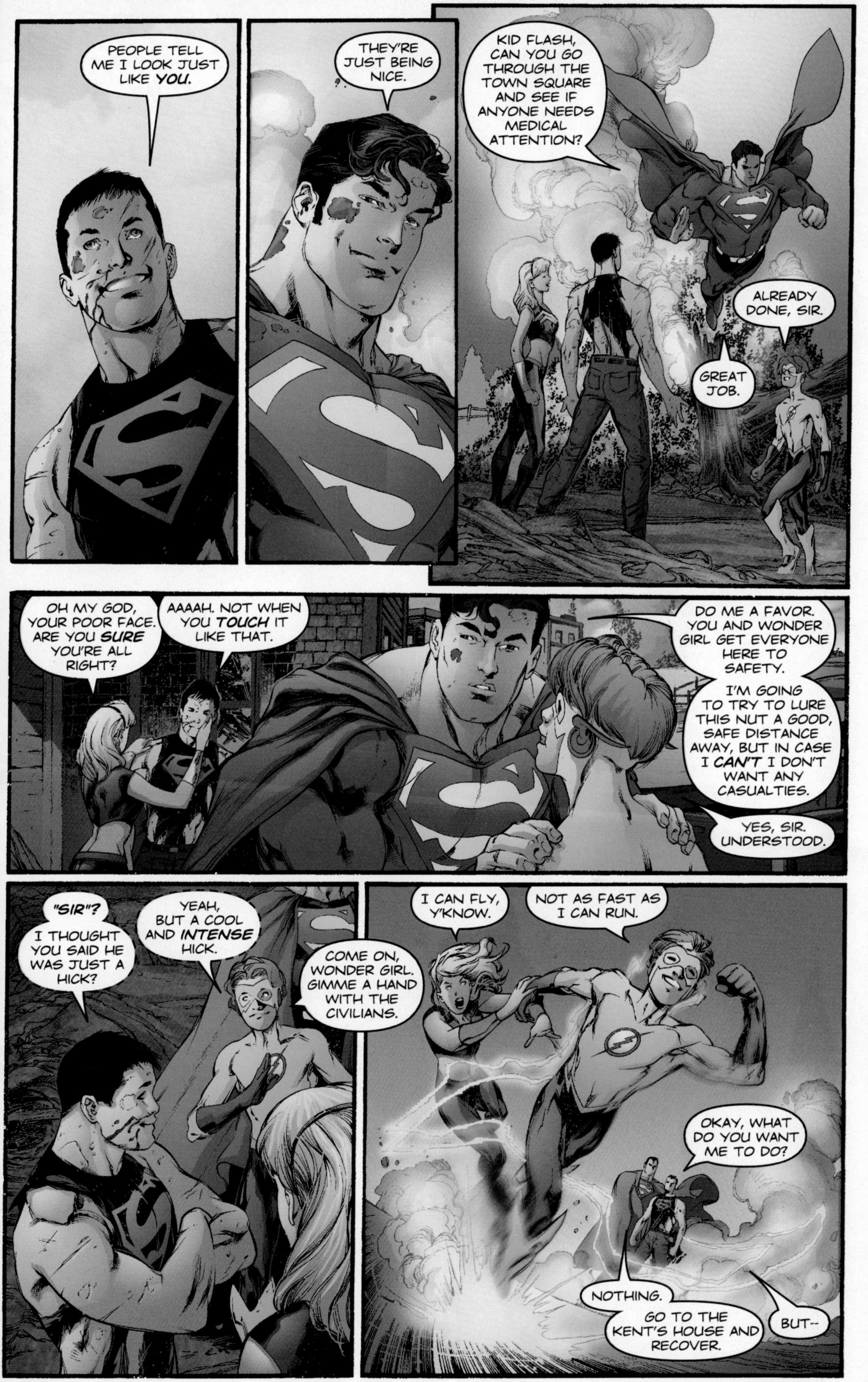
PEOPLE TELL ME I LOOK JUST LIKE YOU.
THEY'RE JUST BEING NICE.
KID FLASH, CAN YOU GO THROUGH THE TOWN SQUARE AND SEE IF ANYONE NEEDS MEDICAL ATTENTION?
ALREADY DONE, SIR.
GREAT JOB.
OH MY GOD, YOUR POOR FACE. ARE YOU SURE YOU'RE ALL RIGHT?
AAAAH. NOT WHEN YOU TOUCH IT LIKE THAT.
DO ME A FAVOR. YOU AND WONDER GIRL GET EVERYONE HERE TO SAFETY.
I'M GOING TO TRY TO LURE THIS NUT A GOOD, SAFE DISTANCE AWAY, BUT IN CASE I CAN'T I DON'T WANT ANY CASUALTIES.
YES, SIR. UNDERSTOOD.
"SIR"? I THOUGHT YOU SAID HE WAS JUST A HICK?
YEAH, BUT A COOL AND INTENSE HICK.
COME ON, WONDER GIRL. GIMME A HAND WITH THE CIVILIANS.
I CAN FLY, Y'KNOW.
NOT AS FAST AS I CAN RUN.
OKAY, WHAT DO YOU WANT ME TO DO?
NOTHING.
GO TO THE KENT'S HOUSE AND RECOVER.
BUT--

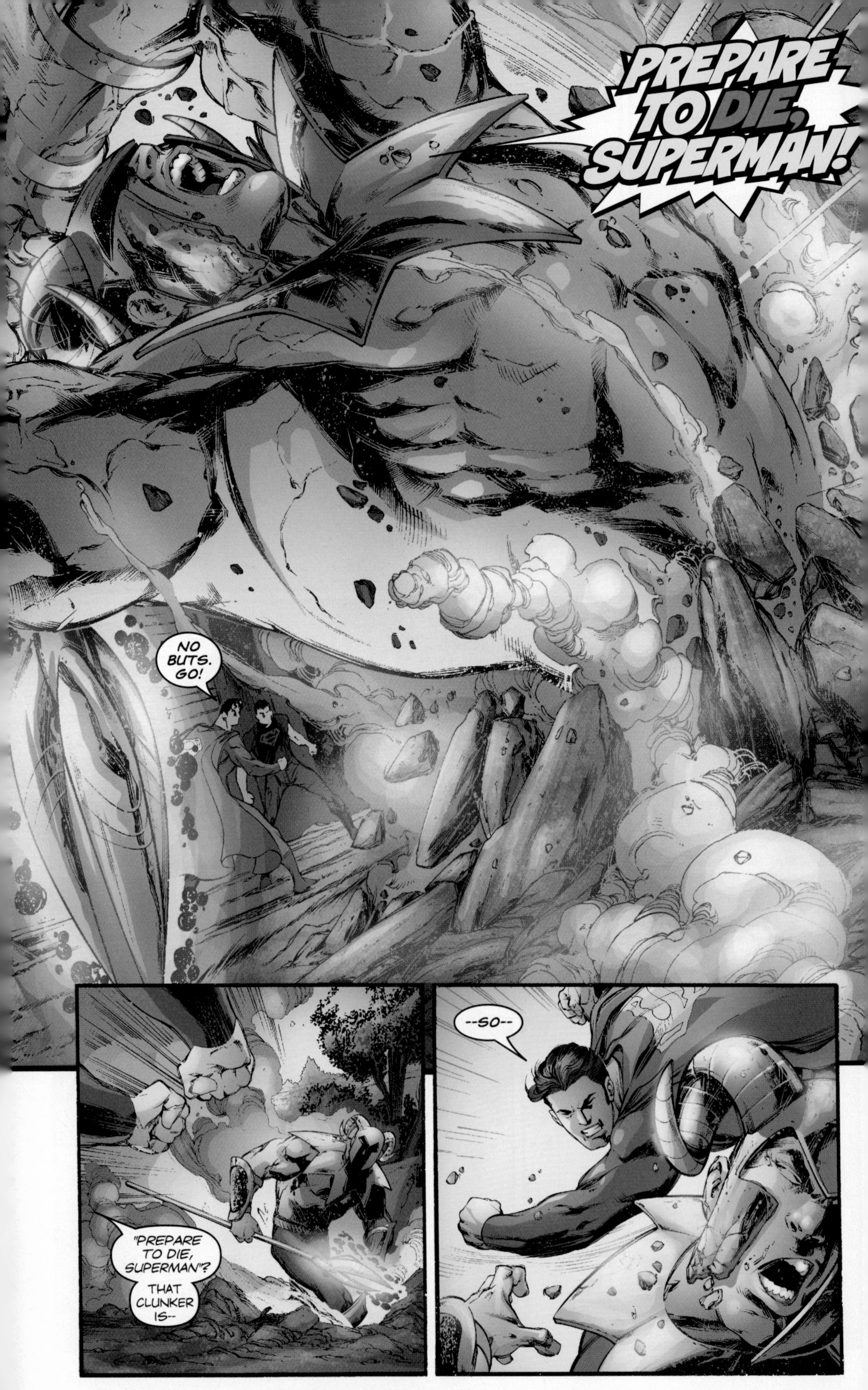
PREPARE TO DIE, SUPERMAN!
NO BUTS. GO!
"PREPARE TO DIE, SUPERMAN"?
THAT CLUNKER IS--
--SO--

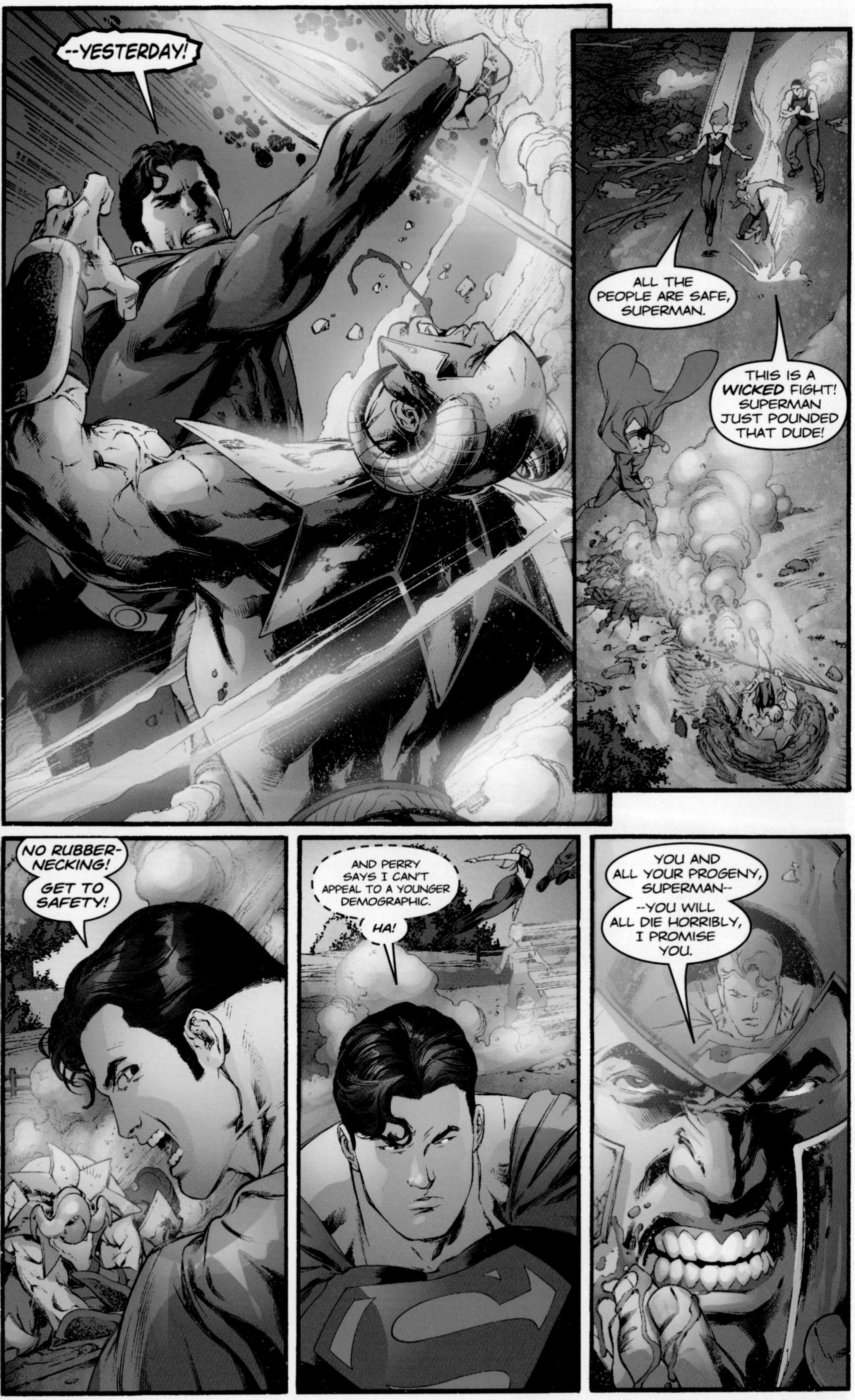
--YESTERDAY!
ALL THE PEOPLE ARE SAFE, SUPERMAN.
THIS IS A *WICKED* FIGHT! SUPERMAN JUST POUNDED THAT DUDE!
NO RUBBER-NECKING!
GET TO SAFETY!
AND PERRY SAYS I CAN'T APPEAL TO A YOUNGER DEMOGRAPHIC.
HA!
YOU AND ALL YOUR PROGENY, SUPERMAN--
--YOU WILL ALL DIE HORRIBLY, I PROMISE YOU.

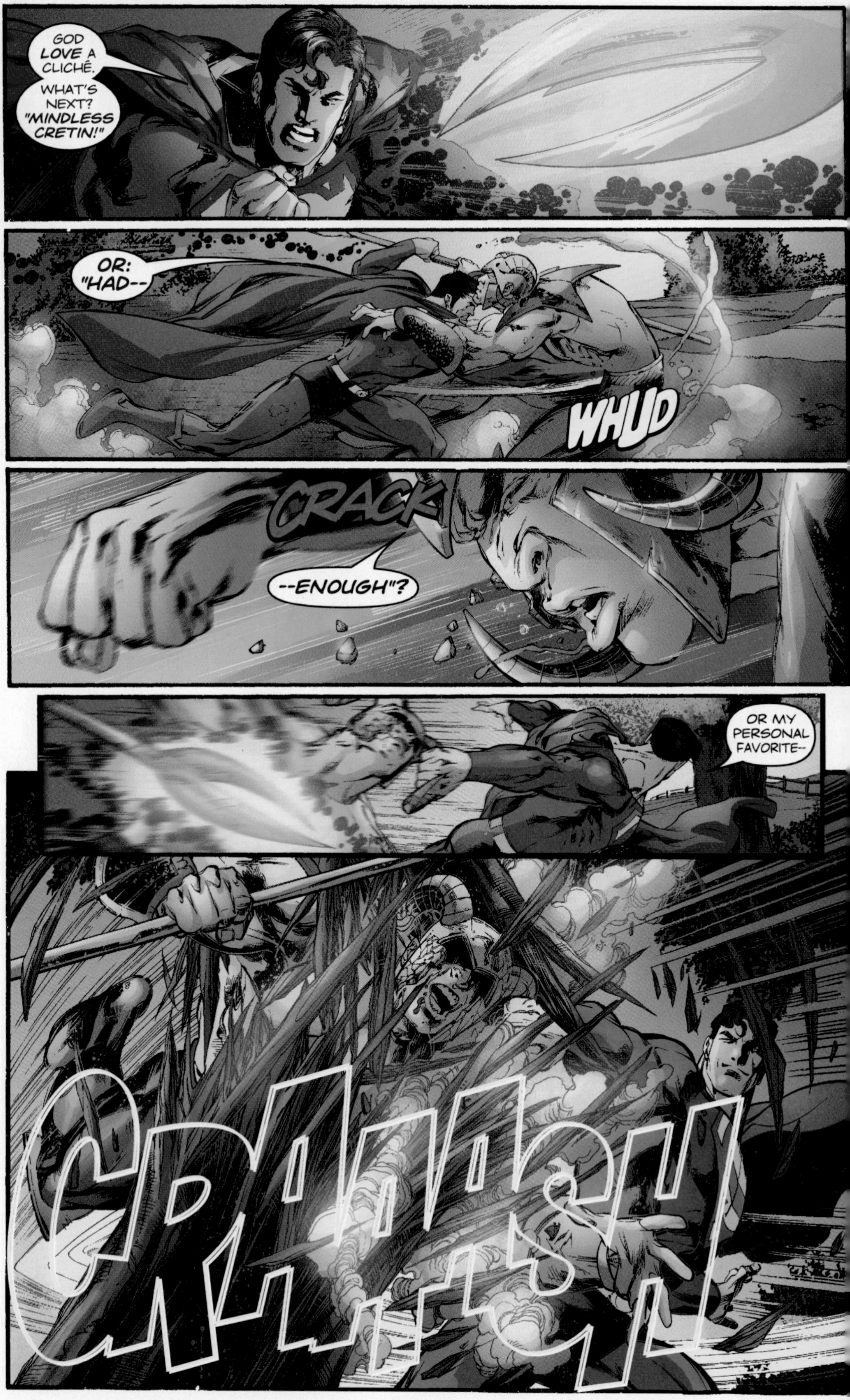
GOD LOVE A CLICHÉ.
WHAT'S NEXT? "MINDLESS CRETIN!"
OR: "HAD--
WHUD
CRACK
--ENOUGH"?
OR MY PERSONAL FAVORITE--
CRAAASH

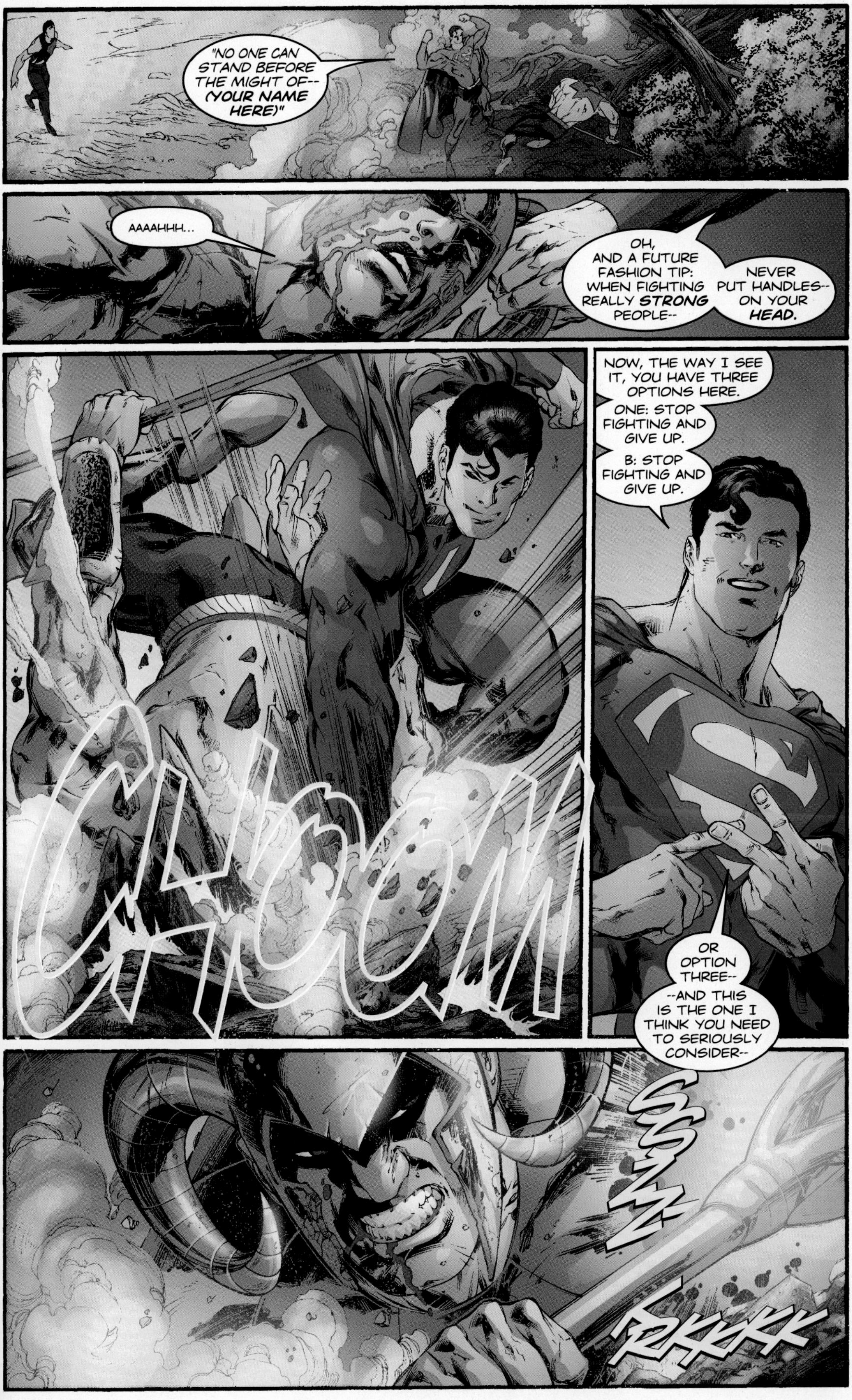

"NO ONE CAN STAND BEFORE THE MIGHT OF-- (YOUR NAME HERE)"
AAAAHHH...
OH, AND A FUTURE FASHION TIP: WHEN FIGHTING REALLY STRONG PEOPLE--
NEVER PUT HANDLES-- ON YOUR HEAD.
CHOOM
NOW, THE WAY I SEE IT, YOU HAVE THREE OPTIONS HERE.
ONE: STOP FIGHTING AND GIVE UP.
B: STOP FIGHTING AND GIVE UP.
OR OPTION THREE--
--AND THIS IS THE ONE I THINK YOU NEED TO SERIOUSLY CONSIDER--
SSSHHH
FRKKKK

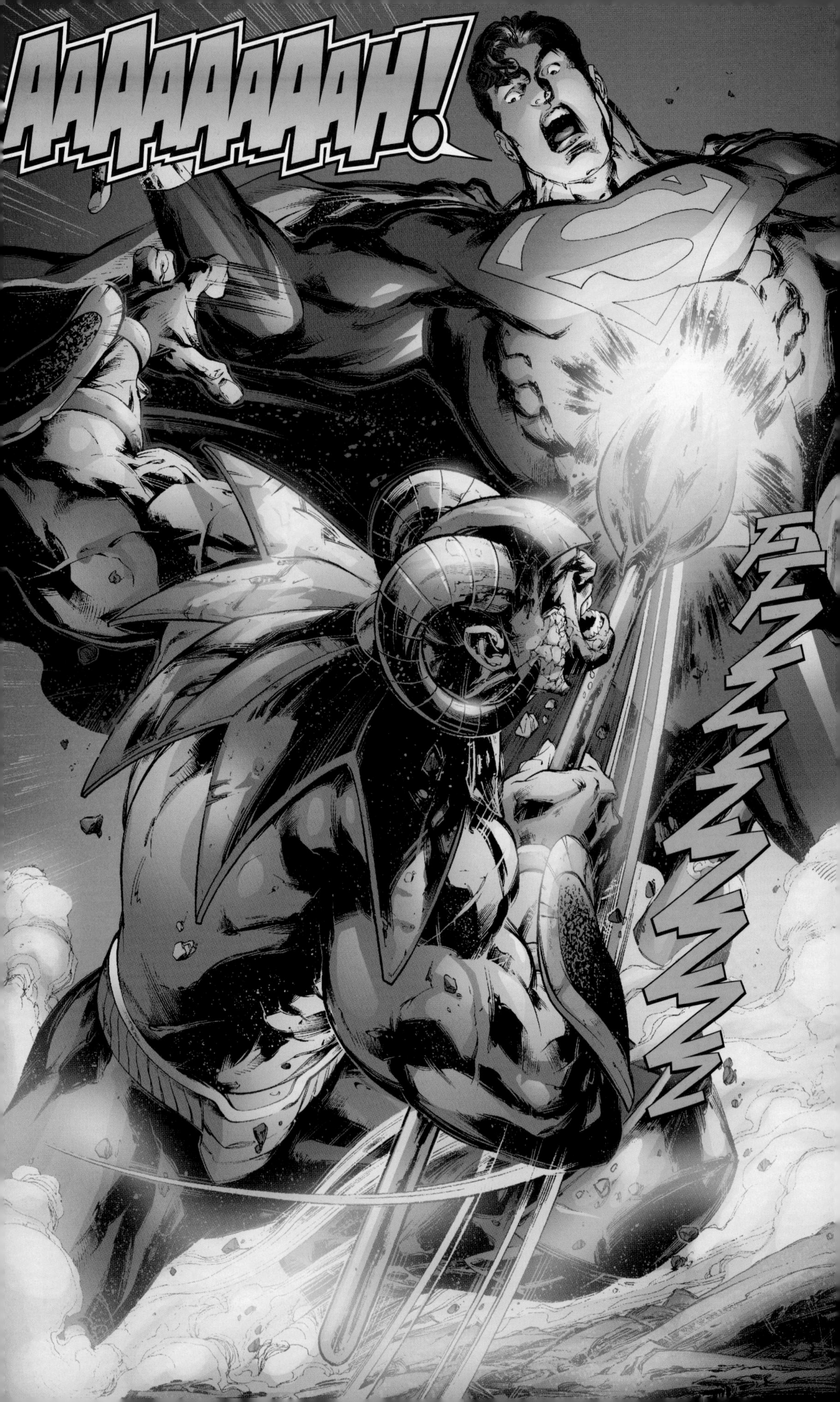
AAAAAAAAH!

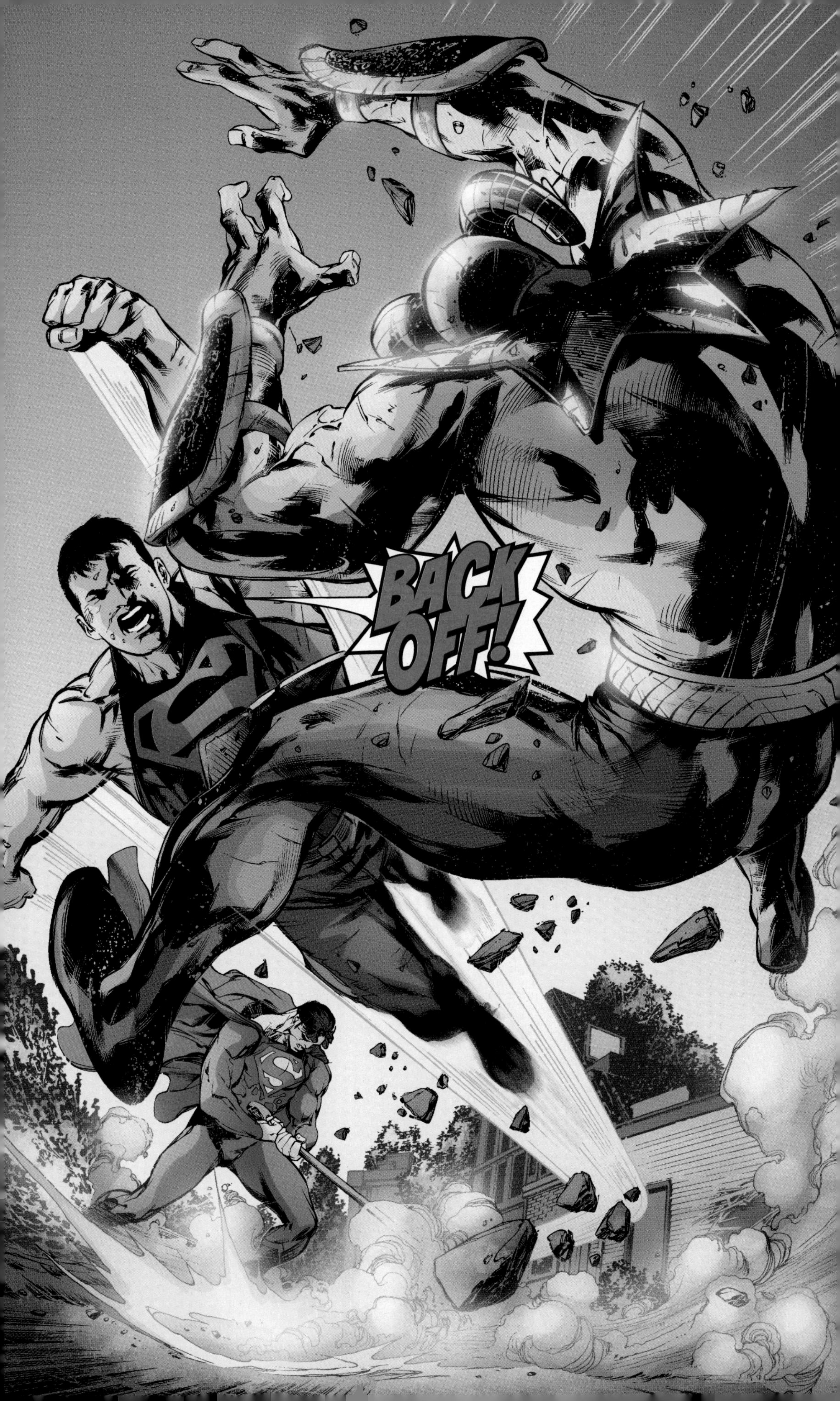
BACK OFF!

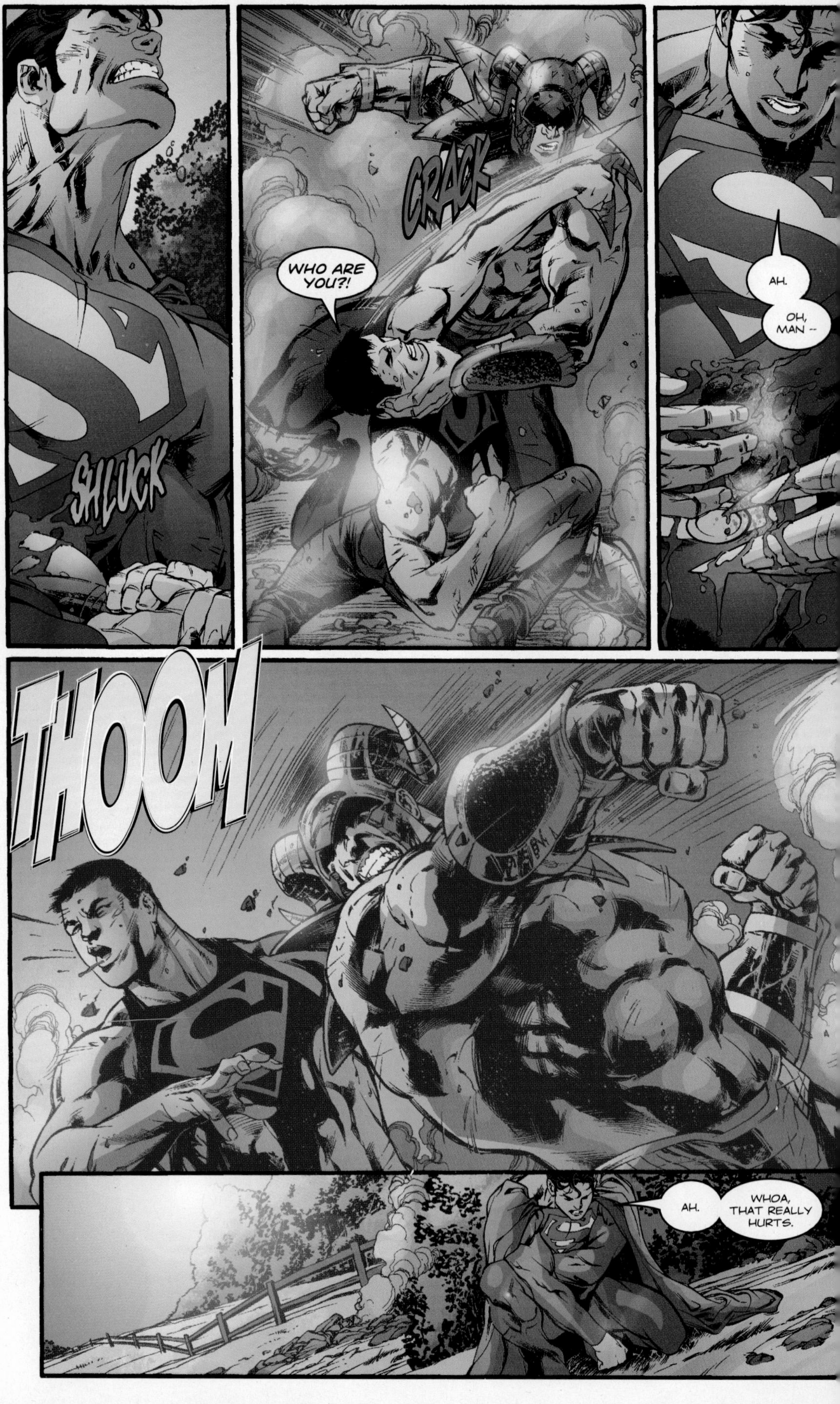
SHLUCK
CRACK
WHO ARE YOU?!
AH.
OH, MAN --
THOOM
AH.
WHOA, THAT REALLY HURTS.

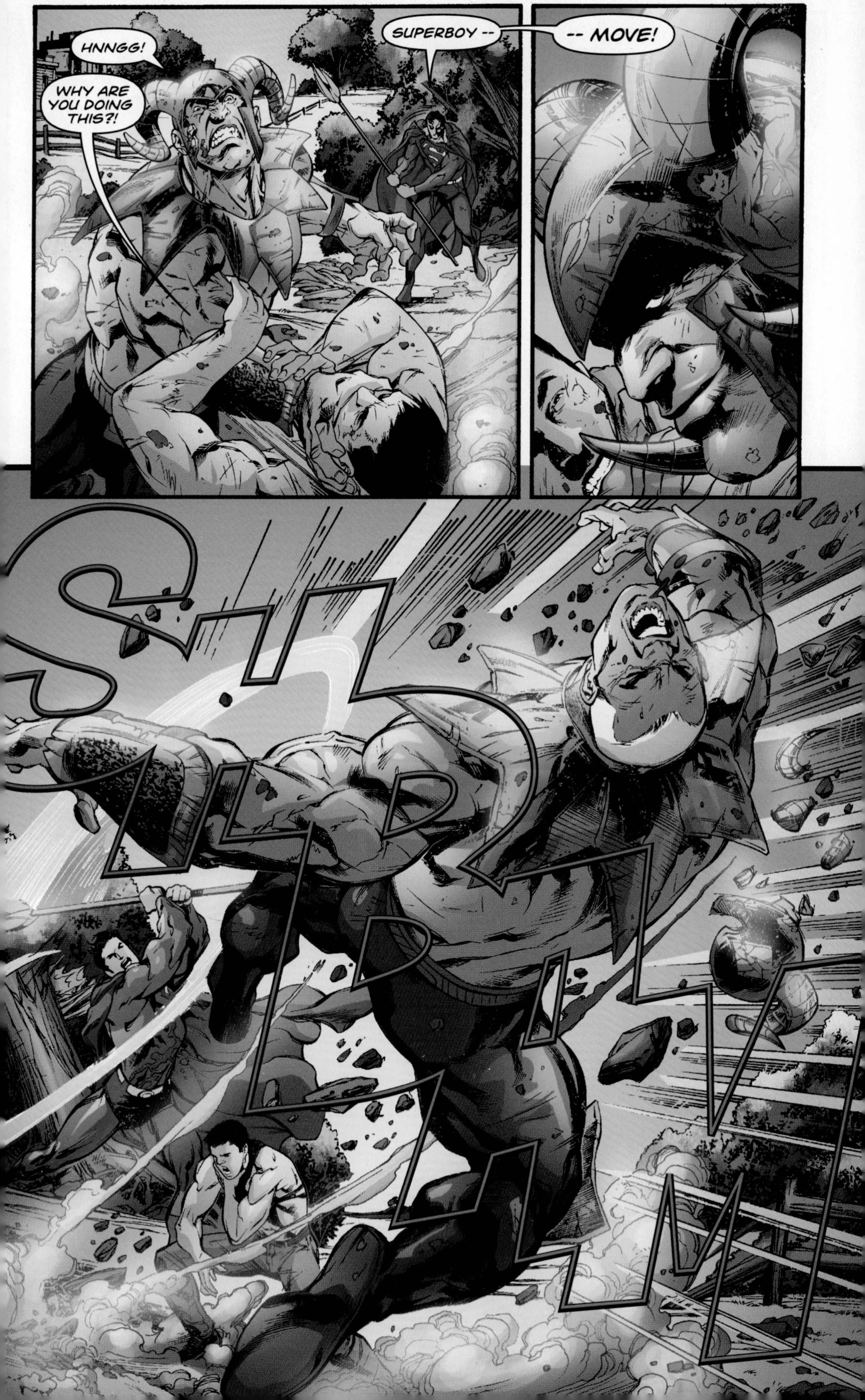

HNNGG!
WHY ARE YOU DOING THIS?!
SUPERBOY --
-- MOVE!

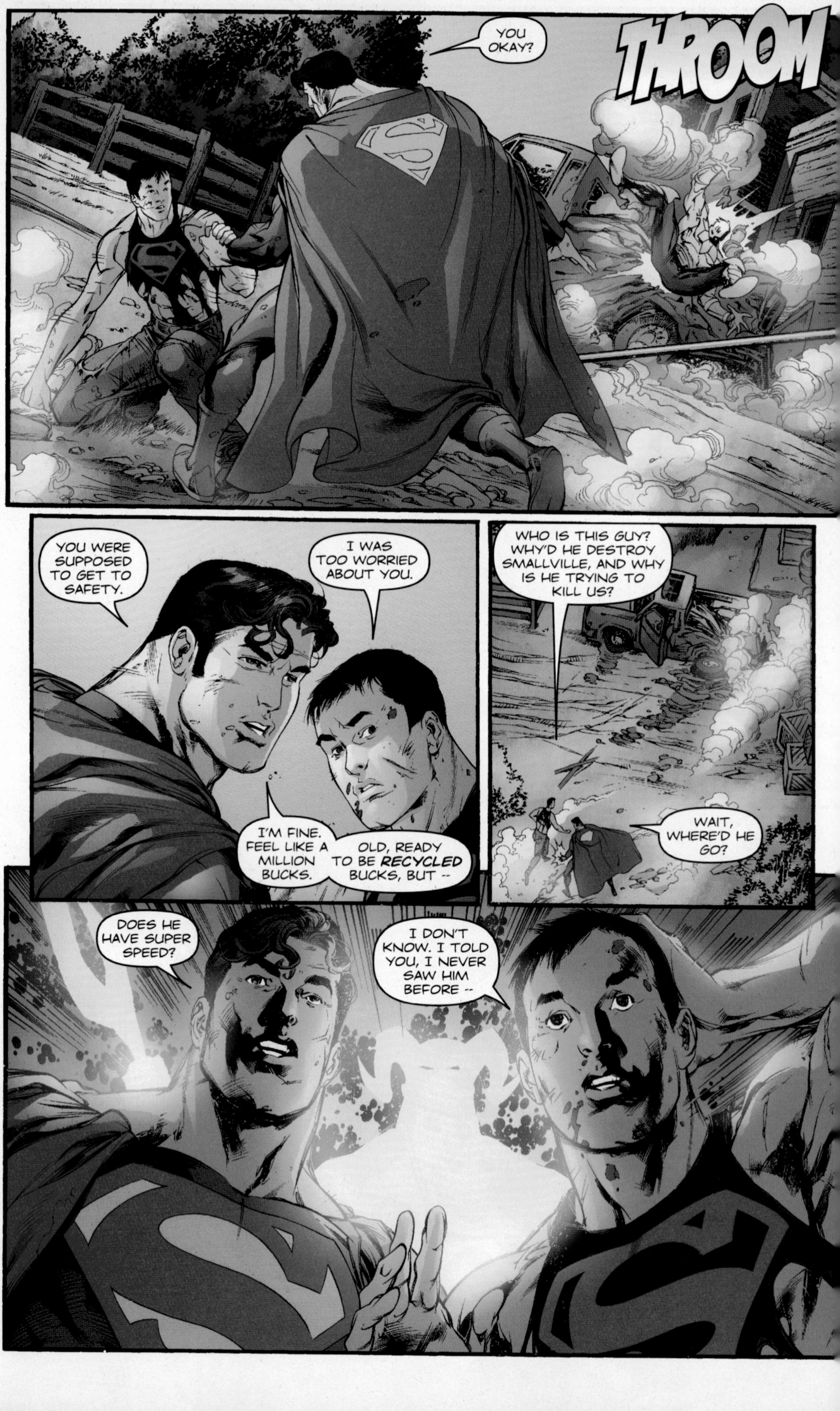
YOU OKAY?
THROOM
YOU WERE SUPPOSED TO GET TO SAFETY.
I WAS TOO WORRIED ABOUT YOU.
I'M FINE. FEEL LIKE A MILLION BUCKS.
OLD, READY TO BE RECYCLED BUCKS, BUT --
WHO IS THIS GUY? WHY'D HE DESTROY SMALLVILLE, AND WHY IS HE TRYING TO KILL US?
WAIT, WHERE'D HE GO?
DOES HE HAVE SUPER SPEED?
I DON'T KNOW. I TOLD YOU, I NEVER SAW HIM BEFORE --

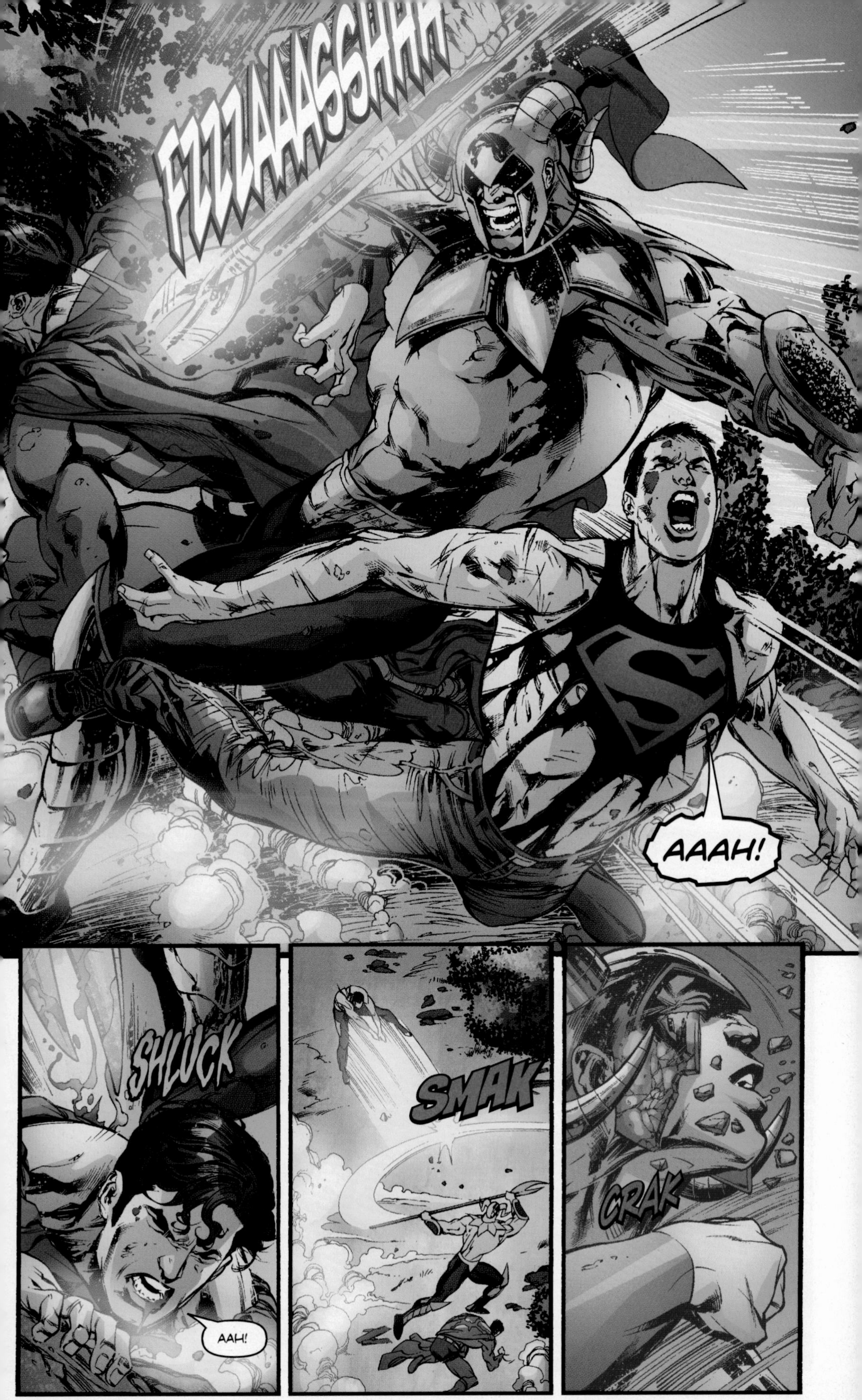
FZZZAAASSHHH
AAAH!
SHLUCK
AAH!
SMAK
CRAK

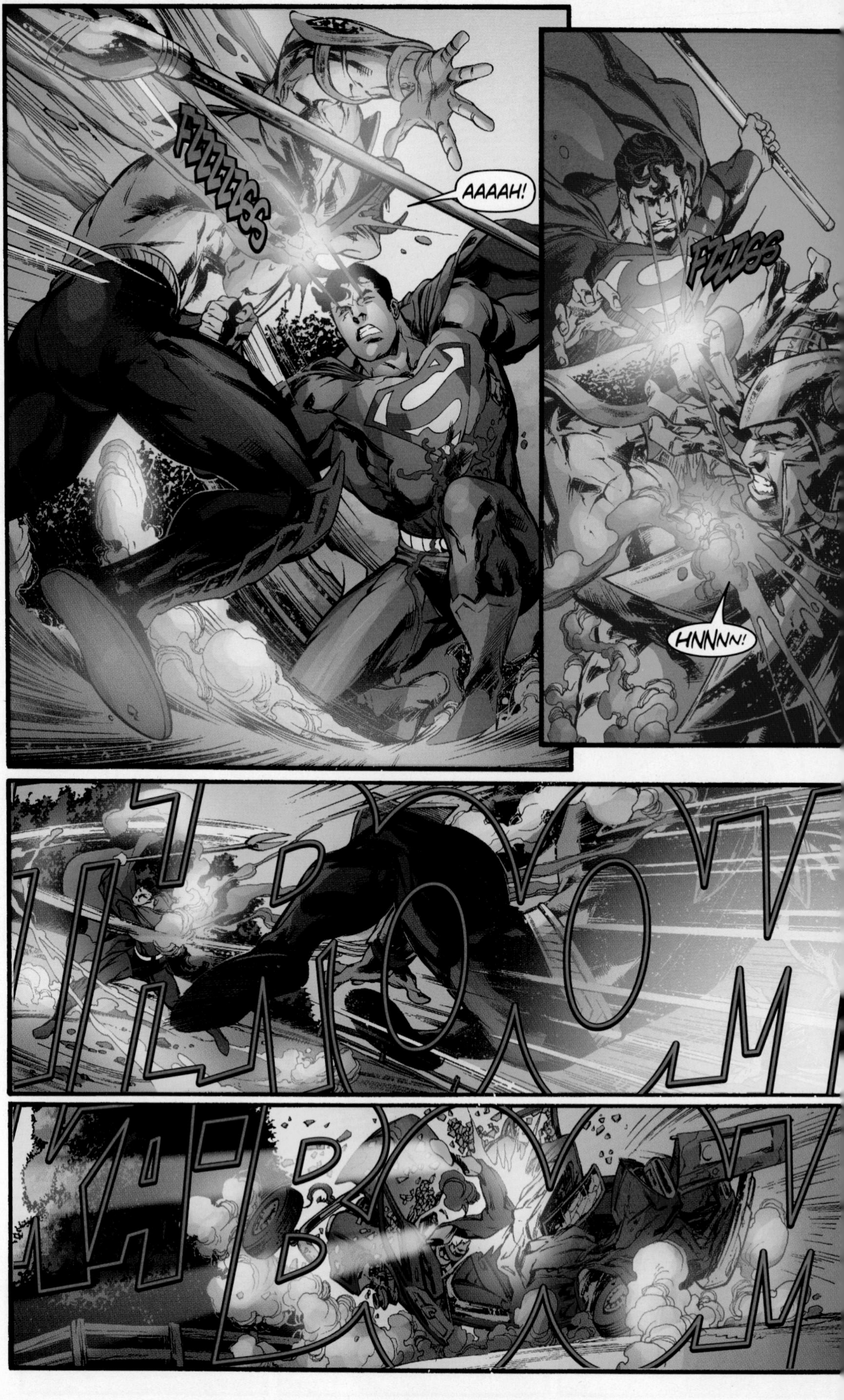

FZZZSS
AAAAH!
FZZZSS
HNNNN!

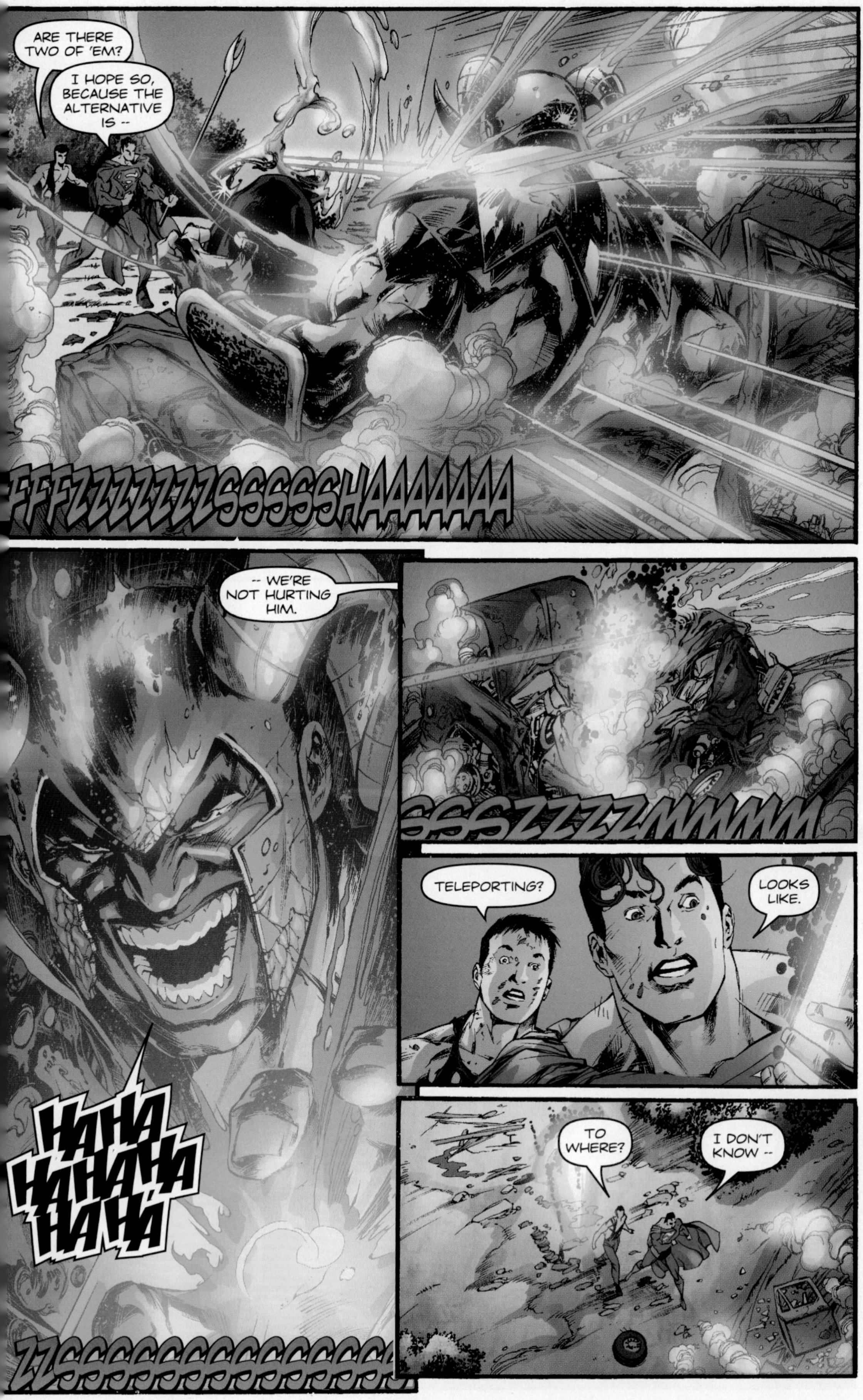
ARE THERE TWO OF 'EM?
I HOPE SO, BECAUSE THE ALTERNATIVE IS --
FFFZZZZZZZSSSSSSHAAAAAAA
-- WE'RE NOT HURTING HIM.
HAHA HAHAHA HAHA
ZZSSSSSSSSSSSSSSSS
SSSZZZZZMMMMM
TELEPORTING?
LOOKS LIKE.
TO WHERE?
I DON'T KNOW --

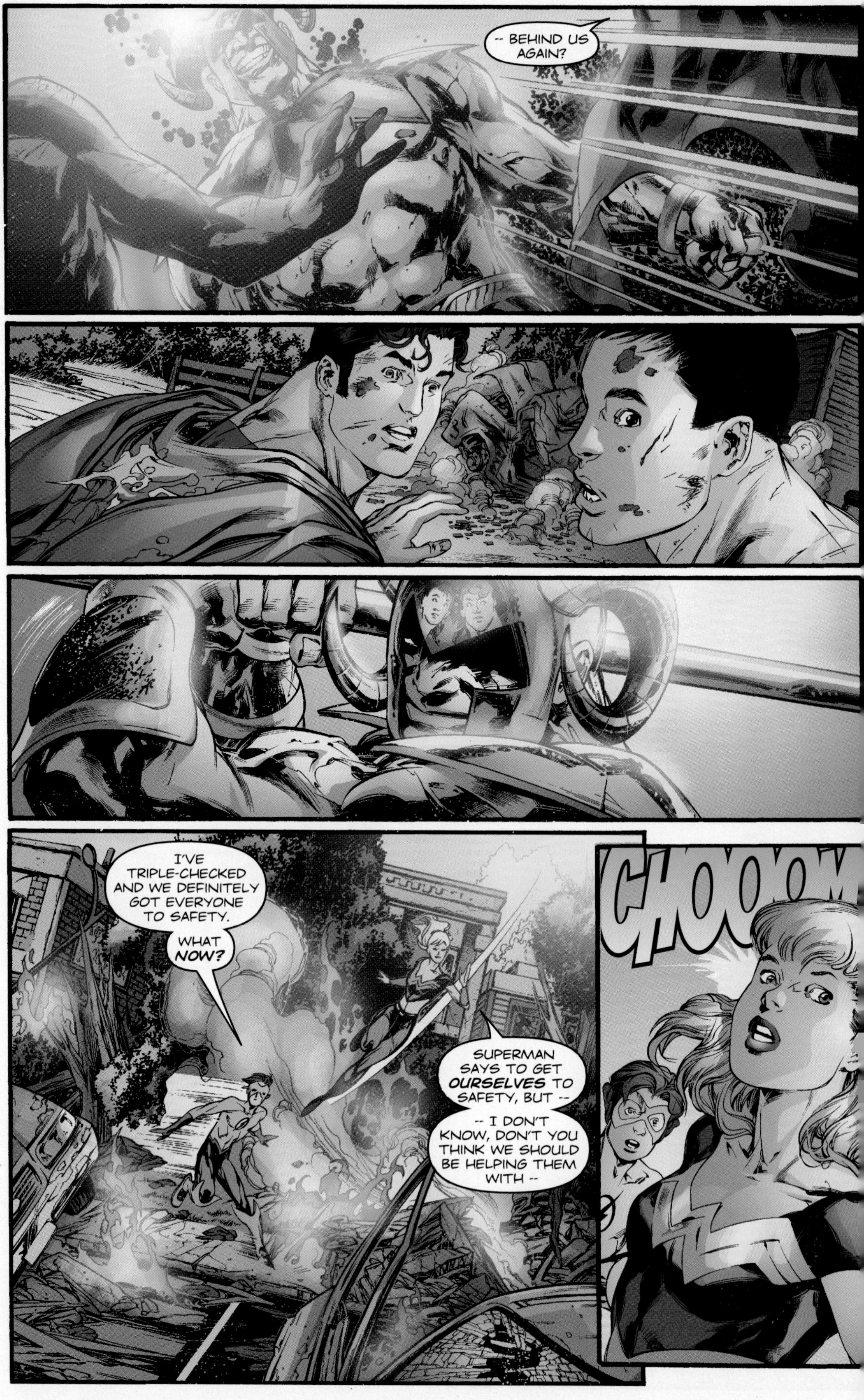
-- BEHIND US AGAIN?
I'VE TRIPLE-CHECKED AND WE DEFINITELY GOT EVERYONE TO SAFETY.
WHAT NOW?
SUPERMAN SAYS TO GET OURSELVES TO SAFETY, BUT --
-- I DON'T KNOW, DON'T YOU THINK WE SHOULD BE HELPING THEM WITH --
CHOOOOM

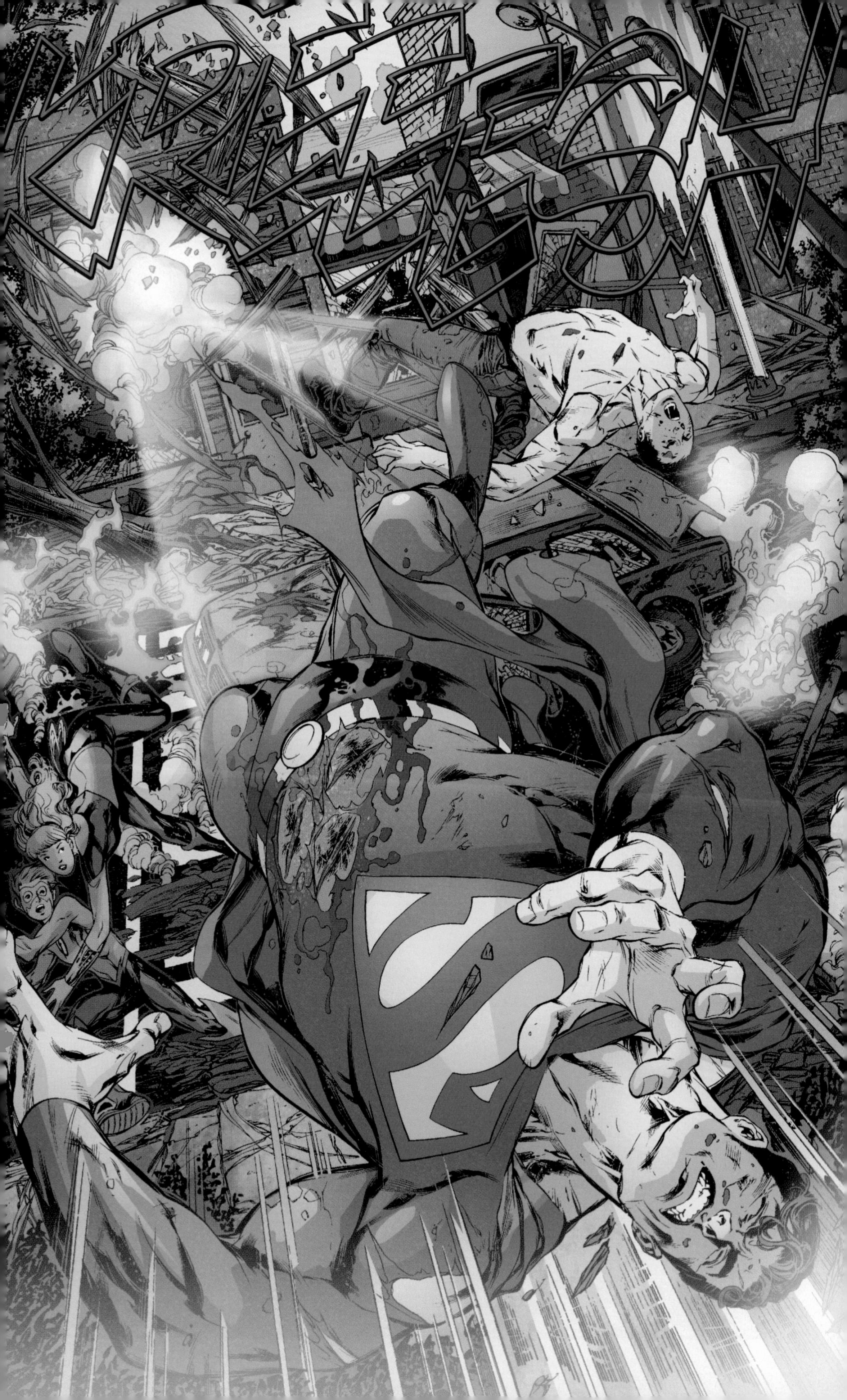

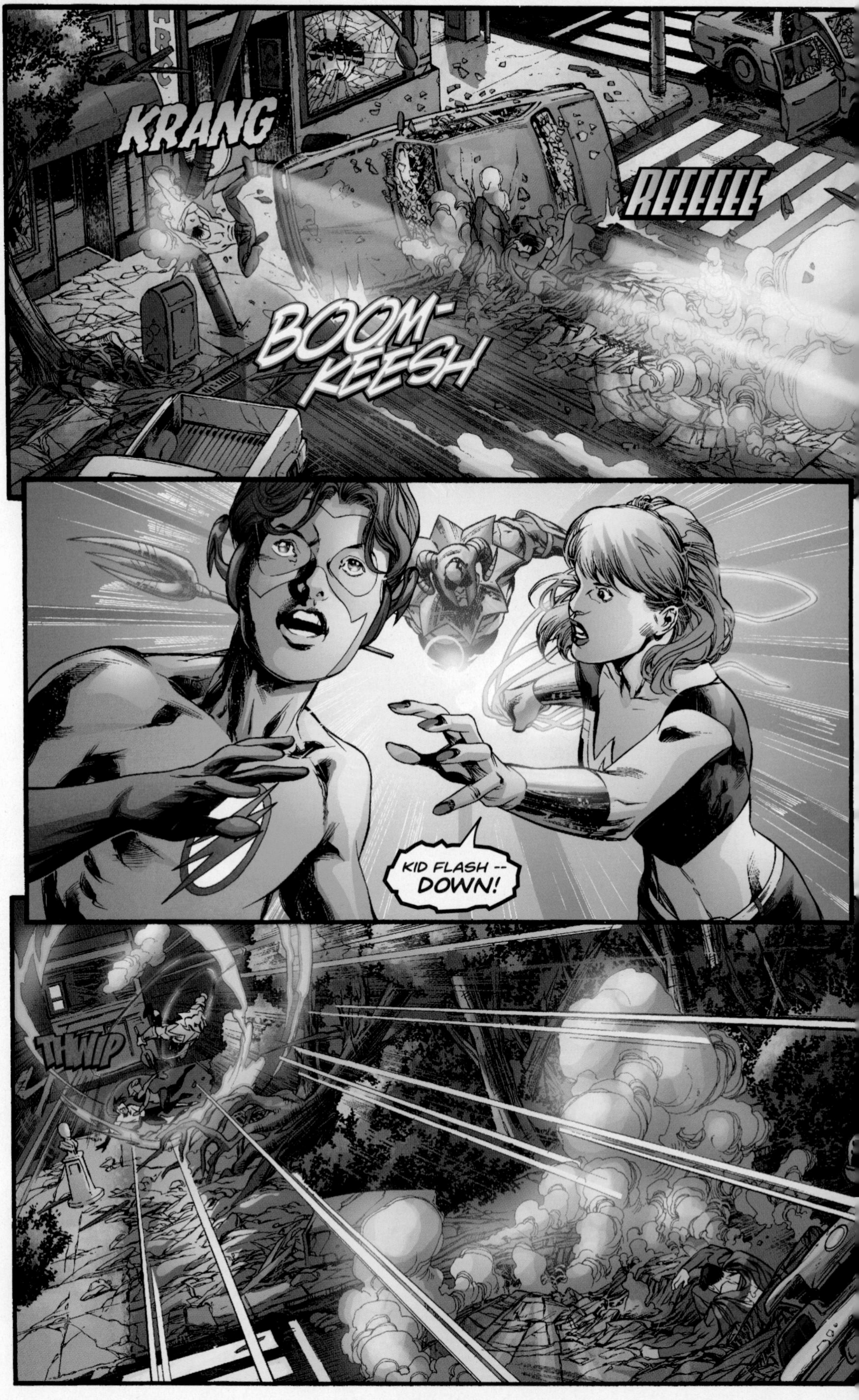
KRANG
REEEEEEE
BOOM-KEESH
KID FLASH -- DOWN!
THWIP

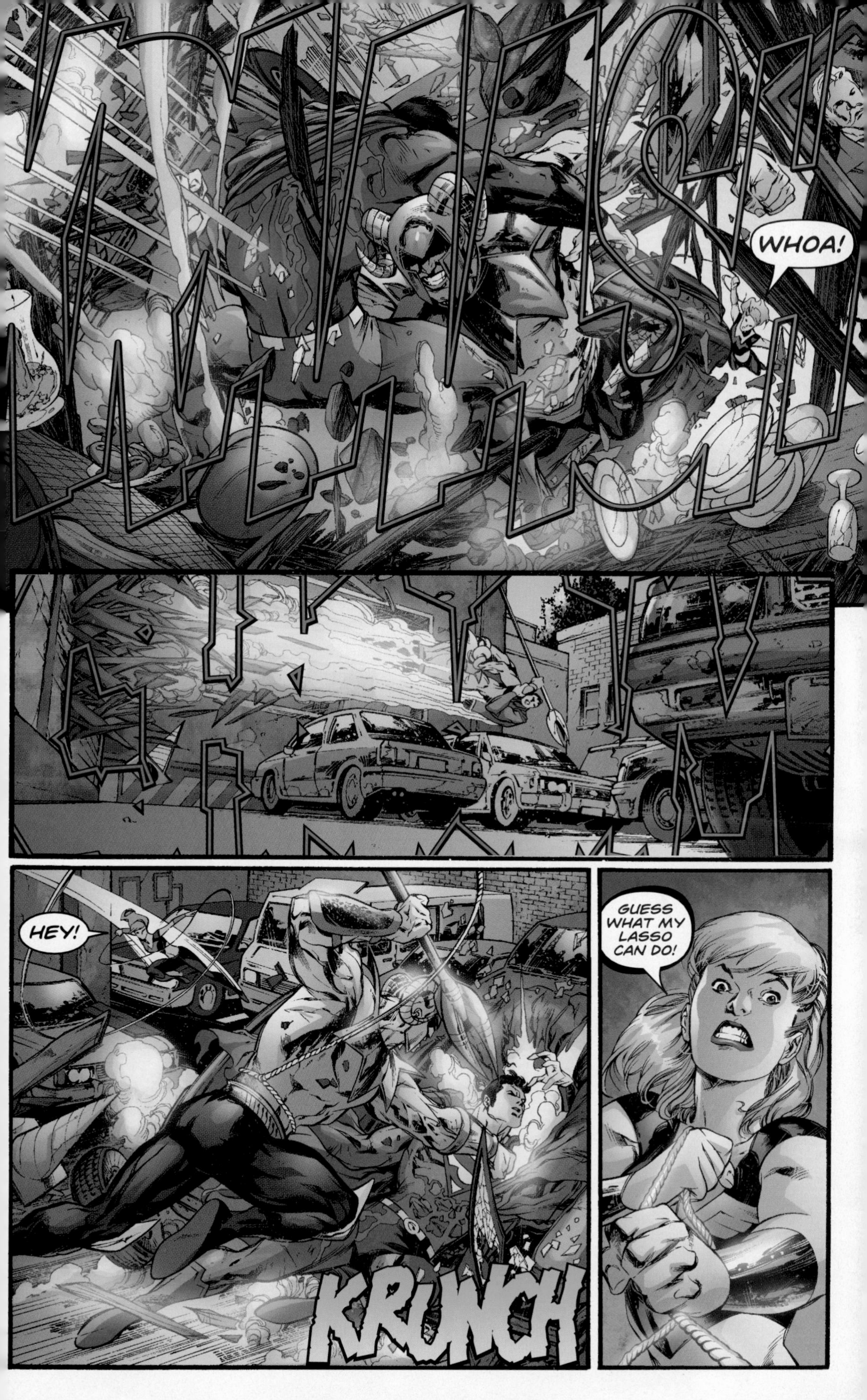
WHOA!
HEY!
KRUNCH
GUESS WHAT MY LASSO CAN DO!

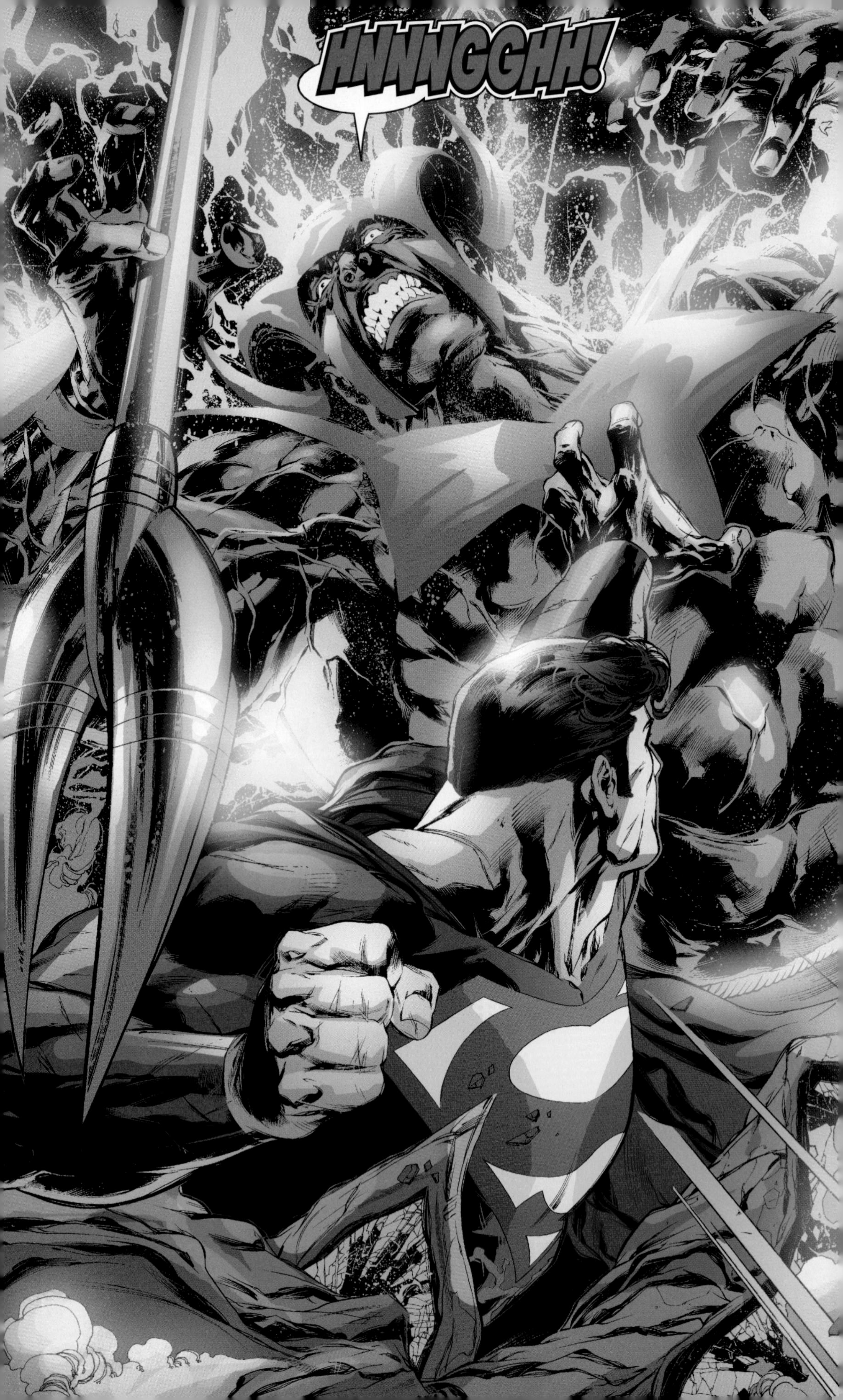
HNNNGGHH!

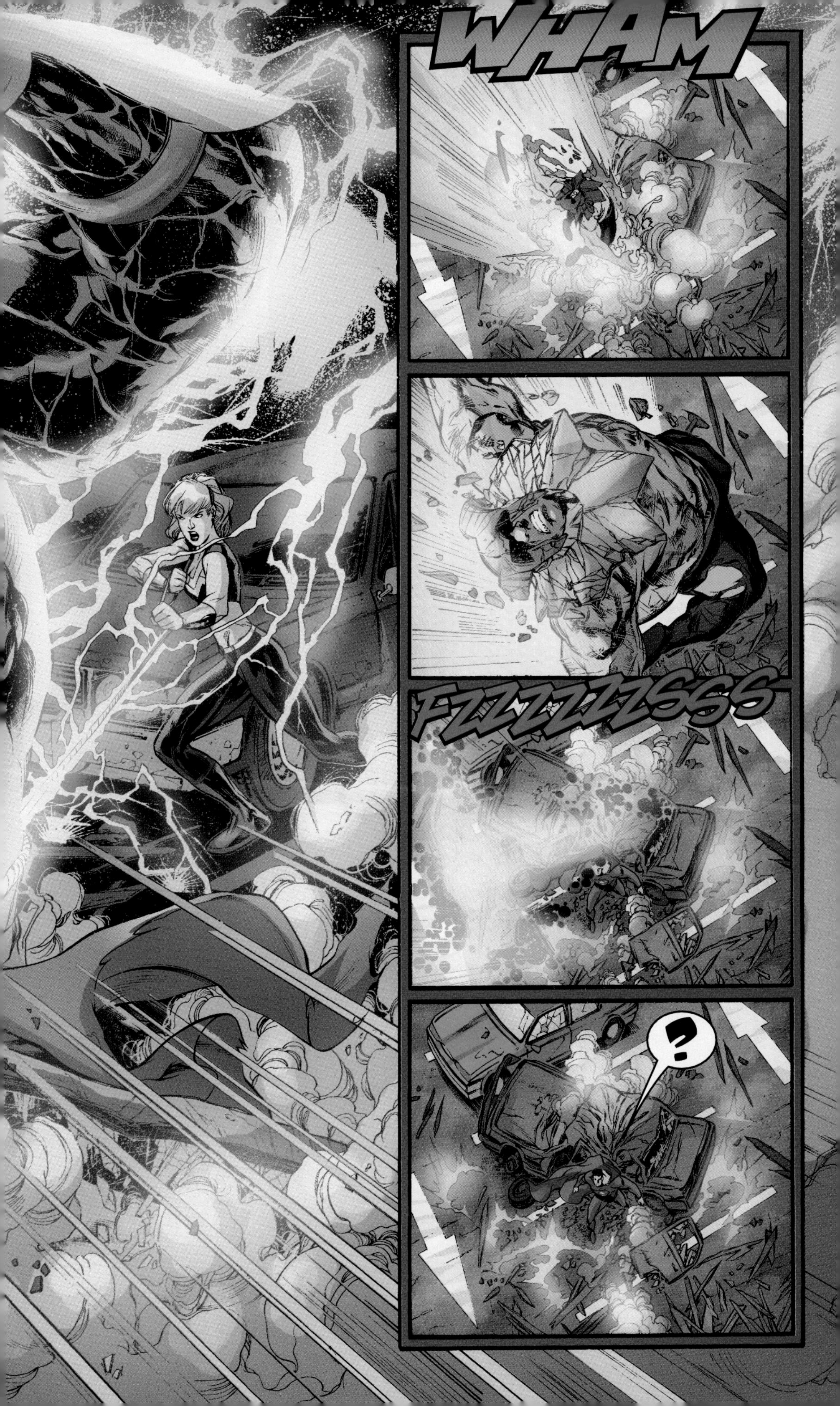
WHAM
FZZZZZZSSS
?

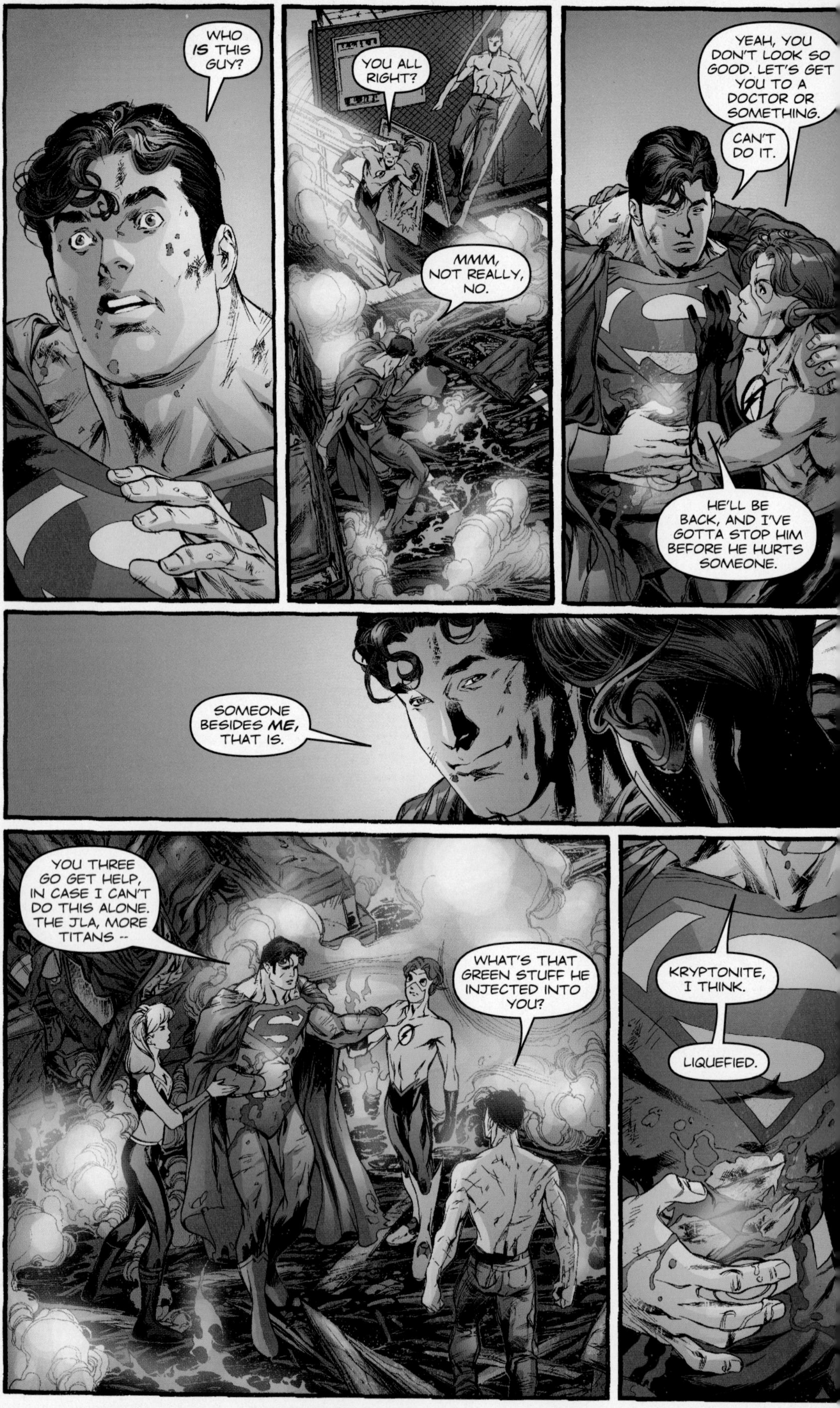
WHO IS THIS GUY?
YOU ALL RIGHT?
MMM, NOT REALLY, NO.
YEAH, YOU DON'T LOOK SO GOOD. LET'S GET YOU TO A DOCTOR OR SOMETHING.
CAN'T DO IT.
HE'LL BE BACK, AND I'VE GOTTA STOP HIM BEFORE HE HURTS SOMEONE.
SOMEONE BESIDES ME, THAT IS.
YOU THREE GO GET HELP, IN CASE I CAN'T DO THIS ALONE. THE JLA, MORE TITANS --
WHAT'S THAT GREEN STUFF HE INJECTED INTO YOU?
KRYPTONITE, I THINK.
LIQUEFIED.

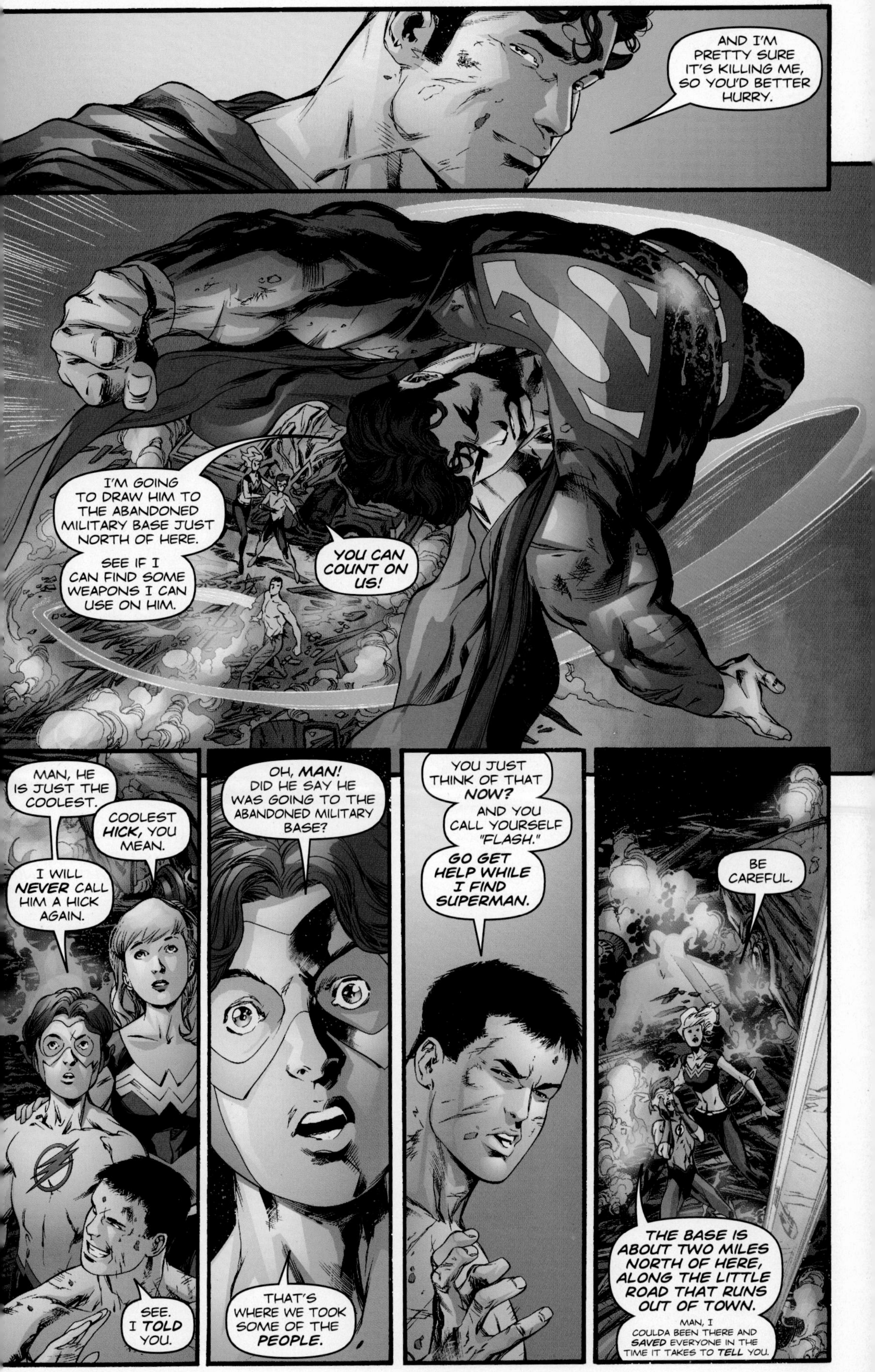

AND I'M PRETTY SURE IT'S KILLING ME, SO YOU'D BETTER HURRY.
I'M GOING TO DRAW HIM TO THE ABANDONED MILITARY BASE JUST NORTH OF HERE.
SEE IF I CAN FIND SOME WEAPONS I CAN USE ON HIM.
YOU CAN COUNT ON US!
MAN, HE IS JUST THE COOLEST.
COOLEST HICK, YOU MEAN.
I WILL NEVER CALL HIM A HICK AGAIN.
SEE. I TOLD YOU.
OH, MAN! DID HE SAY HE WAS GOING TO THE ABANDONED MILITARY BASE?
THAT'S WHERE WE TOOK SOME OF THE PEOPLE.
YOU JUST THINK OF THAT NOW?
AND YOU CALL YOURSELF "FLASH."
GO GET HELP WHILE I FIND SUPERMAN.
BE CAREFUL.
THE BASE IS ABOUT TWO MILES NORTH OF HERE, ALONG THE LITTLE ROAD THAT RUNS OUT OF TOWN.
MAN, I COULDA BEEN THERE AND SAVED EVERYONE IN THE TIME IT TAKES TO TELL YOU.

SAVE *YOURSELVES,* LITTLE ONES.

AND IF YOU CHOOSE TO RETURN WITH THIS SO-CALLED *"HELP"* --

-- BE SURE TO BRING A PAIR OF ADEQUATELY SIZED CASKETS.

HA HA HA HA HA HA

ZOIUDA PARKING

TO THINK ALL THIS TIME I'VE BEEN WORRIED ABOUT DOOMSDAY, AND THEN *THIS* LOSER SHOWS UP AND KICKS MY --

GREAT. THIS STUFF IS USELESS.

SUPERMAN! HE'S RIGHT BEHIND ME!

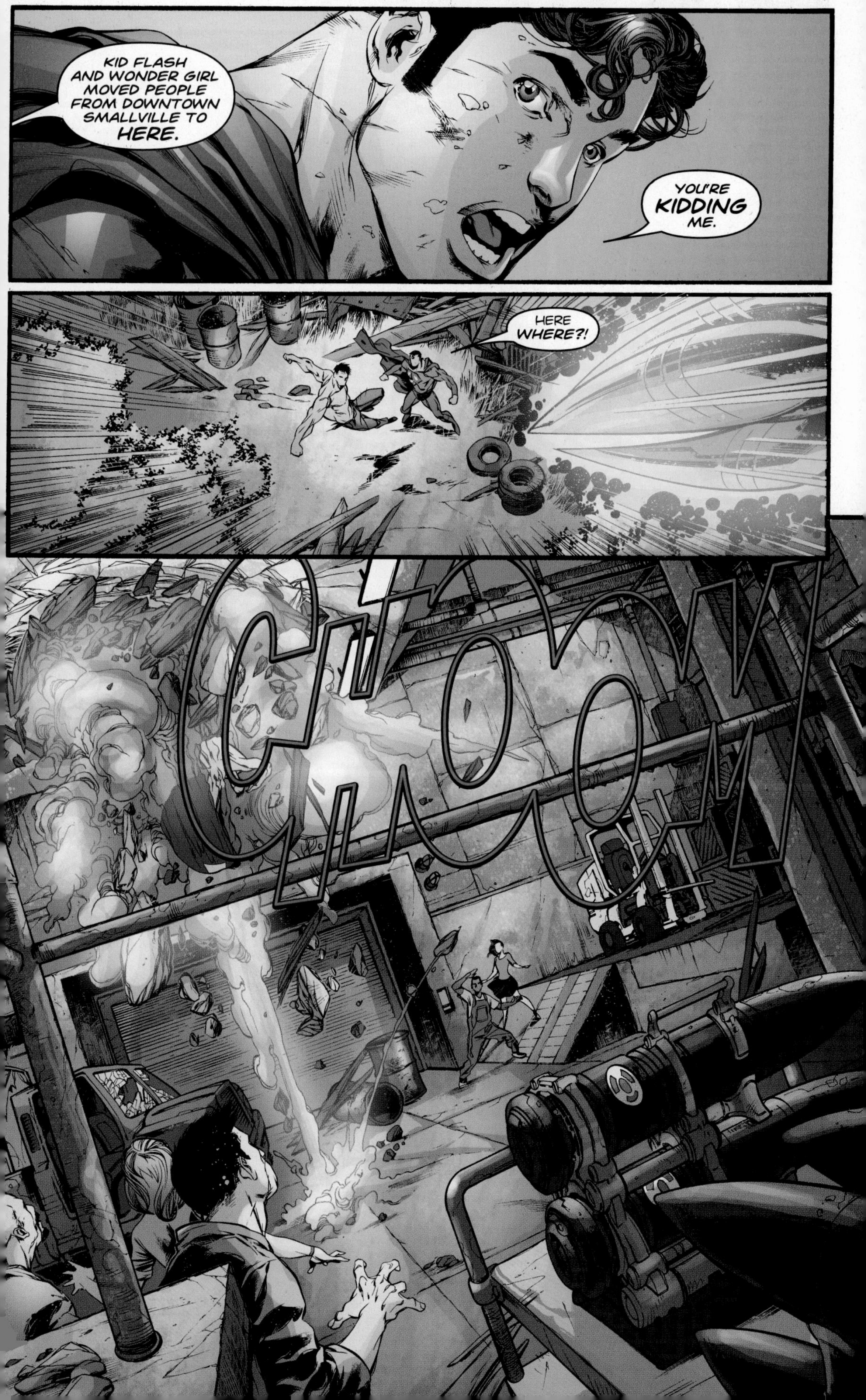
KID FLASH AND WONDER GIRL MOVED PEOPLE FROM DOWNTOWN SMALLVILLE TO HERE.
YOU'RE KIDDING ME.
HERE WHERE?!
CHOOOM

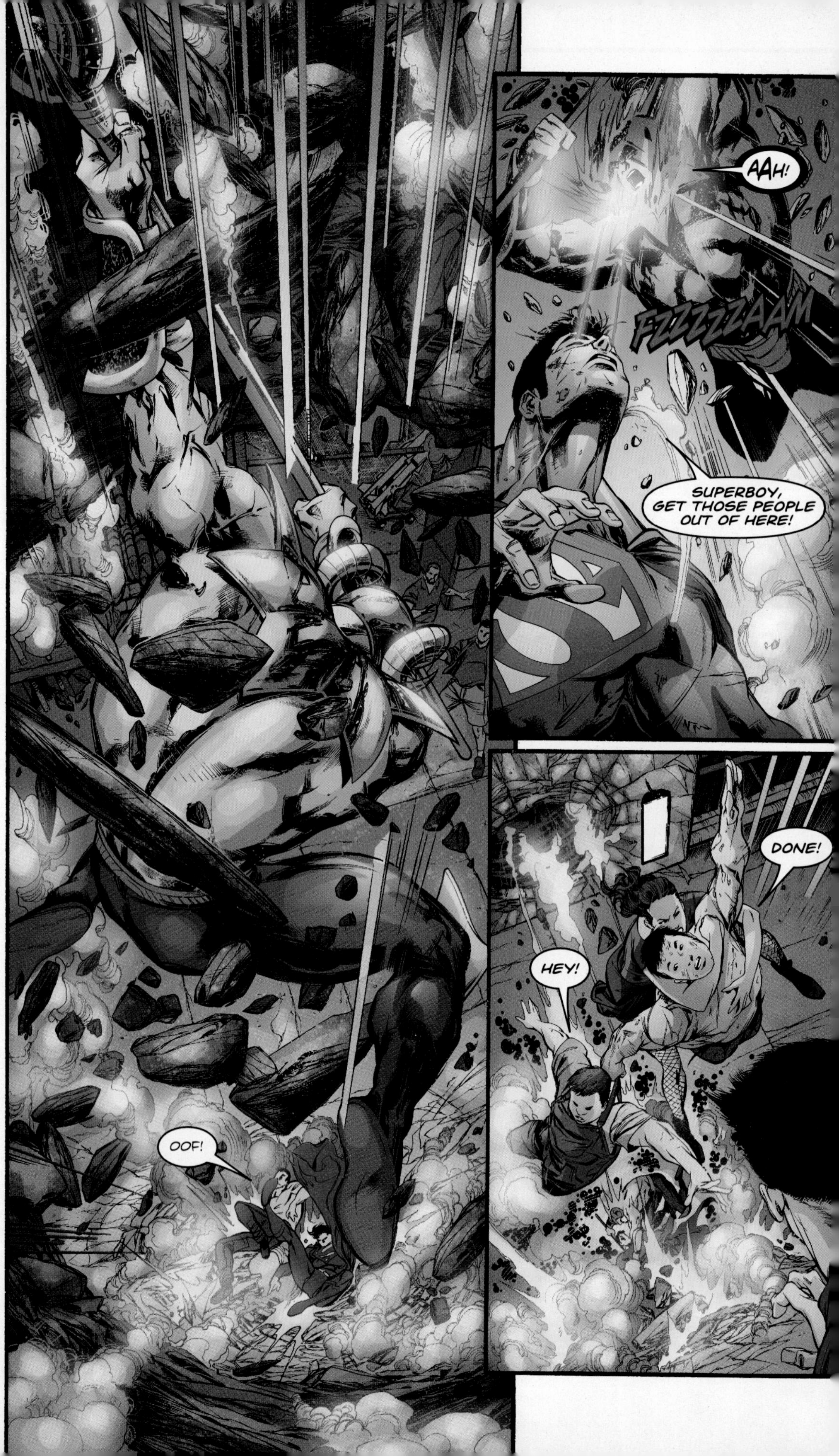
AAH!
FZZZZZAAM
SUPERBOY,
GET THOSE PEOPLE
OUT OF HERE!
DONE!
HEY!
OOF!

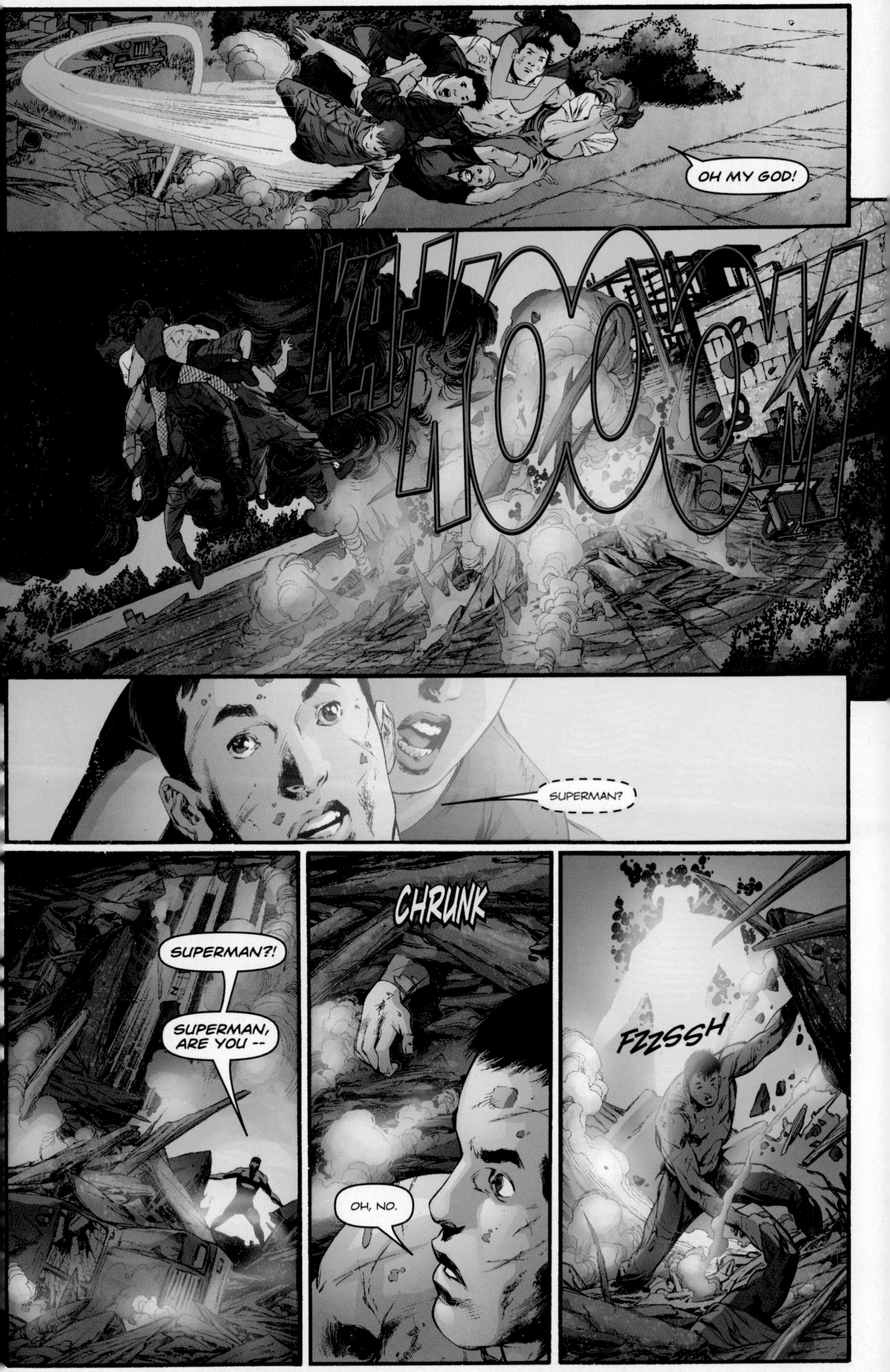
OH MY GOD!
KA-WOOOOM
SUPERMAN?
SUPERMAN?!
SUPERMAN, ARE YOU --
CHRUNK
OH, NO.
FZZSSH

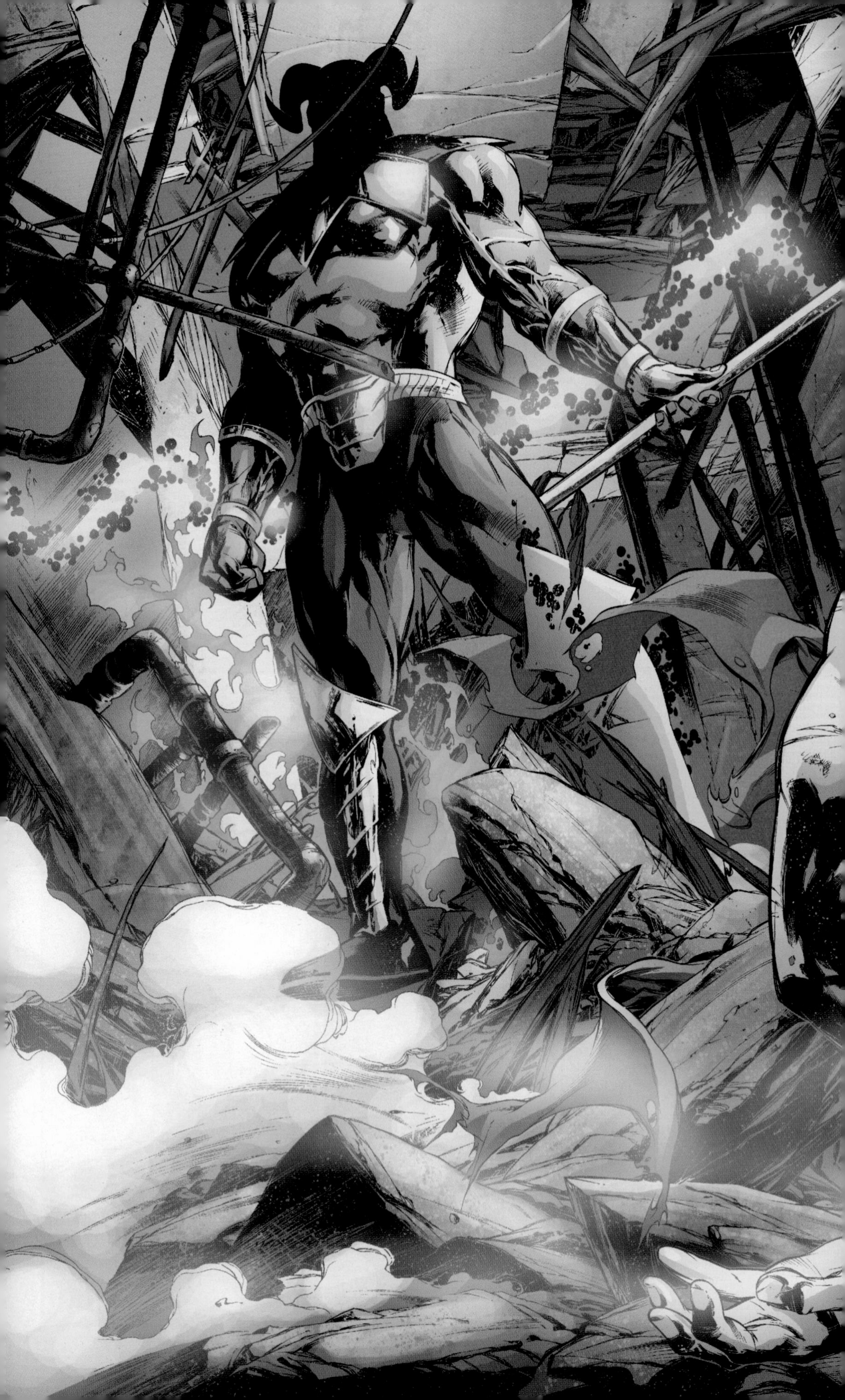

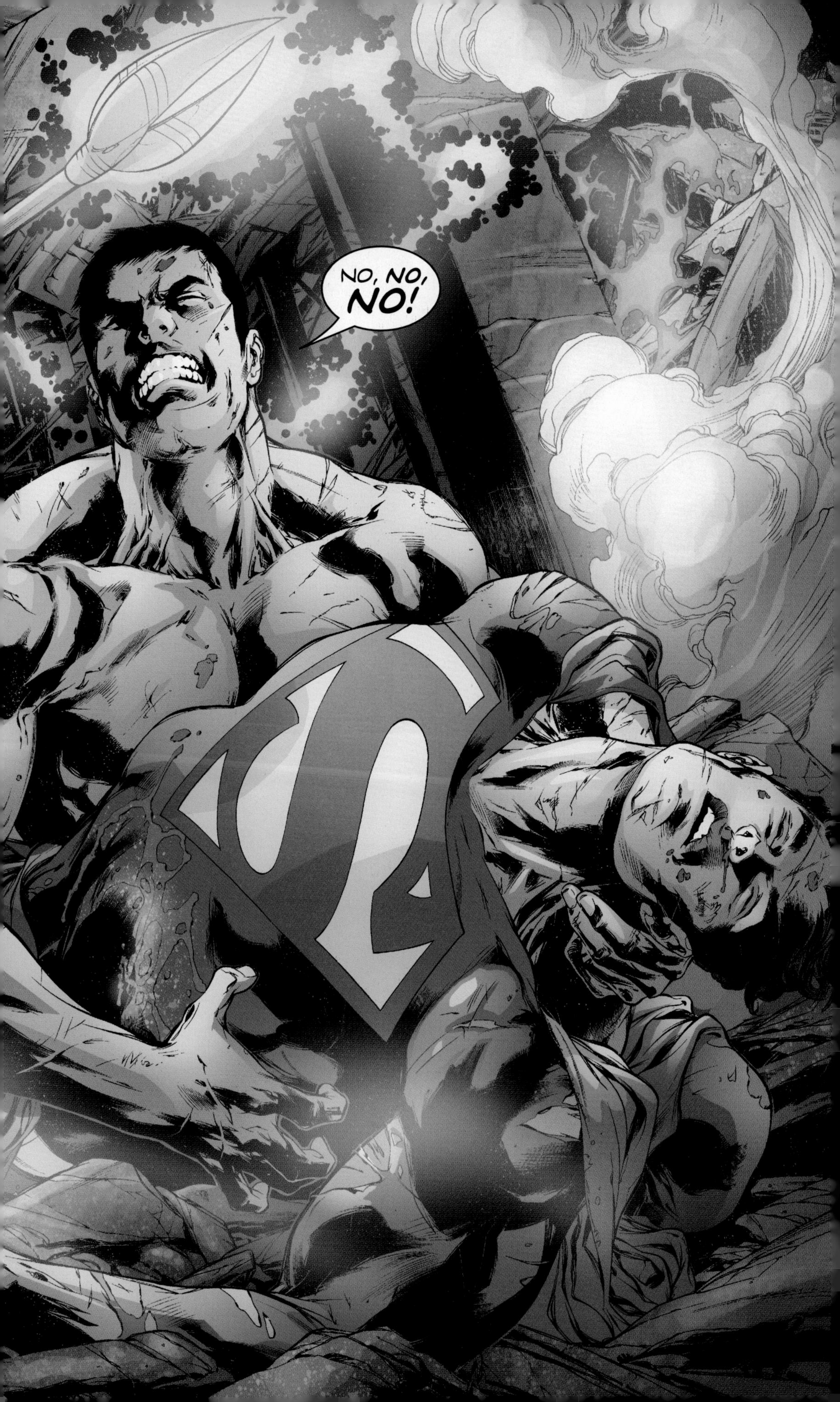
NO, NO, NO!

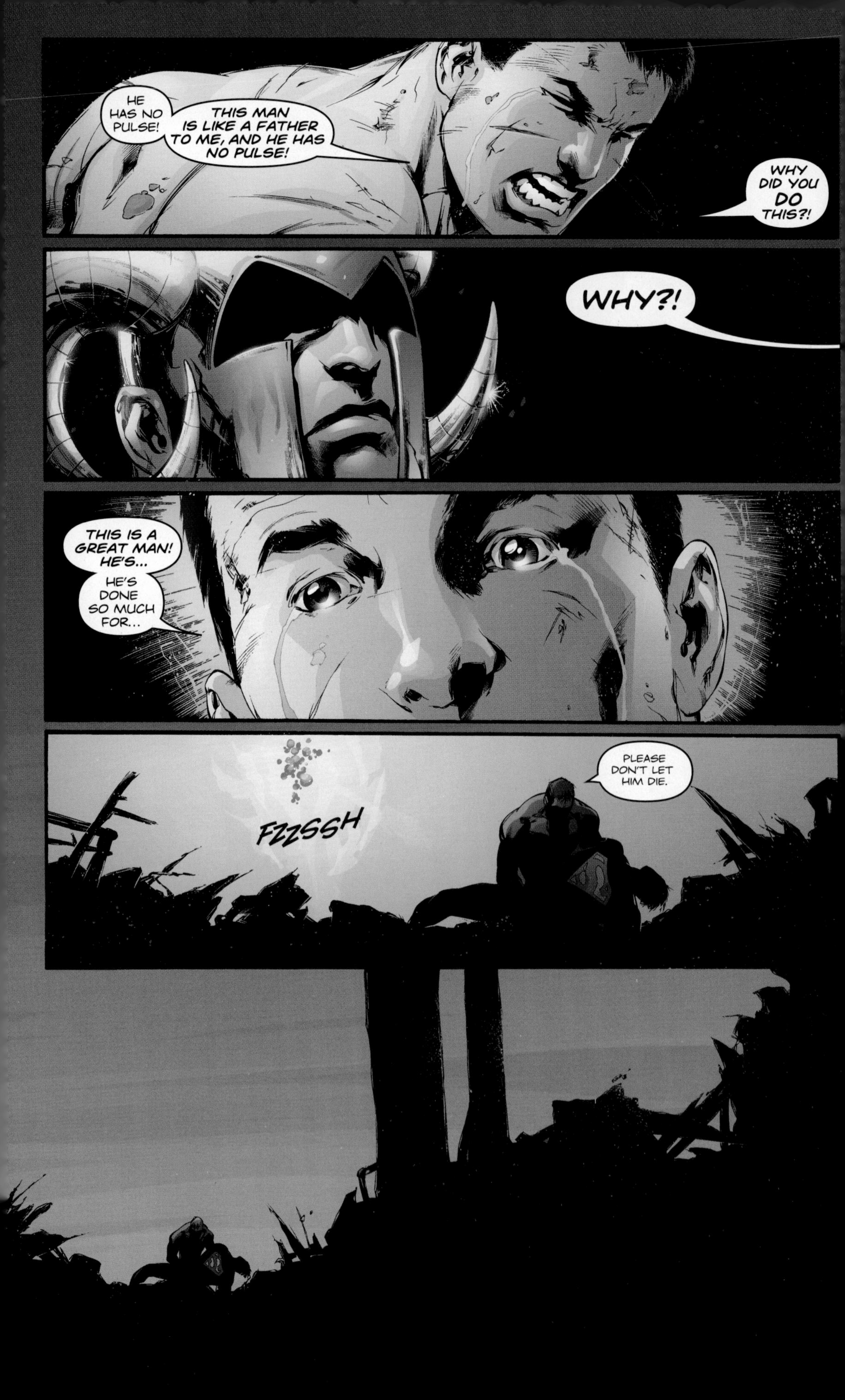
HE HAS NO PULSE!
THIS MAN IS LIKE A FATHER TO ME, AND HE HAS NO PULSE!
WHY DID YOU DO THIS?!
WHY?!
THIS IS A GREAT MAN! HE'S...
HE'S DONE SO MUCH FOR...
FZZSSH
PLEASE DON'T LET HIM DIE.

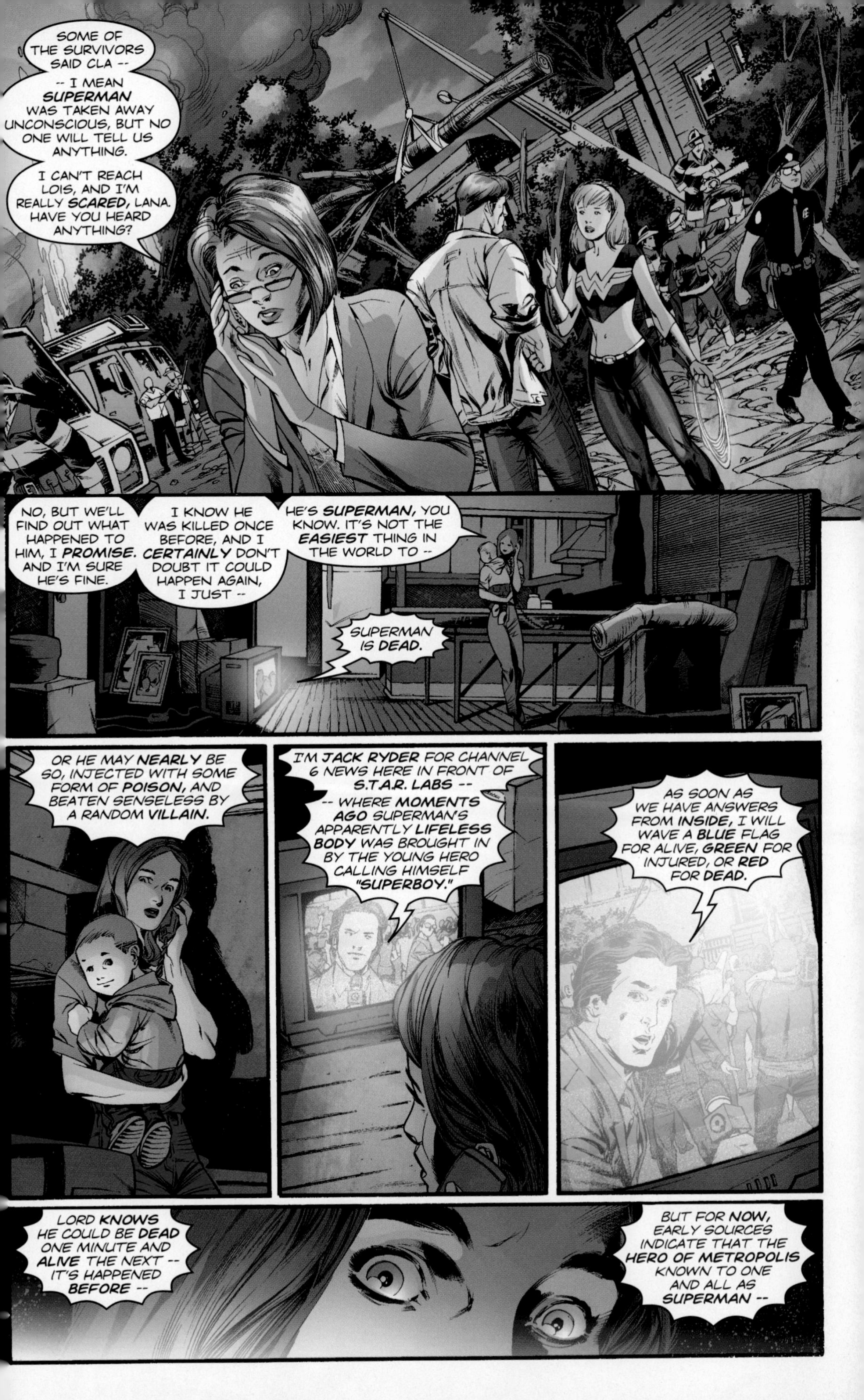
SOME OF THE SURVIVORS SAID CLA --
-- I MEAN **SUPERMAN** WAS TAKEN AWAY UNCONSCIOUS, BUT NO ONE WILL TELL US ANYTHING.
I CAN'T REACH LOIS, AND I'M REALLY **SCARED,** LANA. HAVE YOU HEARD ANYTHING?
NO, BUT WE'LL FIND OUT WHAT HAPPENED TO HIM, I **PROMISE.** AND I'M SURE HE'S FINE.
I KNOW HE WAS KILLED ONCE BEFORE, AND I **CERTAINLY** DON'T DOUBT IT COULD HAPPEN AGAIN, I JUST --
HE'S **SUPERMAN,** YOU KNOW. IT'S NOT THE **EASIEST** THING IN THE WORLD TO --
SUPERMAN IS **DEAD.**
OR HE MAY **NEARLY** BE SO, INJECTED WITH SOME FORM OF **POISON,** AND BEATEN SENSELESS BY A RANDOM **VILLAIN.**
I'M **JACK RYDER** FOR CHANNEL 6 NEWS HERE IN FRONT OF **S.T.A.R. LABS** --
-- WHERE **MOMENTS AGO** SUPERMAN'S APPARENTLY **LIFELESS BODY** WAS BROUGHT IN BY THE YOUNG HERO CALLING HIMSELF **"SUPERBOY."**
AS SOON AS WE HAVE ANSWERS FROM **INSIDE,** I WILL WAVE A **BLUE** FLAG FOR ALIVE, **GREEN** FOR INJURED, OR **RED** FOR **DEAD.**
LORD **KNOWS** HE COULD BE **DEAD** ONE MINUTE AND **ALIVE** THE NEXT -- IT'S HAPPENED **BEFORE** --
BUT FOR **NOW,** EARLY SOURCES INDICATE THAT THE **HERO OF METROPOLIS** KNOWN TO ONE AND ALL AS **SUPERMAN** --

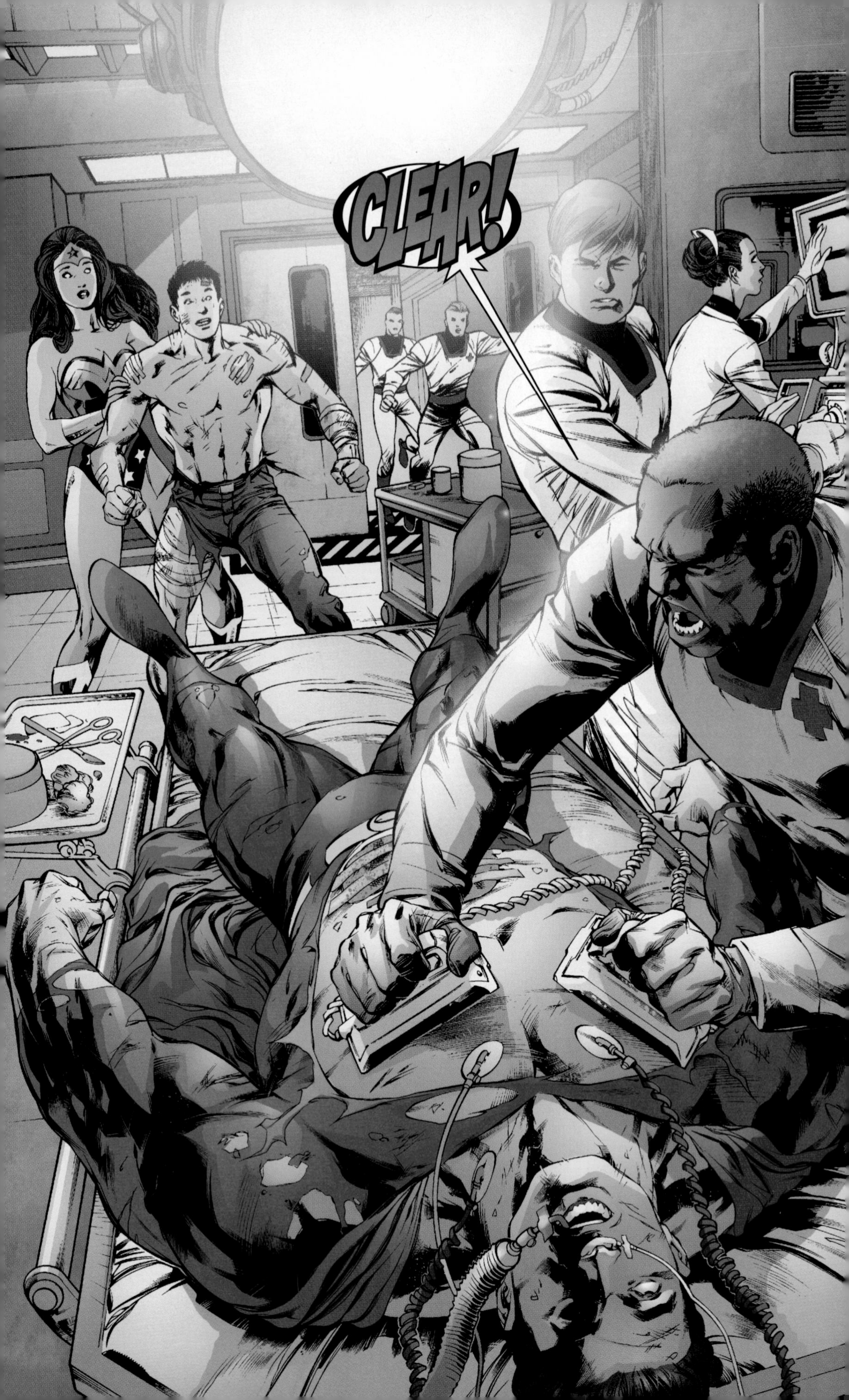
CLEAR!

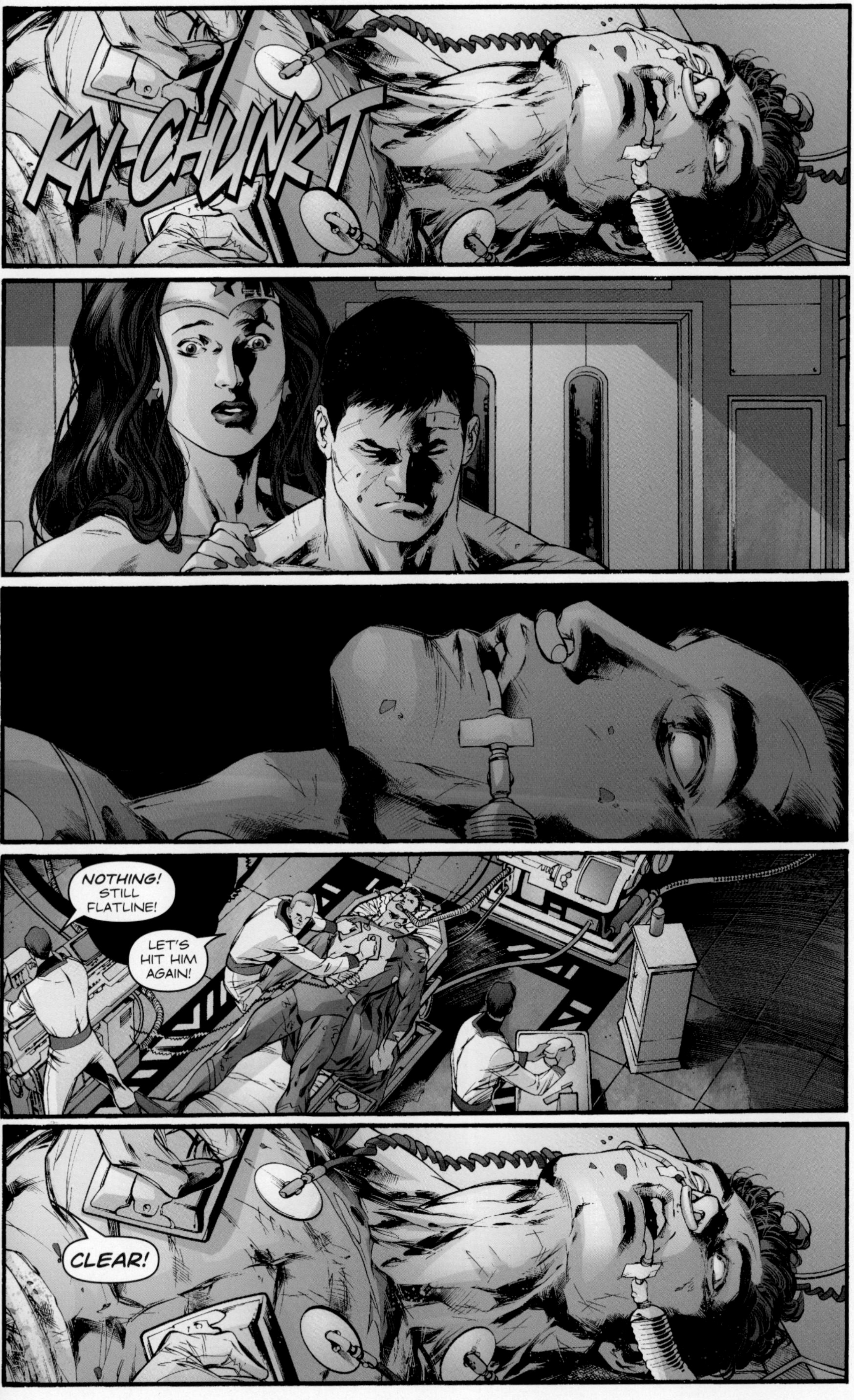
KN-CHUNK T
NOTHING! STILL FLATLINE!
LET'S HIT HIM AGAIN!
CLEAR!

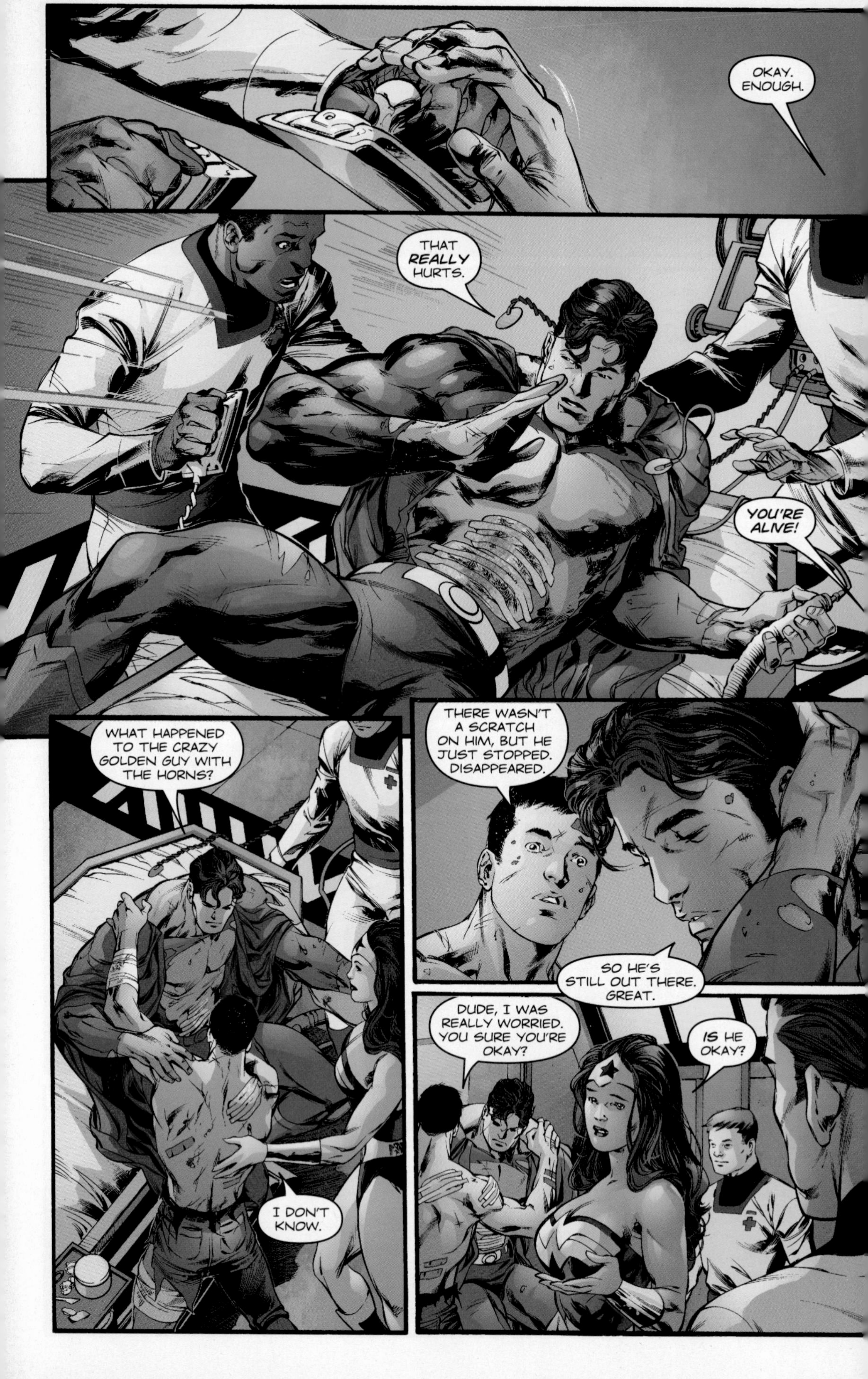
OKAY. ENOUGH.
THAT REALLY HURTS.
YOU'RE ALIVE!
WHAT HAPPENED TO THE CRAZY GOLDEN GUY WITH THE HORNS?
I DON'T KNOW.
THERE WASN'T A SCRATCH ON HIM, BUT HE JUST STOPPED. DISAPPEARED.
SO HE'S STILL OUT THERE. GREAT.
DUDE, I WAS REALLY WORRIED. YOU SURE YOU'RE OKAY?
IS HE OKAY?

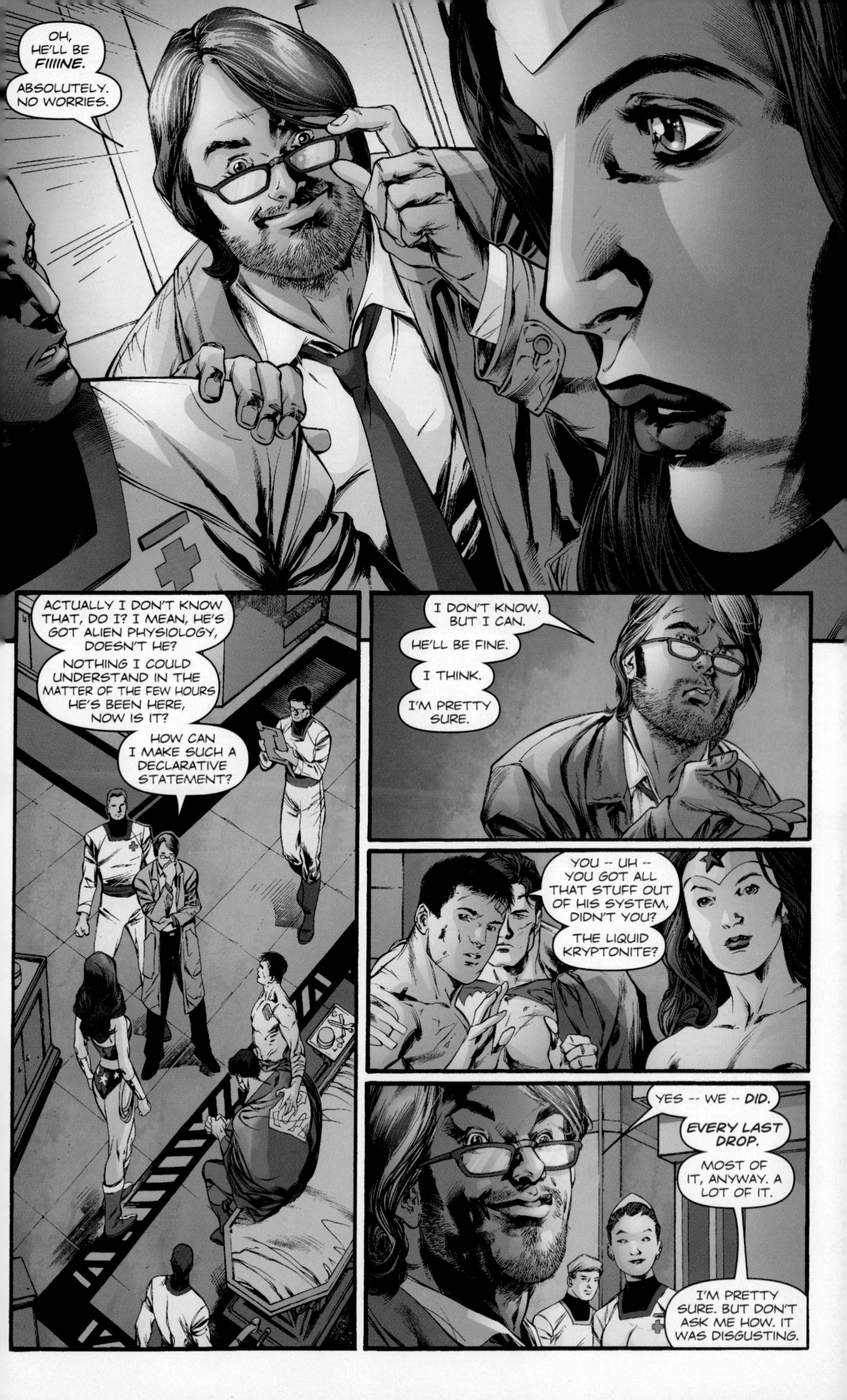
OH, HE'LL BE ***FIIIINE.***
ABSOLUTELY. NO WORRIES.
ACTUALLY I DON'T KNOW THAT, DO I? I MEAN, HE'S GOT ALIEN PHYSIOLOGY, DOESN'T HE?
NOTHING I COULD UNDERSTAND IN THE MATTER OF THE FEW HOURS HE'S BEEN HERE, NOW IS IT?
HOW CAN I MAKE SUCH A DECLARATIVE STATEMENT?
I DON'T KNOW, BUT I CAN.
HE'LL BE FINE.
I THINK.
I'M PRETTY SURE.
YOU -- UH -- YOU GOT ALL THAT STUFF OUT OF HIS SYSTEM, DIDN'T YOU?
THE LIQUID KRYPTONITE?
YES -- WE -- ***DID.***
EVERY LAST DROP.
MOST OF IT, ANYWAY. A LOT OF IT.
I'M PRETTY SURE. BUT DON'T ASK ME HOW. IT WAS DISGUSTING.

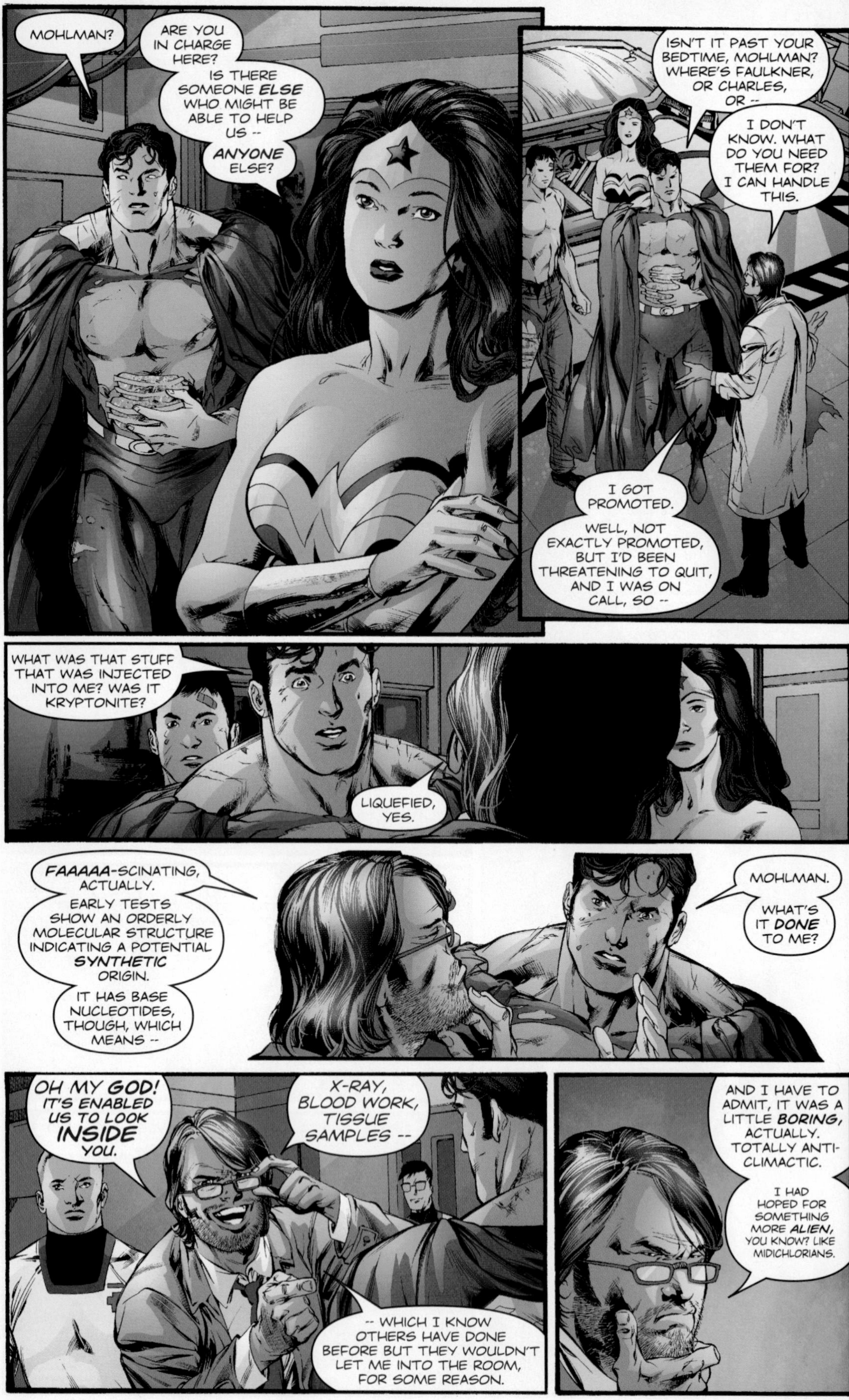

MOHLMAN?
ARE YOU IN CHARGE HERE?
IS THERE SOMEONE ELSE WHO MIGHT BE ABLE TO HELP US --
ANYONE ELSE?
ISN'T IT PAST YOUR BEDTIME, MOHLMAN? WHERE'S FAULKNER, OR CHARLES, OR --
I DON'T KNOW. WHAT DO YOU NEED THEM FOR? I CAN HANDLE THIS.
I GOT PROMOTED.
WELL, NOT EXACTLY PROMOTED, BUT I'D BEEN THREATENING TO QUIT, AND I WAS ON CALL, SO --
WHAT WAS THAT STUFF THAT WAS INJECTED INTO ME? WAS IT KRYPTONITE?
LIQUEFIED, YES.
FAAAAA-SCINATING, ACTUALLY.
EARLY TESTS SHOW AN ORDERLY MOLECULAR STRUCTURE INDICATING A POTENTIAL SYNTHETIC ORIGIN.
IT HAS BASE NUCLEOTIDES, THOUGH, WHICH MEANS --
MOHLMAN.
WHAT'S IT DONE TO ME?
OH MY GOD! IT'S ENABLED US TO LOOK INSIDE YOU.
X-RAY, BLOOD WORK, TISSUE SAMPLES --
-- WHICH I KNOW OTHERS HAVE DONE BEFORE BUT THEY WOULDN'T LET ME INTO THE ROOM, FOR SOME REASON.
AND I HAVE TO ADMIT, IT WAS A LITTLE BORING, ACTUALLY. TOTALLY ANTI-CLIMACTIC.
I HAD HOPED FOR SOMETHING MORE ALIEN, YOU KNOW? LIKE MIDICHLORIANS.

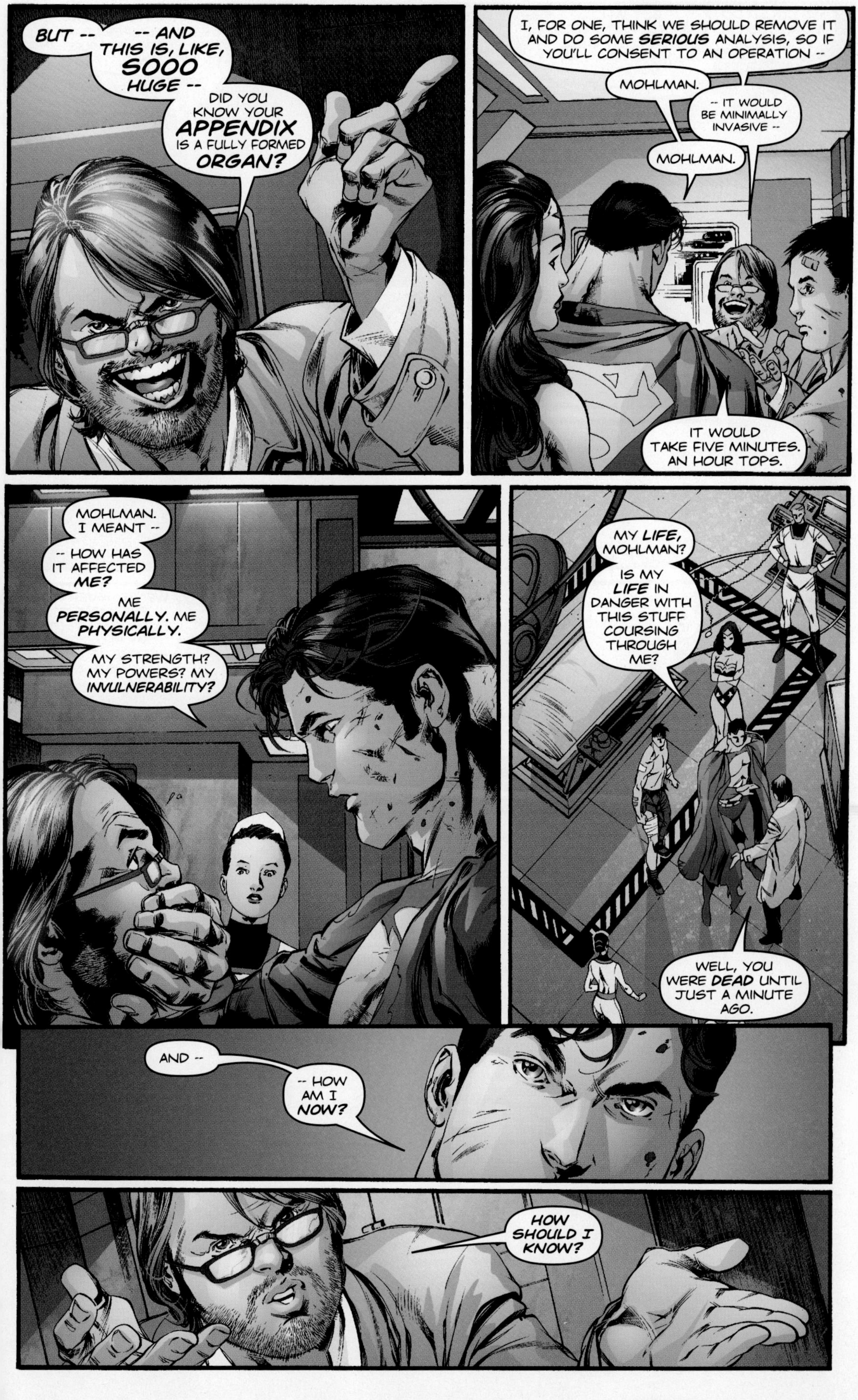
BUT --
-- AND THIS IS, LIKE, SOOO HUGE --
DID YOU KNOW YOUR APPENDIX IS A FULLY FORMED ORGAN?
I, FOR ONE, THINK WE SHOULD REMOVE IT AND DO SOME SERIOUS ANALYSIS, SO IF YOU'LL CONSENT TO AN OPERATION --
MOHLMAN.
-- IT WOULD BE MINIMALLY INVASIVE --
MOHLMAN.
IT WOULD TAKE FIVE MINUTES. AN HOUR TOPS.
MOHLMAN. I MEANT --
-- HOW HAS IT AFFECTED ME?
ME PERSONALLY. ME PHYSICALLY.
MY STRENGTH? MY POWERS? MY INVULNERABILITY?
MY LIFE, MOHLMAN?
IS MY LIFE IN DANGER WITH THIS STUFF COURSING THROUGH ME?
WELL, YOU WERE DEAD UNTIL JUST A MINUTE AGO.
AND --
-- HOW AM I NOW?
HOW SHOULD I KNOW?

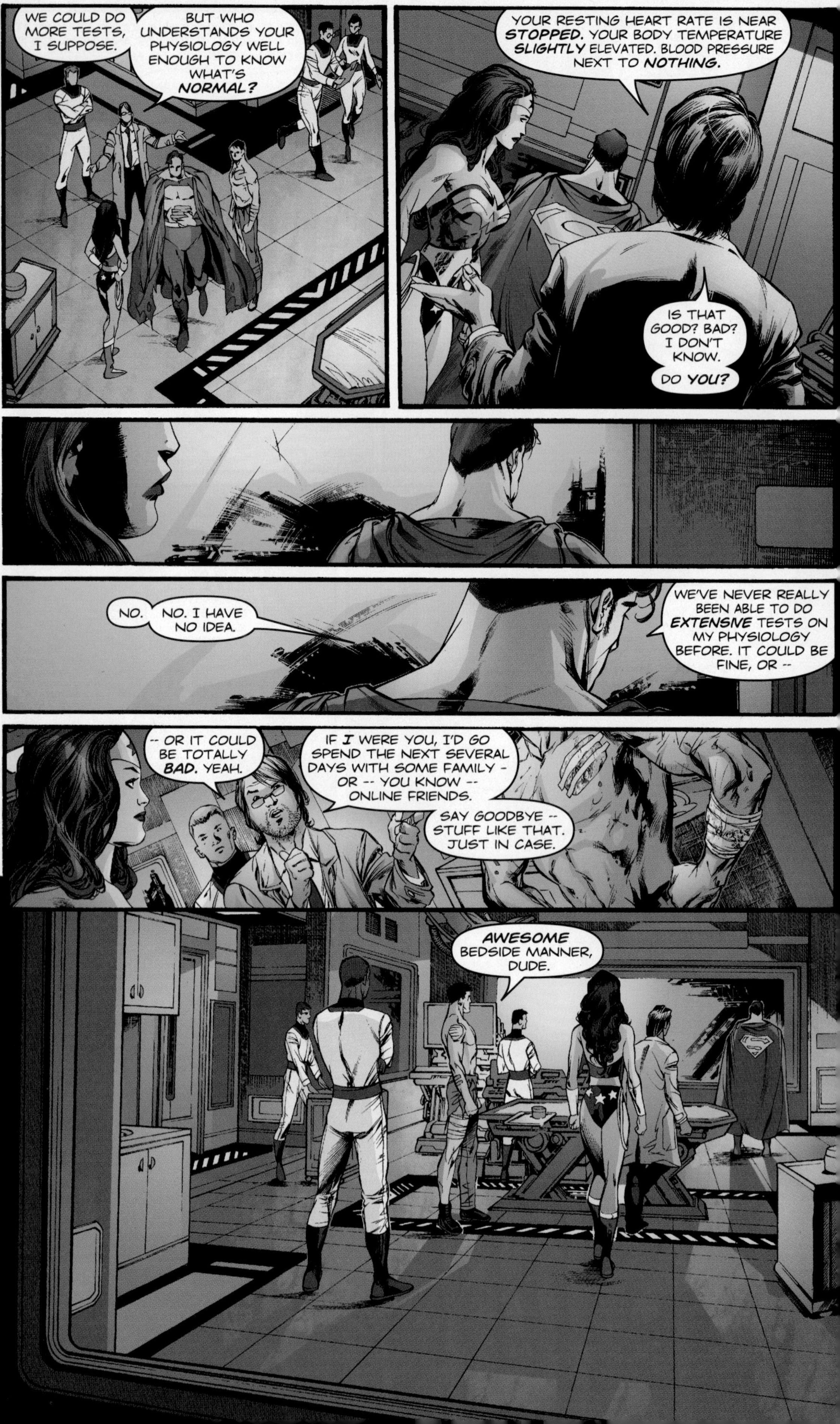
WE COULD DO MORE TESTS, I SUPPOSE.
BUT WHO UNDERSTANDS YOUR PHYSIOLOGY WELL ENOUGH TO KNOW WHAT'S NORMAL?
YOUR RESTING HEART RATE IS NEAR STOPPED. YOUR BODY TEMPERATURE SLIGHTLY ELEVATED. BLOOD PRESSURE NEXT TO NOTHING.
IS THAT GOOD? BAD? I DON'T KNOW.
DO YOU?
NO.
NO. I HAVE NO IDEA.
WE'VE NEVER REALLY BEEN ABLE TO DO EXTENSIVE TESTS ON MY PHYSIOLOGY BEFORE. IT COULD BE FINE, OR --
-- OR IT COULD BE TOTALLY BAD. YEAH.
IF I WERE YOU, I'D GO SPEND THE NEXT SEVERAL DAYS WITH SOME FAMILY -- OR -- YOU KNOW -- ONLINE FRIENDS.
SAY GOODBYE -- STUFF LIKE THAT. JUST IN CASE.
AWESOME BEDSIDE MANNER, DUDE.

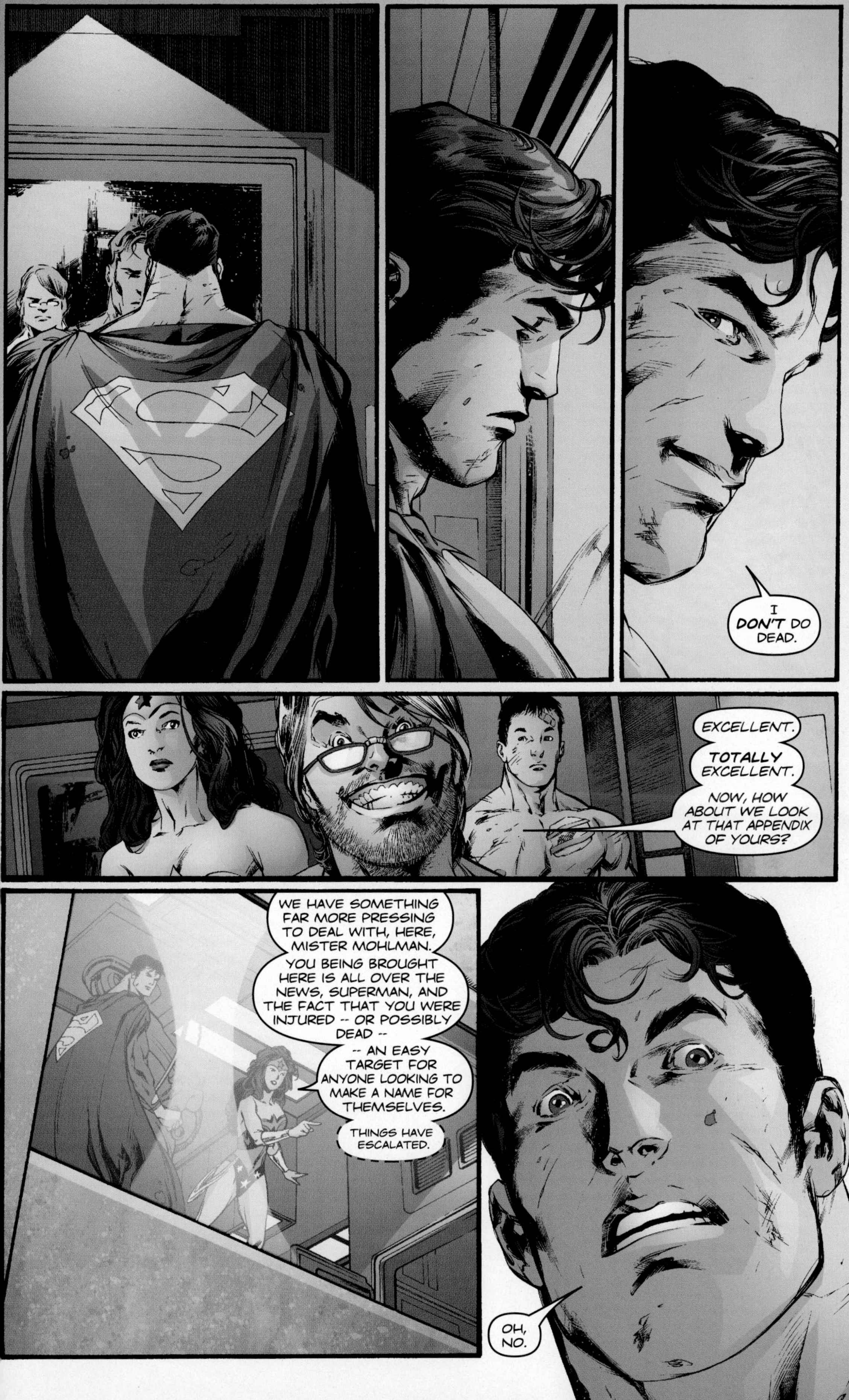

I DON'T DO DEAD.
EXCELLENT.
TOTALLY EXCELLENT.
NOW, HOW ABOUT WE LOOK AT THAT APPENDIX OF YOURS?
WE HAVE SOMETHING FAR MORE PRESSING TO DEAL WITH, HERE, MISTER MOHLMAN.
YOU BEING BROUGHT HERE IS ALL OVER THE NEWS, SUPERMAN, AND THE FACT THAT YOU WERE INJURED -- OR POSSIBLY DEAD --
-- AN EASY TARGET FOR ANYONE LOOKING TO MAKE A NAME FOR THEMSELVES.
THINGS HAVE ESCALATED.
OH, NO.

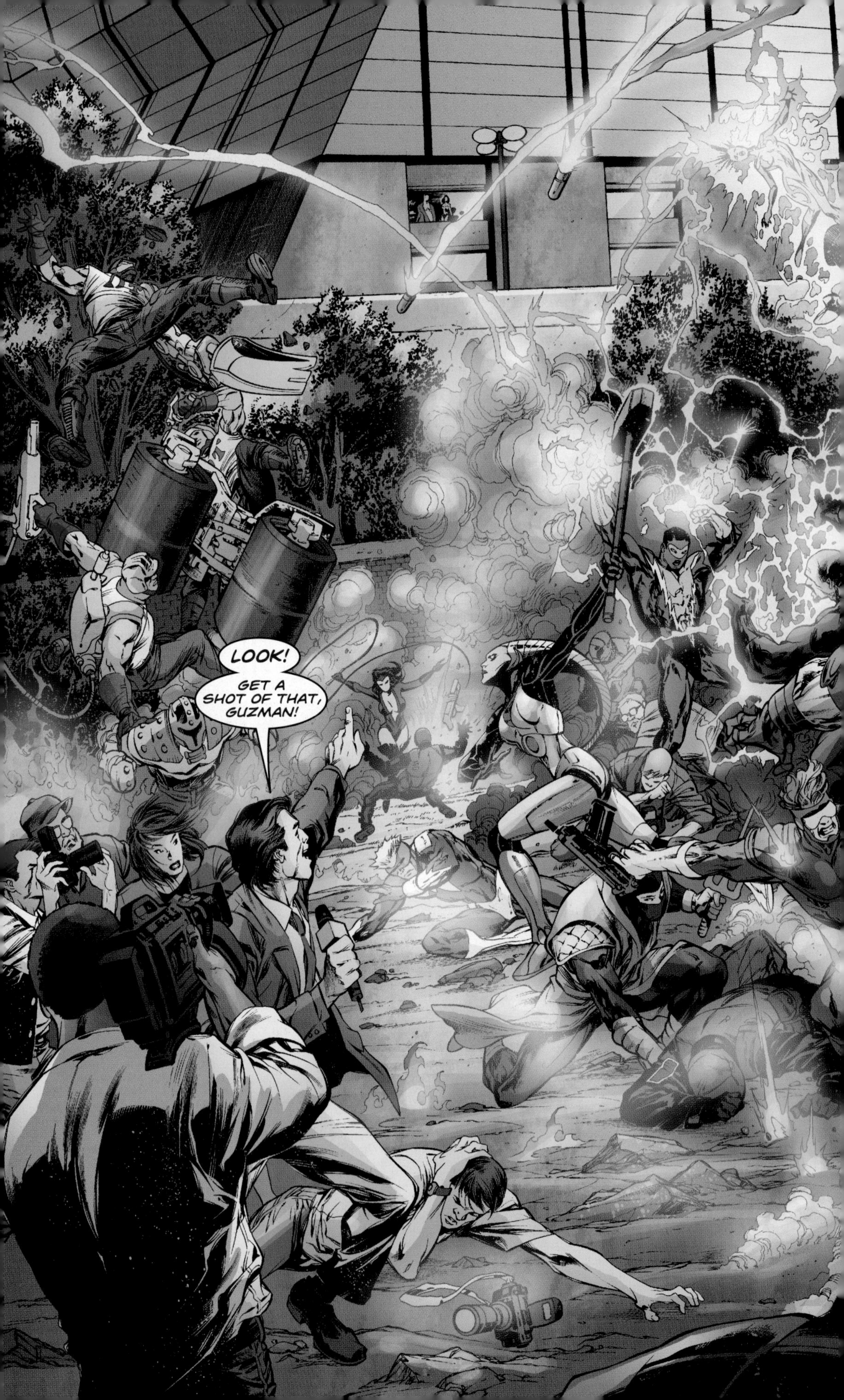
LOOK!
GET A SHOT OF THAT, GUZMAN!

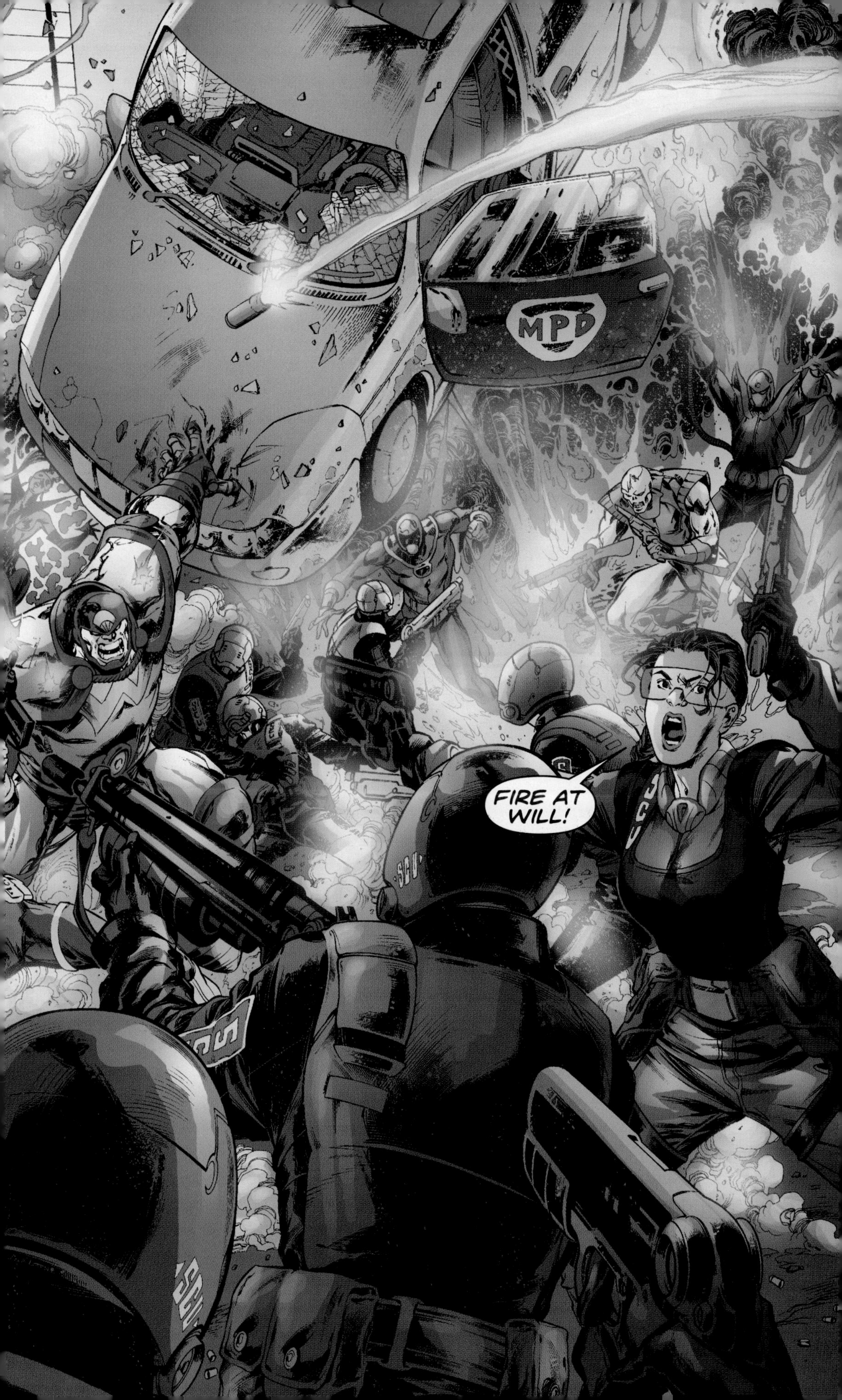
FIRE AT WILL!
MPD

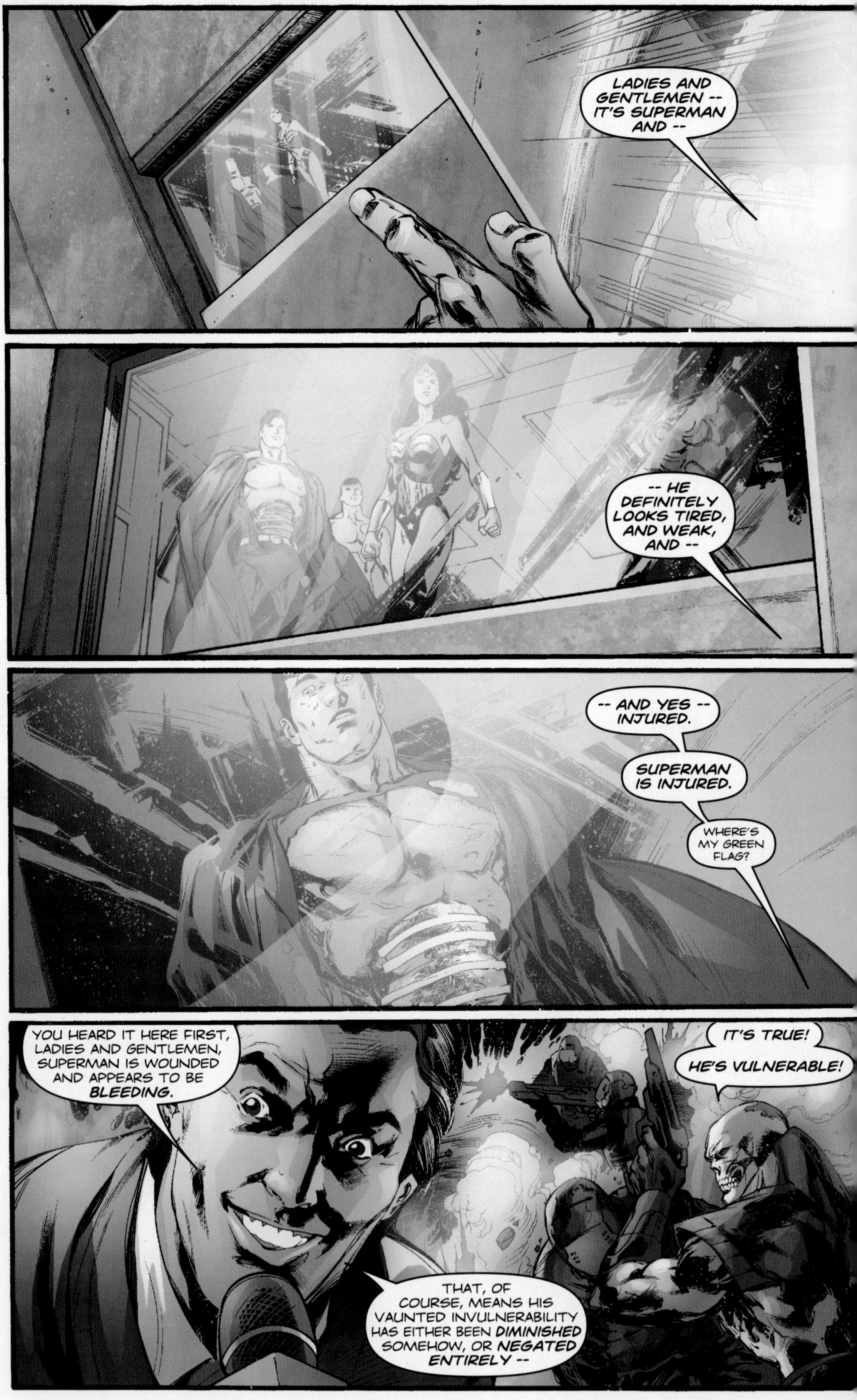
LADIES AND GENTLEMEN -- IT'S SUPERMAN AND --
-- HE DEFINITELY LOOKS TIRED, AND WEAK, AND --
-- AND YES -- INJURED.
SUPERMAN IS INJURED.
WHERE'S MY GREEN FLAG?
YOU HEARD IT HERE FIRST, LADIES AND GENTLEMEN, SUPERMAN IS WOUNDED AND APPEARS TO BE BLEEDING.
IT'S TRUE!
HE'S VULNERABLE!
THAT, OF COURSE, MEANS HIS VAUNTED INVULNERABILITY HAS EITHER BEEN DIMINISHED SOMEHOW, OR NEGATED ENTIRELY --

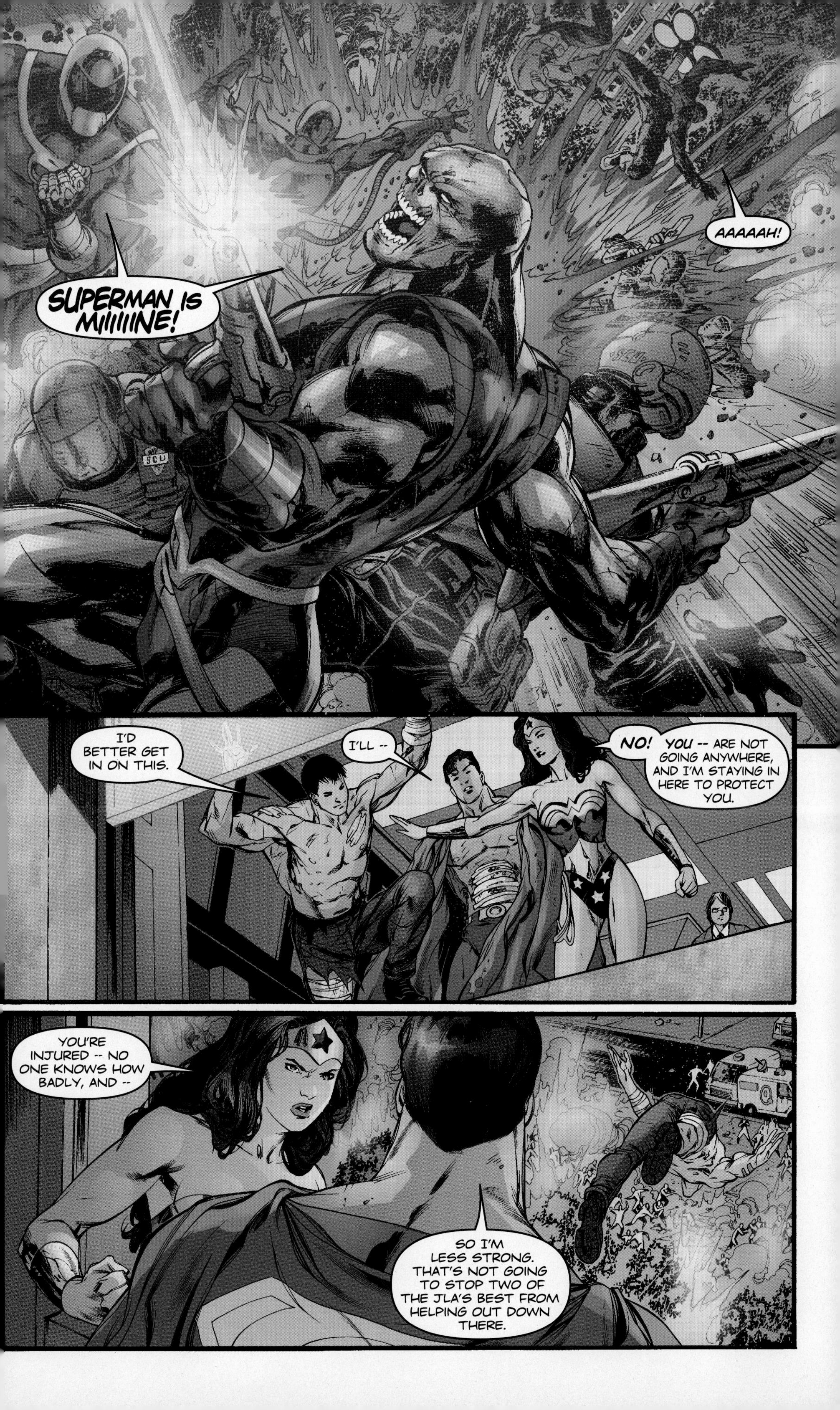
AAAAAH!
SUPERMAN IS MIIIIINE!
I'D BETTER GET IN ON THIS.
I'LL --
NO! YOU -- ARE NOT GOING ANYWHERE, AND I'M STAYING IN HERE TO PROTECT YOU.
YOU'RE INJURED -- NO ONE KNOWS HOW BADLY, AND --
SO I'M LESS STRONG. THAT'S NOT GOING TO STOP TWO OF THE JLA'S BEST FROM HELPING OUT DOWN THERE.

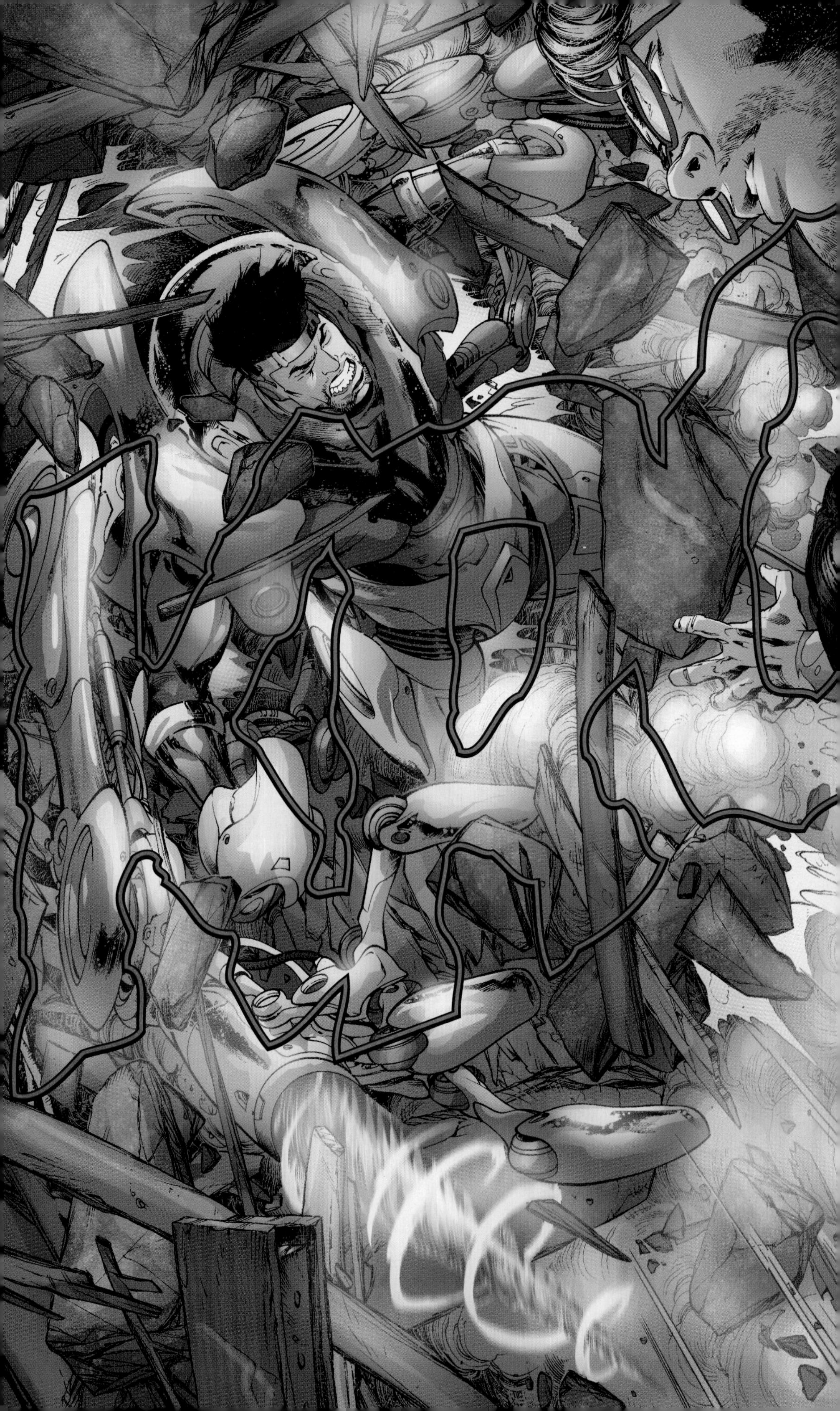

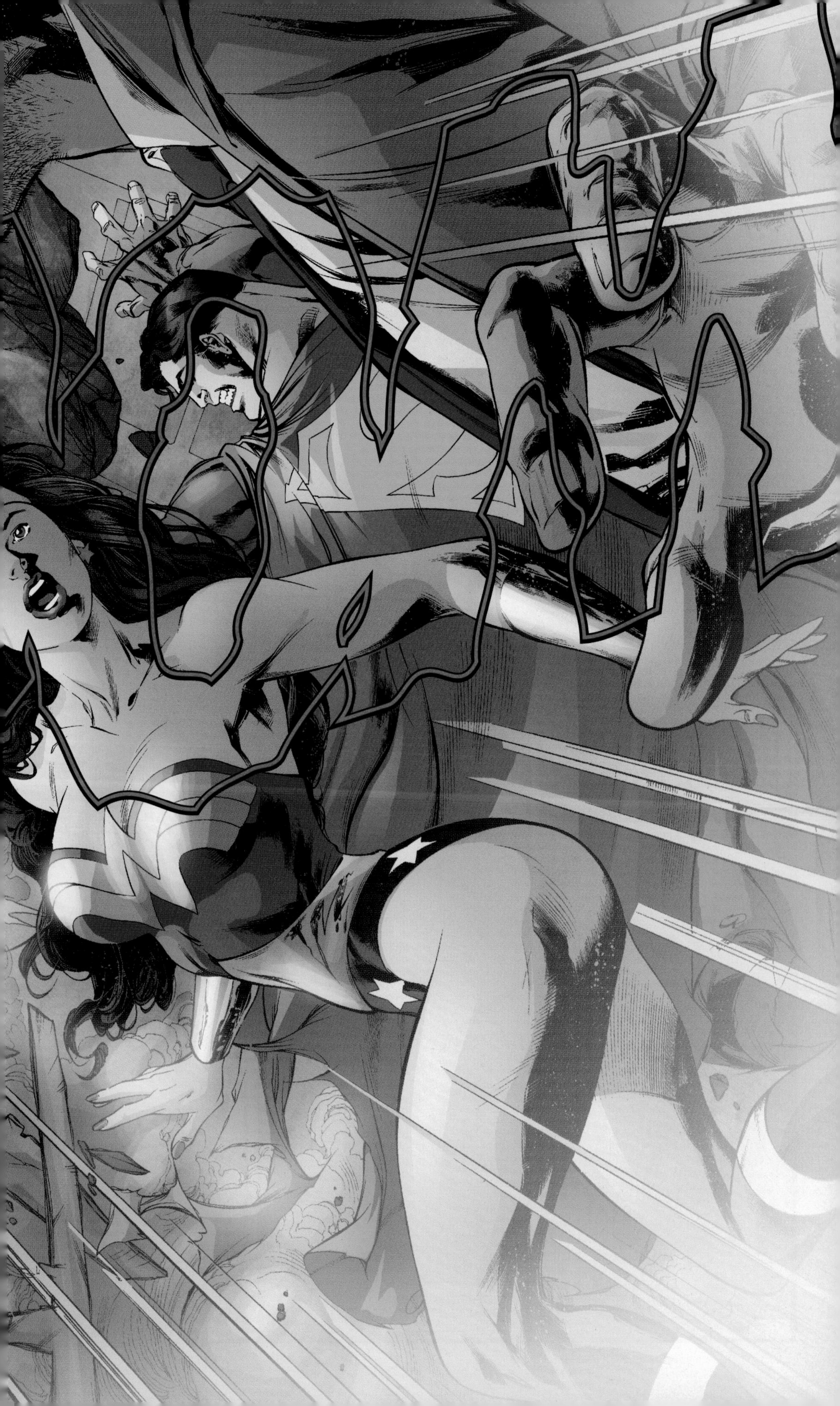

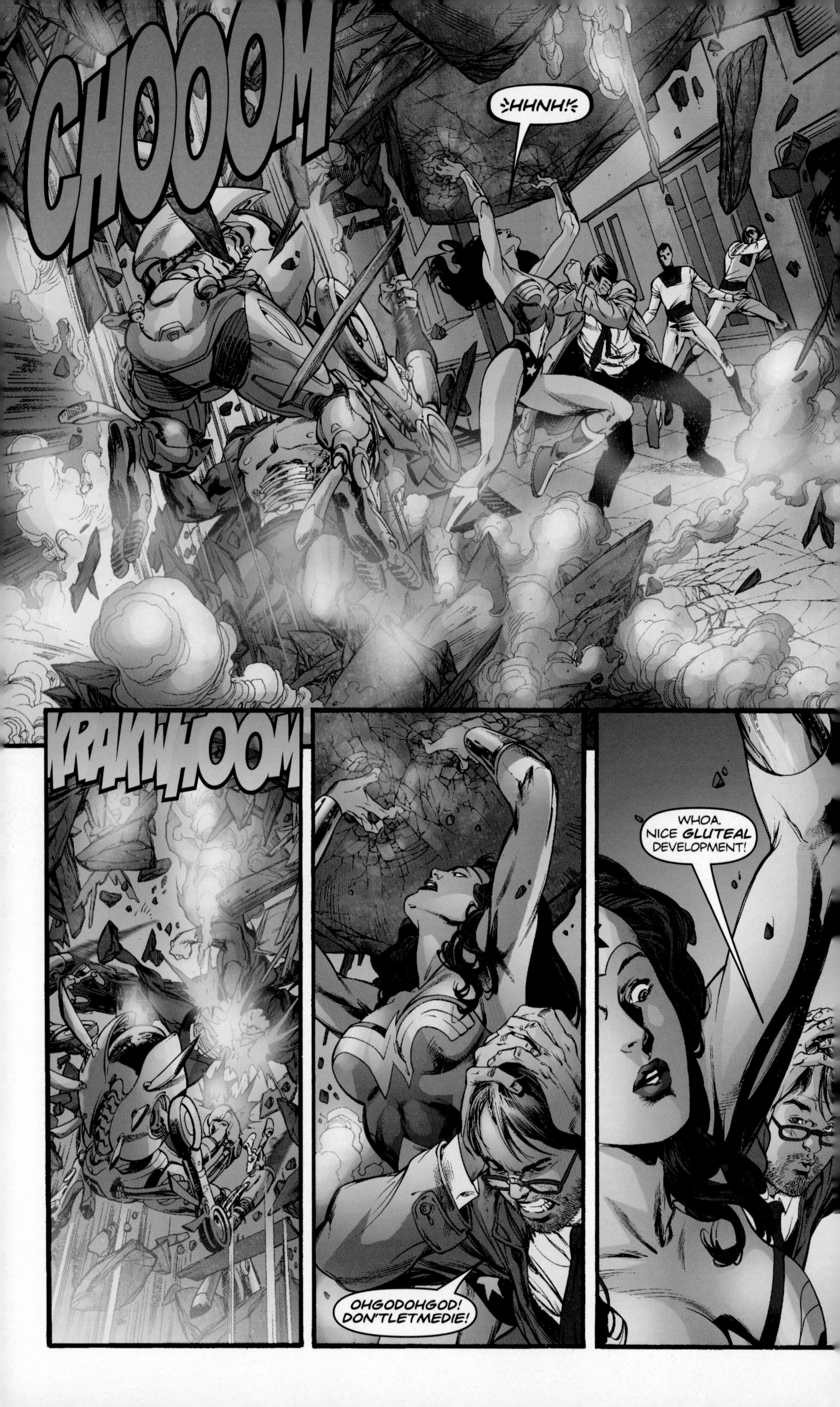
CHOOOM
HHNH!
KRAKWHOOM
OHGODOHGOD! DON'TLETMEDIE!
WHOA. NICE GLUTEAL DEVELOPMENT!

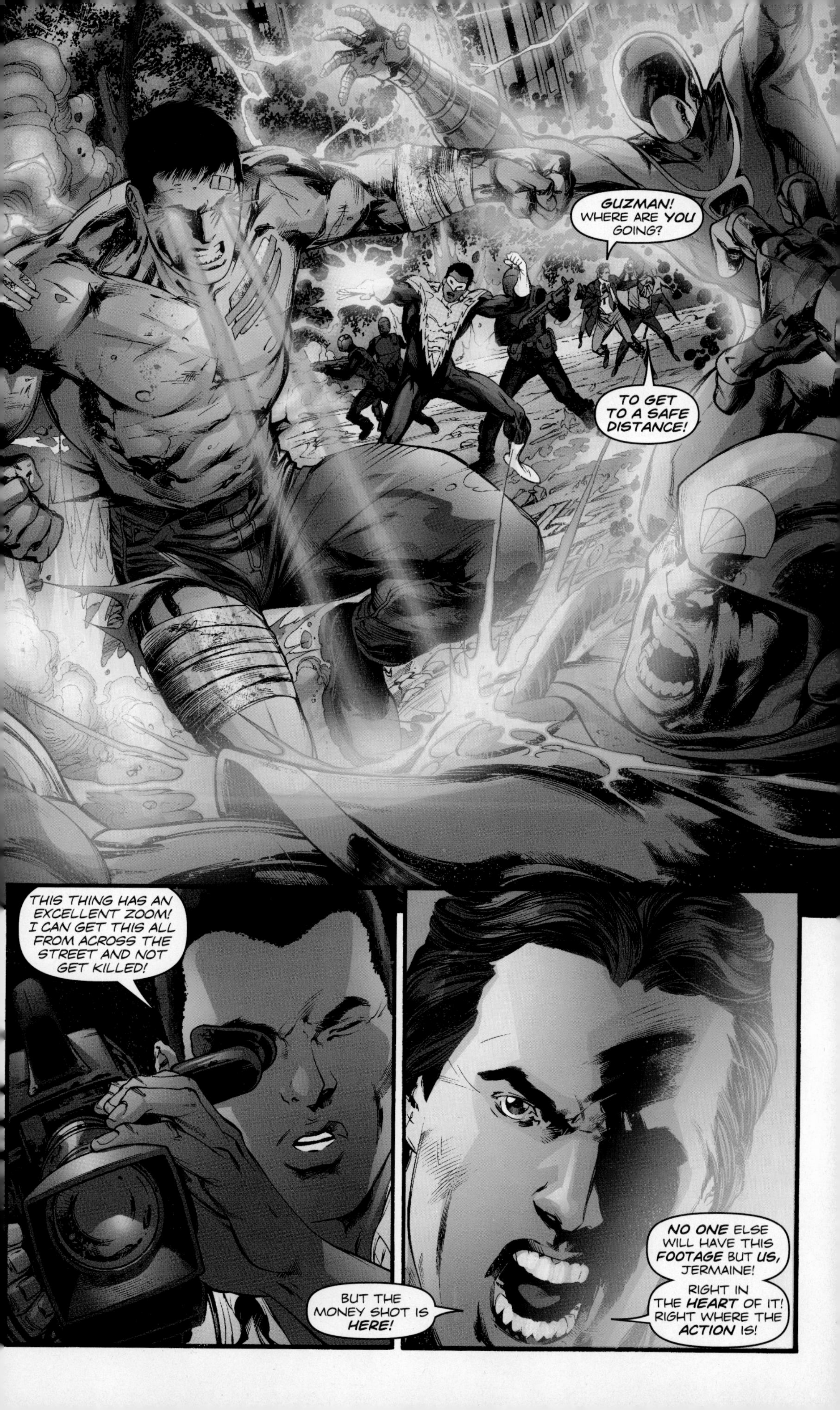
GUZMAN! WHERE ARE YOU GOING?
TO GET TO A SAFE DISTANCE!
THIS THING HAS AN EXCELLENT ZOOM! I CAN GET THIS ALL FROM ACROSS THE STREET AND NOT GET KILLED!
BUT THE MONEY SHOT IS HERE!
NO ONE ELSE WILL HAVE THIS FOOTAGE BUT US, JERMAINE!
RIGHT IN THE HEART OF IT! RIGHT WHERE THE ACTION IS!

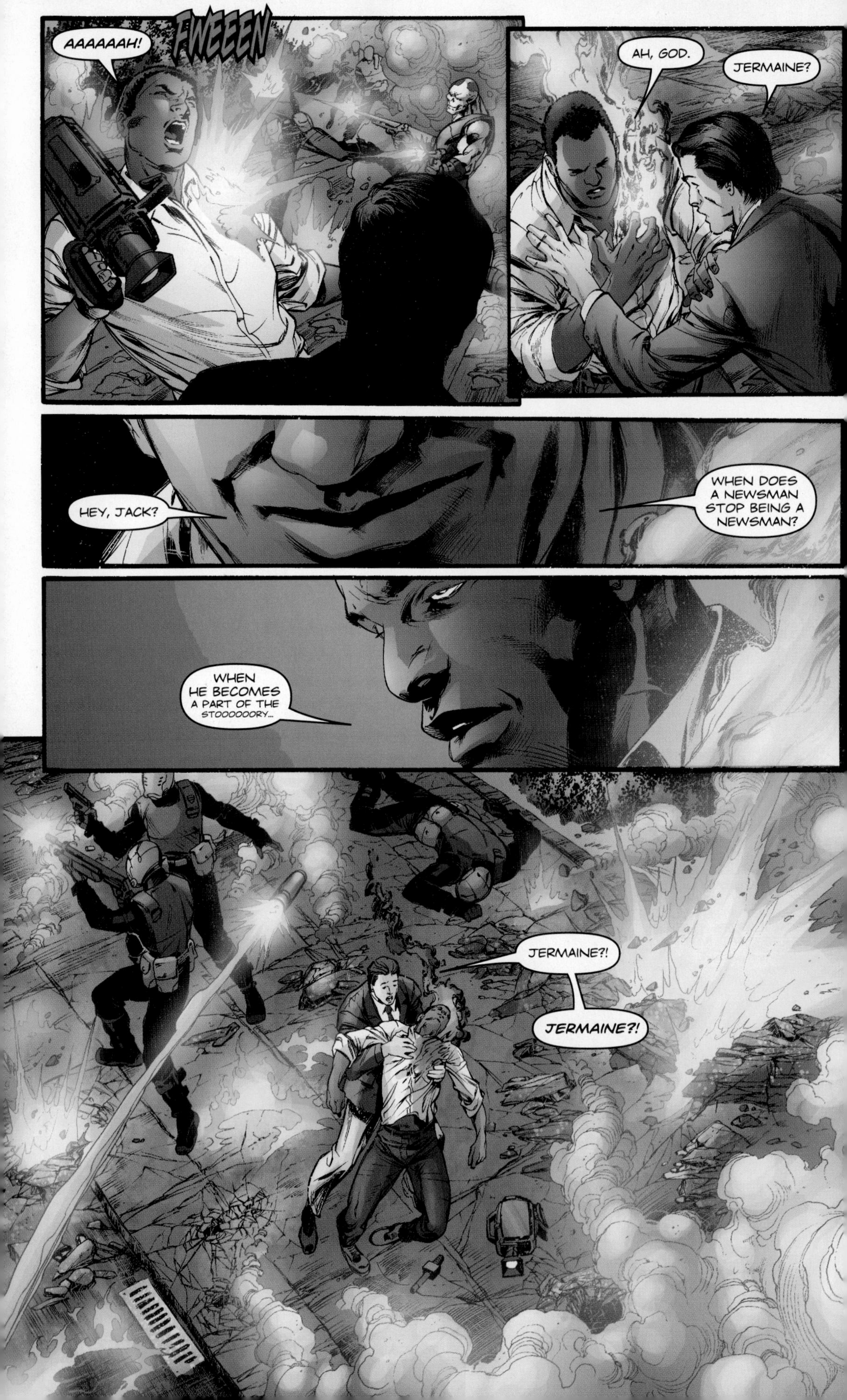
AAAAAAH!
FWEEEN
AH, GOD.
JERMAINE?
HEY, JACK?
WHEN DOES A NEWSMAN STOP BEING A NEWSMAN?
WHEN HE BECOMES A PART OF THE STOOOOOORY...
JERMAINE?!
JERMAINE?!

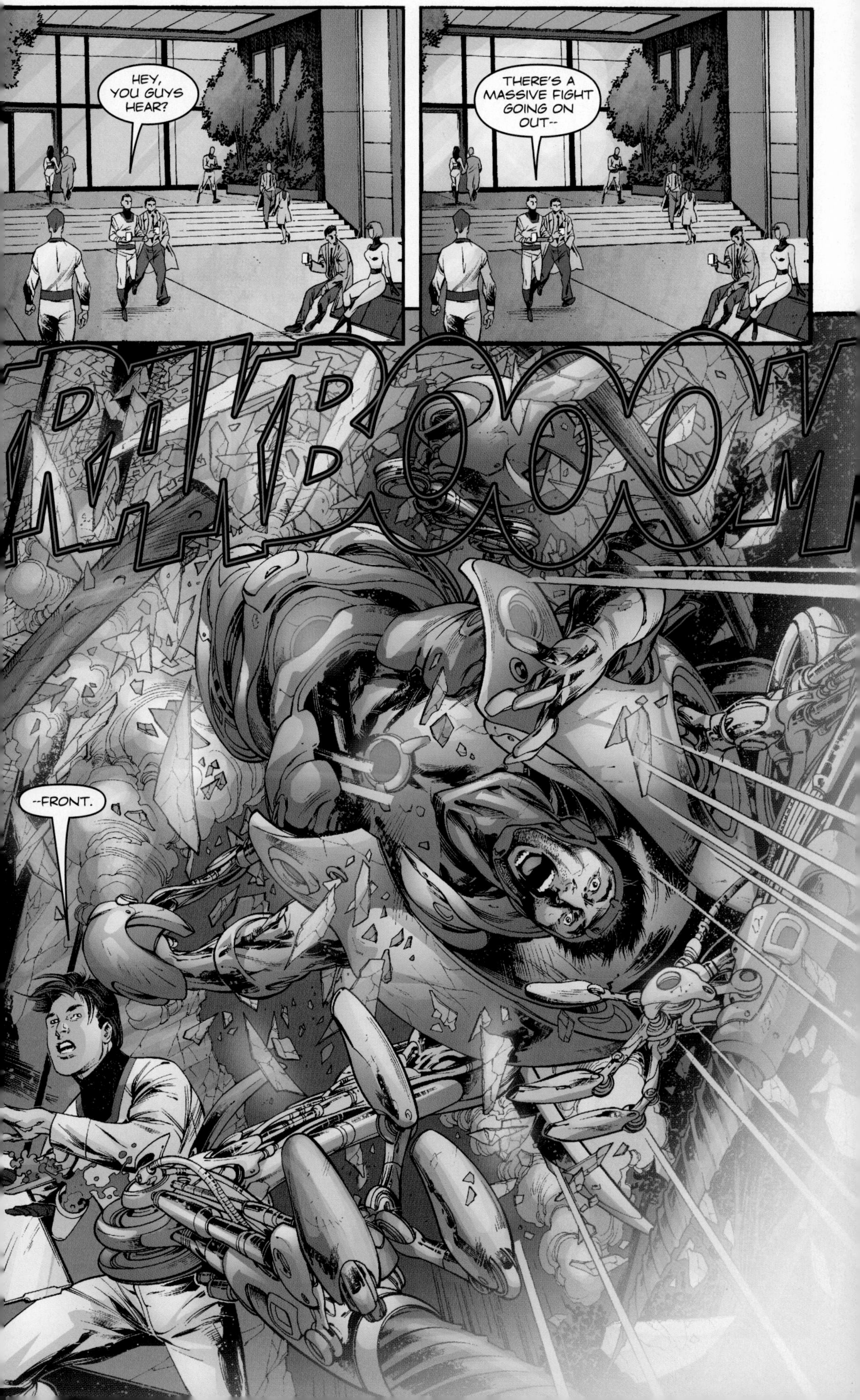
HEY, YOU GUYS HEAR?
THERE'S A MASSIVE FIGHT GOING ON OUT--
KRAKBOOOOM
--FRONT.

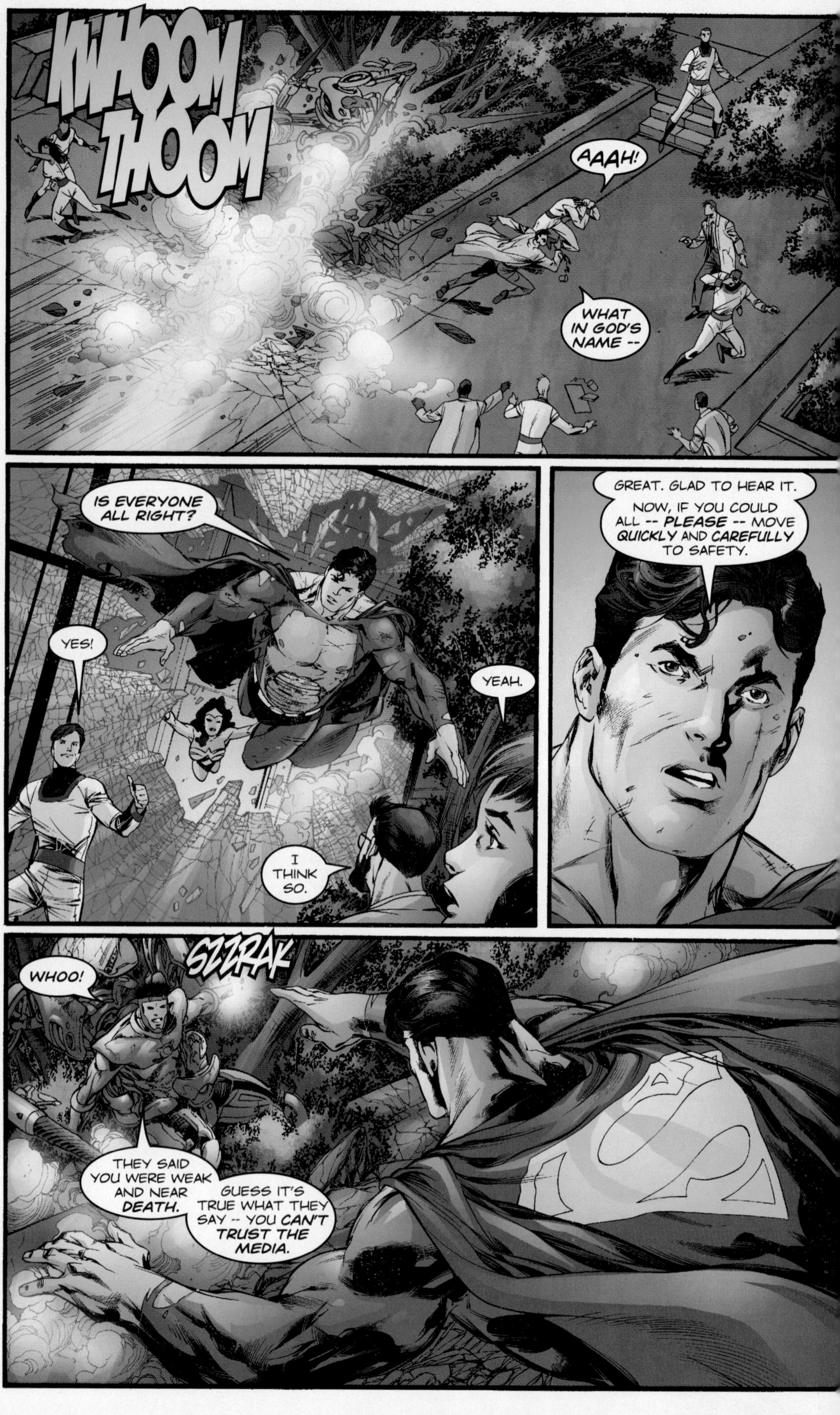
KWHOOM
THOOM
AAAH!
WHAT IN GOD'S NAME --
IS EVERYONE ALL RIGHT?
YES!
YEAH.
I THINK SO.
GREAT. GLAD TO HEAR IT.
NOW, IF YOU COULD ALL -- PLEASE -- MOVE QUICKLY AND CAREFULLY TO SAFETY.
SZZRAK
WHOO!
THEY SAID YOU WERE WEAK AND NEAR DEATH.
GUESS IT'S TRUE WHAT THEY SAY -- YOU CAN'T TRUST THE MEDIA.

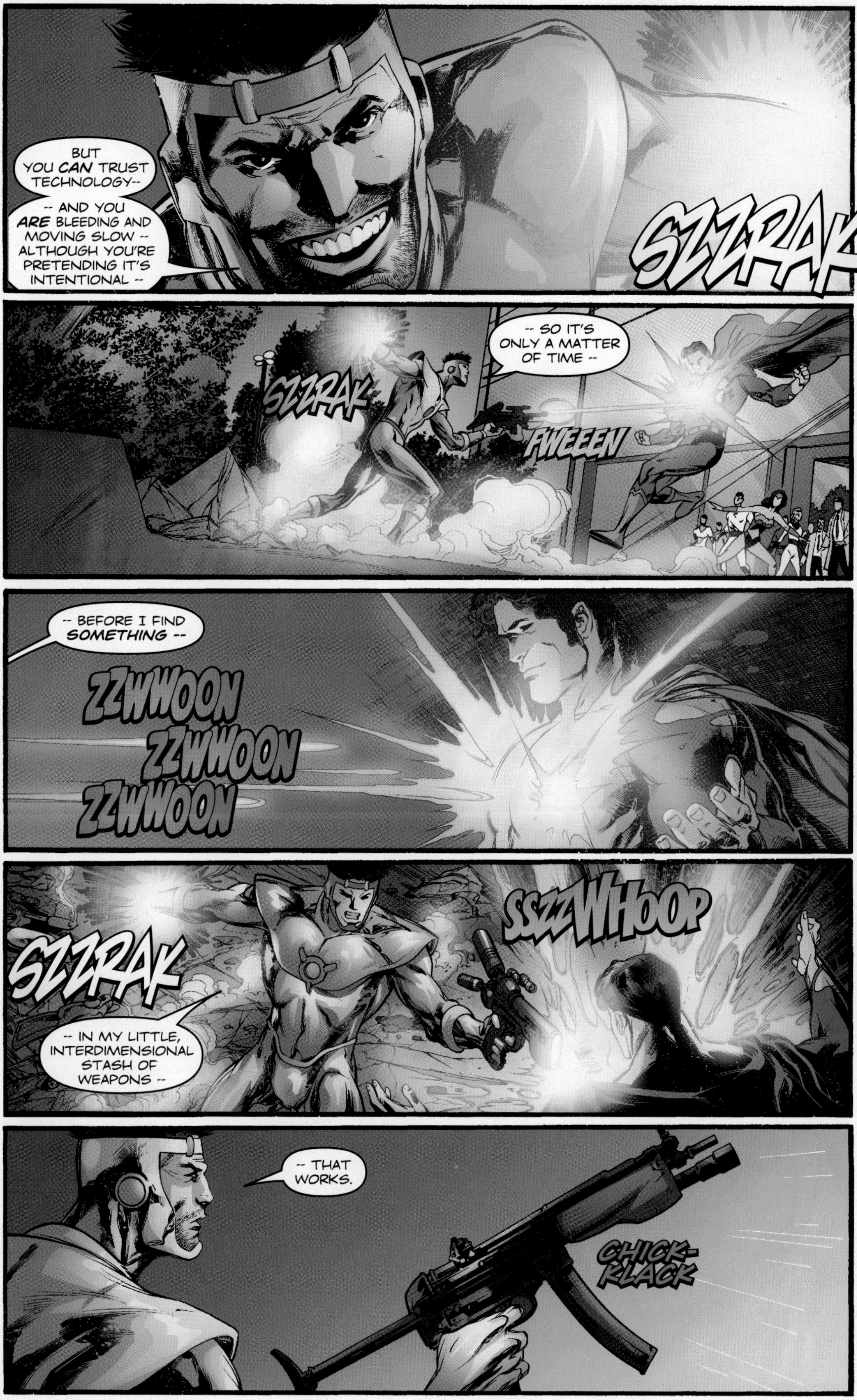
BUT YOU CAN TRUST TECHNOLOGY--
-- AND YOU ARE BLEEDING AND MOVING SLOW -- ALTHOUGH YOU'RE PRETENDING IT'S INTENTIONAL --
SZZRAK
-- SO IT'S ONLY A MATTER OF TIME --
SZZRAK
FWEEEN
-- BEFORE I FIND SOMETHING --
ZZWWOON
ZZWWOON
ZZWWOON
SZZRAK
SSZZWHOOP
-- IN MY LITTLE, INTERDIMENSIONAL STASH OF WEAPONS --
-- THAT WORKS.
CHICK-KLACK

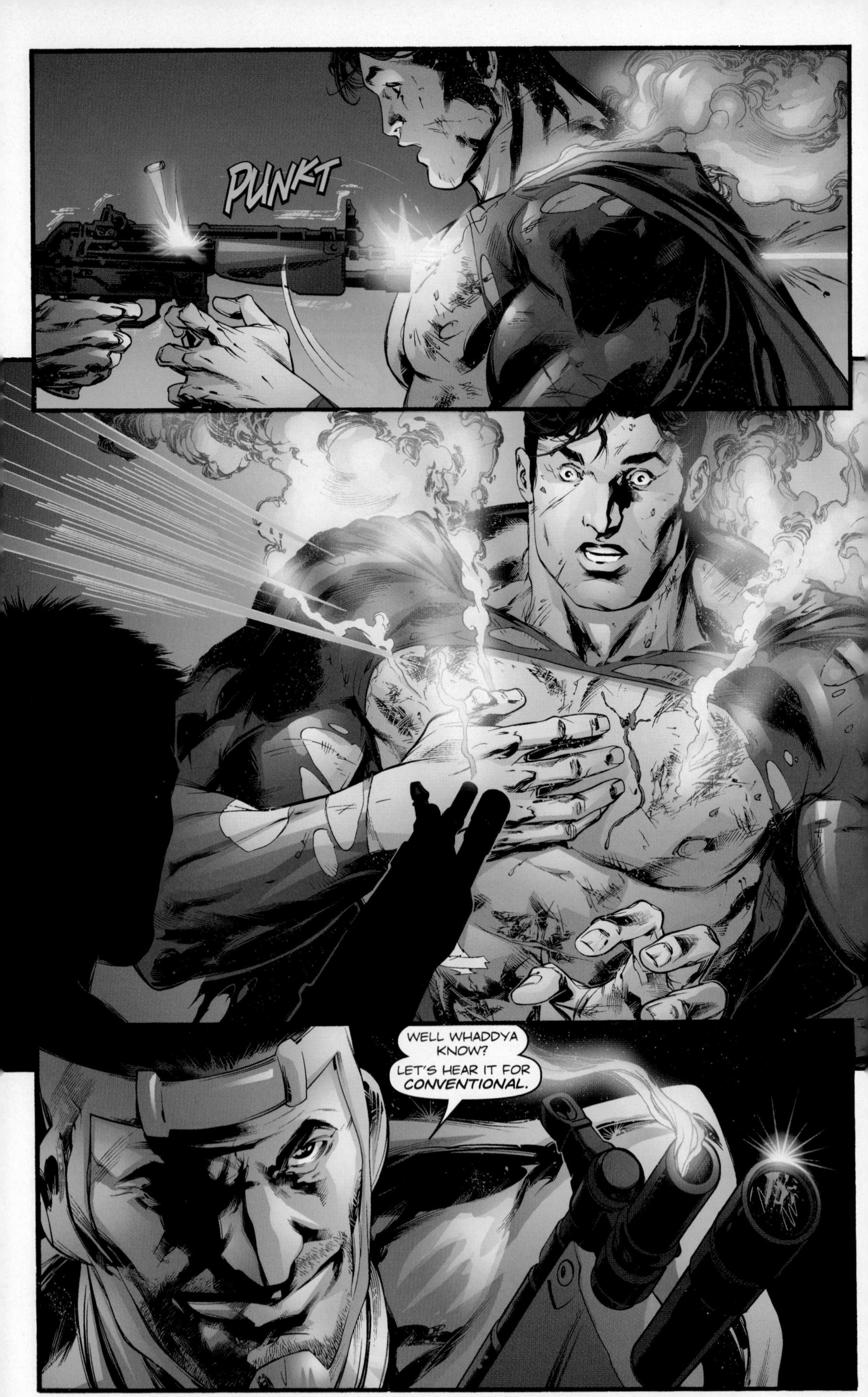
PUNKT
WELL WHADDYA KNOW?
LET'S HEAR IT FOR CONVENTIONAL.

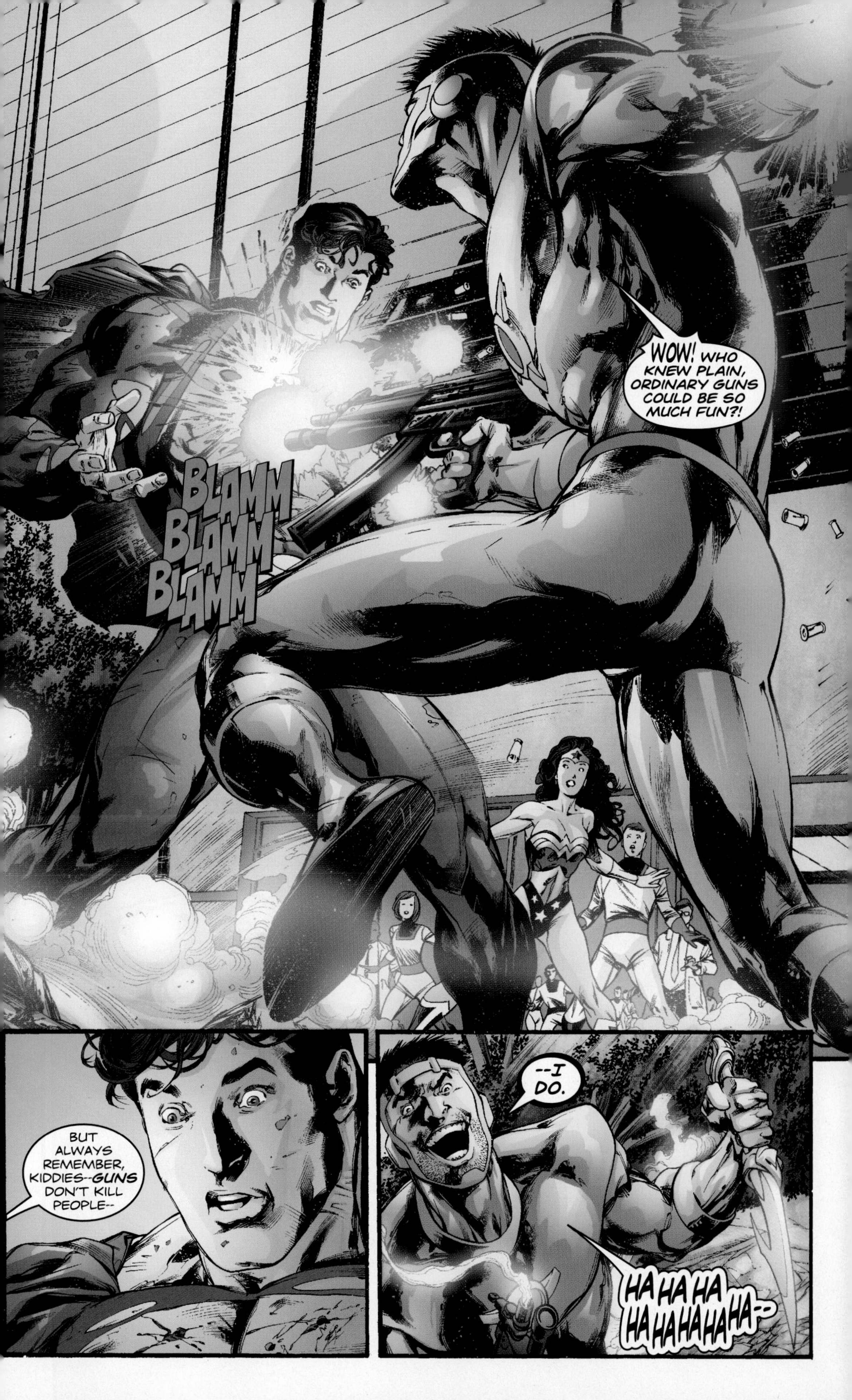
WOW! WHO KNEW PLAIN, ORDINARY GUNS COULD BE SO MUCH FUN?!
BLAMM BLAMM BLAMM
BUT ALWAYS REMEMBER, KIDDIES--GUNS DON'T KILL PEOPLE--
--I DO.
HA HA HA HA HA HA HA HA-

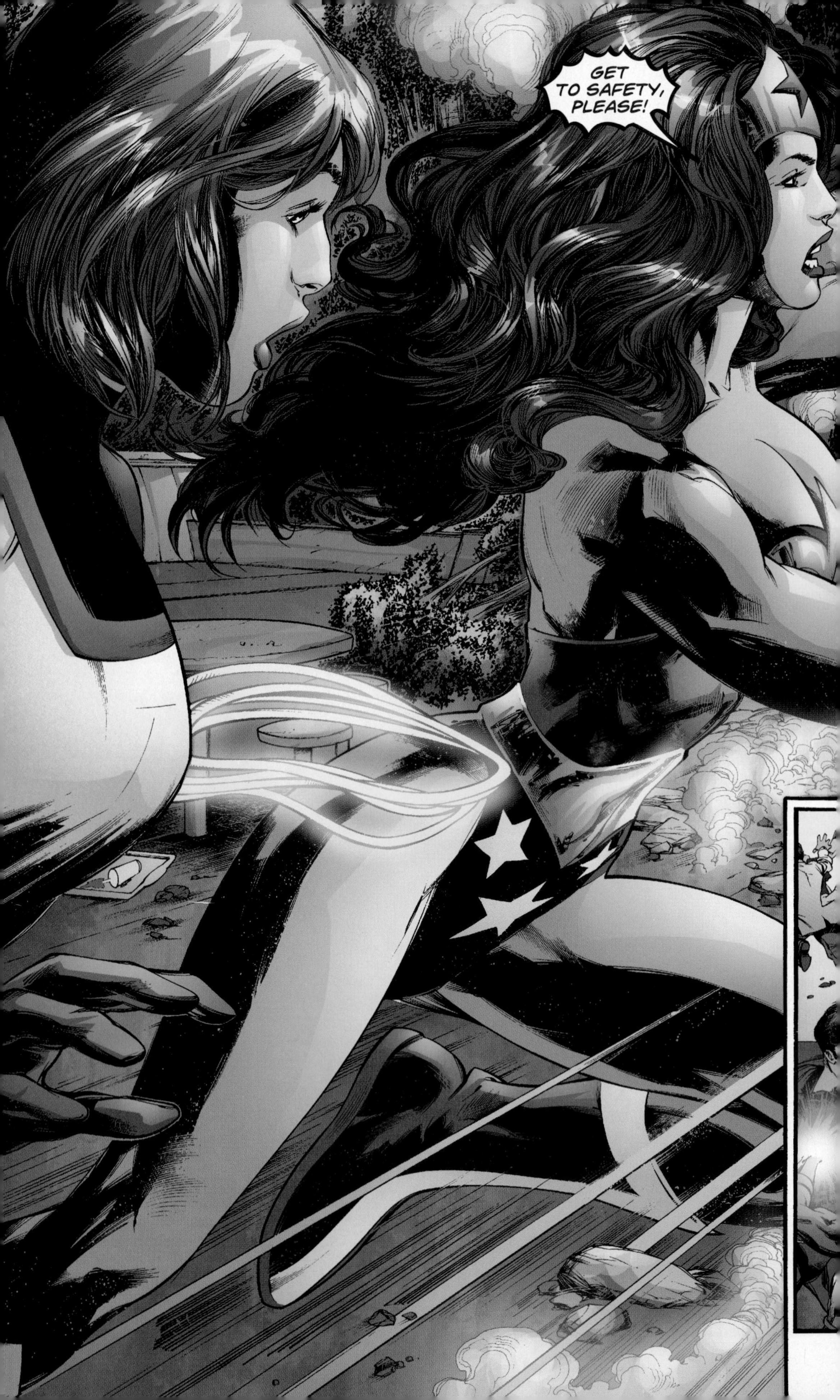
GET
TO SAFETY,
PLEASE!

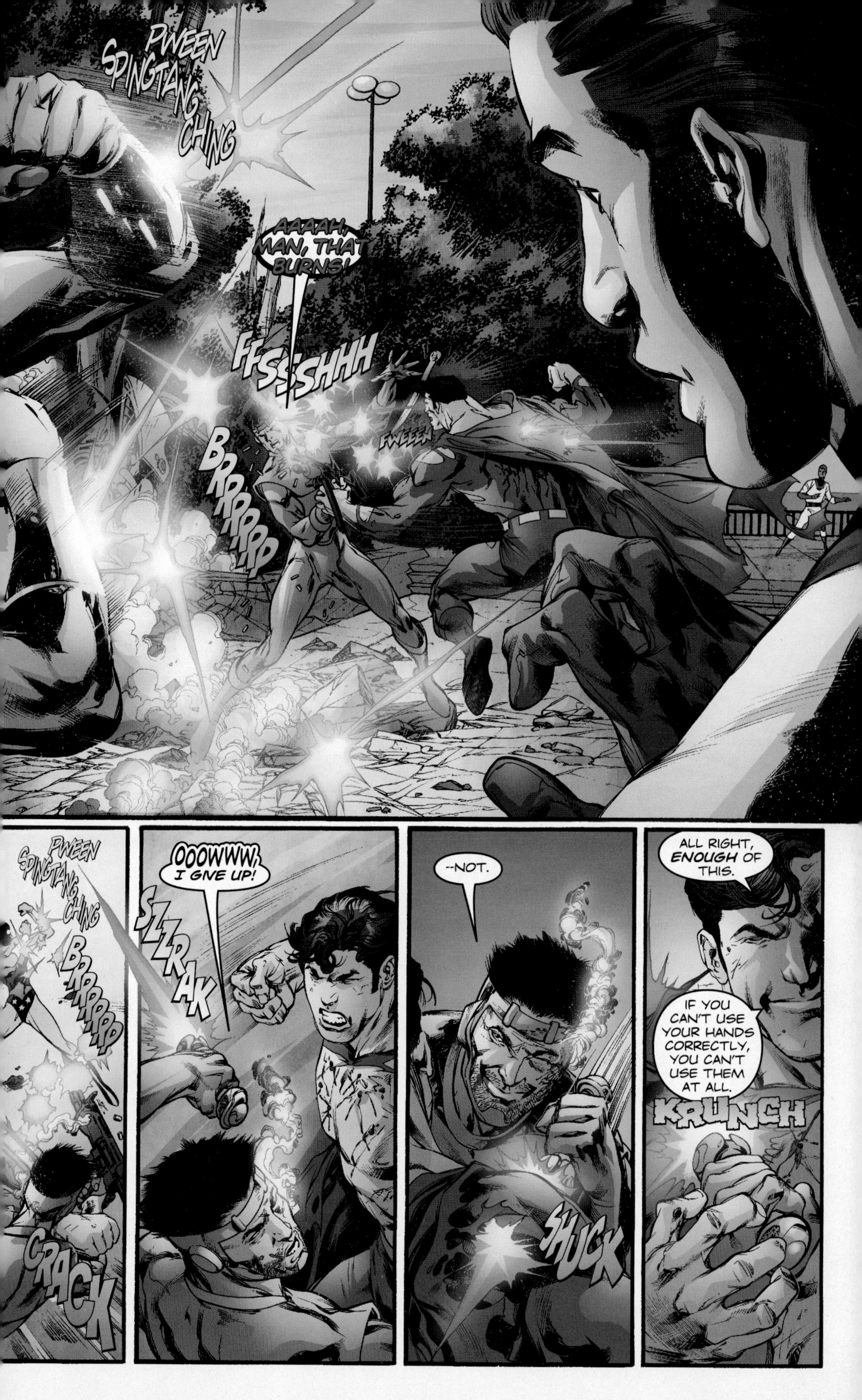
PWEEN
SPINGTANG
CHING
AAAAH, MAN, THAT BURNS!
FFSSSHHH
FWEEEN
BRRRRRP
PWEEN
SPINGTANG
CHING
BRRRRRP
CRACK
OOOWWW! I GIVE UP!
SZZRAK
--NOT.
SHUCK
ALL RIGHT, ENOUGH OF THIS.
IF YOU CAN'T USE YOUR HANDS CORRECTLY, YOU CAN'T USE THEM AT ALL.
KRUNCH

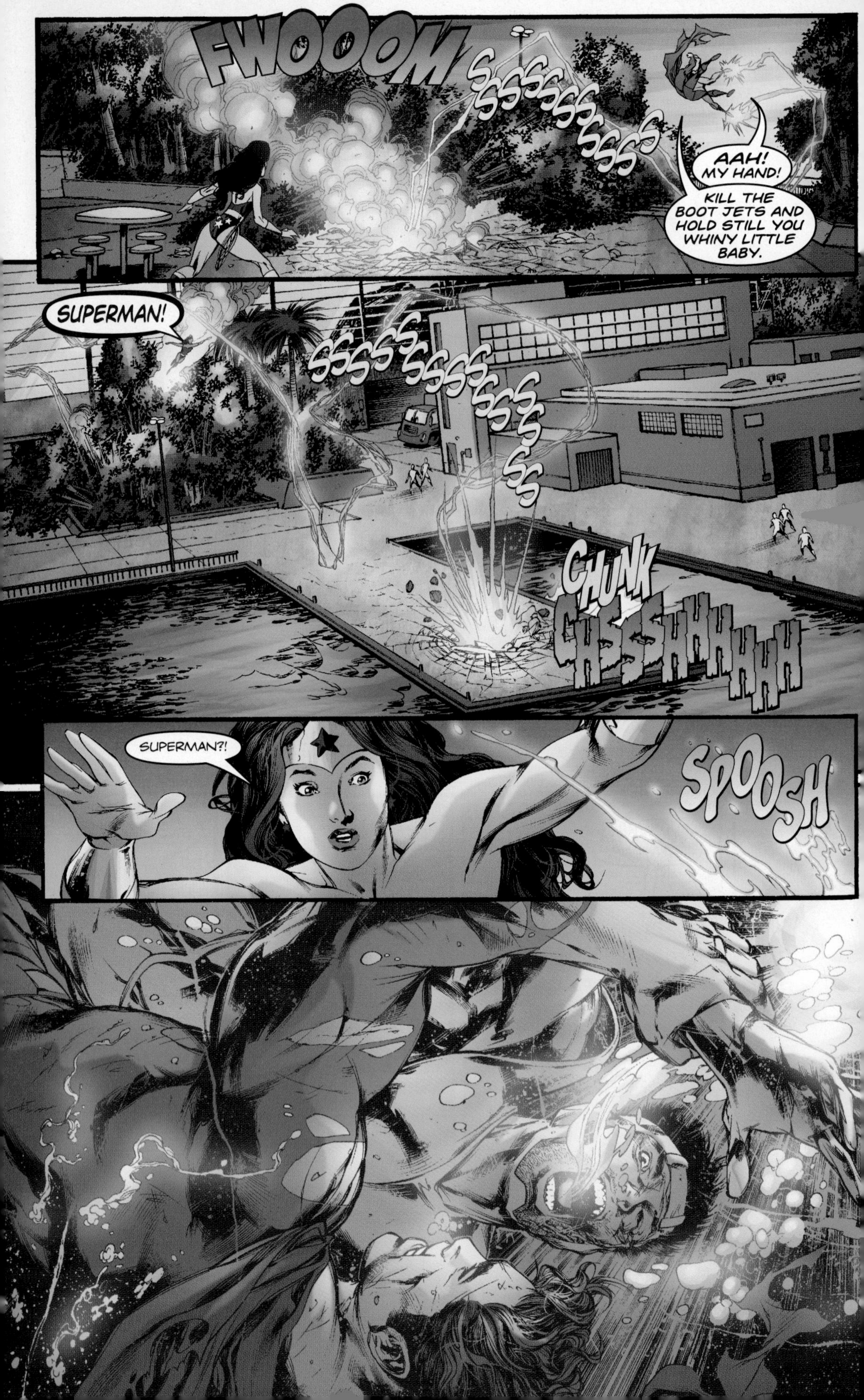
FWOOOM
SSSSSSSSSSSSSSS
AAH! MY HAND!
KILL THE BOOT JETS AND HOLD STILL YOU WHINY LITTLE BABY.
SUPERMAN!
SSSSSSSSSSSSSSS
CHUNK
CHSSSHHHHHH
SUPERMAN?!
SPOOSH

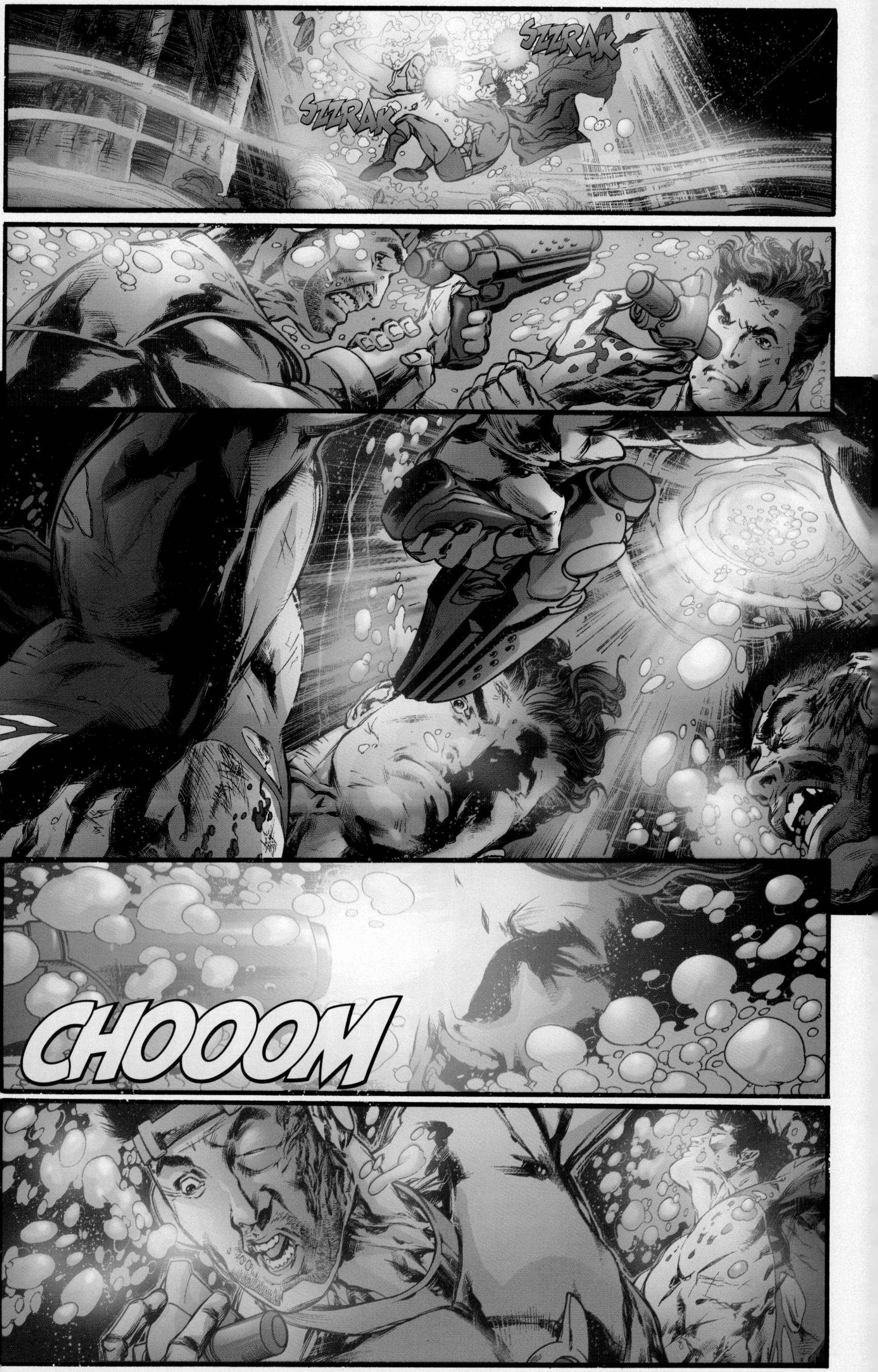
SZZZRAK
SZZZRAK
CHOOOM

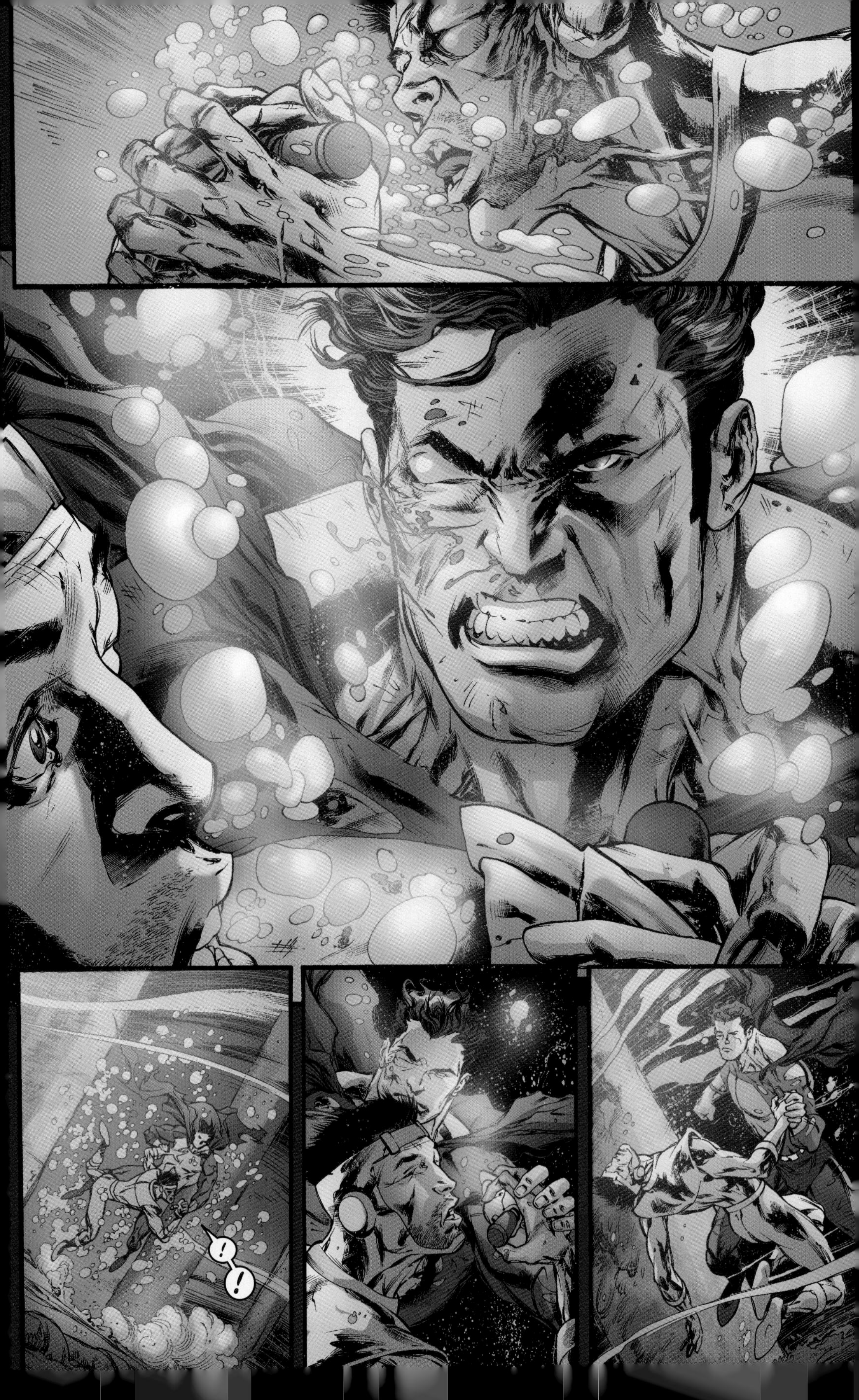
!
!

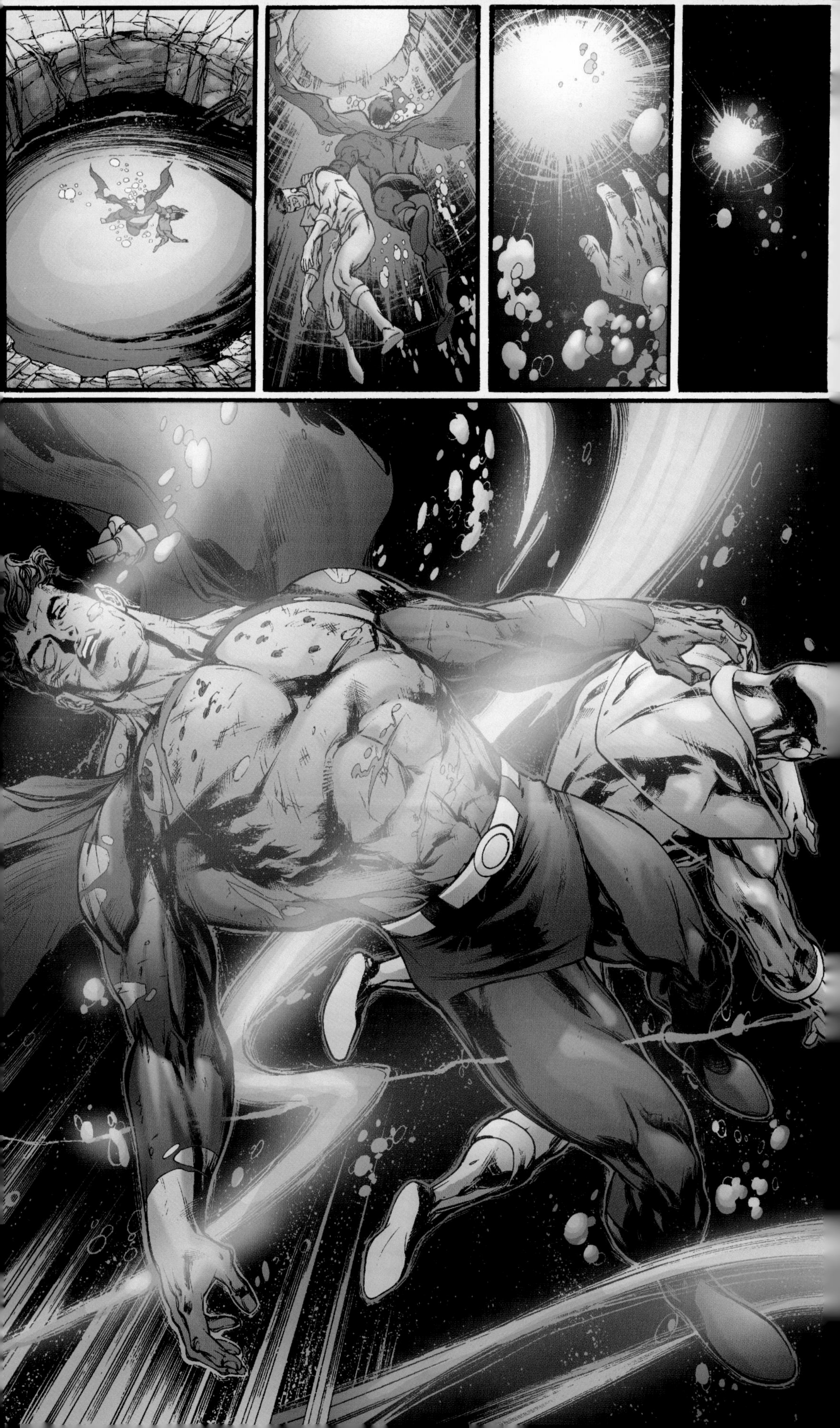

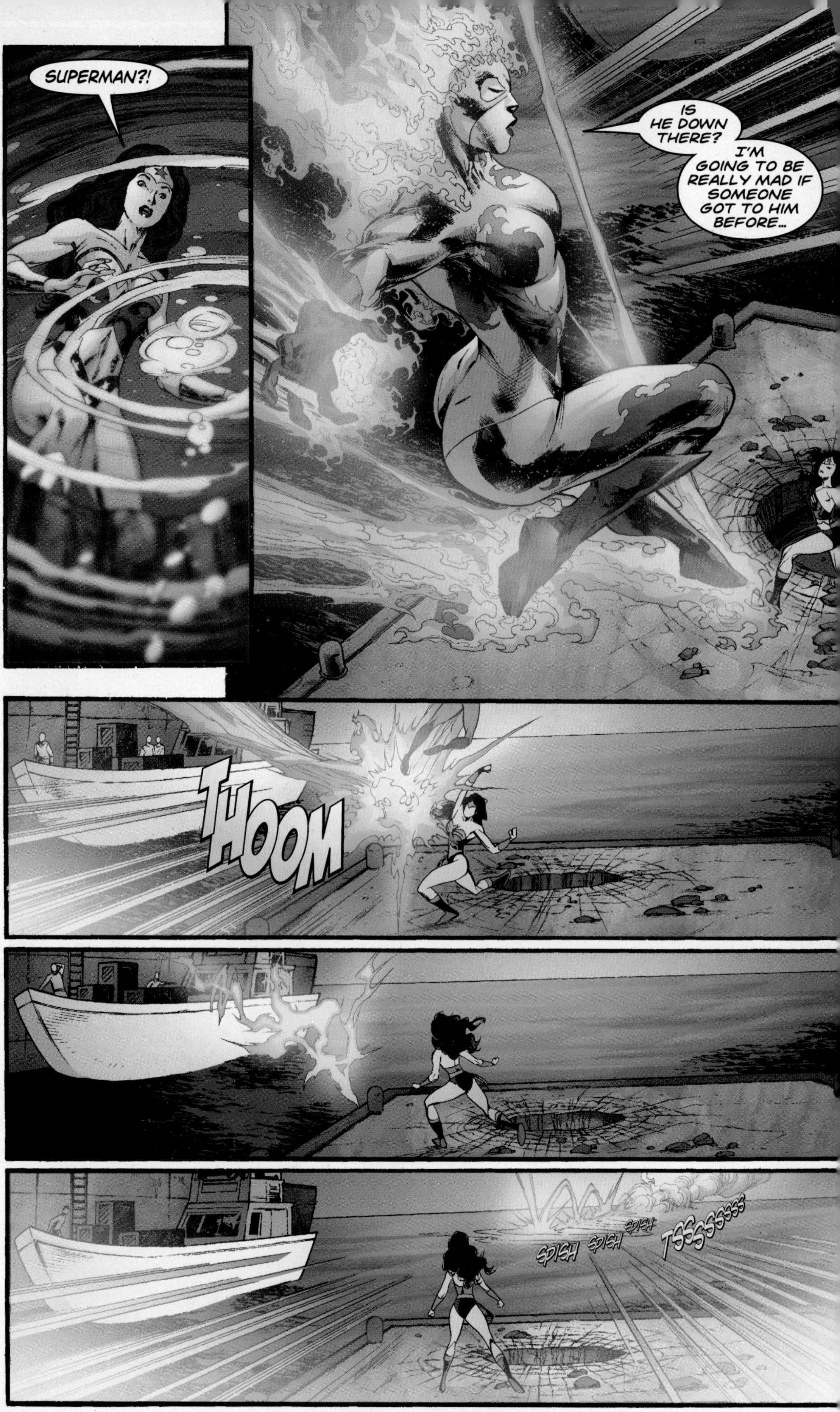
SUPERMAN?!
IS HE DOWN THERE?
I'M GOING TO BE REALLY MAD IF SOMEONE GOT TO HIM BEFORE...
THOOM
SPISH SPISH SPISH
TSSSSSSS

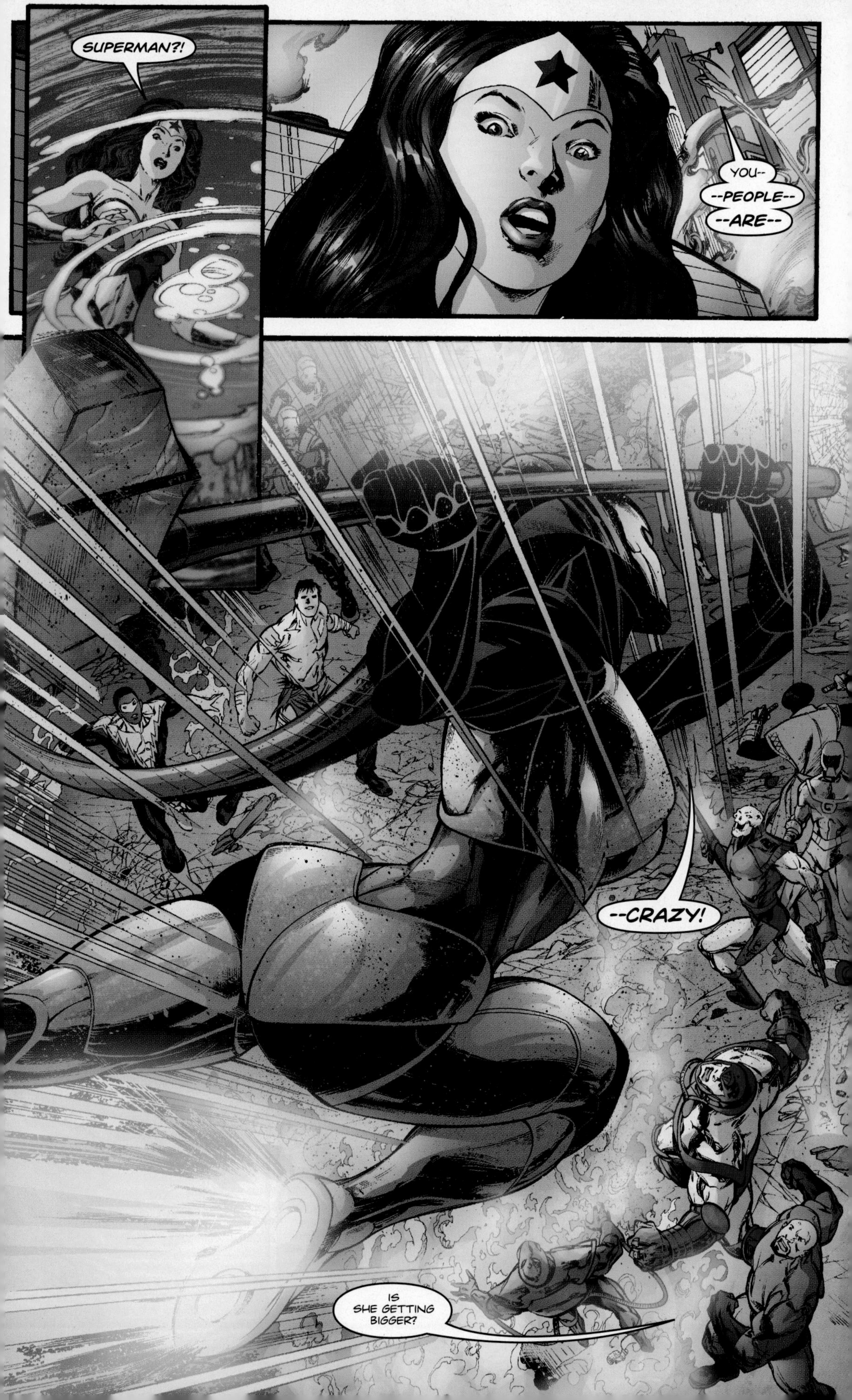
SUPERMAN?!
YOU--
--PEOPLE--
--ARE--
--CRAZY!
IS SHE GETTING BIGGER?

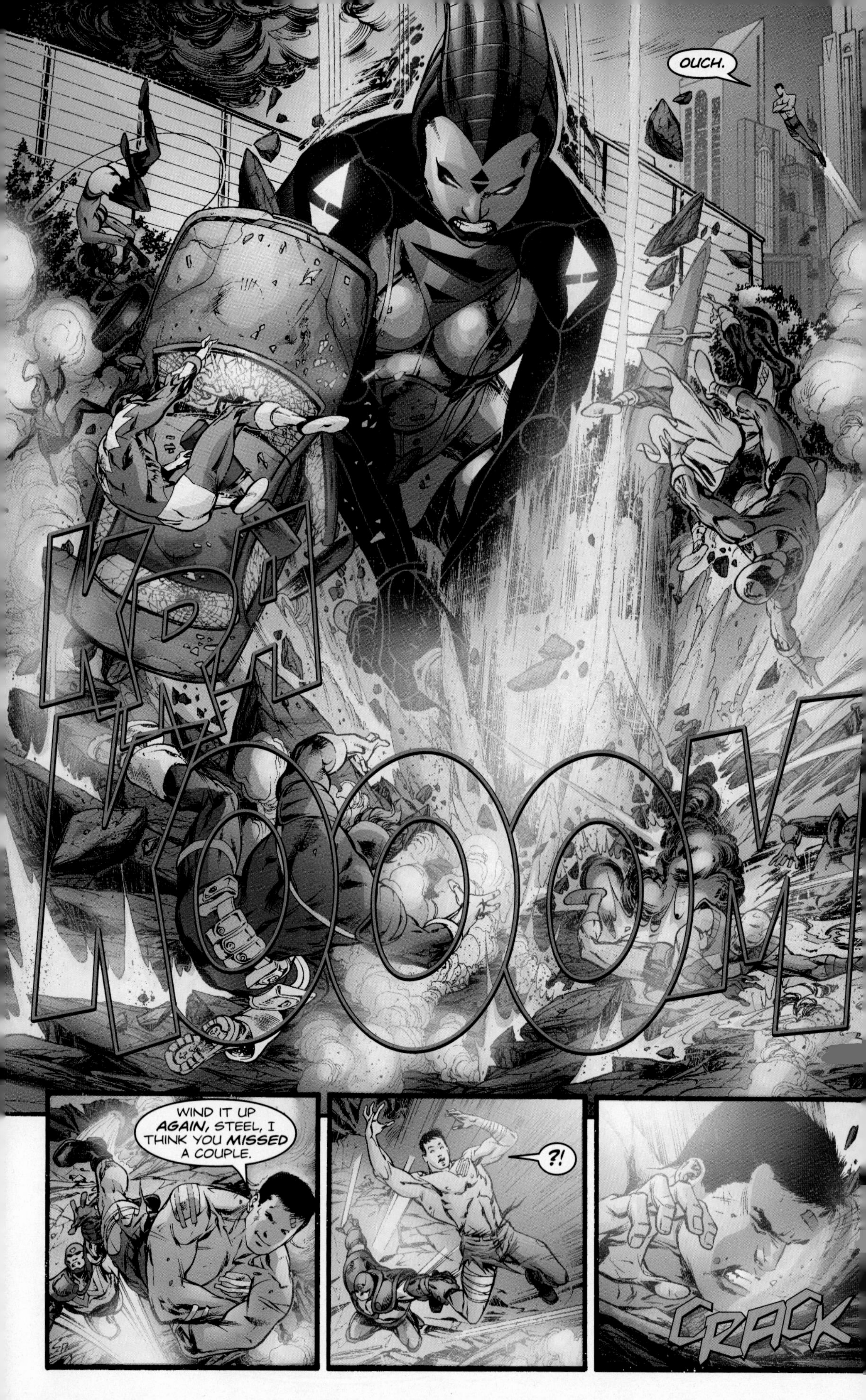
OUCH.
KRA
KOOOM
WIND IT UP AGAIN, STEEL, I THINK YOU MISSED A COUPLE.
?!
CRACK

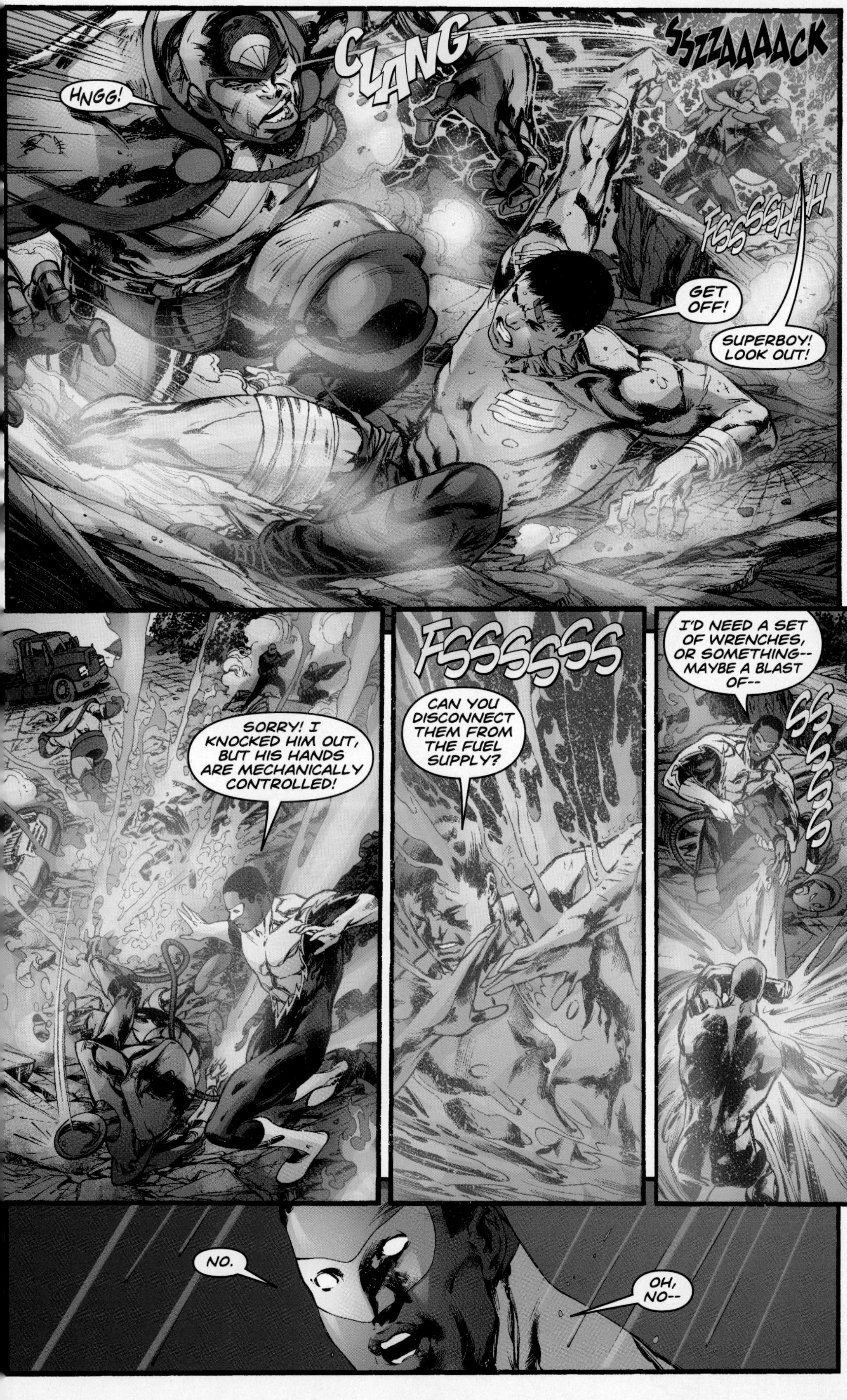

CLANG
SSZZAAAACK
HNGG!
FSSSSHHH
GET OFF!
SUPERBOY! LOOK OUT!
SORRY! I KNOCKED HIM OUT, BUT HIS HANDS ARE MECHANICALLY CONTROLLED!
FSSSSSSS
CAN YOU DISCONNECT THEM FROM THE FUEL SUPPLY?
I'D NEED A SET OF WRENCHES, OR SOMETHING-- MAYBE A BLAST OF--
SSSSSSSS
NO.
OH, NO--

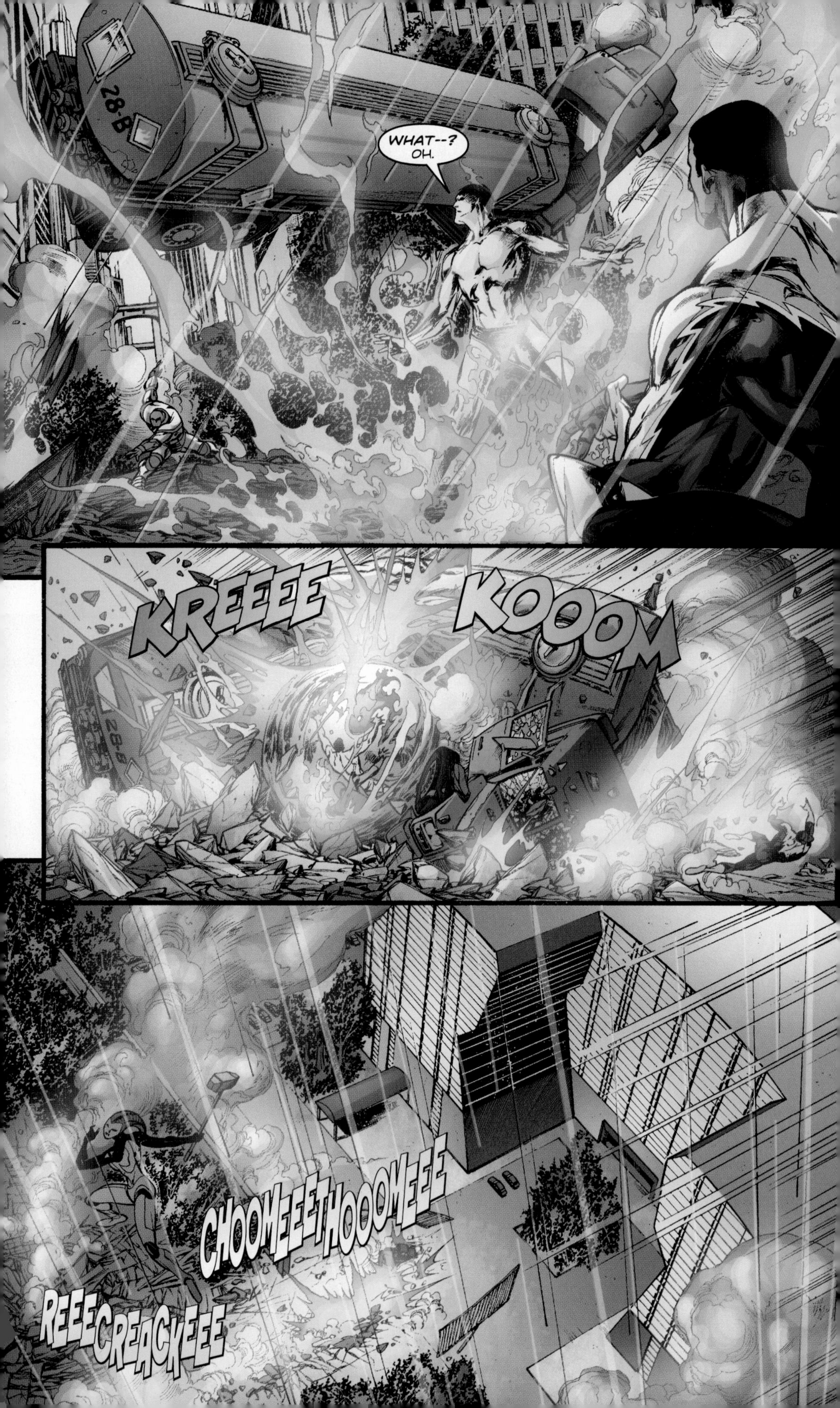
WHAT--?
OH.
KREEEE
KOOOM
CHOOMEEETHOOOMEEE
REEECREACKEEE

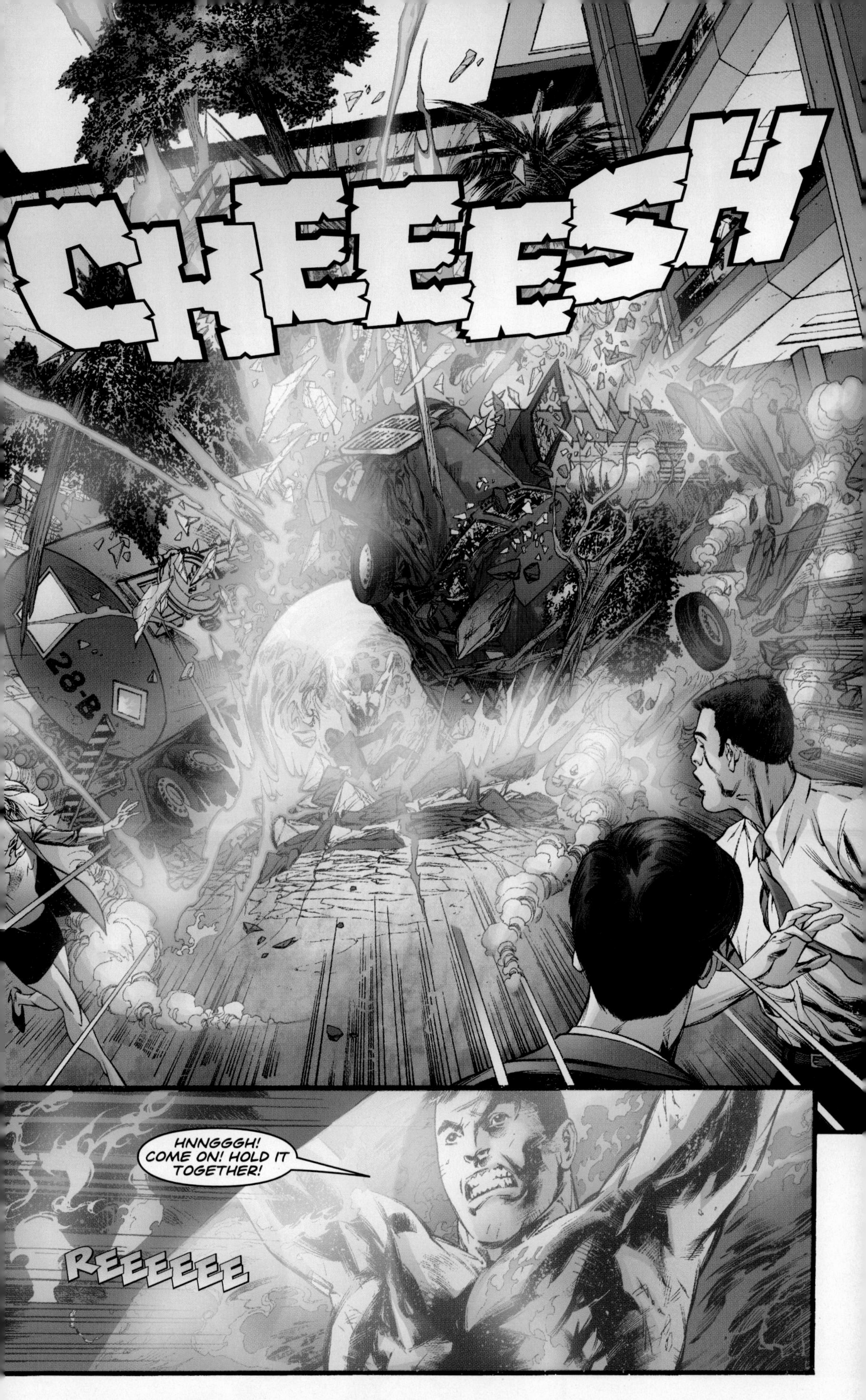
CHEEESH
28-B
HNNGGGH! COME ON! HOLD IT TOGETHER!
REEEEEE

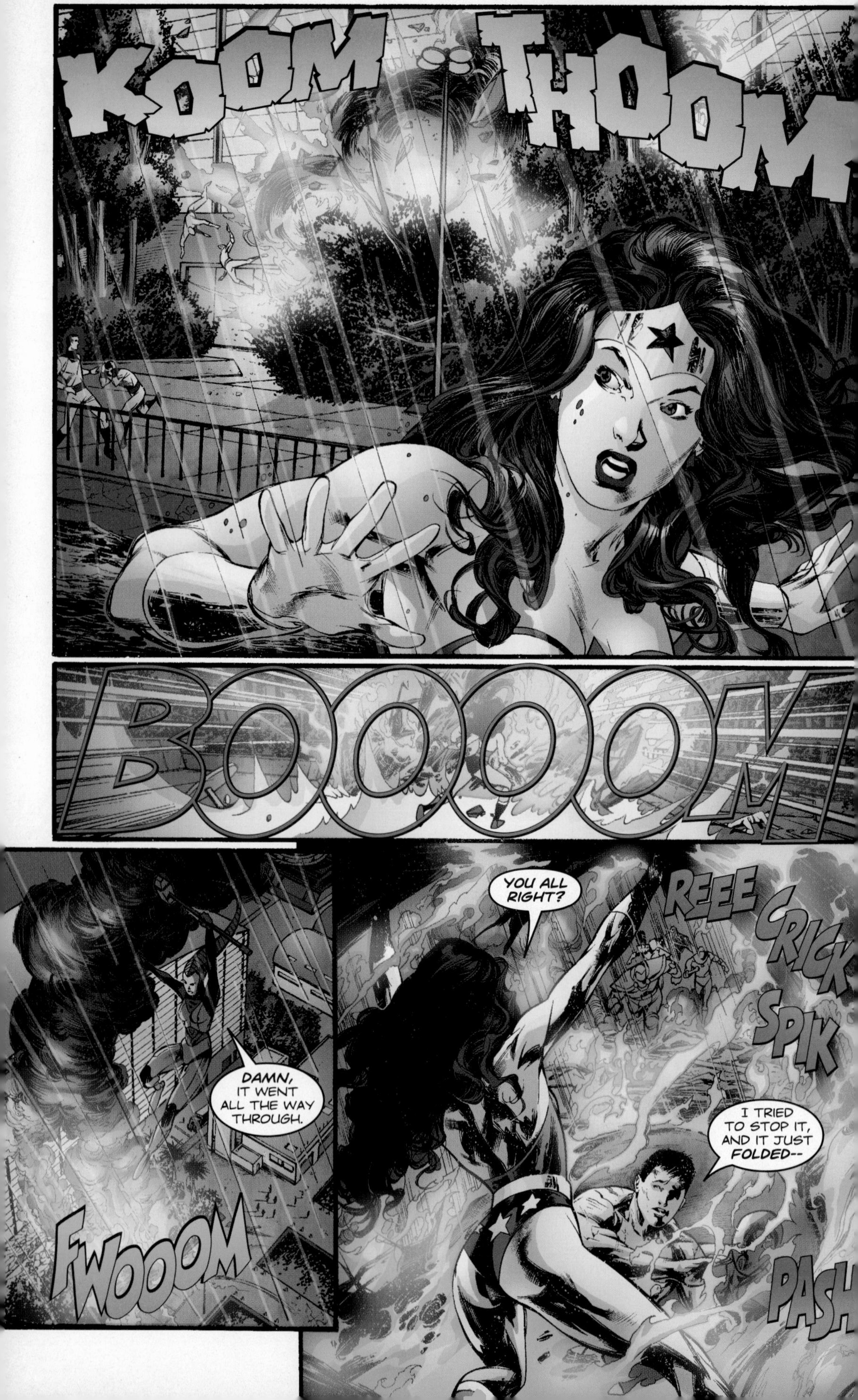
KOOM
THOOM
BOOOOM
DAMN, IT WENT ALL THE WAY THROUGH.
FWOOOM
YOU ALL RIGHT?
REEE
CRICK
SPIK
I TRIED TO STOP IT, AND IT JUST FOLDED--
PASH

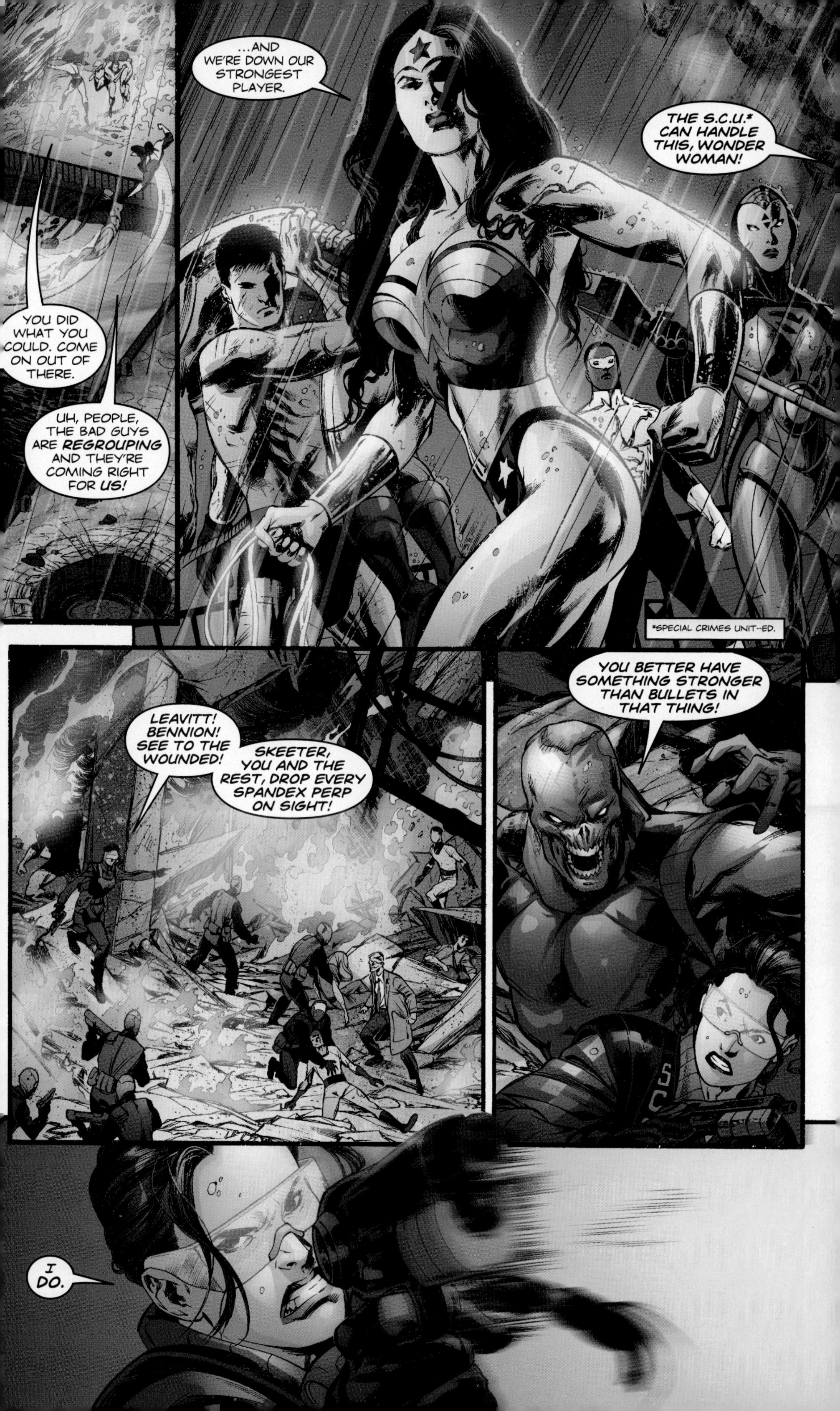
...AND WE'RE DOWN OUR STRONGEST PLAYER.
YOU DID WHAT YOU COULD. COME ON OUT OF THERE.
UH, PEOPLE, THE BAD GUYS ARE REGROUPING AND THEY'RE COMING RIGHT FOR US!
THE S.C.U.* CAN HANDLE THIS, WONDER WOMAN!
*SPECIAL CRIMES UNIT--ED.
LEAVITT! BENNION! SEE TO THE WOUNDED!
SKEETER, YOU AND THE REST, DROP EVERY SPANDEX PERP ON SIGHT!
YOU BETTER HAVE SOMETHING STRONGER THAN BULLETS IN THAT THING!
I DO.

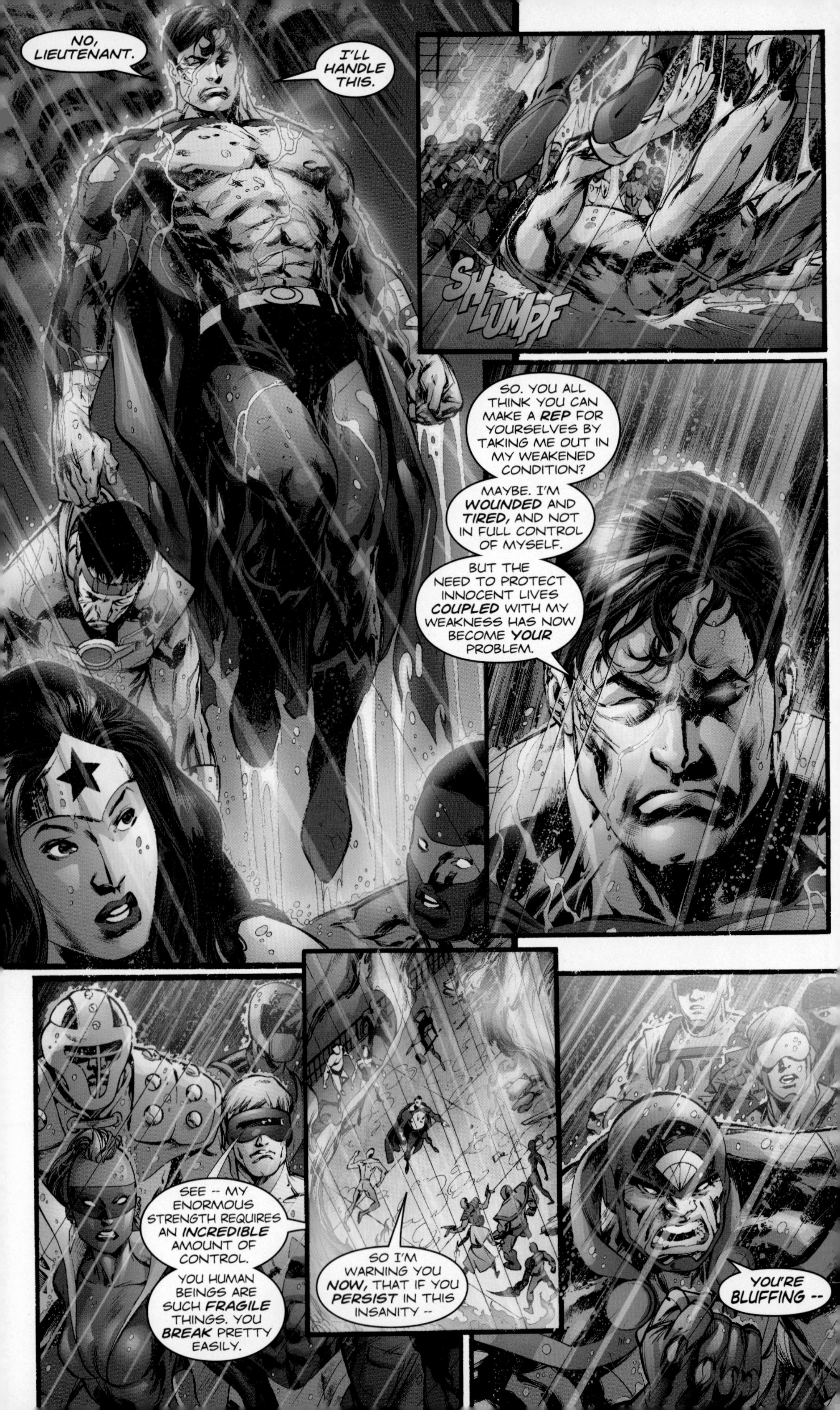
NO, LIEUTENANT.
I'LL HANDLE THIS.
SHLUMPF
SO. YOU ALL THINK YOU CAN MAKE A **REP** FOR YOURSELVES BY TAKING ME OUT IN MY WEAKENED CONDITION?
MAYBE. I'M **WOUNDED** AND **TIRED,** AND NOT IN FULL CONTROL OF MYSELF.
BUT THE NEED TO PROTECT INNOCENT LIVES **COUPLED** WITH MY WEAKNESS HAS NOW BECOME **YOUR** PROBLEM.
SEE -- MY ENORMOUS STRENGTH REQUIRES AN **INCREDIBLE** AMOUNT OF CONTROL.
YOU HUMAN BEINGS ARE SUCH **FRAGILE** THINGS. YOU **BREAK** PRETTY EASILY.
SO I'M WARNING YOU **NOW,** THAT IF YOU **PERSIST** IN THIS INSANITY --
YOU'RE BLUFFING --

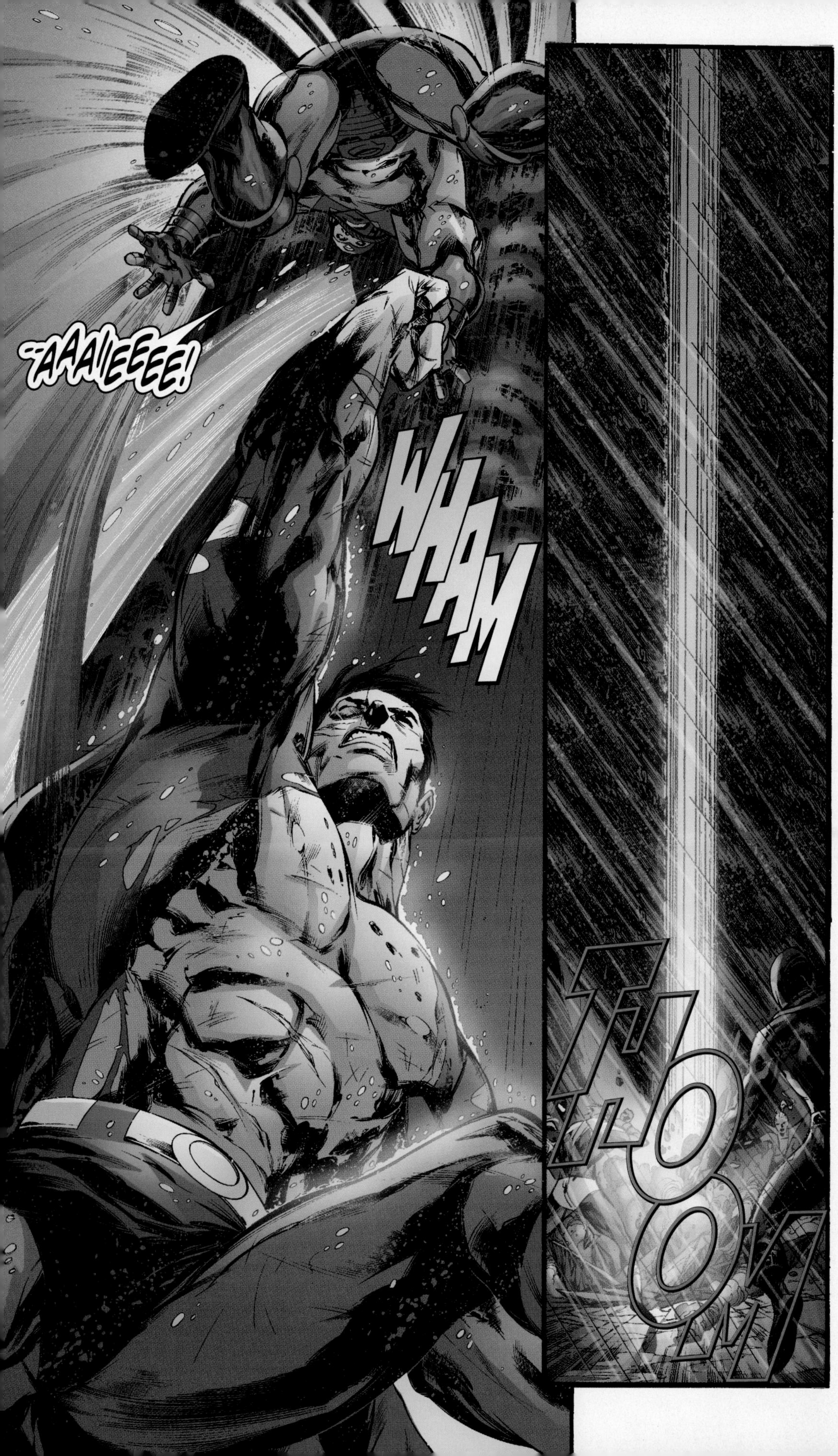
-AAAIIEEEEE!
WHAM
THOOM

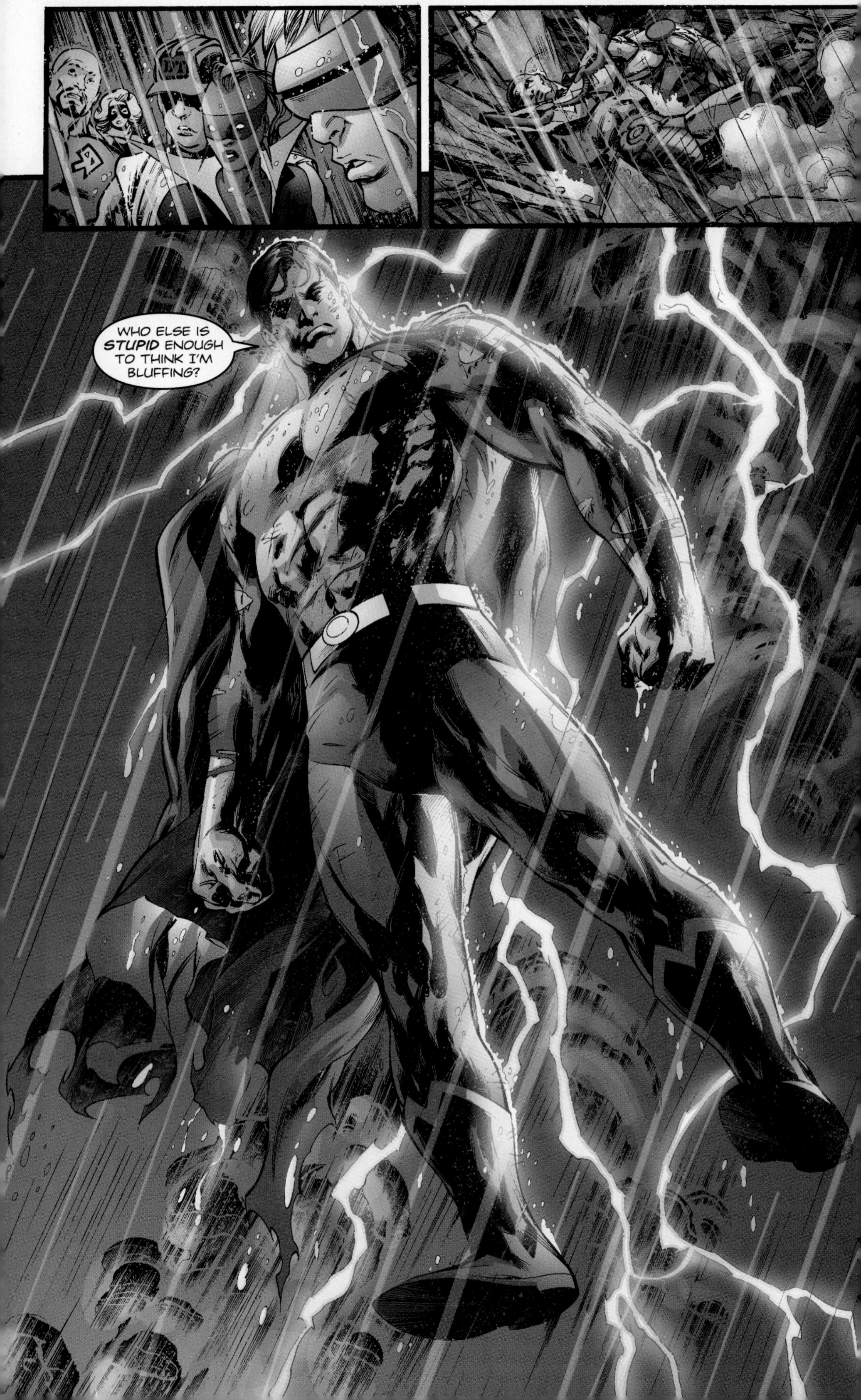
WHO ELSE IS STUPID ENOUGH TO THINK I'M BLUFFING?

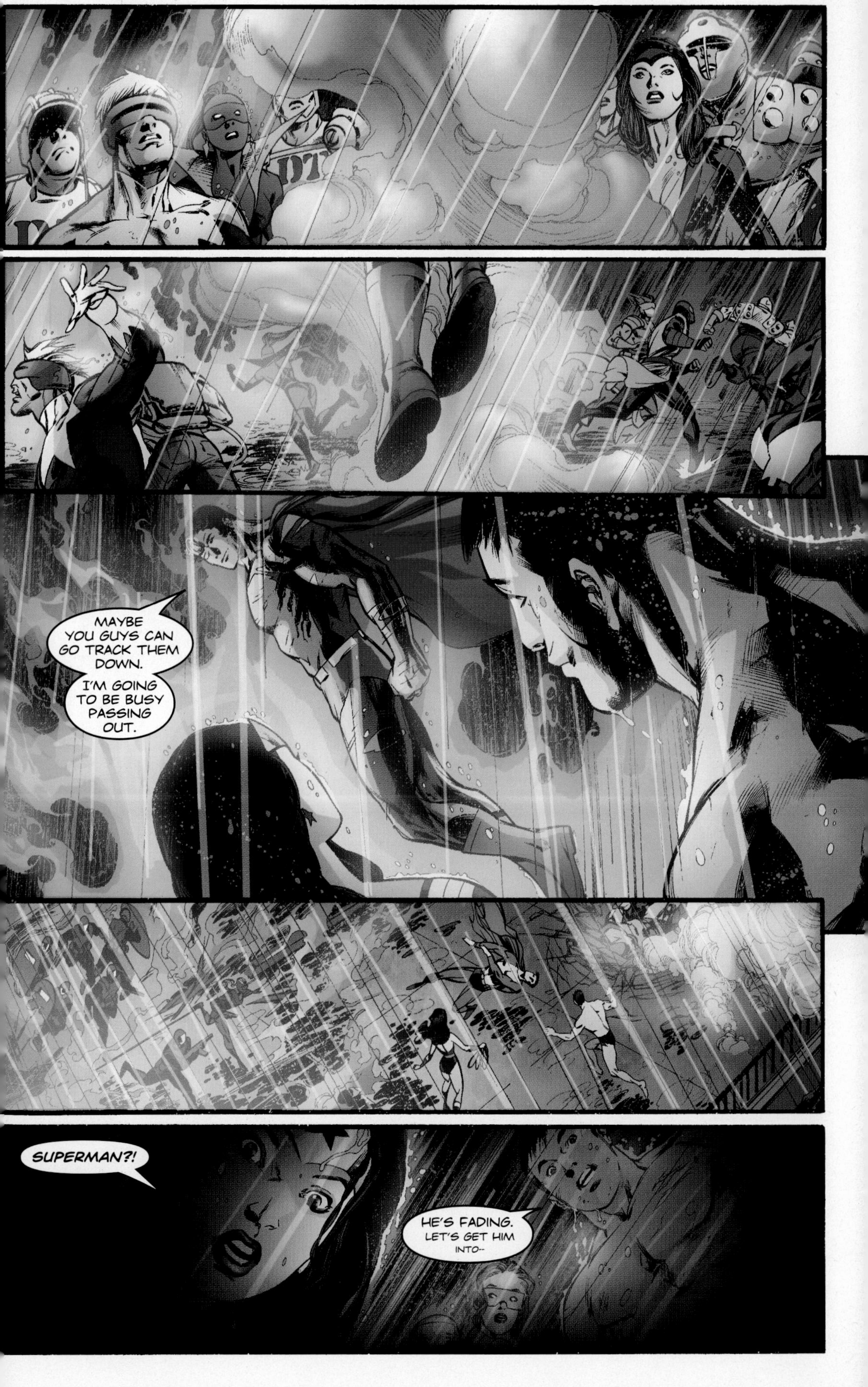
MAYBE YOU GUYS CAN GO TRACK THEM DOWN.
I'M GOING TO BE BUSY PASSING OUT.
SUPERMAN?!
HE'S FADING. LET'S GET HIM INTO--

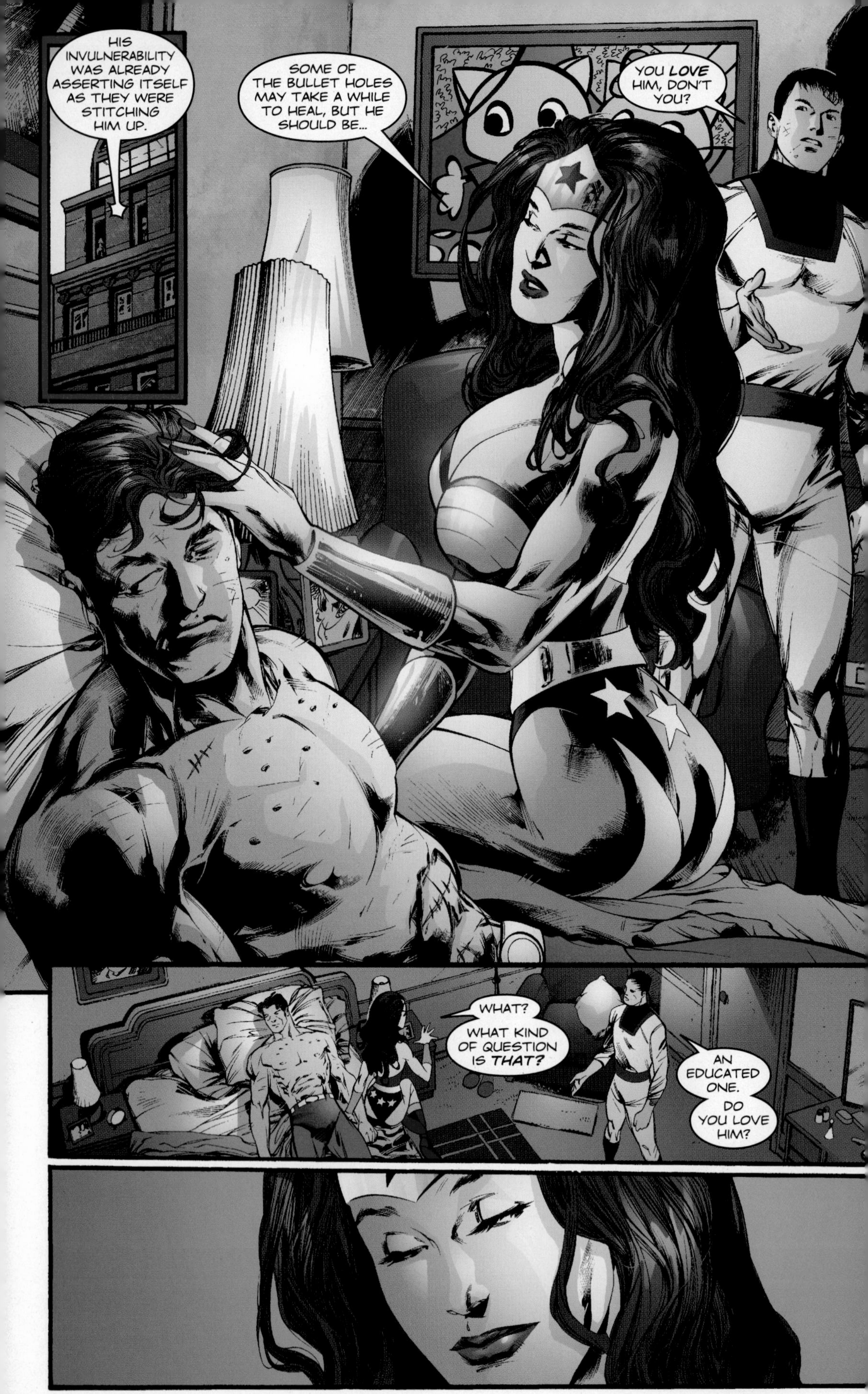
HIS INVULNERABILITY WAS ALREADY ASSERTING ITSELF AS THEY WERE STITCHING HIM UP.
SOME OF THE BULLET HOLES MAY TAKE A WHILE TO HEAL, BUT HE SHOULD BE...
YOU LOVE HIM, DON'T YOU?
WHAT?
WHAT KIND OF QUESTION IS THAT?
AN EDUCATED ONE.
DO YOU LOVE HIM?

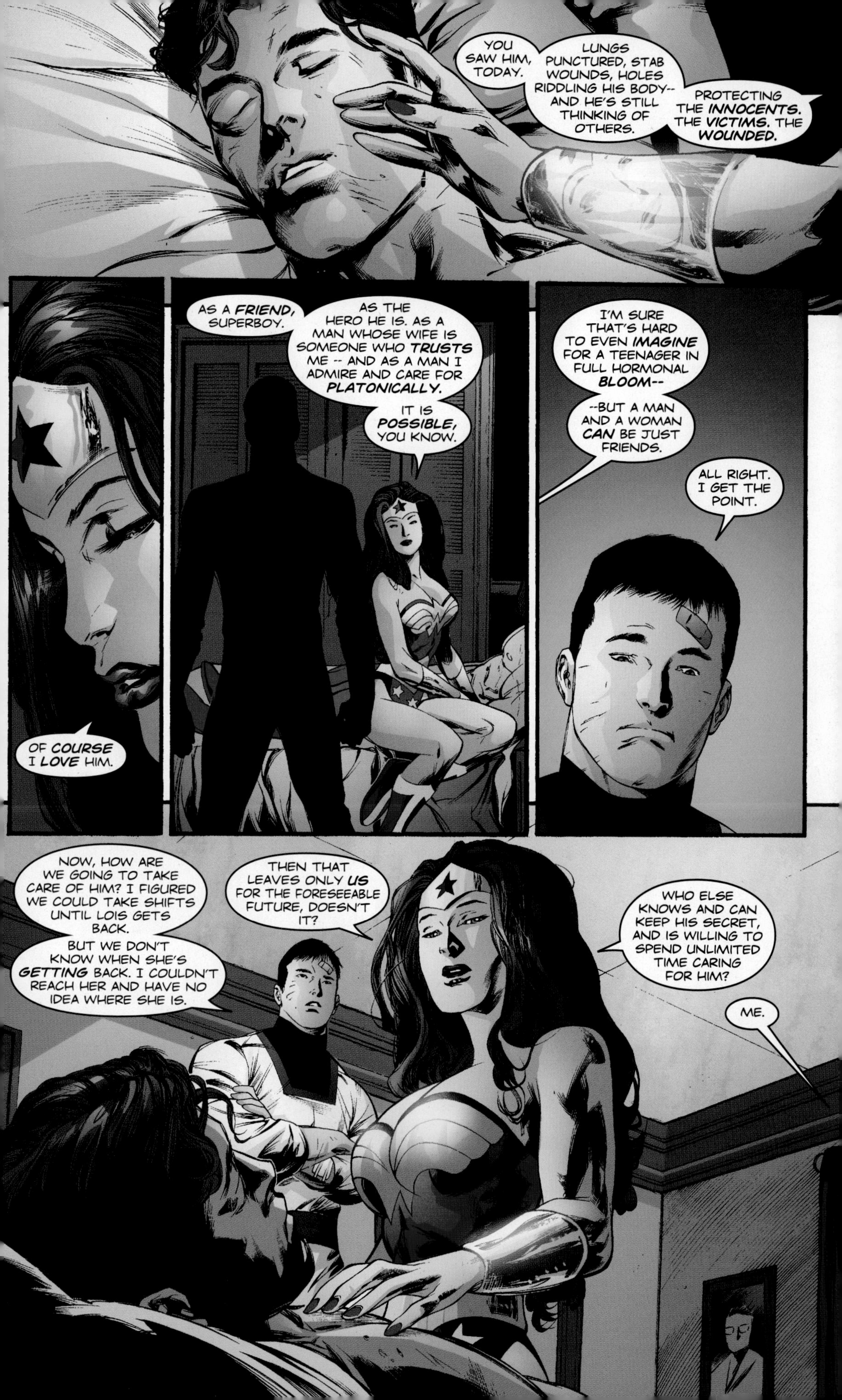

YOU SAW HIM, TODAY.
LUNGS PUNCTURED, STAB WOUNDS, HOLES RIDDLING HIS BODY-- AND HE'S STILL THINKING OF OTHERS.
PROTECTING THE INNOCENTS. THE VICTIMS. THE WOUNDED.
OF COURSE I LOVE HIM.
AS A FRIEND, SUPERBOY.
AS THE HERO HE IS. AS A MAN WHOSE WIFE IS SOMEONE WHO TRUSTS ME -- AND AS A MAN I ADMIRE AND CARE FOR PLATONICALLY.
IT IS POSSIBLE, YOU KNOW.
I'M SURE THAT'S HARD TO EVEN IMAGINE FOR A TEENAGER IN FULL HORMONAL BLOOM--
--BUT A MAN AND A WOMAN CAN BE JUST FRIENDS.
ALL RIGHT. I GET THE POINT.
NOW, HOW ARE WE GOING TO TAKE CARE OF HIM? I FIGURED WE COULD TAKE SHIFTS UNTIL LOIS GETS BACK.
BUT WE DON'T KNOW WHEN SHE'S GETTING BACK. I COULDN'T REACH HER AND HAVE NO IDEA WHERE SHE IS.
THEN THAT LEAVES ONLY US FOR THE FORESEEABLE FUTURE, DOESN'T IT?
WHO ELSE KNOWS AND CAN KEEP HIS SECRET, AND IS WILLING TO SPEND UNLIMITED TIME CARING FOR HIM?
ME.

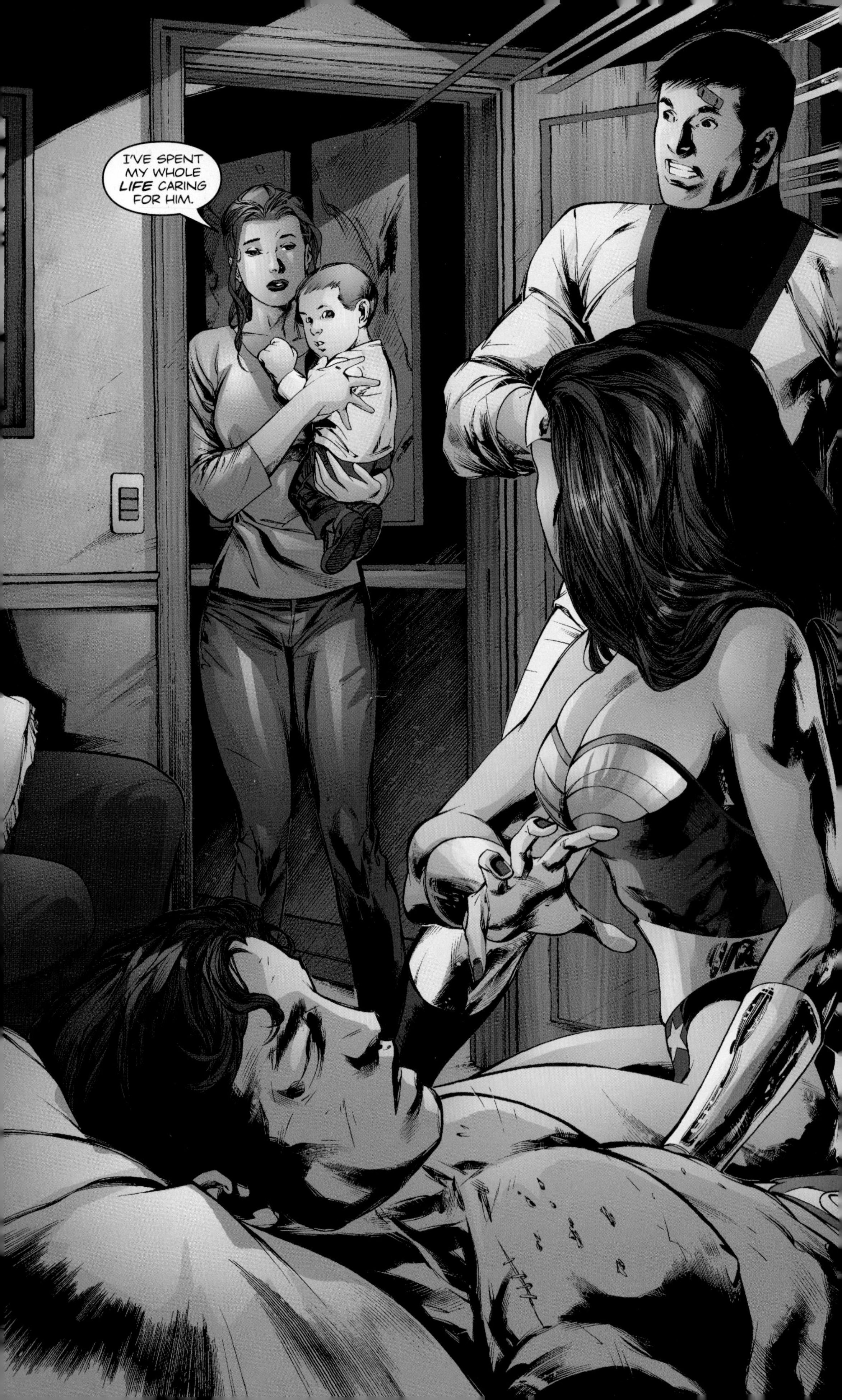
I'VE SPENT MY WHOLE LIFE CARING FOR HIM.

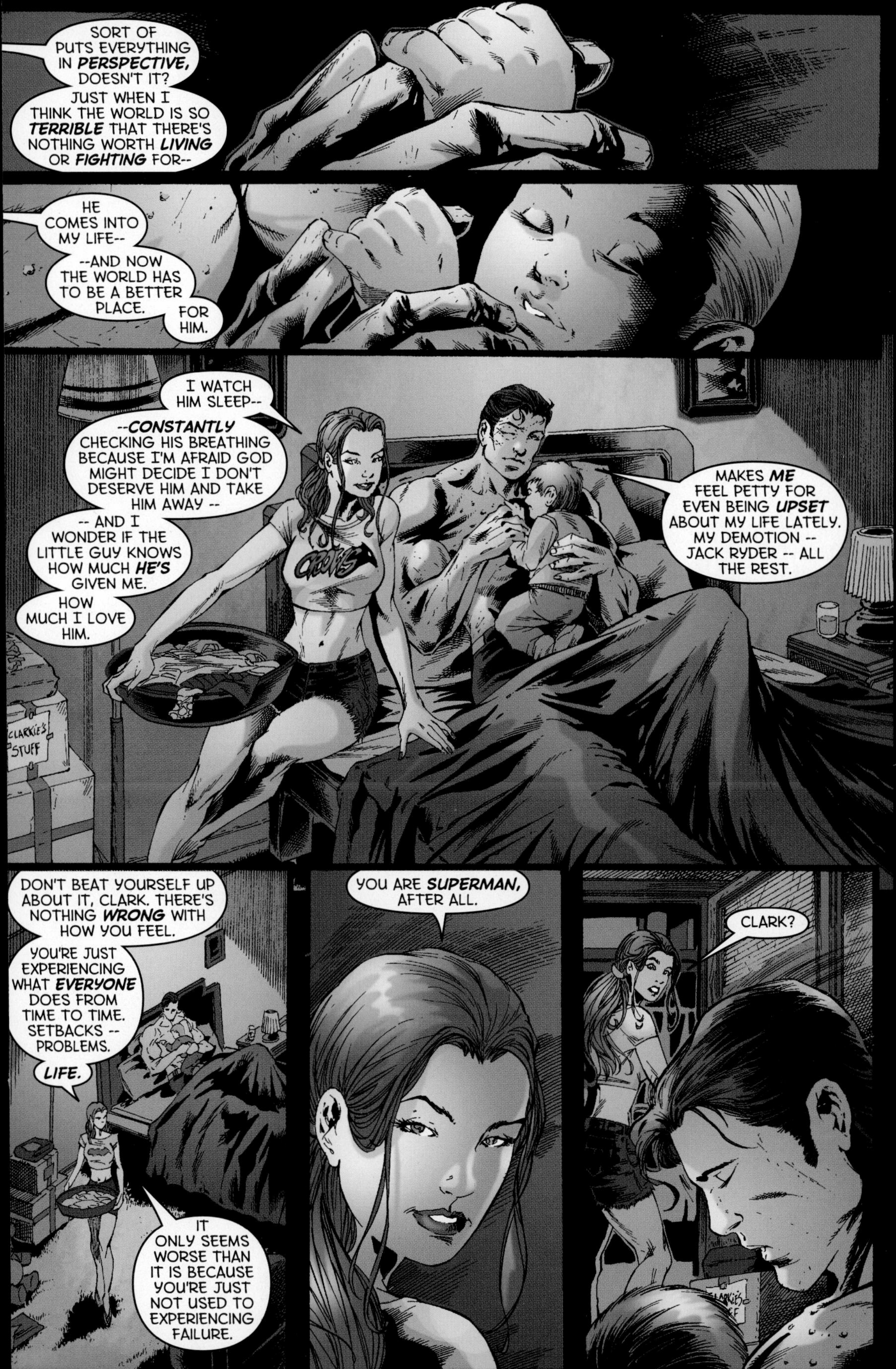
SORT OF PUTS EVERYTHING IN PERSPECTIVE, DOESN'T IT?
JUST WHEN I THINK THE WORLD IS SO TERRIBLE THAT THERE'S NOTHING WORTH LIVING OR FIGHTING FOR--
HE COMES INTO MY LIFE--
--AND NOW THE WORLD HAS TO BE A BETTER PLACE.
FOR HIM.
I WATCH HIM SLEEP--
--CONSTANTLY CHECKING HIS BREATHING BECAUSE I'M AFRAID GOD MIGHT DECIDE I DON'T DESERVE HIM AND TAKE HIM AWAY --
-- AND I WONDER IF THE LITTLE GUY KNOWS HOW MUCH HE'S GIVEN ME.
HOW MUCH I LOVE HIM.
MAKES ME FEEL PETTY FOR EVEN BEING UPSET ABOUT MY LIFE LATELY. MY DEMOTION -- JACK RYDER -- ALL THE REST.
CLARKIE'S STUFF
DON'T BEAT YOURSELF UP ABOUT IT, CLARK. THERE'S NOTHING WRONG WITH HOW YOU FEEL.
YOU'RE JUST EXPERIENCING WHAT EVERYONE DOES FROM TIME TO TIME. SETBACKS -- PROBLEMS.
LIFE.
IT ONLY SEEMS WORSE THAN IT IS BECAUSE YOU'RE JUST NOT USED TO EXPERIENCING FAILURE.
YOU ARE SUPERMAN, AFTER ALL.
CLARK?

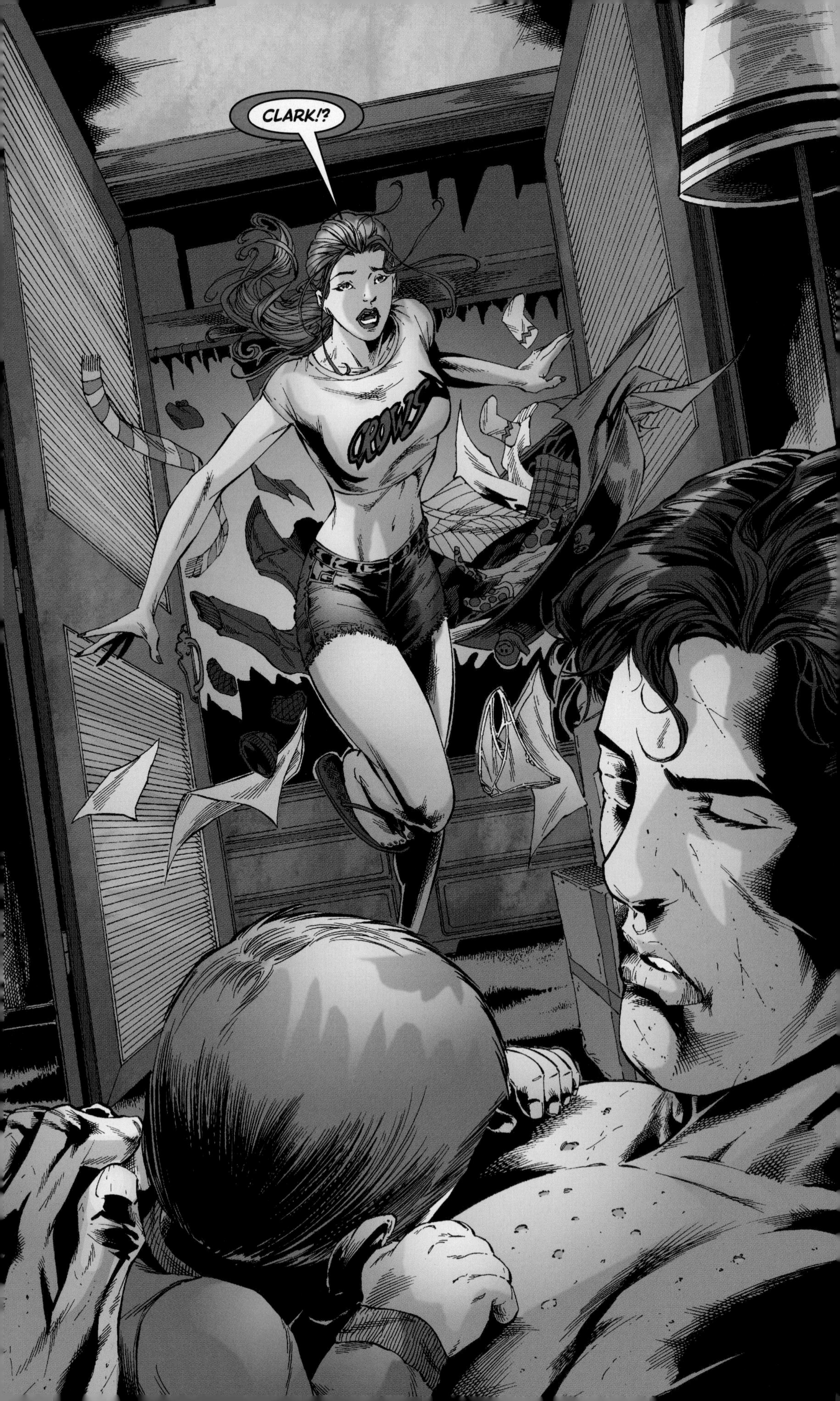
CLARK!?
CROWS

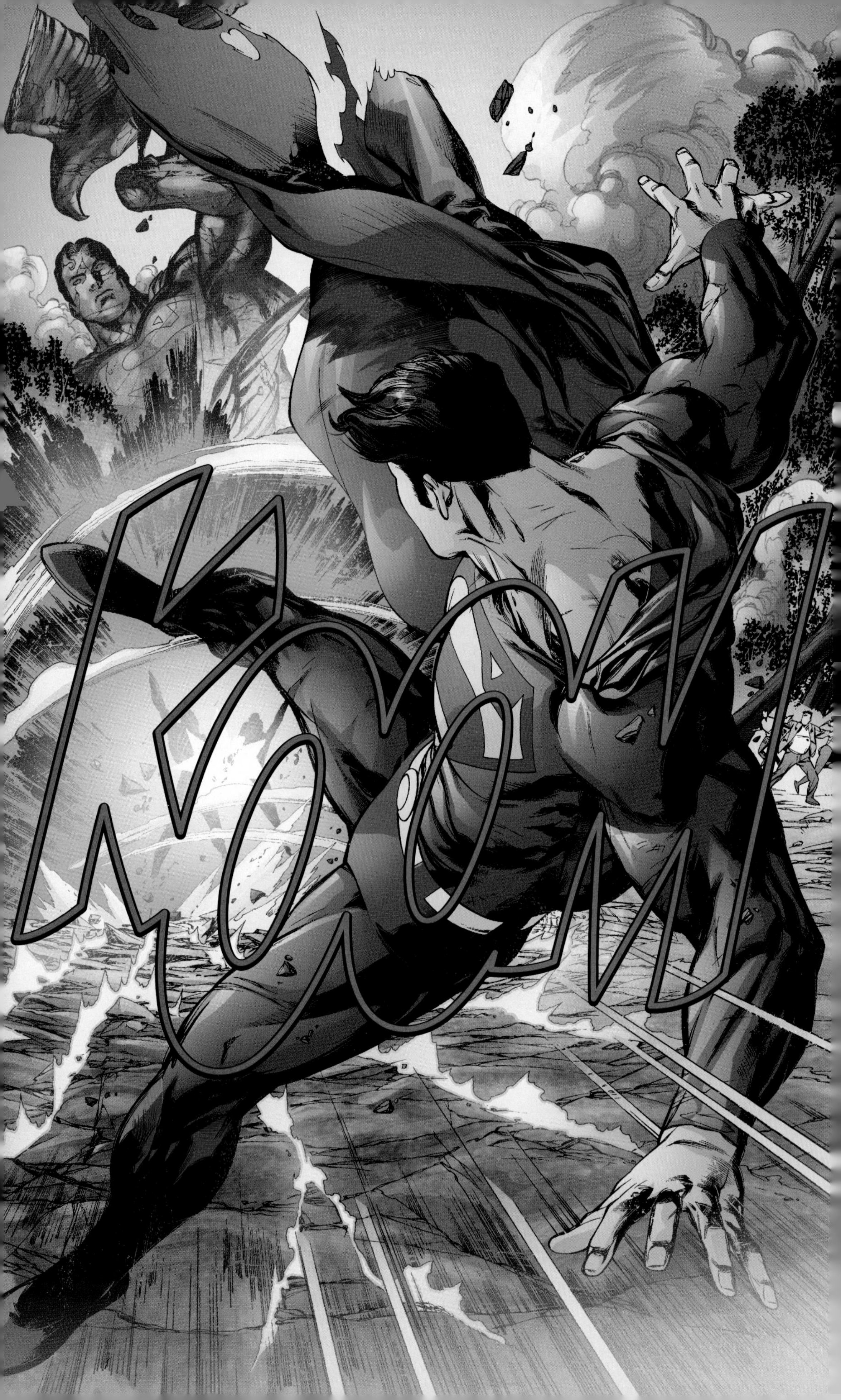

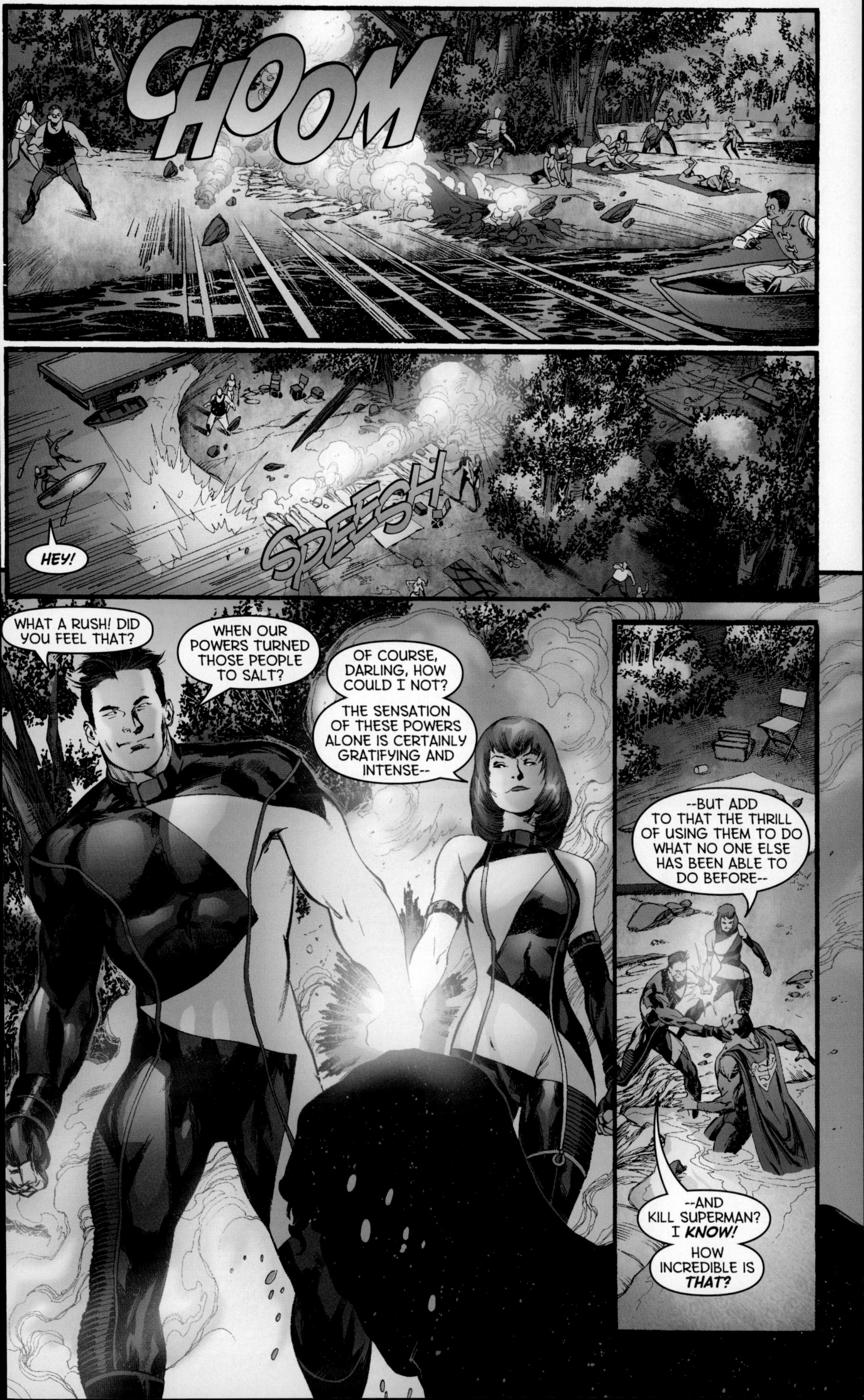
CHOOM
SPEESH!
HEY!
WHAT A RUSH! DID YOU FEEL THAT?
WHEN OUR POWERS TURNED THOSE PEOPLE TO SALT?
OF COURSE, DARLING, HOW COULD I NOT?
THE SENSATION OF THESE POWERS ALONE IS CERTAINLY GRATIFYING AND INTENSE--
--BUT ADD TO THAT THE THRILL OF USING THEM TO DO WHAT NO ONE ELSE HAS BEEN ABLE TO DO BEFORE--
--AND KILL SUPERMAN? I KNOW!
HOW INCREDIBLE IS THAT?

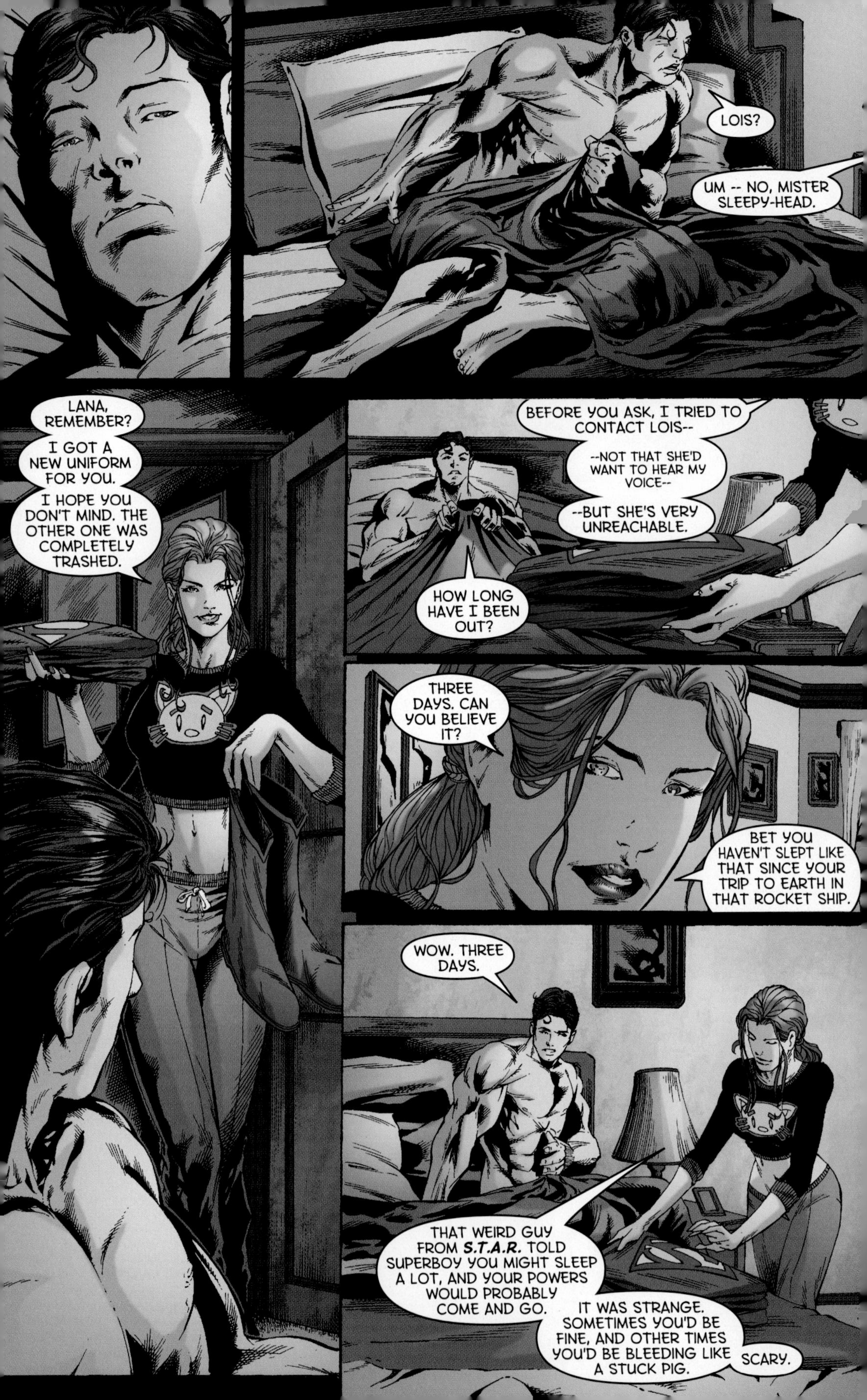
LOIS?
UM -- NO, MISTER SLEEPY-HEAD.
LANA, REMEMBER?
I GOT A NEW UNIFORM FOR YOU.
I HOPE YOU DON'T MIND. THE OTHER ONE WAS COMPLETELY TRASHED.
BEFORE YOU ASK, I TRIED TO CONTACT LOIS--
--NOT THAT SHE'D WANT TO HEAR MY VOICE--
--BUT SHE'S VERY UNREACHABLE.
HOW LONG HAVE I BEEN OUT?
THREE DAYS. CAN YOU BELIEVE IT?
BET YOU HAVEN'T SLEPT LIKE THAT SINCE YOUR TRIP TO EARTH IN THAT ROCKET SHIP.
WOW. THREE DAYS.
THAT WEIRD GUY FROM *S.T.A.R.* TOLD SUPERBOY YOU MIGHT SLEEP A LOT, AND YOUR POWERS WOULD PROBABLY COME AND GO.
IT WAS STRANGE. SOMETIMES YOU'D BE FINE, AND OTHER TIMES YOU'D BE BLEEDING LIKE A STUCK PIG.
SCARY.

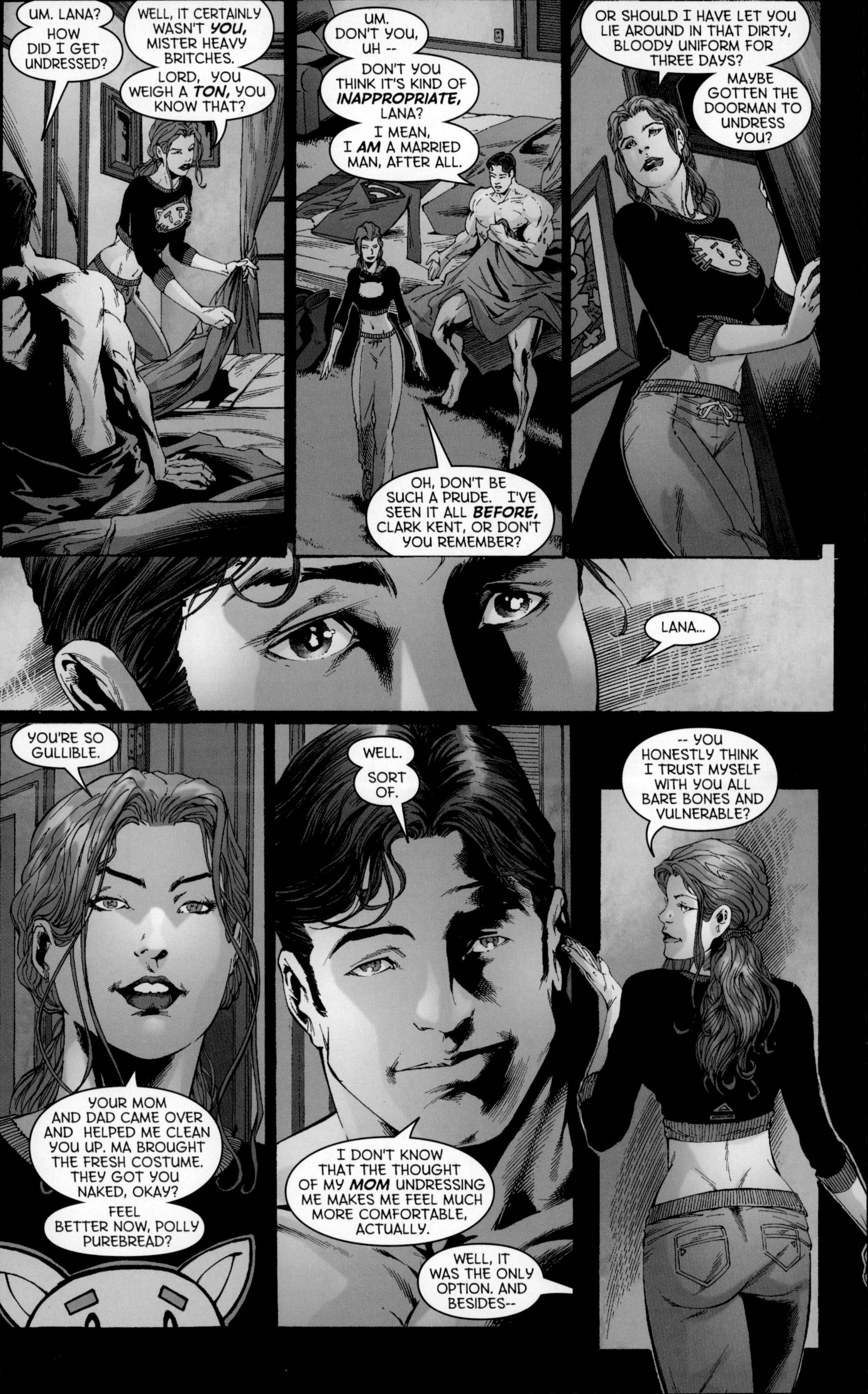
UM. LANA? HOW DID I GET UNDRESSED?
WELL, IT CERTAINLY WASN'T YOU, MISTER HEAVY BRITCHES.
LORD, YOU WEIGH A TON, YOU KNOW THAT?
UM. DON'T YOU, UH --
DON'T YOU THINK IT'S KIND OF INAPPROPRIATE, LANA?
I MEAN, I AM A MARRIED MAN, AFTER ALL.
OH, DON'T BE SUCH A PRUDE. I'VE SEEN IT ALL BEFORE, CLARK KENT, OR DON'T YOU REMEMBER?
OR SHOULD I HAVE LET YOU LIE AROUND IN THAT DIRTY, BLOODY UNIFORM FOR THREE DAYS?
MAYBE GOTTEN THE DOORMAN TO UNDRESS YOU?
LANA...
YOU'RE SO GULLIBLE.
YOUR MOM AND DAD CAME OVER AND HELPED ME CLEAN YOU UP. MA BROUGHT THE FRESH COSTUME. THEY GOT YOU NAKED, OKAY?
FEEL BETTER NOW, POLLY PUREBREAD?
WELL. SORT OF.
I DON'T KNOW THAT THE THOUGHT OF MY MOM UNDRESSING ME MAKES ME FEEL MUCH MORE COMFORTABLE, ACTUALLY.
WELL, IT WAS THE ONLY OPTION. AND BESIDES--
-- YOU HONESTLY THINK I TRUST MYSELF WITH YOU ALL BARE BONES AND VULNERABLE?

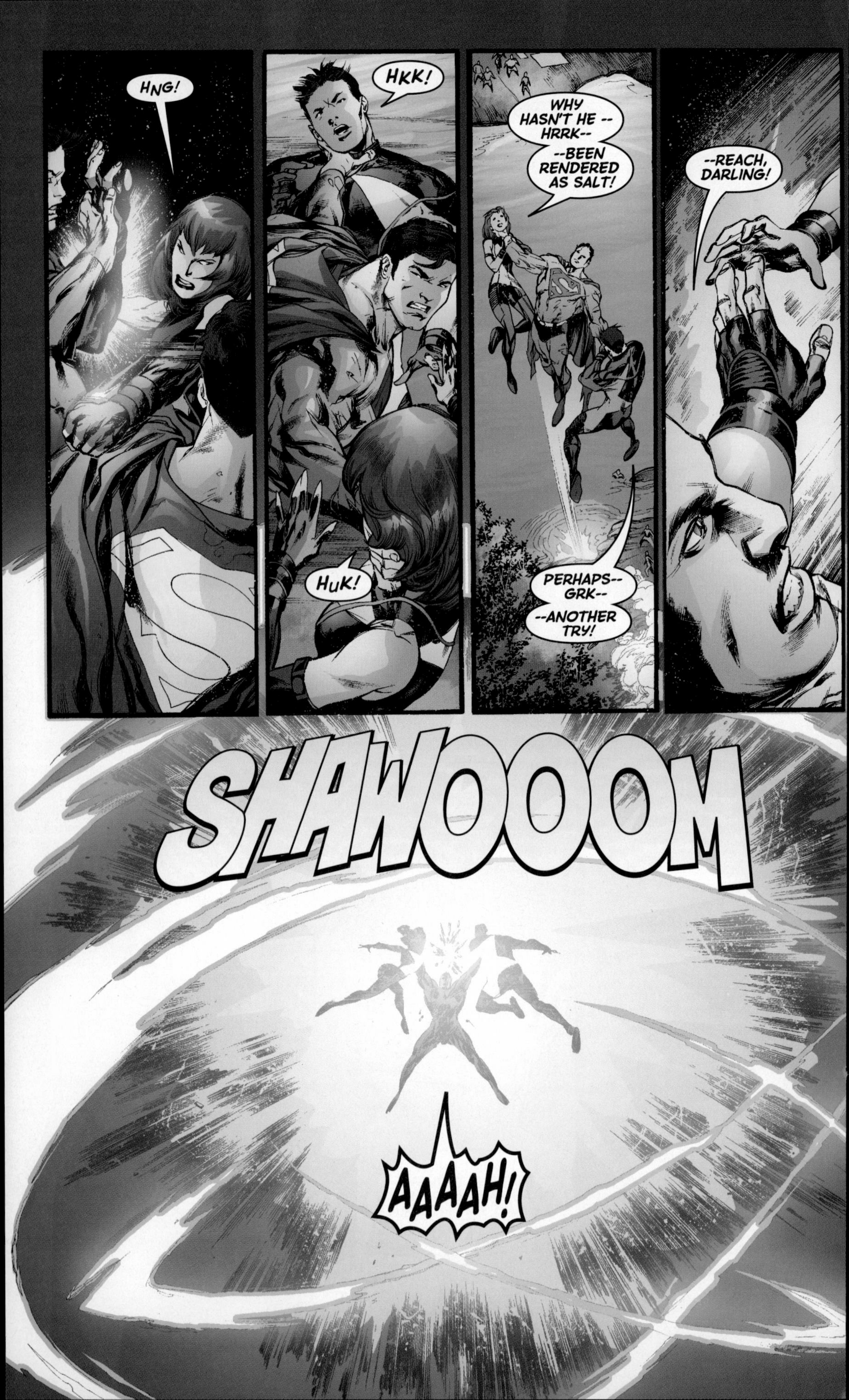
HNG!
HKK!
HUK!
WHY HASN'T HE -- HRRK--
--BEEN RENDERED AS SALT!
PERHAPS-- GRK--
--ANOTHER TRY!
--REACH, DARLING!
SHAWOOOM
AAAAH!

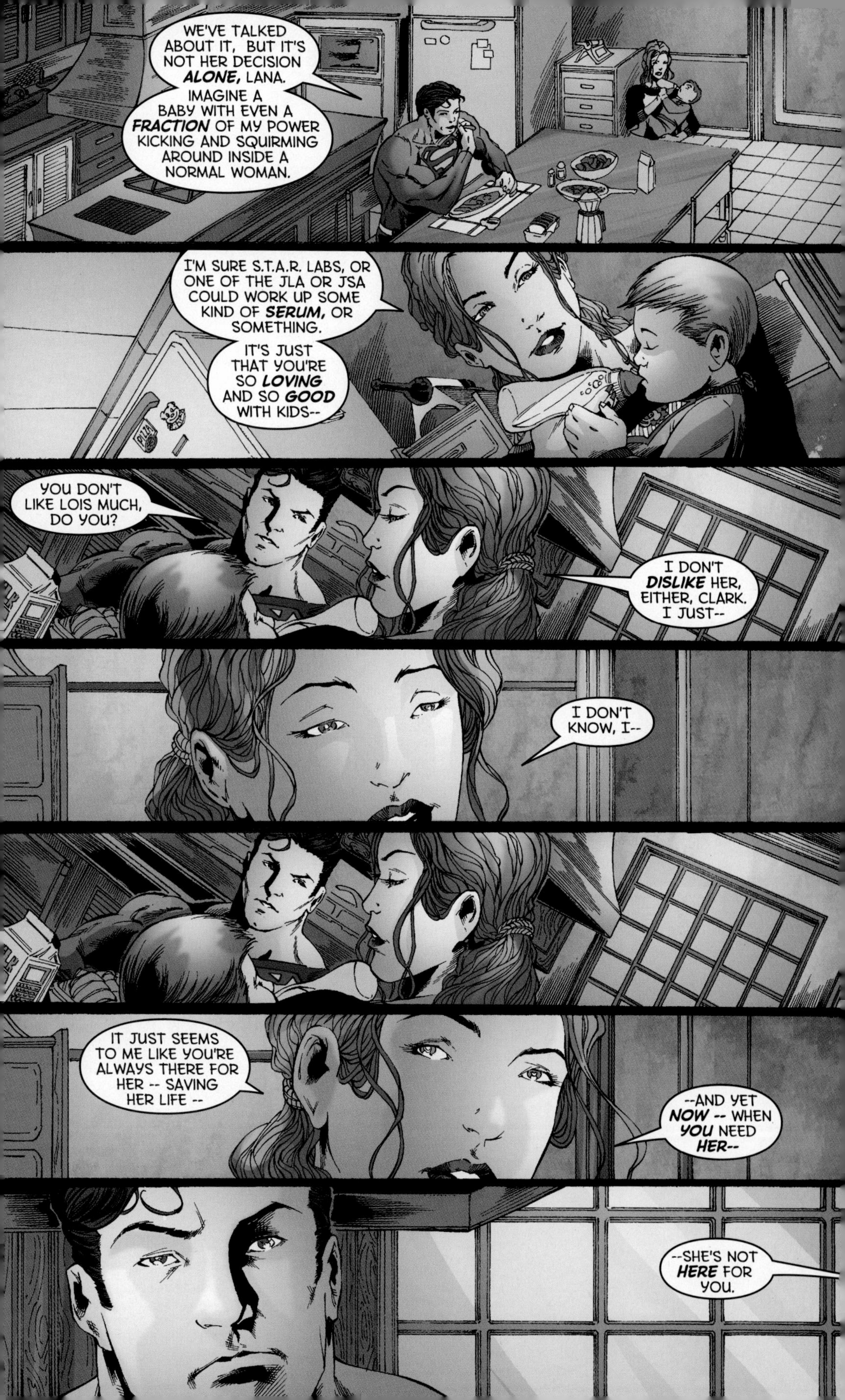
WE'VE TALKED ABOUT IT, BUT IT'S NOT HER DECISION ALONE, LANA.
IMAGINE A BABY WITH EVEN A FRACTION OF MY POWER KICKING AND SQUIRMING AROUND INSIDE A NORMAL WOMAN.
I'M SURE S.T.A.R. LABS, OR ONE OF THE JLA OR JSA COULD WORK UP SOME KIND OF SERUM, OR SOMETHING.
IT'S JUST THAT YOU'RE SO LOVING AND SO GOOD WITH KIDS--
PIZZA
YOU DON'T LIKE LOIS MUCH, DO YOU?
I DON'T DISLIKE HER, EITHER, CLARK. I JUST--
I DON'T KNOW, I--
IT JUST SEEMS TO ME LIKE YOU'RE ALWAYS THERE FOR HER -- SAVING HER LIFE --
--AND YET NOW -- WHEN YOU NEED HER--
--SHE'S NOT HERE FOR YOU.

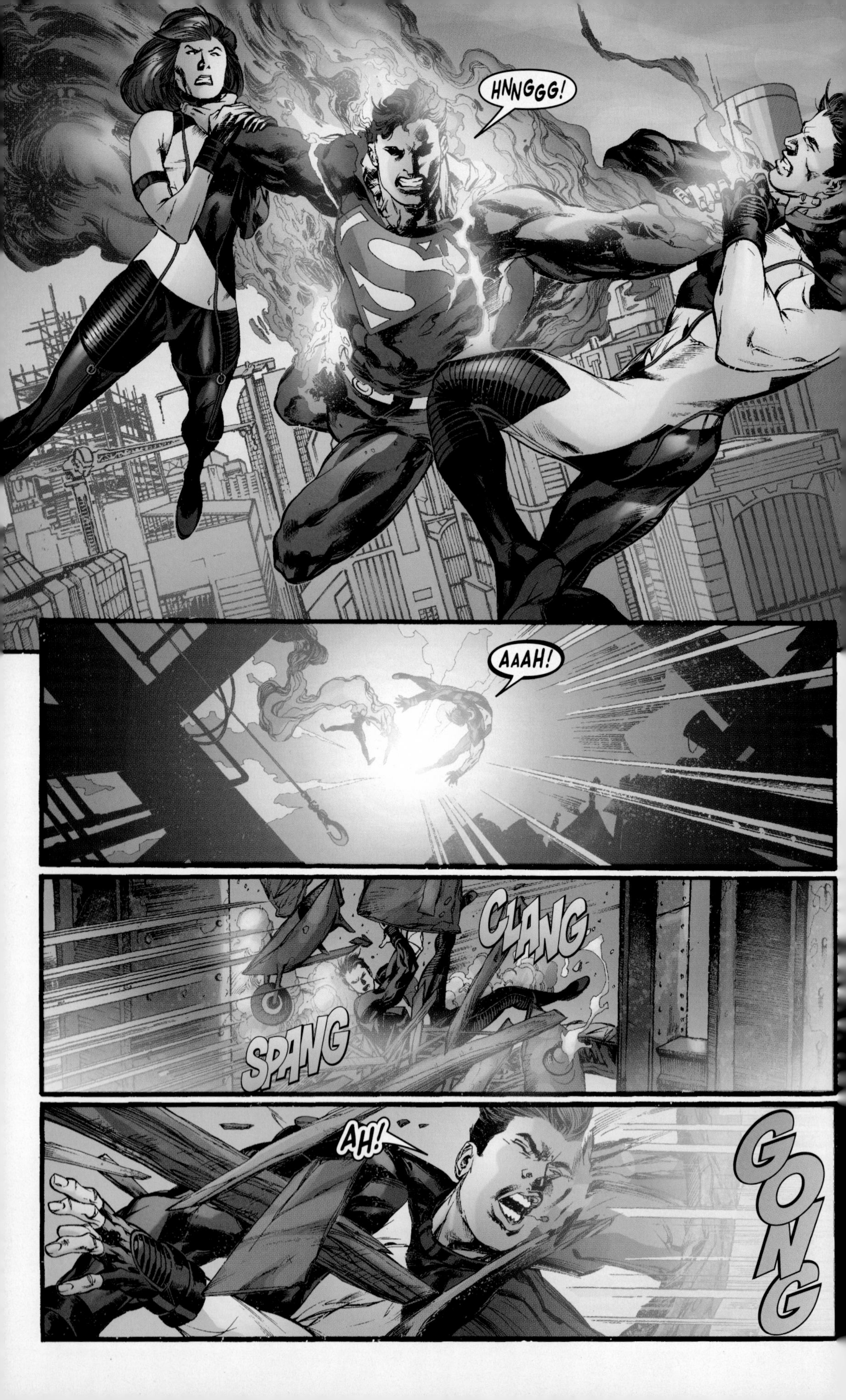
HNNGGG!
AAAH!
CLANG
SPANG
AH!
GONG

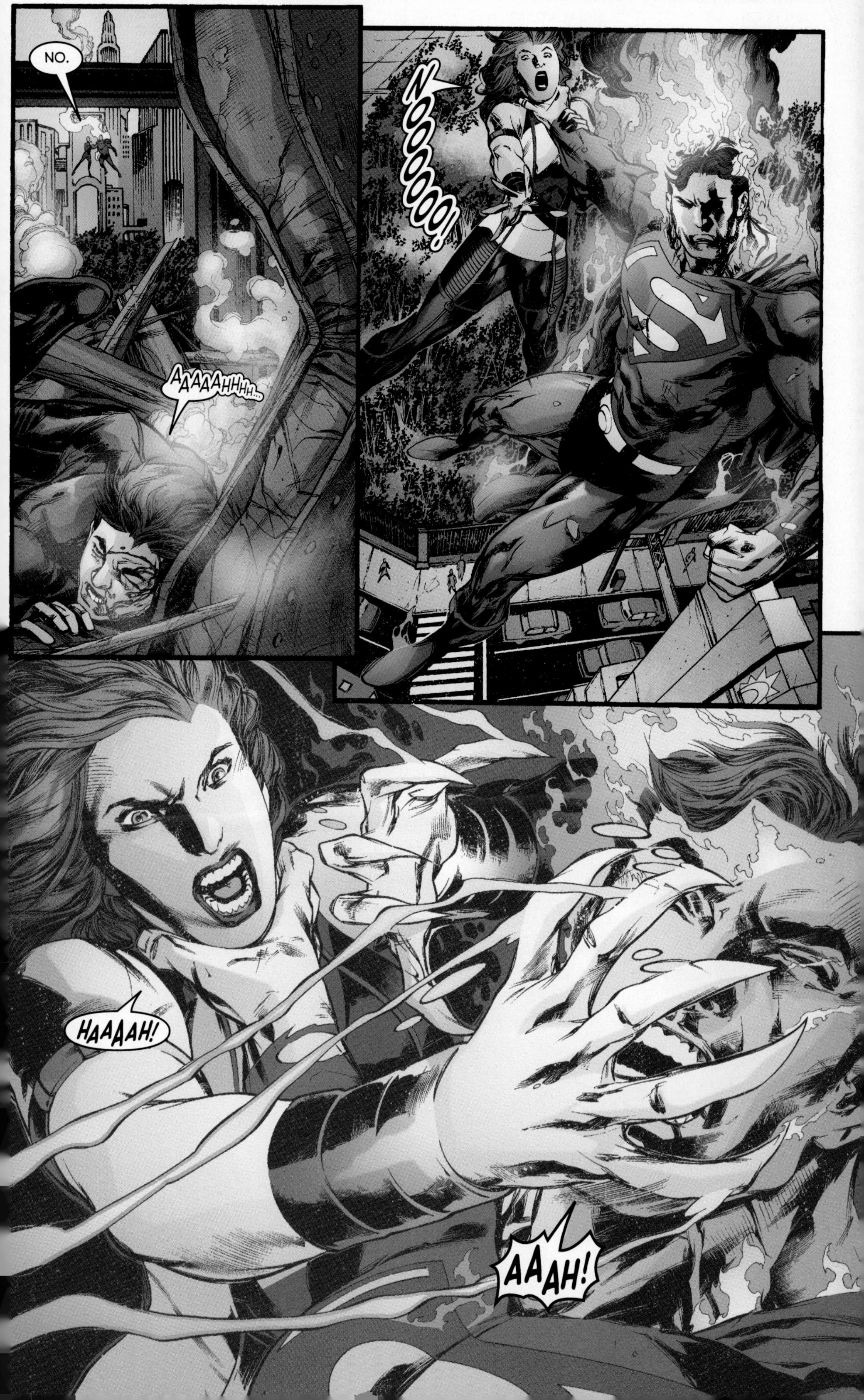
NO.
AAAAAHHHH...
NOOOOOOO!
HAAAAH!
AAAH!

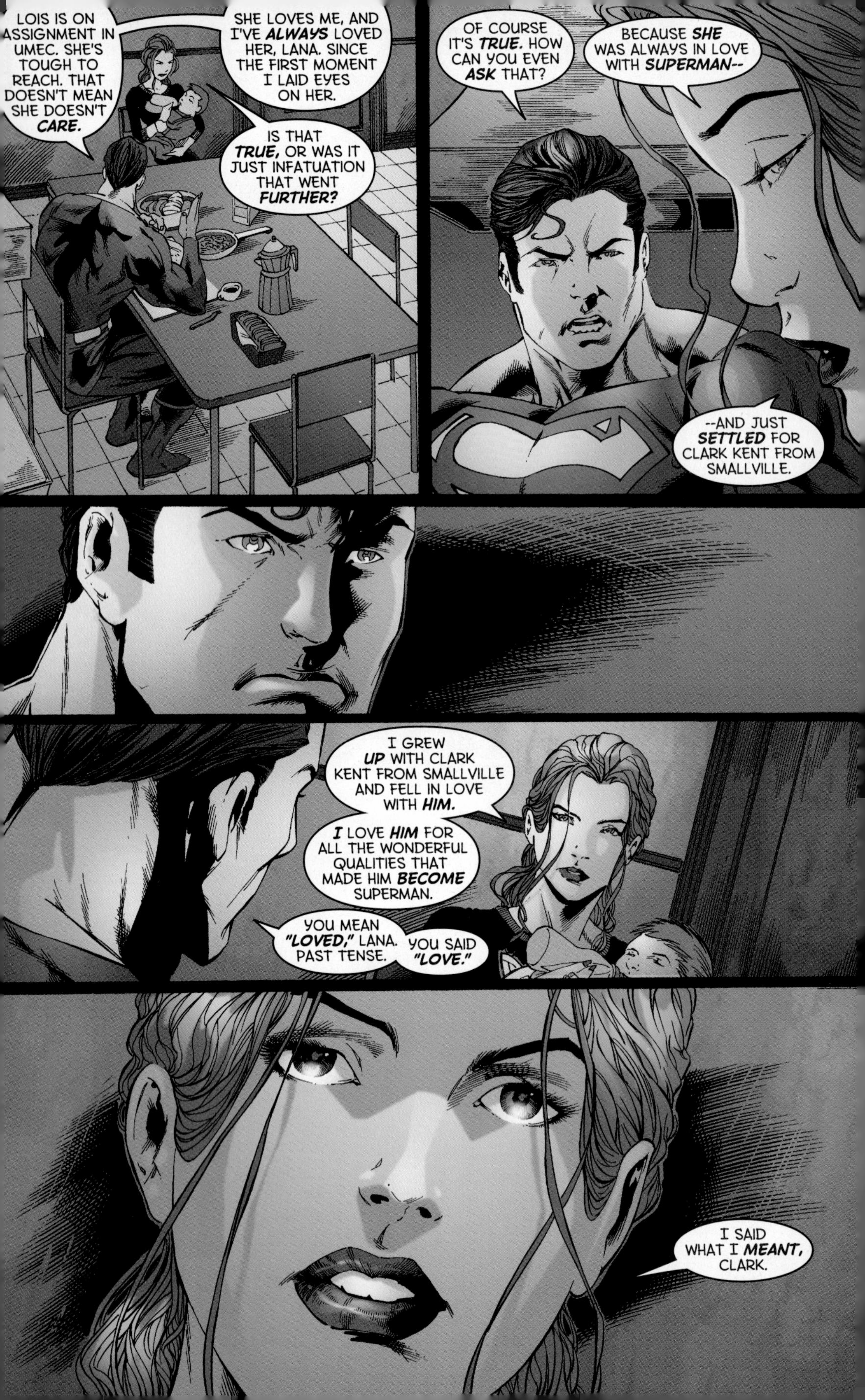
LOIS IS ON ASSIGNMENT IN UMEC. SHE'S TOUGH TO REACH. THAT DOESN'T MEAN SHE DOESN'T **CARE.**
SHE LOVES ME, AND I'VE **ALWAYS** LOVED HER, LANA. SINCE THE FIRST MOMENT I LAID EYES ON HER.
IS THAT **TRUE,** OR WAS IT JUST INFATUATION THAT WENT **FURTHER?**
OF COURSE IT'S **TRUE.** HOW CAN YOU EVEN **ASK** THAT?
BECAUSE **SHE** WAS ALWAYS IN LOVE WITH **SUPERMAN--**
--AND JUST **SETTLED** FOR CLARK KENT FROM SMALLVILLE.
I GREW **UP** WITH CLARK KENT FROM SMALLVILLE AND FELL IN LOVE WITH **HIM.**
I LOVE **HIM** FOR ALL THE WONDERFUL QUALITIES THAT MADE HIM **BECOME** SUPERMAN.
YOU MEAN **"LOVED,"** LANA. PAST TENSE.
YOU SAID **"LOVE."**
I SAID WHAT I **MEANT,** CLARK.

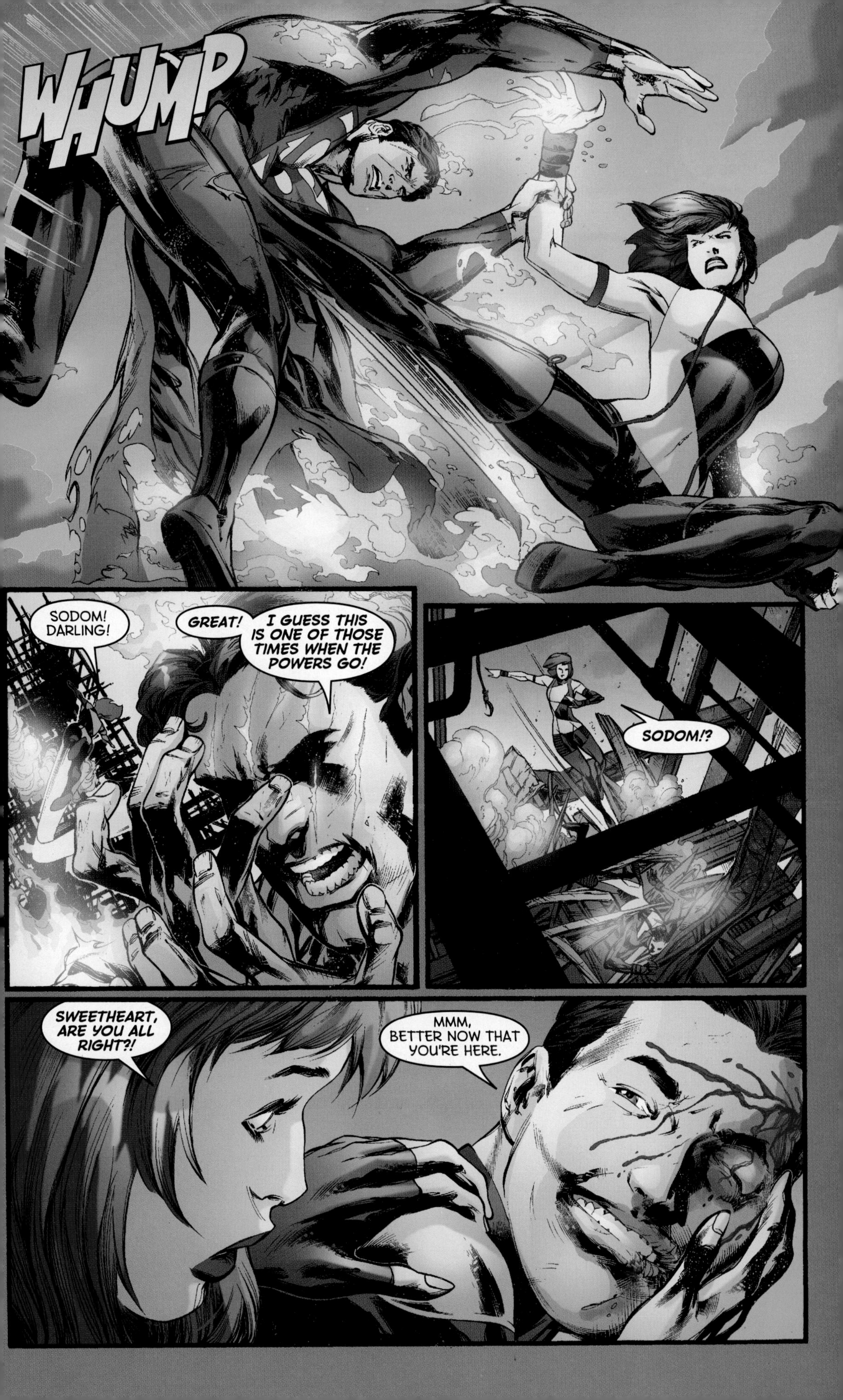
WHUMP
SODOM! DARLING!
GREAT!
I GUESS THIS IS ONE OF THOSE TIMES WHEN THE POWERS GO!
SODOM!?
SWEETHEART, ARE YOU ALL RIGHT?!
MMM, BETTER NOW THAT YOU'RE HERE.

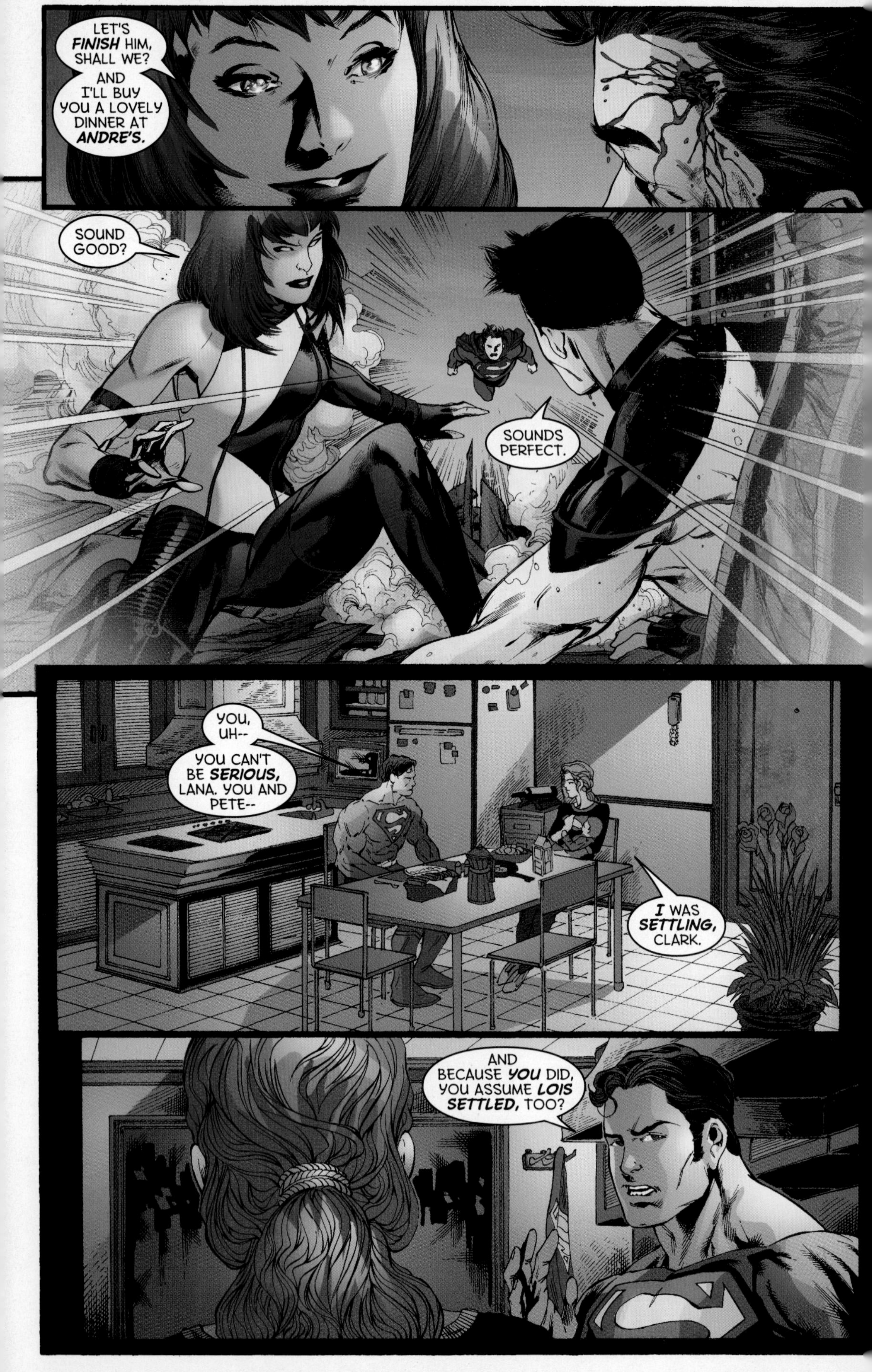
LET'S FINISH HIM, SHALL WE?
AND I'LL BUY YOU A LOVELY DINNER AT ANDRE'S.
SOUND GOOD?
SOUNDS PERFECT.
YOU, UH--
YOU CAN'T BE SERIOUS, LANA. YOU AND PETE--
I WAS SETTLING, CLARK.
AND BECAUSE YOU DID, YOU ASSUME LOIS SETTLED, TOO?

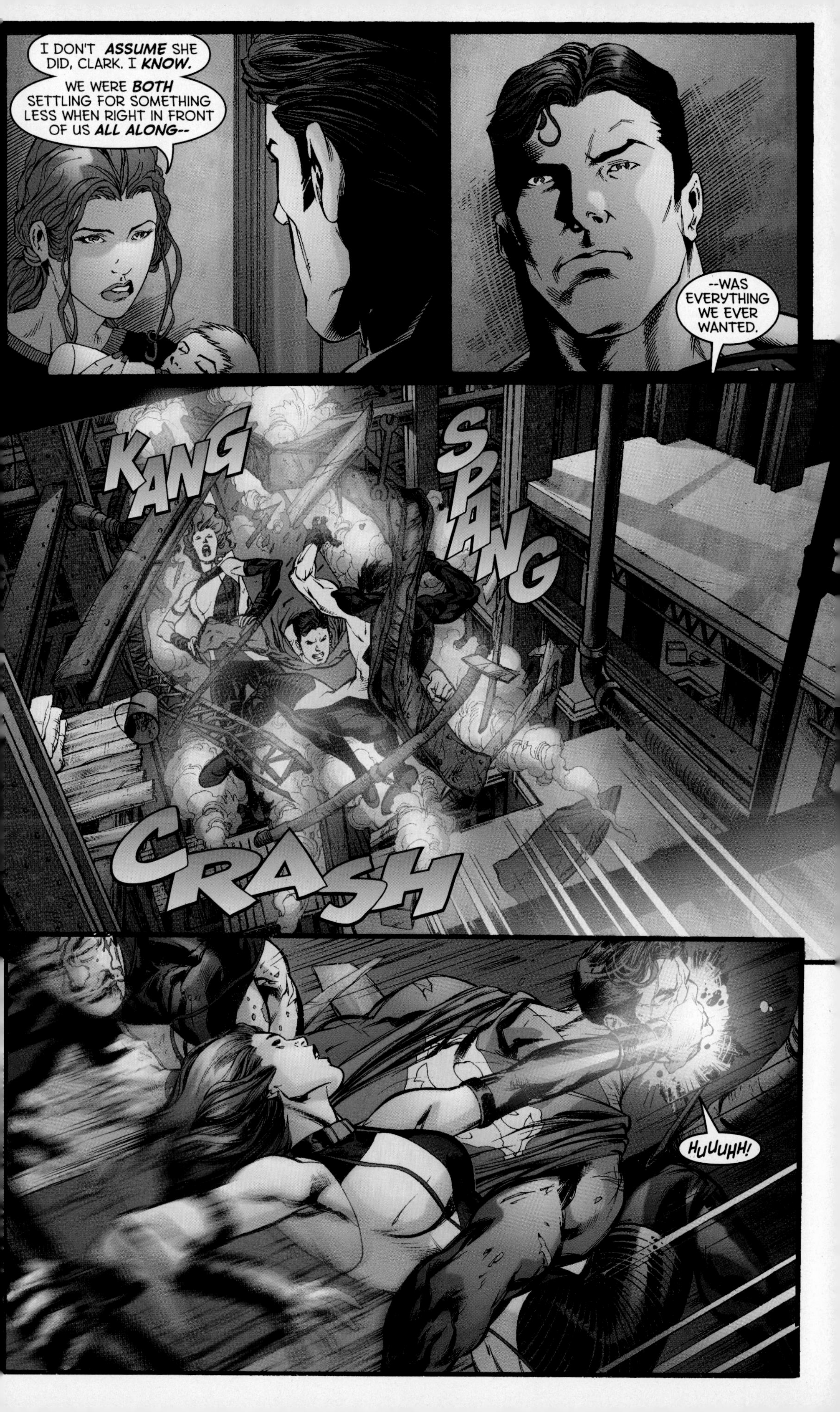
I DON'T ASSUME SHE DID, CLARK. I KNOW.
WE WERE BOTH SETTLING FOR SOMETHING LESS WHEN RIGHT IN FRONT OF US ALL ALONG--
--WAS EVERYTHING WE EVER WANTED.
KANG
SPANG
CRASH
HUUUHH!

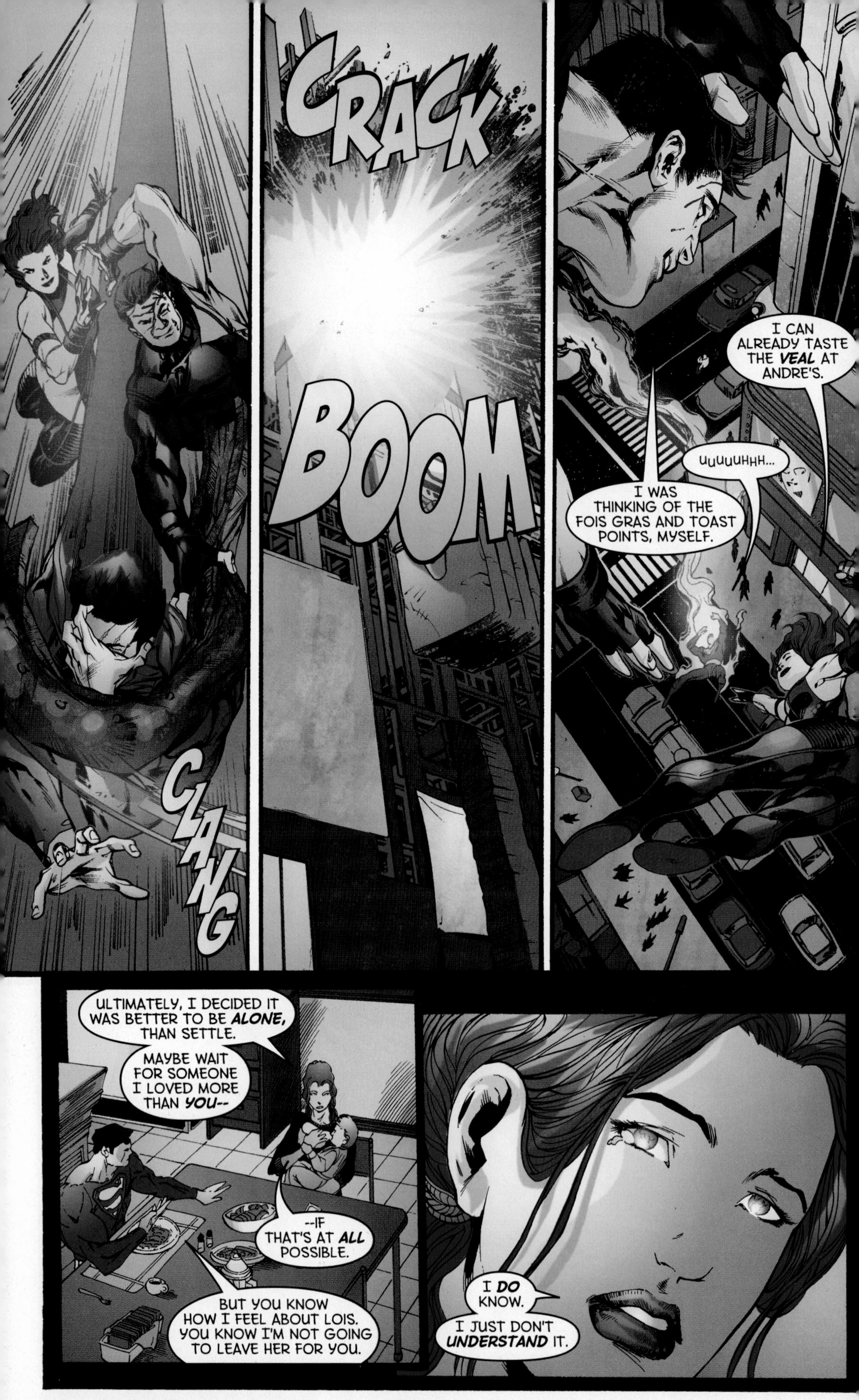
CLANG
CRACK
BOOM
I CAN ALREADY TASTE THE VEAL AT ANDRE'S.
UUUUUHHH...
I WAS THINKING OF THE FOIS GRAS AND TOAST POINTS, MYSELF.
ULTIMATELY, I DECIDED IT WAS BETTER TO BE ALONE, THAN SETTLE.
MAYBE WAIT FOR SOMEONE I LOVED MORE THAN YOU--
--IF THAT'S AT ALL POSSIBLE.
BUT YOU KNOW HOW I FEEL ABOUT LOIS. YOU KNOW I'M NOT GOING TO LEAVE HER FOR YOU.
I DO KNOW.
I JUST DON'T UNDERSTAND IT.

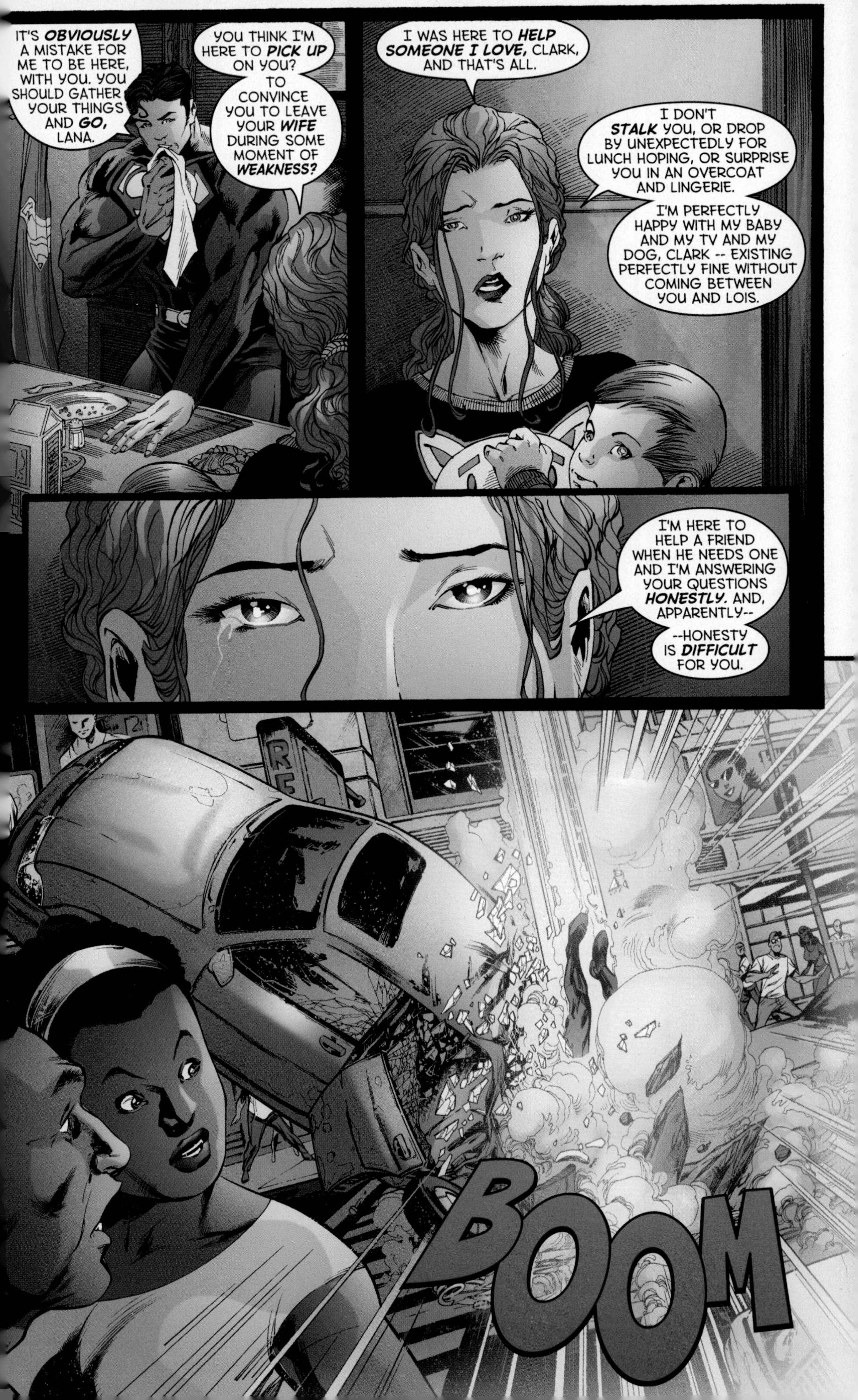
IT'S OBVIOUSLY A MISTAKE FOR ME TO BE HERE, WITH YOU. YOU SHOULD GATHER YOUR THINGS AND GO, LANA.
YOU THINK I'M HERE TO PICK UP ON YOU?
TO CONVINCE YOU TO LEAVE YOUR WIFE DURING SOME MOMENT OF WEAKNESS?
I WAS HERE TO HELP SOMEONE I LOVE, CLARK, AND THAT'S ALL.
I DON'T STALK YOU, OR DROP BY UNEXPECTEDLY FOR LUNCH HOPING, OR SURPRISE YOU IN AN OVERCOAT AND LINGERIE.
I'M PERFECTLY HAPPY WITH MY BABY AND MY TV AND MY DOG, CLARK -- EXISTING PERFECTLY FINE WITHOUT COMING BETWEEN YOU AND LOIS.
I'M HERE TO HELP A FRIEND WHEN HE NEEDS ONE AND I'M ANSWERING YOUR QUESTIONS HONESTLY. AND, APPARENTLY--
--HONESTY IS DIFFICULT FOR YOU.
BOOM

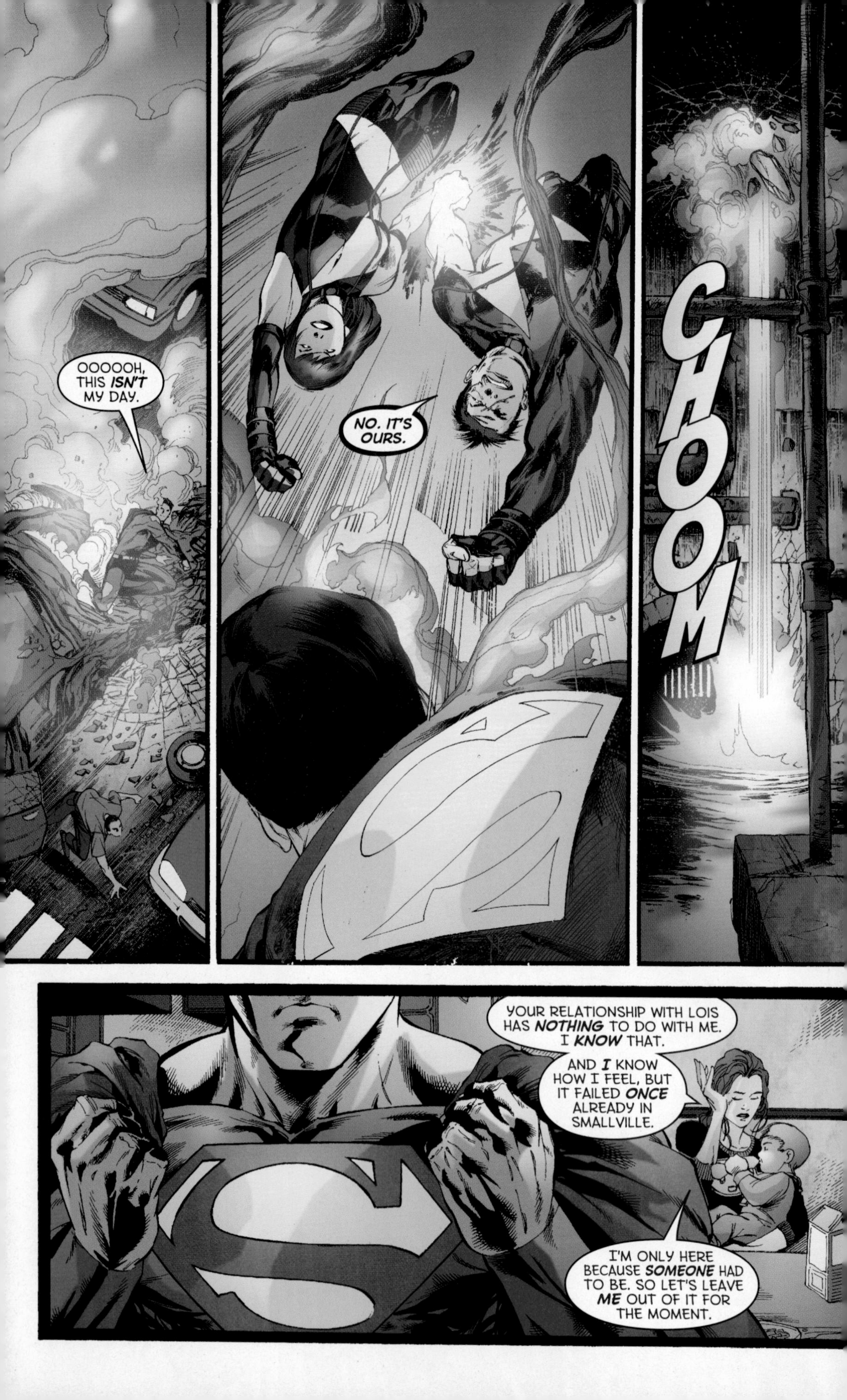
OOOOOH, THIS *ISN'T* MY DAY.
NO. IT'S OURS.
CHOOM
YOUR RELATIONSHIP WITH LOIS HAS *NOTHING* TO DO WITH ME. I *KNOW* THAT.
AND *I* KNOW HOW I FEEL, BUT IT FAILED *ONCE* ALREADY IN SMALLVILLE.
I'M ONLY HERE BECAUSE *SOMEONE* HAD TO BE. SO LET'S LEAVE *ME* OUT OF IT FOR THE MOMENT.

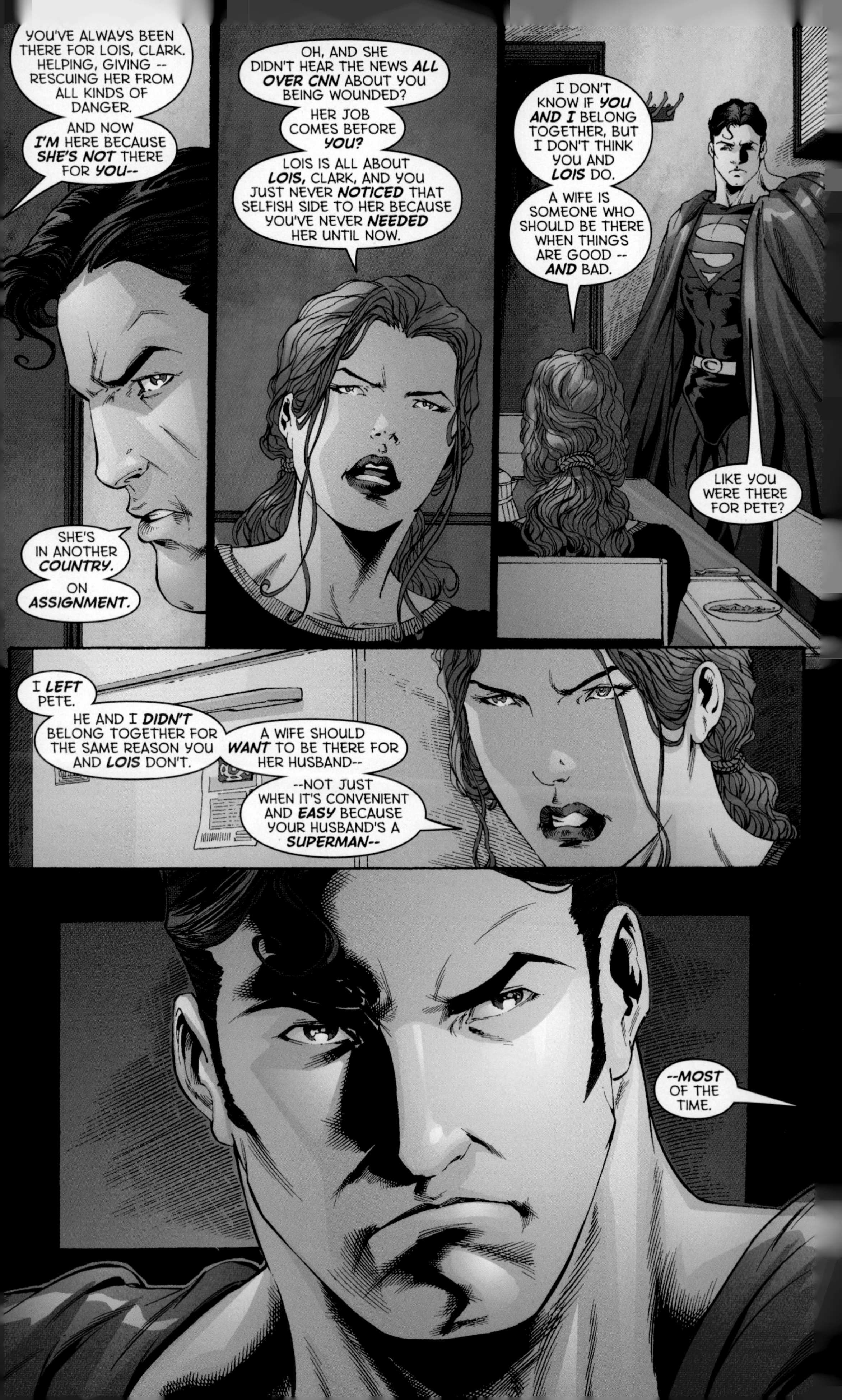

YOU'VE ALWAYS BEEN THERE FOR LOIS, CLARK. HELPING, GIVING -- RESCUING HER FROM ALL KINDS OF DANGER.
AND NOW I'M HERE BECAUSE SHE'S NOT THERE FOR YOU--
SHE'S IN ANOTHER COUNTRY.
ON ASSIGNMENT.
OH, AND SHE DIDN'T HEAR THE NEWS ALL OVER CNN ABOUT YOU BEING WOUNDED?
HER JOB COMES BEFORE YOU?
LOIS IS ALL ABOUT LOIS, CLARK, AND YOU JUST NEVER NOTICED THAT SELFISH SIDE TO HER BECAUSE YOU'VE NEVER NEEDED HER UNTIL NOW.
I DON'T KNOW IF YOU AND I BELONG TOGETHER, BUT I DON'T THINK YOU AND LOIS DO.
A WIFE IS SOMEONE WHO SHOULD BE THERE WHEN THINGS ARE GOOD -- AND BAD.
LIKE YOU WERE THERE FOR PETE?
I LEFT PETE.
HE AND I DIDN'T BELONG TOGETHER FOR THE SAME REASON YOU AND LOIS DON'T.
A WIFE SHOULD WANT TO BE THERE FOR HER HUSBAND--
--NOT JUST WHEN IT'S CONVENIENT AND EASY BECAUSE YOUR HUSBAND'S A SUPERMAN--
--MOST OF THE TIME.

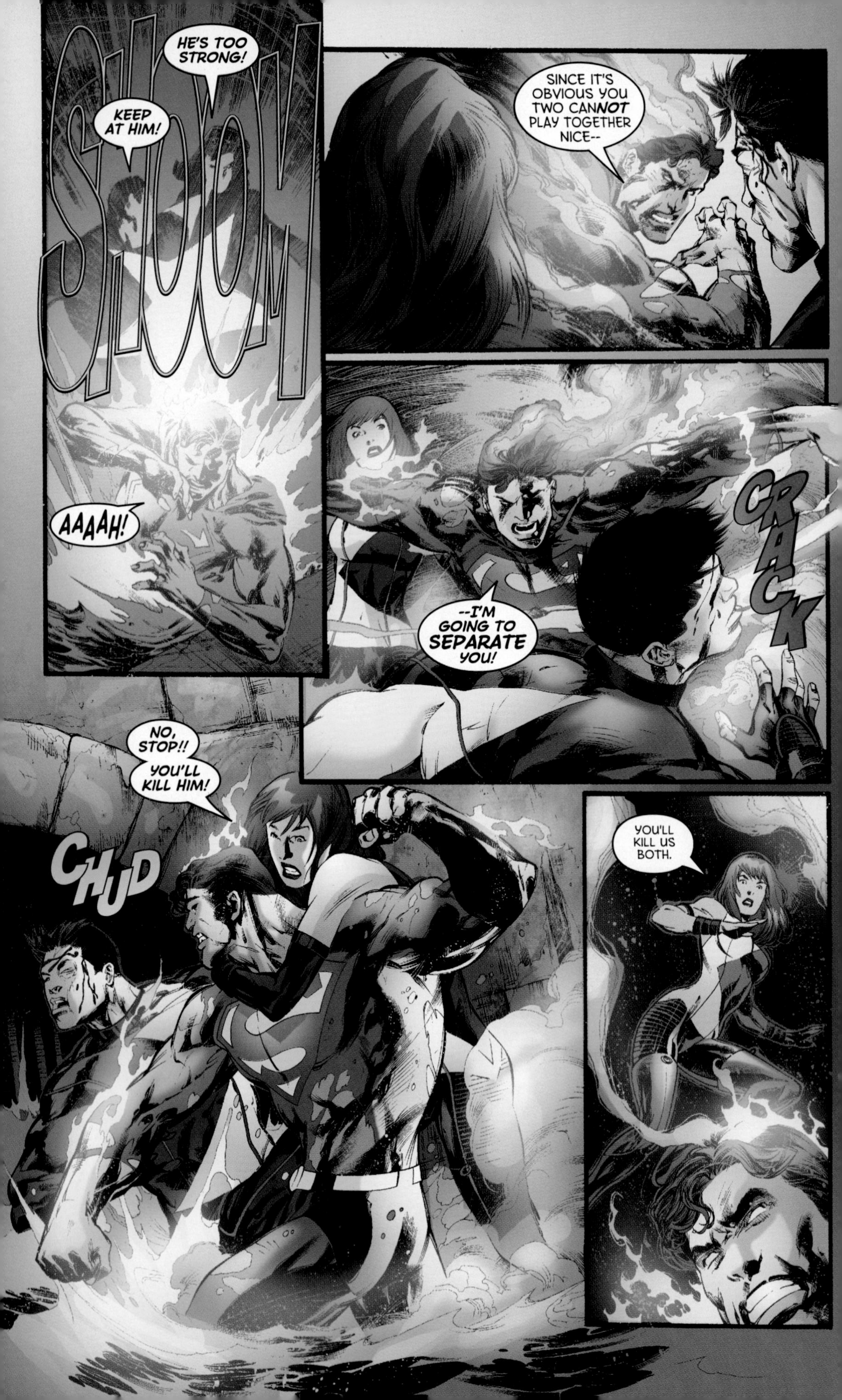
SHOOOM
HE'S TOO STRONG!
KEEP AT HIM!
AAAAH!
SINCE IT'S OBVIOUS YOU TWO CAN*NOT* PLAY TOGETHER NICE--
--I'M GOING TO **SEPARATE** YOU!
CRACK
NO, STOP!!
YOU'LL KILL HIM!
CHUD
YOU'LL KILL US BOTH.

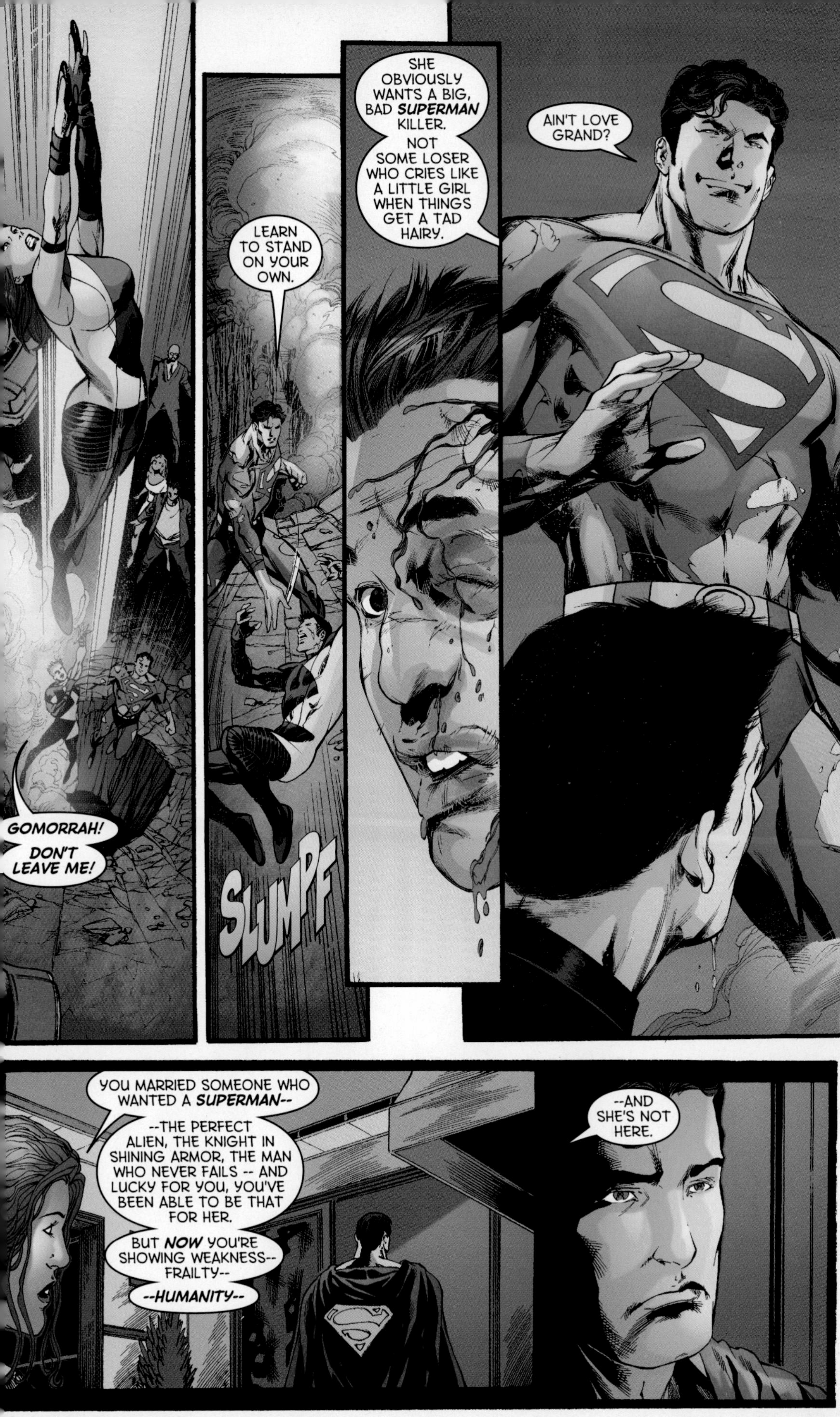
GOMORRAH!
DON'T LEAVE ME!
LEARN TO STAND ON YOUR OWN.
SLUMPF
SHE OBVIOUSLY WANTS A BIG, BAD SUPERMAN KILLER.
NOT SOME LOSER WHO CRIES LIKE A LITTLE GIRL WHEN THINGS GET A TAD HAIRY.
AIN'T LOVE GRAND?
YOU MARRIED SOMEONE WHO WANTED A SUPERMAN--
--THE PERFECT ALIEN, THE KNIGHT IN SHINING ARMOR, THE MAN WHO NEVER FAILS -- AND LUCKY FOR YOU, YOU'VE BEEN ABLE TO BE THAT FOR HER.
BUT NOW YOU'RE SHOWING WEAKNESS-- FRAILTY--
--HUMANITY--
--AND SHE'S NOT HERE.

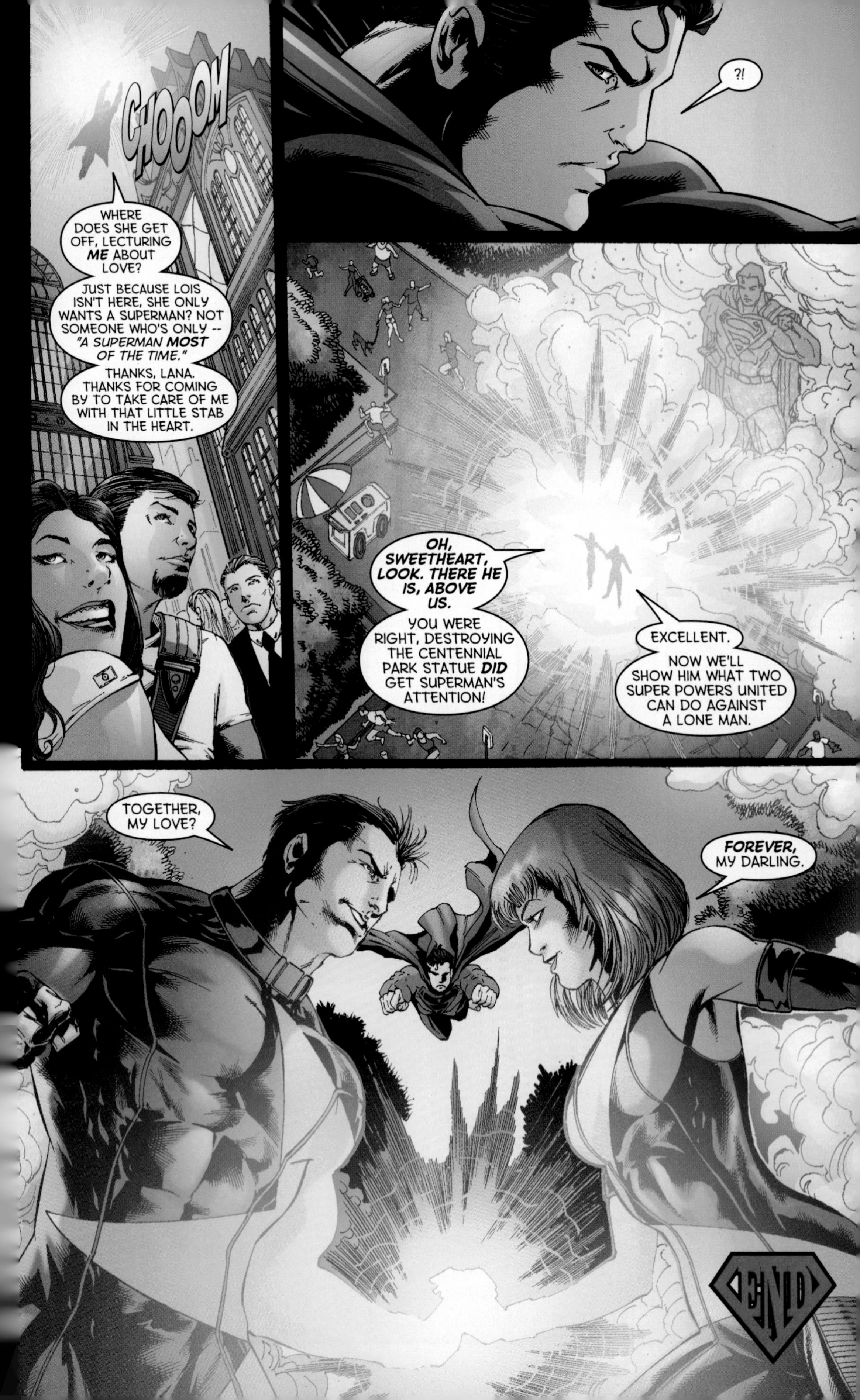
CHOOOM
?!
WHERE DOES SHE GET OFF, LECTURING ME ABOUT LOVE?
JUST BECAUSE LOIS ISN'T HERE, SHE ONLY WANTS A SUPERMAN? NOT SOMEONE WHO'S ONLY -- "A SUPERMAN MOST OF THE TIME."
THANKS, LANA. THANKS FOR COMING BY TO TAKE CARE OF ME WITH THAT LITTLE STAB IN THE HEART.
OH, SWEETHEART, LOOK. THERE HE IS, ABOVE US.
YOU WERE RIGHT, DESTROYING THE CENTENNIAL PARK STATUE DID GET SUPERMAN'S ATTENTION!
EXCELLENT.
NOW WE'LL SHOW HIM WHAT TWO SUPER POWERS UNITED CAN DO AGAINST A LONE MAN.
TOGETHER, MY LOVE?
FOREVER, MY DARLING.
END

COVER GALLERY

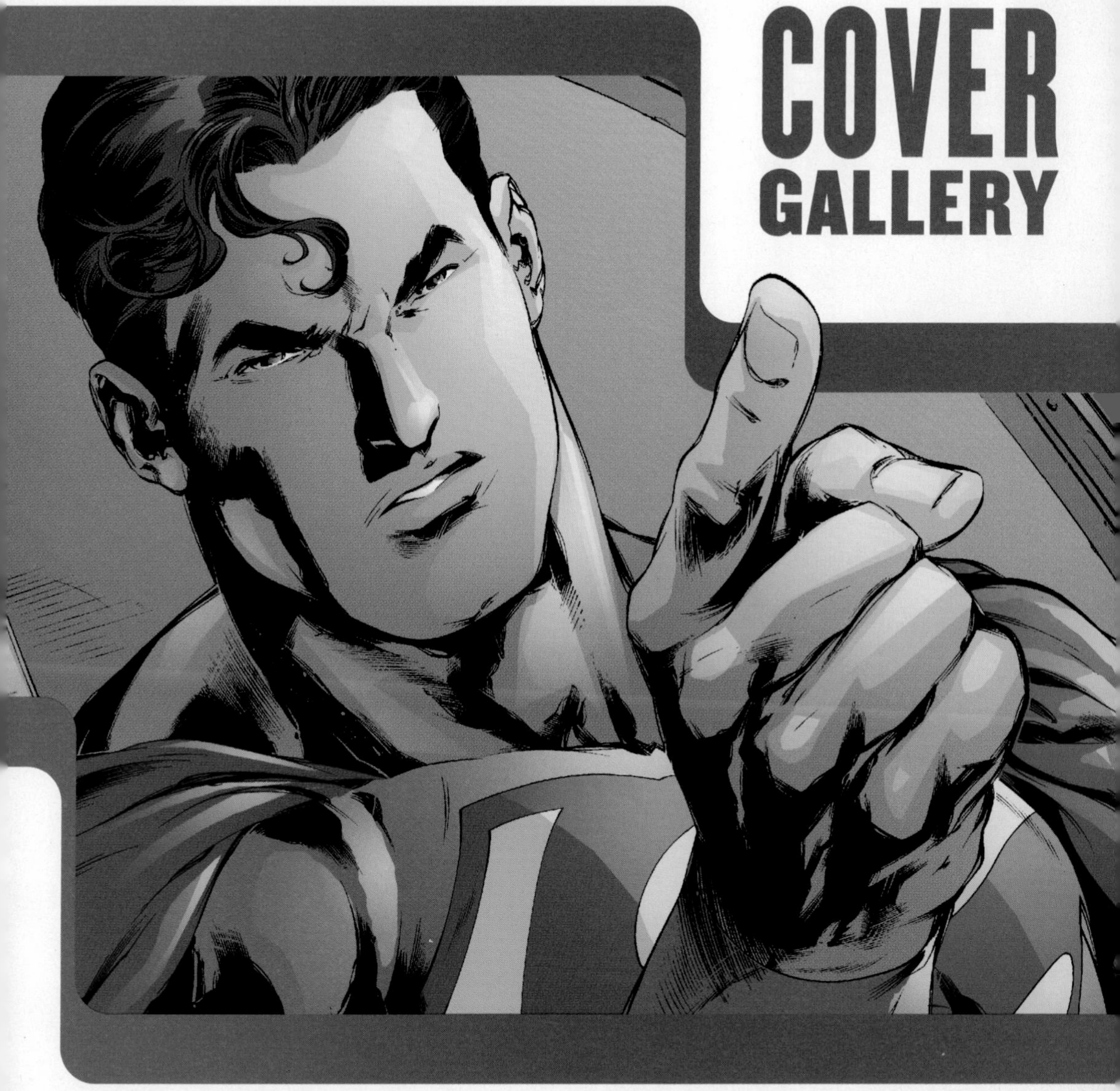

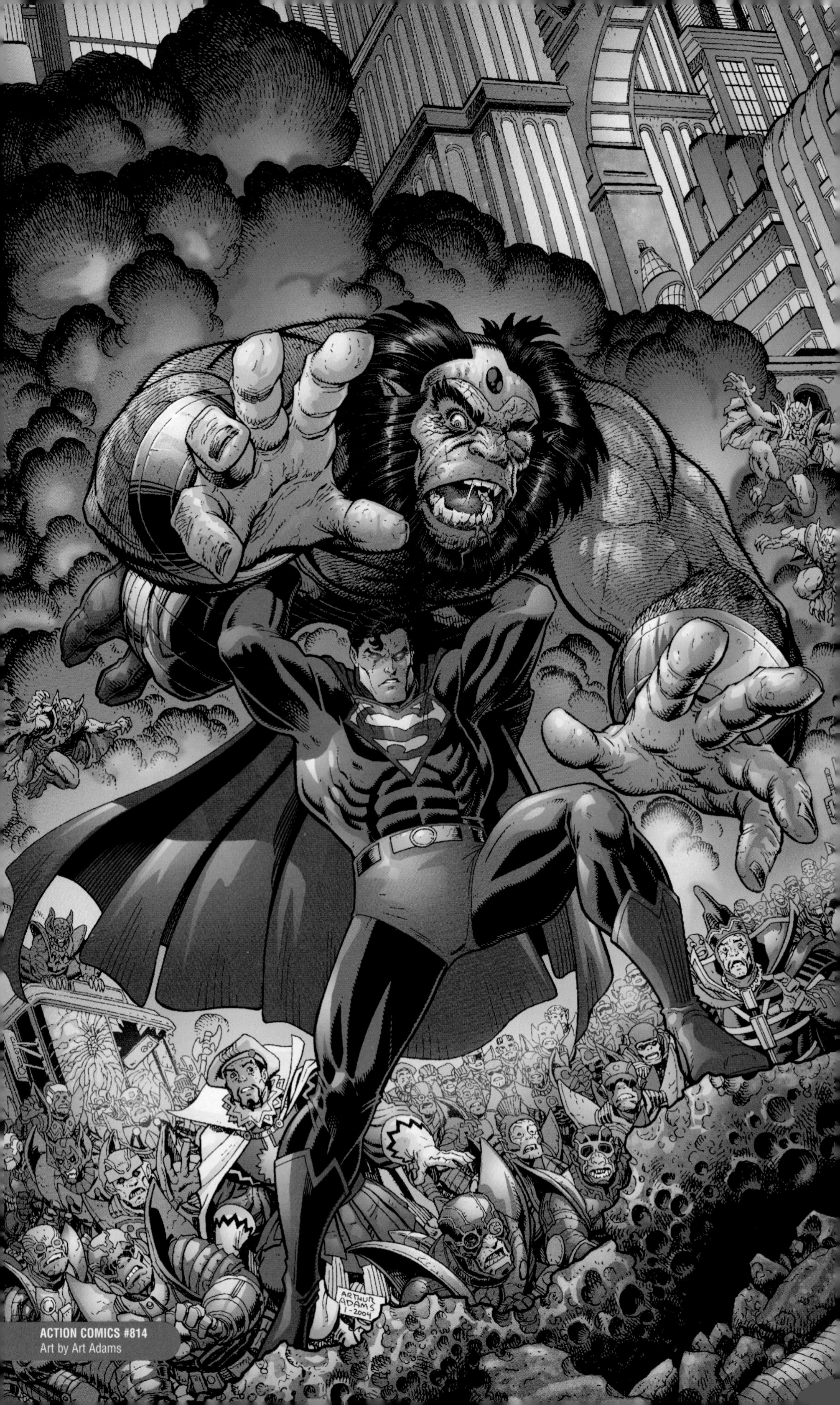
ARTHUR
ADAMS
1-2004

ACTION COMICS #814
Art by Art Adams

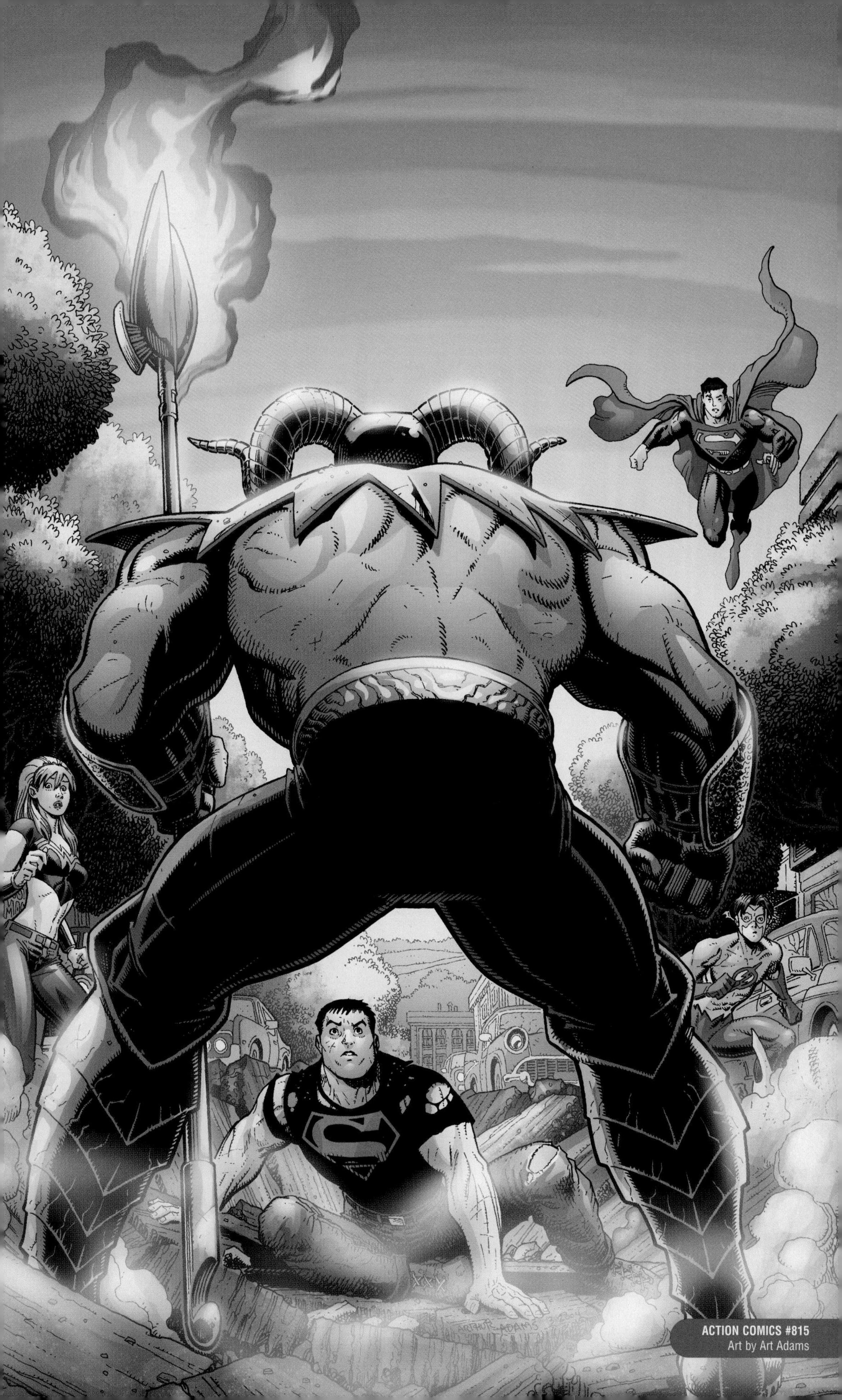

ACTION COMICS #815
Art by Art Adams

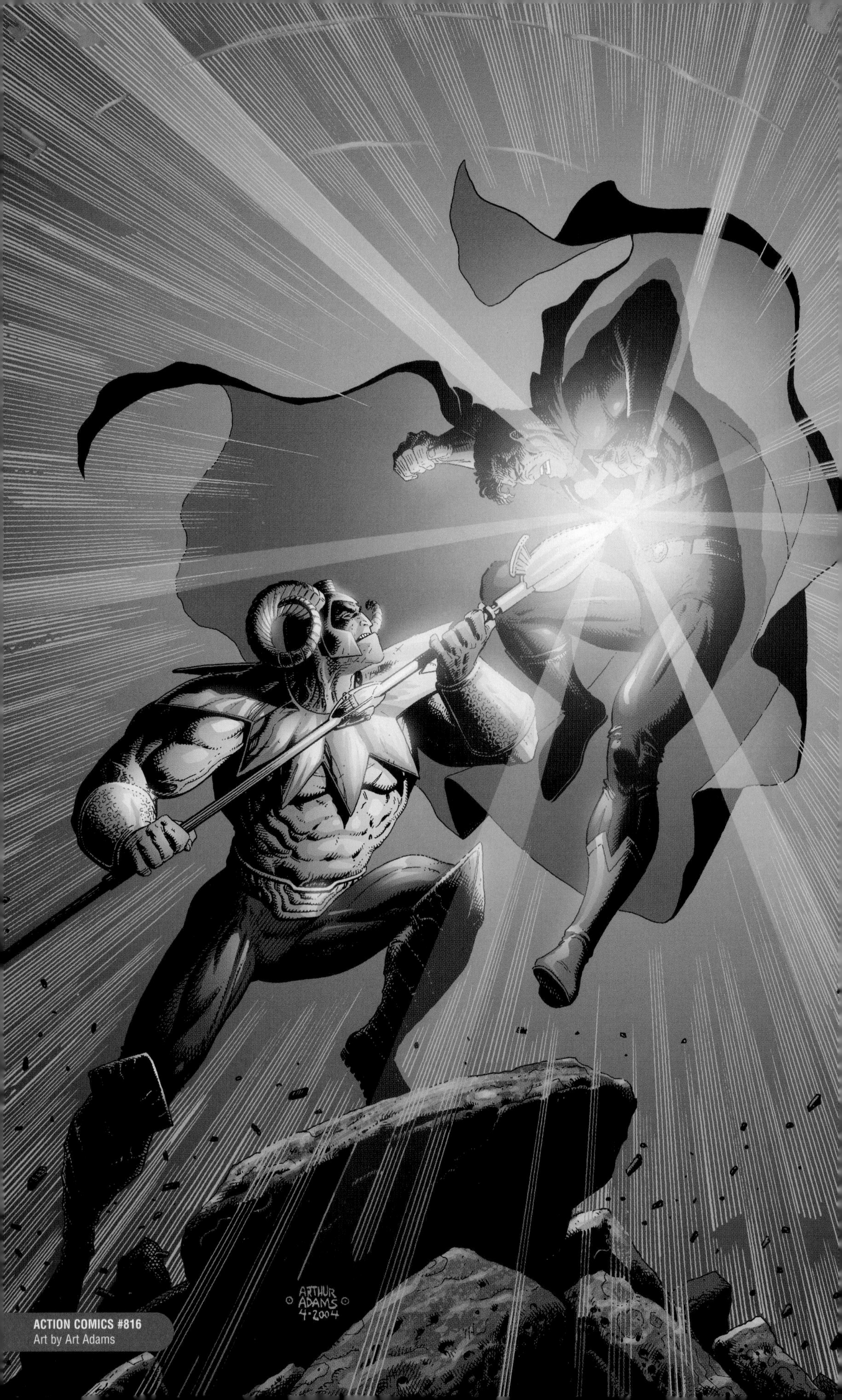
ARTHUR
ADAMS
4·2004

ACTION COMICS #816
Art by Art Adams

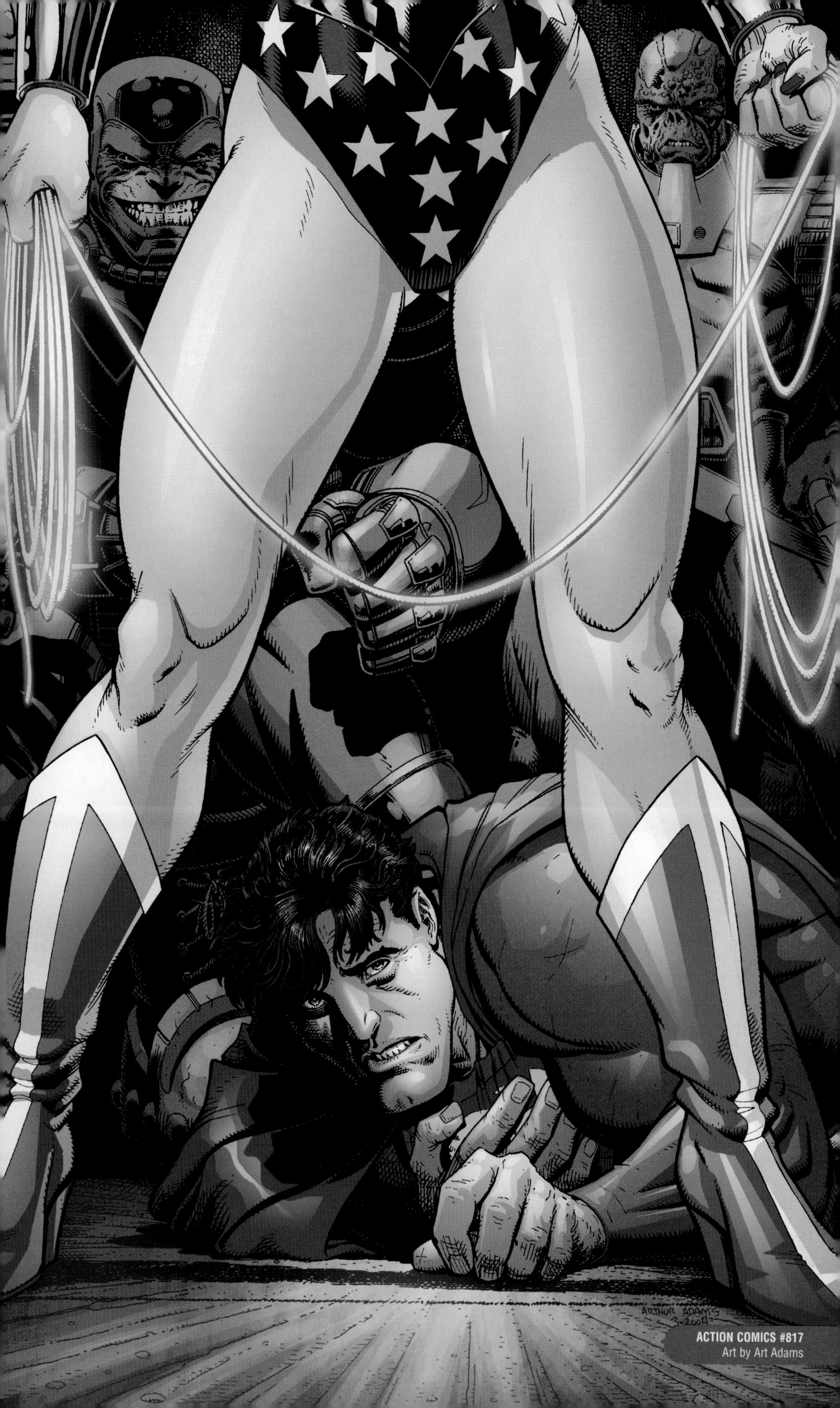
ARTHUR ADAMS
3-2004

ACTION COMICS #817
Art by Art Adams

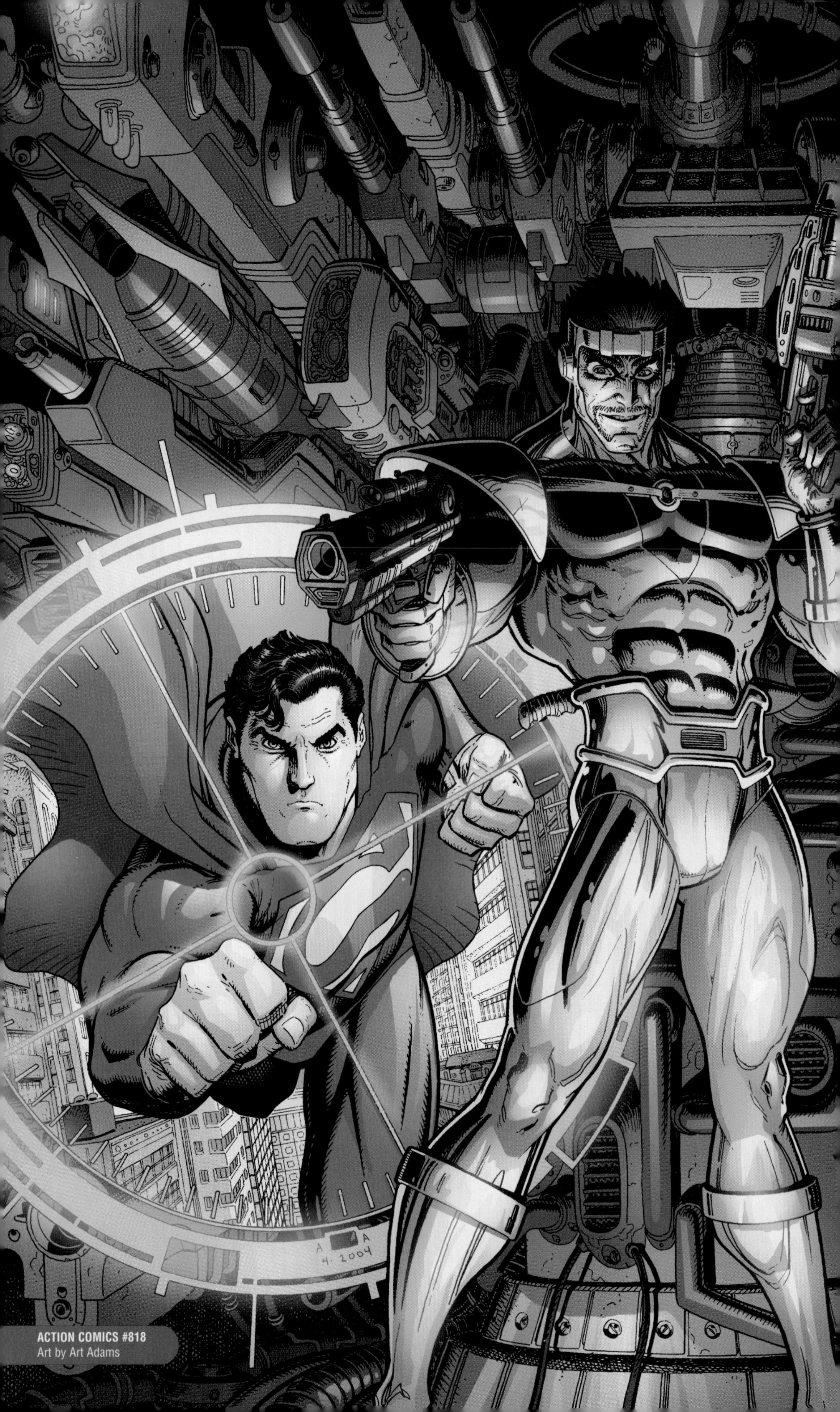

ACTION COMICS #818
Art by Art Adams

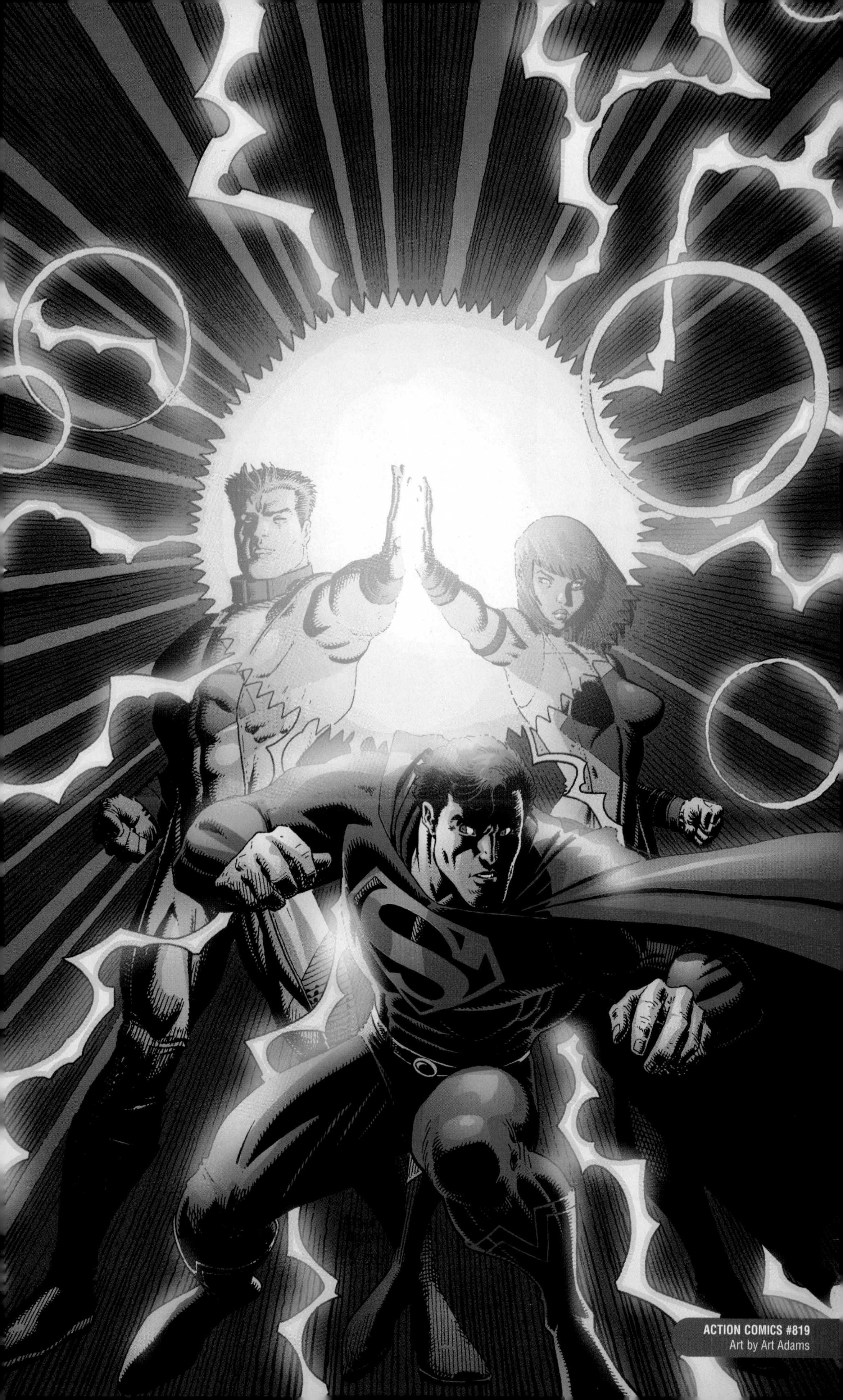

ACTION COMICS #819
Art by Art Adams

GOG

Real Name: **William** (last name unknown)
Occupation: **Fanatic**
Base of Operations: **Mobile**
Height: **6' 3"**
Weight: **210 lbs.**
Eyes: **White**
Hair: **None**
First Appearance: **NEW YEAR'S EVIL: GOG #1** (February, 1998)

Decades into the future, a young boy named William became the lone survivor of a cataclysmic event that resulted in the destruction of Kansas. Rescued by Superman, the boy grew up convinced that he had survived to become the Man of Steel's disciple. But when Superman confessed to him years later that the tragedy was a consequence of his choice to distance himself from mankind's affairs, Willaim was devastated, and suddenly viewed his savior as an "antichrist."

It was at that time when the Quintessence — cosmic immortals including the Phantom Stranger, the New Gods' Highfather, Ganthet of the Guardians, Zeus and the wizard Shazam — bestowed immeasurable power and knowledge upon William, so that he might journey to the past and avert the disaster in Kansas. Instead, he decided to accelerate the event, and thereby publicly expose Superman as the ultimate evil. Armed with a staff powerful enough to rival even the Quintessence's might, William assumed the mantle of Gog and began traveling further and further back in time, murdering Superman countless times along the way. The present-day Man of Steel, aided by Batman, Wonder Woman and their counterparts from an undetermined future, barely thwarted Gog's mission, but his threat has since resurfaced.

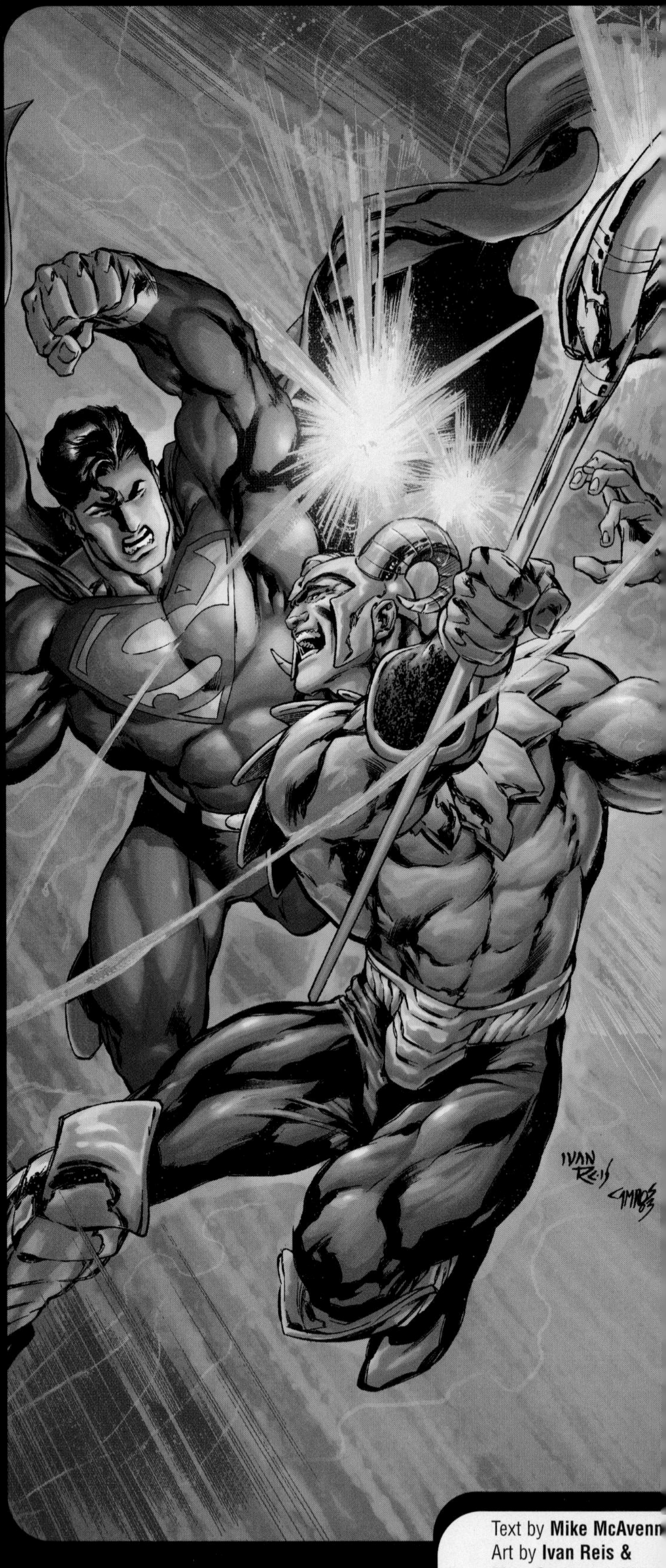
IVAN Reis
CAMPOS

Text by **Mike McAvennie**
Art by **Ivan Reis & Marc Campos, with Dave Stewart**

SUPERMAN LIBRARY

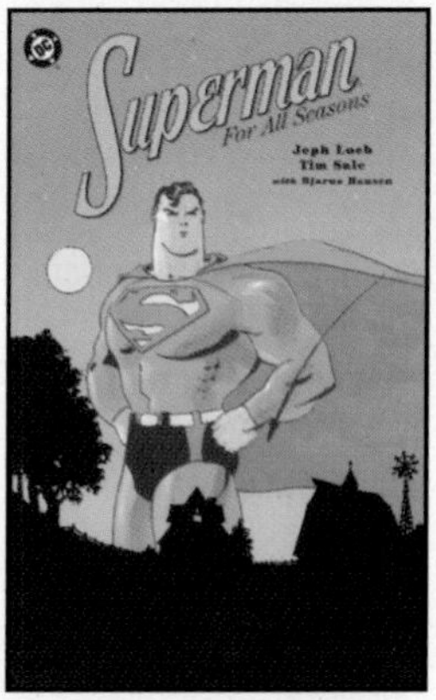
Superman
For All Seasons
Jeph Loeb
Tim Sale

SUPERMAN
FOR ALL SEASONS

Jeph Loeb/Tim Sale

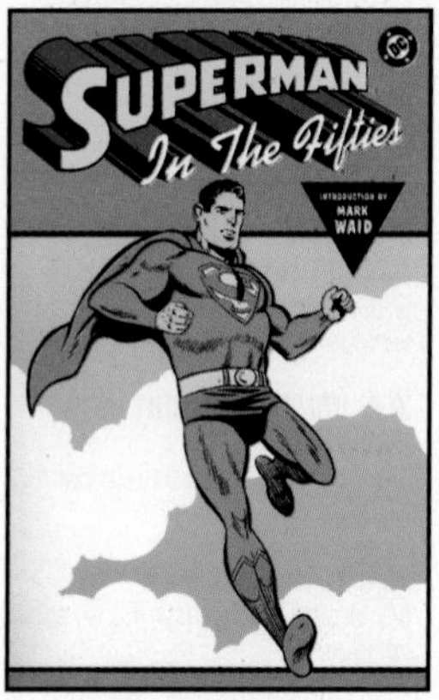
SUPERMAN
In The Fifties
INTRODUCTION BY
MARK
WAID

SUPERMAN IN THE FIFTIES
SUPERMAN IN THE SIXIES
SUPERMAN IN THE SEVENTIES

various

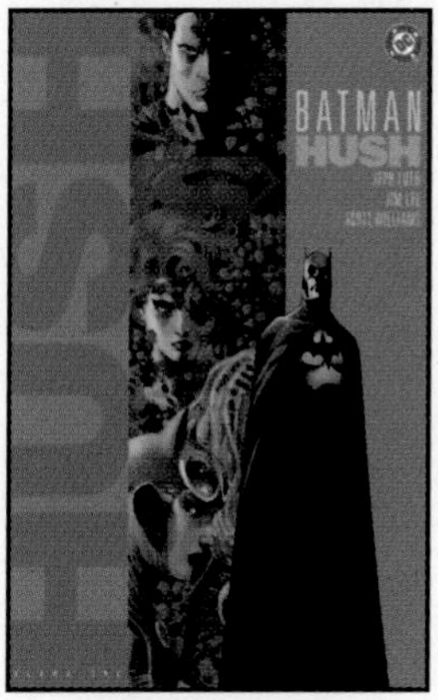
BATMAN
HUSH

BATMAN: HUSH
VOLUMES 1 & 2

Jeph Loeb/Jim Lee/Scott Williams

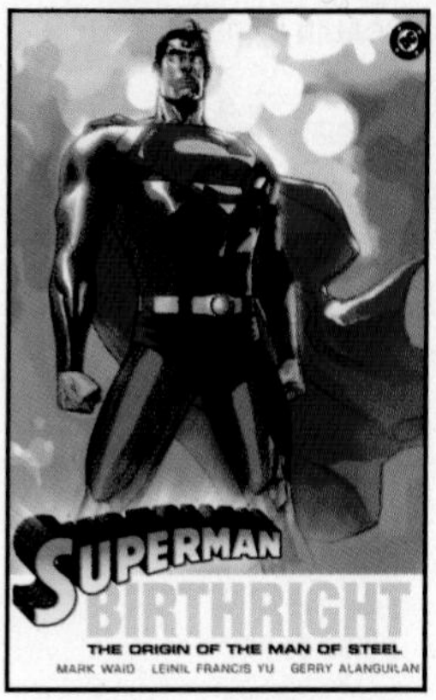
SUPERMAN
BIRTHRIGHT
THE ORIGIN OF THE MAN OF STEEL
MARK WAID LEINIL FRANCIS YU GERRY ALANGUILAN

SUPERMAN: BIRTHRIGHT

Mark Waid/Leinil Francis Yu/
Gerry Alanguilan

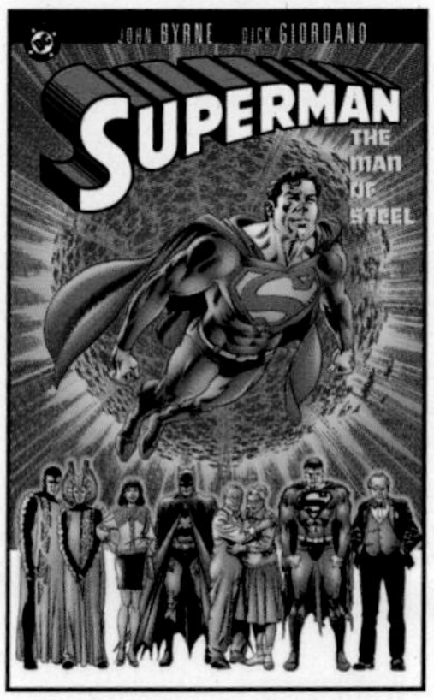
JOHN BYRNE DICK GIORDANO
SUPERMAN
THE
man
OF
STEEL

SUPERMAN: MAN OF STEEL
VOLUMES 1 - 3

John Byrne/Marv Wolfman/
Jerry Ordway

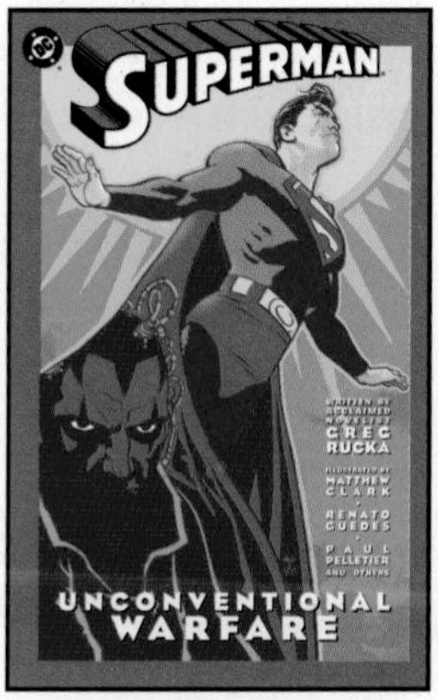
SUPERMAN
GREG
RUCKA
MATTHEW
CLARK
UNCONVENTIONAL
WARFARE

SUPERMAN:
UNCONVENTIONAL WARFARE

Greg Rucka/various

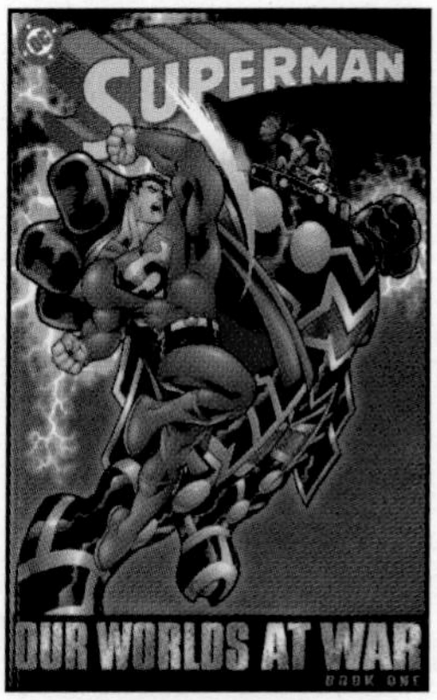
SUPERMAN
OUR WORLDS AT WAR

SUPERMAN:
OUR WORLDS AT WAR
VOLUMES 1 & 2

various

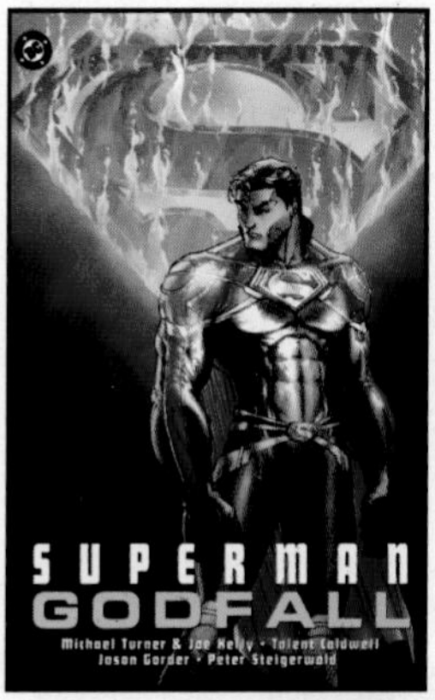
SUPERMAN
GODFALL

SUPERMAN: GODFALL

Michael Turner/Joe Kelly/Talent Caldwell/
Jason Gorder/Peter Steigerwald

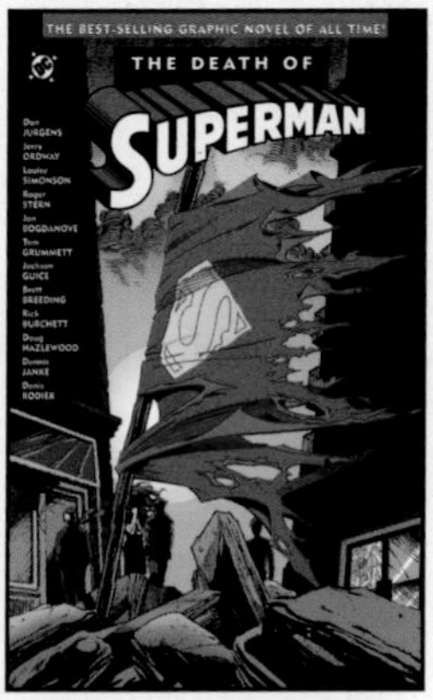
THE BEST-SELLING GRAPHIC NOVEL OF ALL TIME!
THE DEATH OF
SUPERMAN

DEATH OF SUPERMAN

various

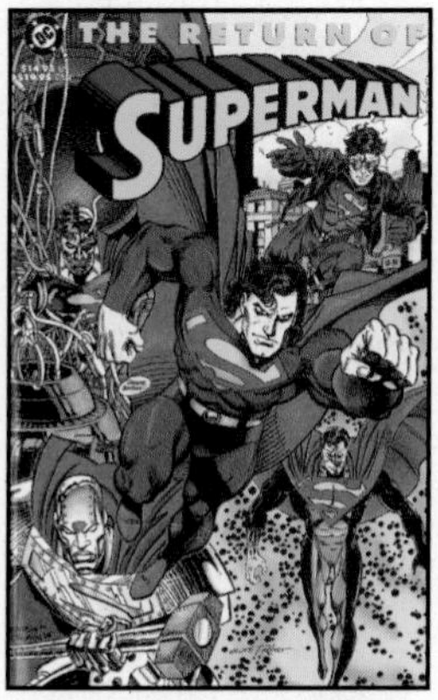
THE RETURN OF
SUPERMAN

RETURN OF SUPERMAN

various

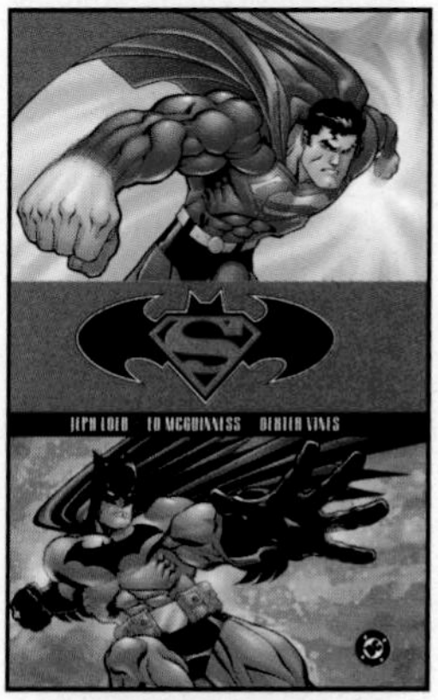

SUPERMAN/BATMAN:
PUBLIC ENEMIES

Jeph Loeb/Ed McGuinness/
Dexter Vines

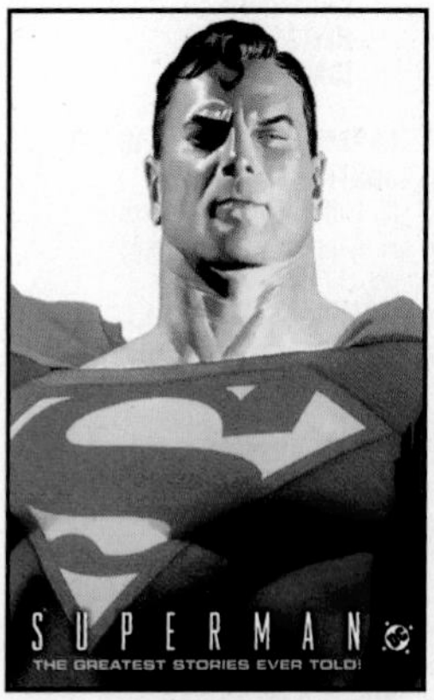
SUPERMAN
THE GREATEST STORIES EVER TOLD!

SUPERMAN:
THE GREATEST STORIES
EVER TOLD!

various

THE STARS OF THE DC UNIVERSE CAN ALSO BE FOUND IN THESE BOOKS:

TO FIND MORE COLLECTED EDITIONS AND MONTHLY COMIC BOOKS FROM DC COMICS, CALL 1-888-COMIC BOOK FOR THE NEAREST COMICS SHOP OR GO TO YOUR LOCAL BOOK STORE.